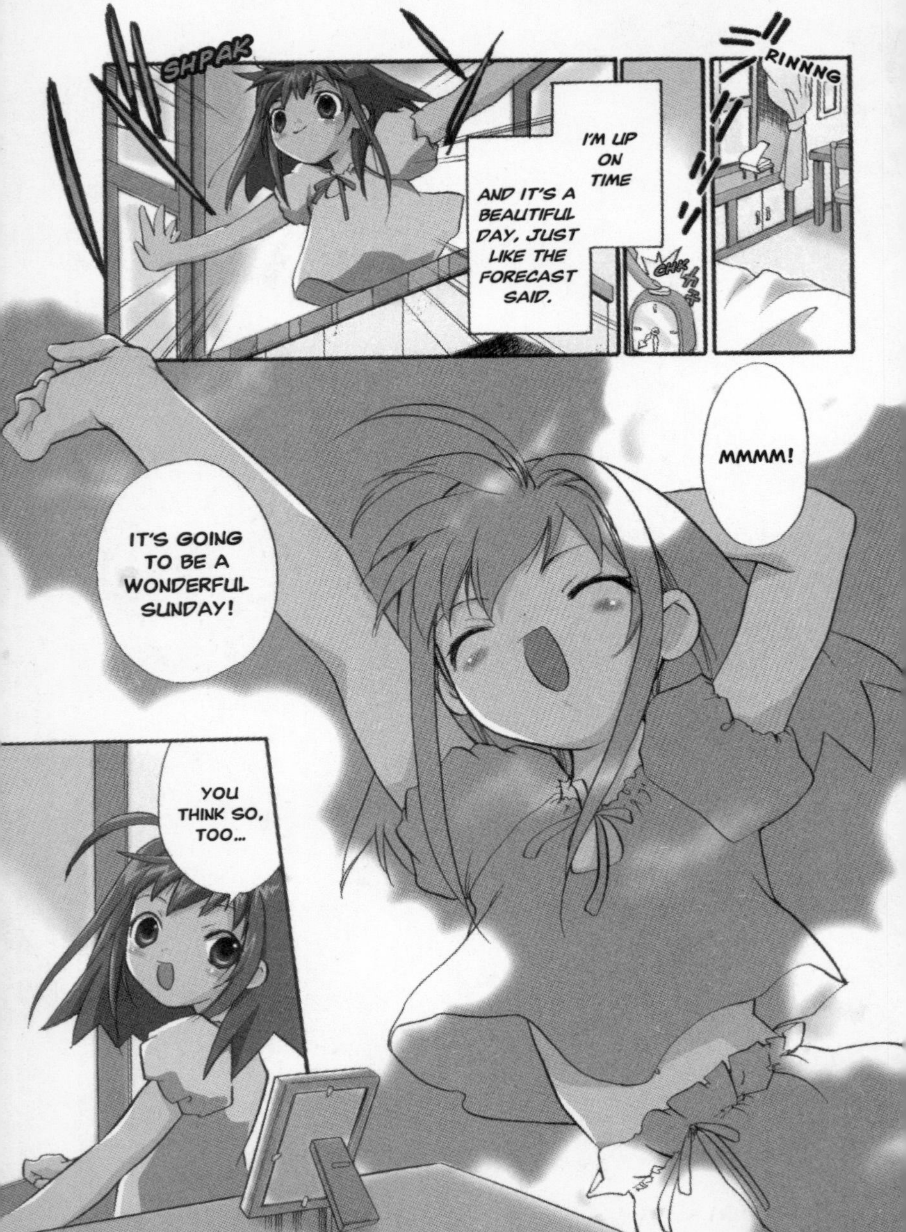
RINNNG
CHK
SHPAK
I'M UP ON TIME
AND IT'S A BEAUTIFUL DAY, JUST LIKE THE FORECAST SAID.
MMMM!
IT'S GOING TO BE A WONDERFUL SUNDAY!
YOU THINK SO, TOO...

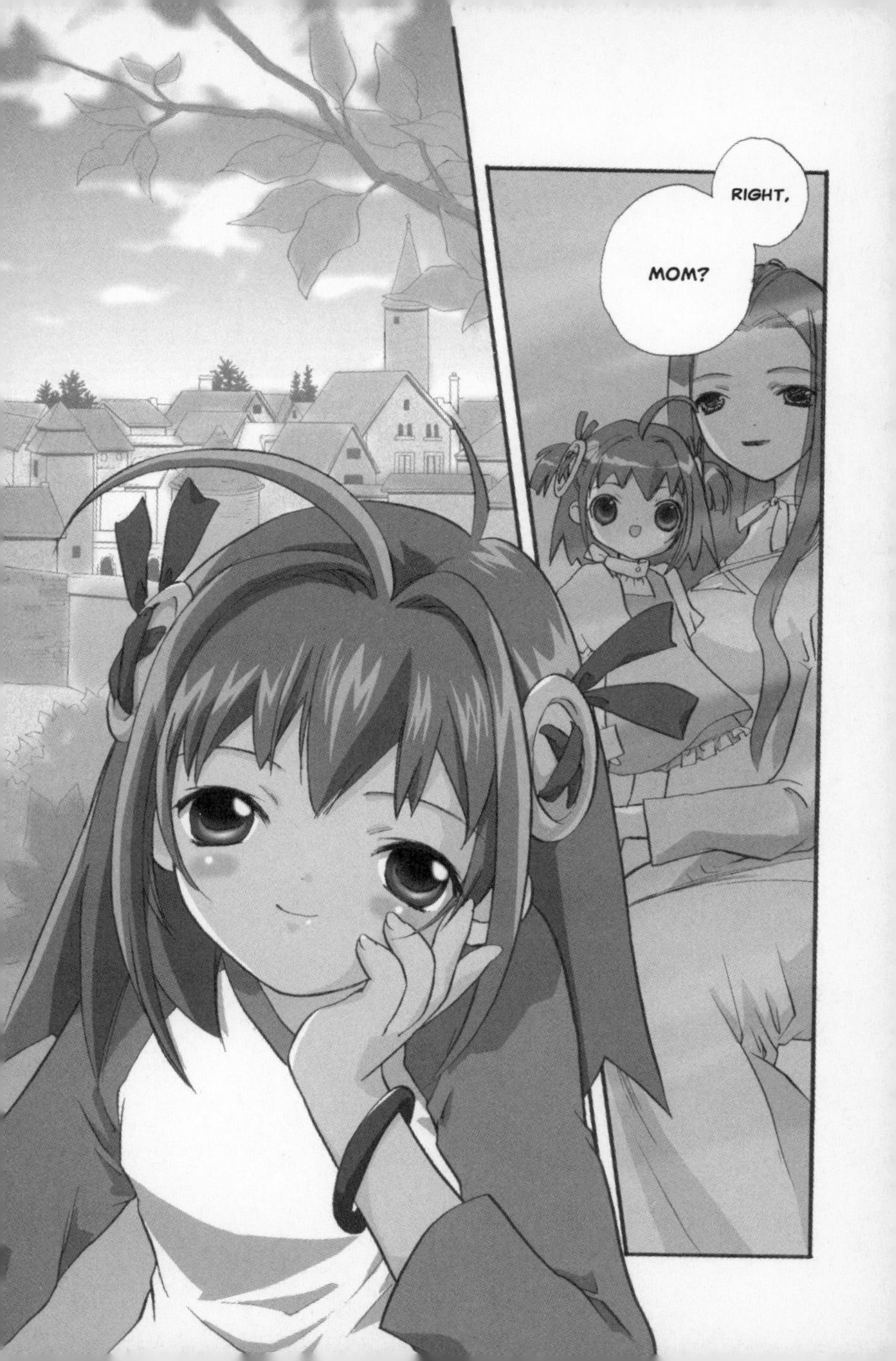
RIGHT,
MOM?

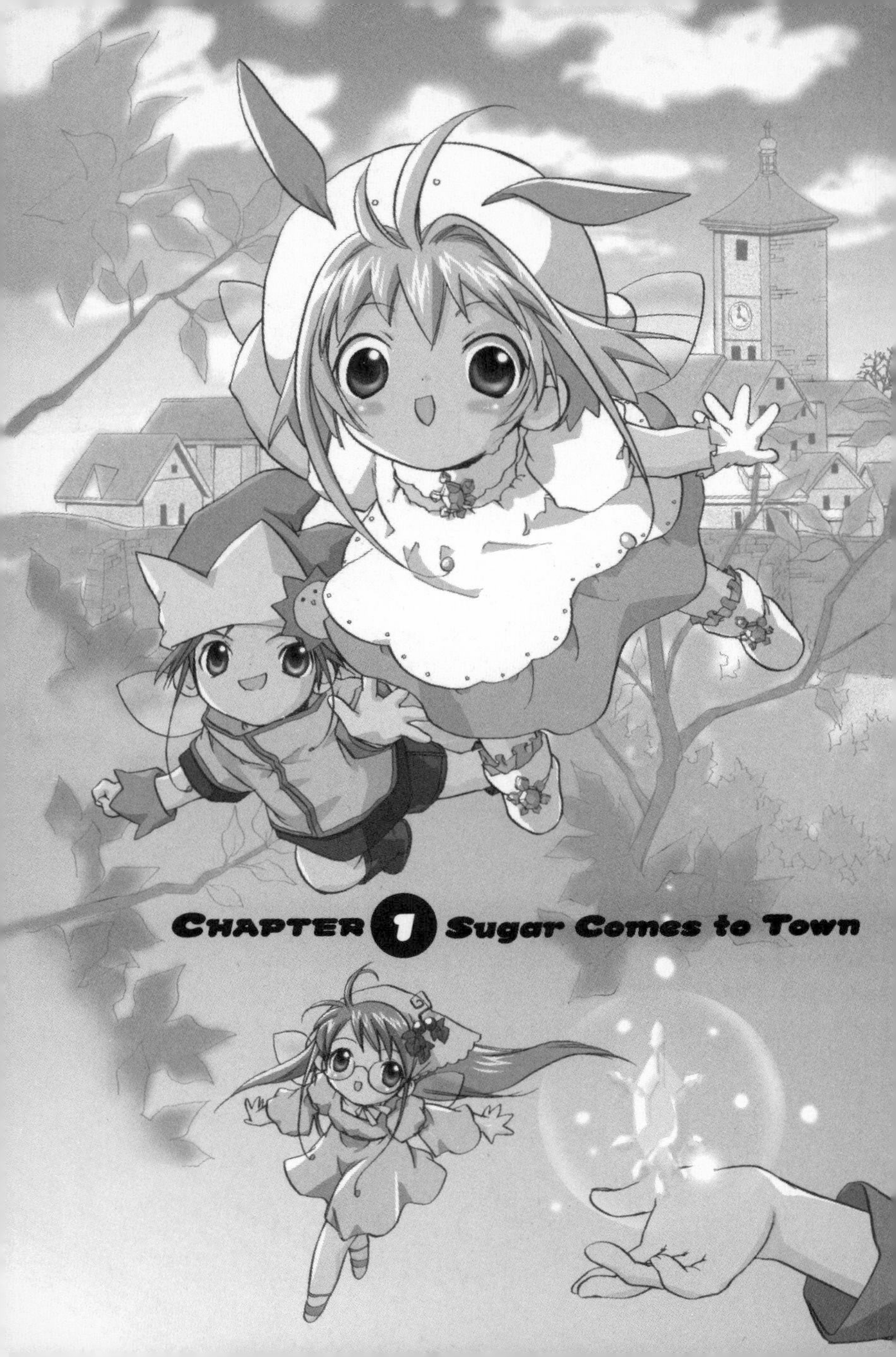

CHAPTER 1 Sugar Comes to Town

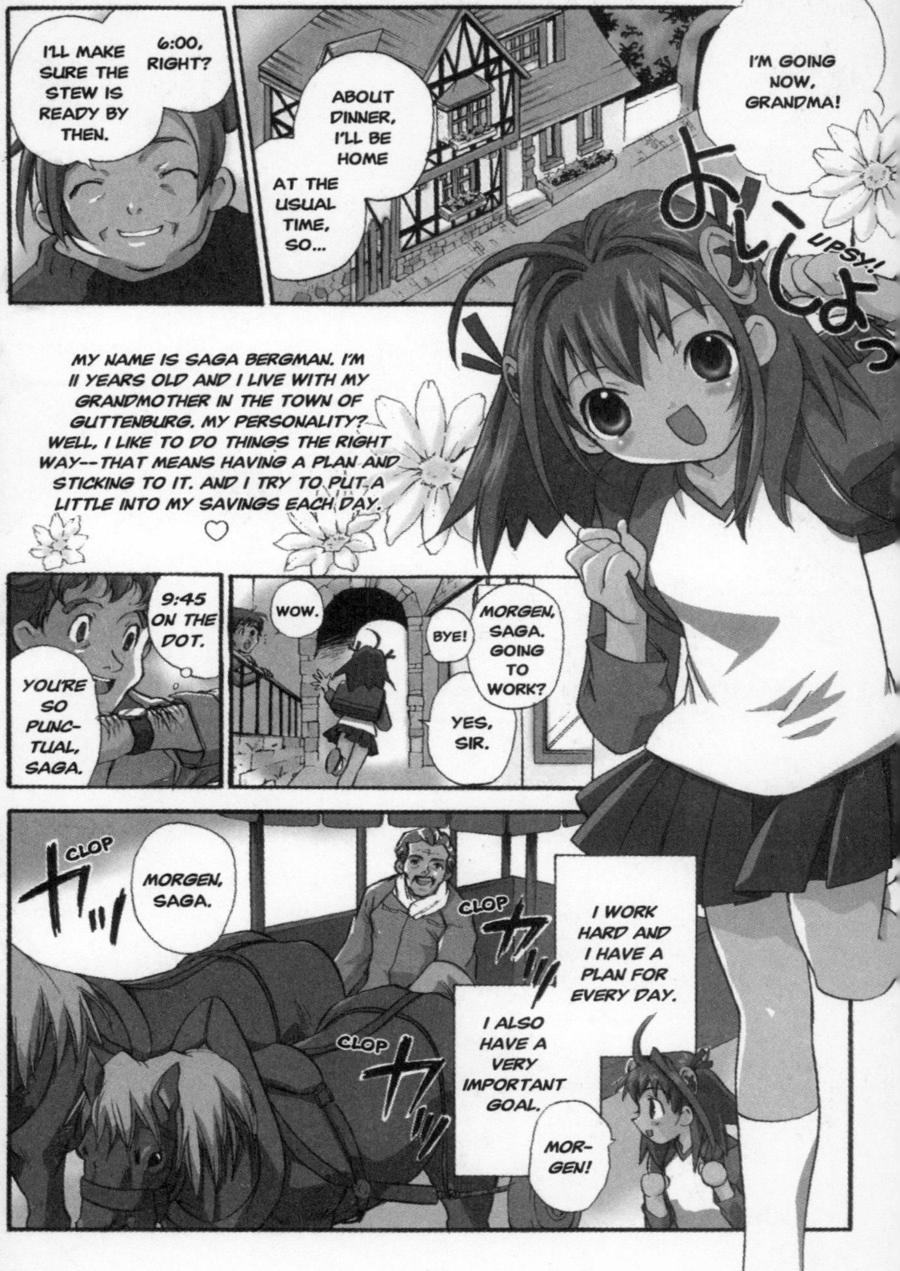

I'M GOING NOW, GRANDMA!
おいしょっ
UPSY!
ABOUT DINNER, I'LL BE HOME
AT THE USUAL TIME, SO...
6:00, RIGHT?
I'LL MAKE SURE THE STEW IS READY BY THEN.
MY NAME IS SAGA BERGMAN. I'M 11 YEARS OLD AND I LIVE WITH MY GRANDMOTHER IN THE TOWN OF GUTTENBURG. MY PERSONALITY? WELL, I LIKE TO DO THINGS THE RIGHT WAY--THAT MEANS HAVING A PLAN AND STICKING TO IT. AND I TRY TO PUT A LITTLE INTO MY SAVINGS EACH DAY. ♡
MORGEN, SAGA. GOING TO WORK?
BYE!
WOW.
YES, SIR.
9:45 ON THE DOT.
YOU'RE SO PUNC-TUAL, SAGA.
I WORK HARD AND I HAVE A PLAN FOR EVERY DAY.
I ALSO HAVE A VERY IMPORTANT GOAL.
MOR-GEN!
CLOP
CLOP
MORGEN, SAGA.
CLOP

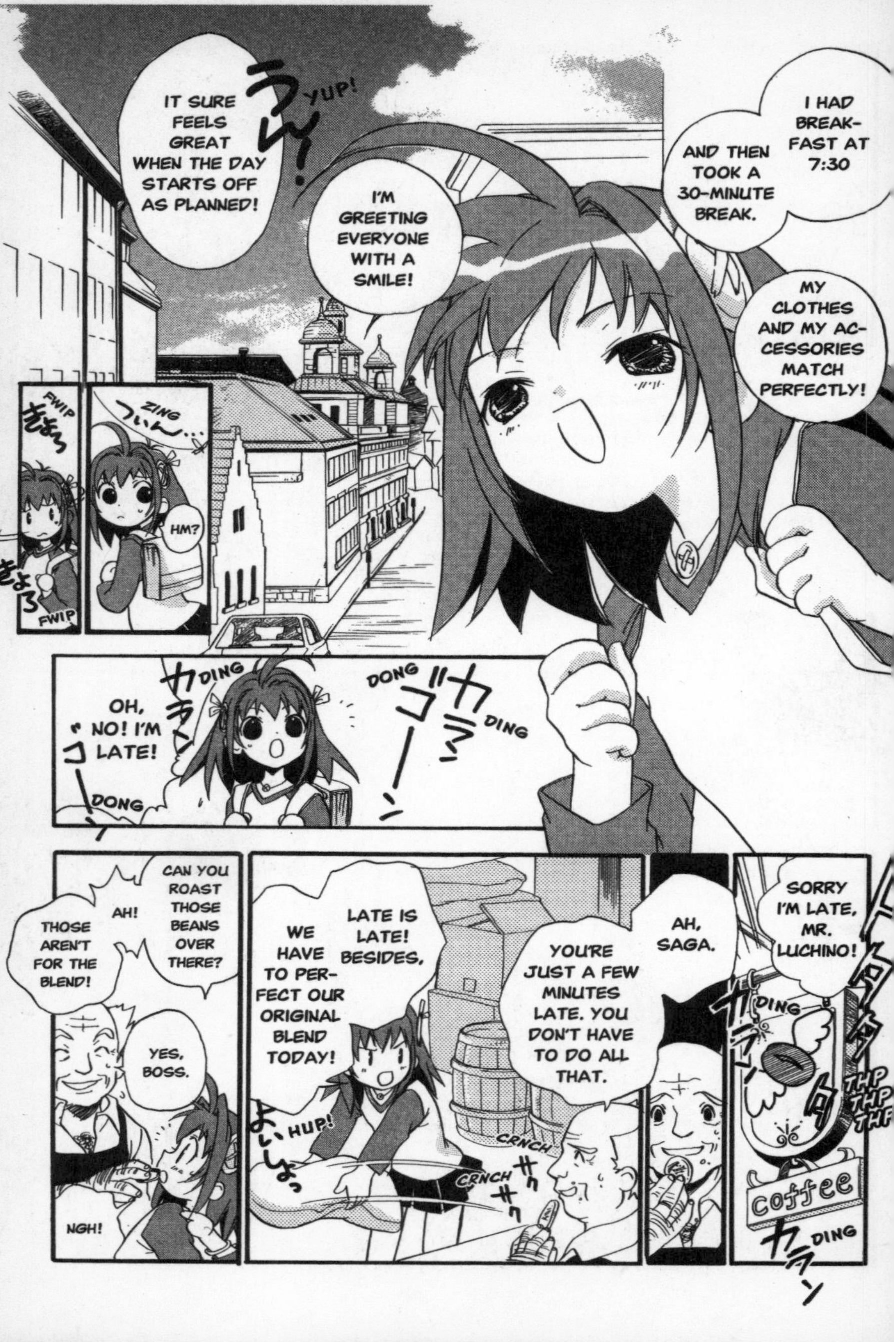
I HAD BREAK-FAST AT 7:30
AND THEN TOOK A 30-MINUTE BREAK.
MY CLOTHES AND MY AC-CESSORIES MATCH PERFECTLY!
I'M GREETING EVERYONE WITH A SMILE!
YUP!
IT SURE FEELS GREAT WHEN THE DAY STARTS OFF AS PLANNED!
ZING
HM?
FWIP
FWIP
DONG
DING
OH, NO! I'M LATE!
DING
DONG
SORRY I'M LATE, MR. LUCHINO!
DING
coffee
THP THP THP
DING
AH, SAGA.
YOU'RE JUST A FEW MINUTES LATE. YOU DON'T HAVE TO DO ALL THAT.
CRNCH
CRNCH
LATE IS LATE! BESIDES,
WE HAVE TO PER-FECT OUR ORIGINAL BLEND TODAY!
HUP!
CAN YOU ROAST THOSE BEANS OVER THERE?
AH!
THOSE AREN'T FOR THE BLEND!
YES, BOSS.
NGH!

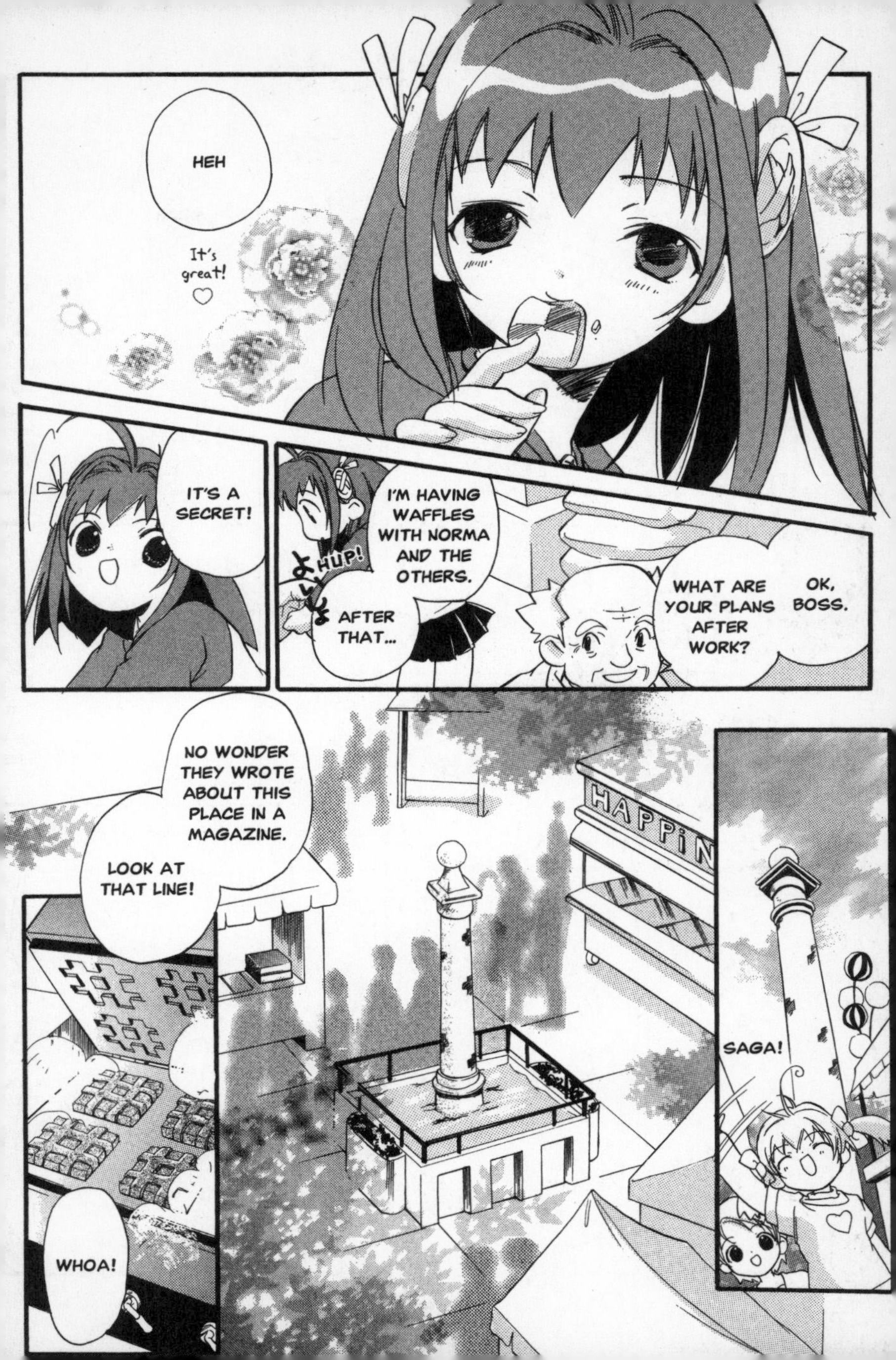
HEH
It's great!
OK, BOSS.
WHAT ARE YOUR PLANS AFTER WORK?
I'M HAVING WAFFLES WITH NORMA AND THE OTHERS.
HUP!
AFTER THAT...
IT'S A SECRET!
SAGA!
HAPPIN
NO WONDER THEY WROTE ABOUT THIS PLACE IN A MAGAZINE.
LOOK AT THAT LINE!
WHOA!

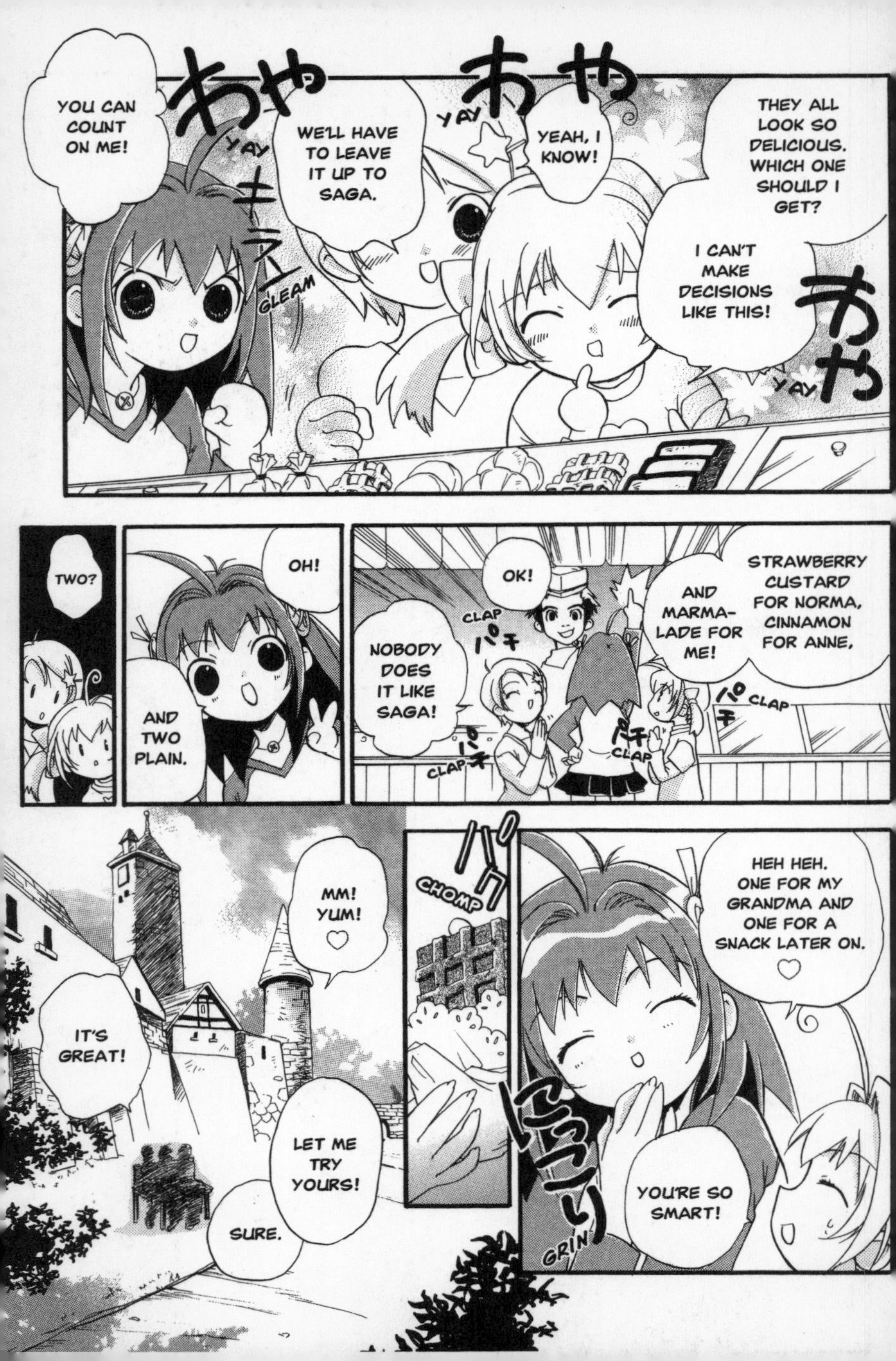

THEY ALL LOOK SO DELICIOUS. WHICH ONE SHOULD I GET?
I CAN'T MAKE DECISIONS LIKE THIS!
YAY
YEAH, I KNOW!
YAY
WE'LL HAVE TO LEAVE IT UP TO SAGA.
YOU CAN COUNT ON ME!
YAY
GLEAM
STRAWBERRY CUSTARD FOR NORMA, CINNAMON FOR ANNE,
AND MARMA-LADE FOR ME!
OK!
CLAP
CLAP
NOBODY DOES IT LIKE SAGA!
CLAP
CLAP
OH!
AND TWO PLAIN.
TWO?
HEH HEH. ONE FOR MY GRANDMA AND ONE FOR A SNACK LATER ON. ♡
CHOMP
YOU'RE SO SMART!
GRIN
MM! YUM! ♡
IT'S GREAT!
LET ME TRY YOURS!
SURE.

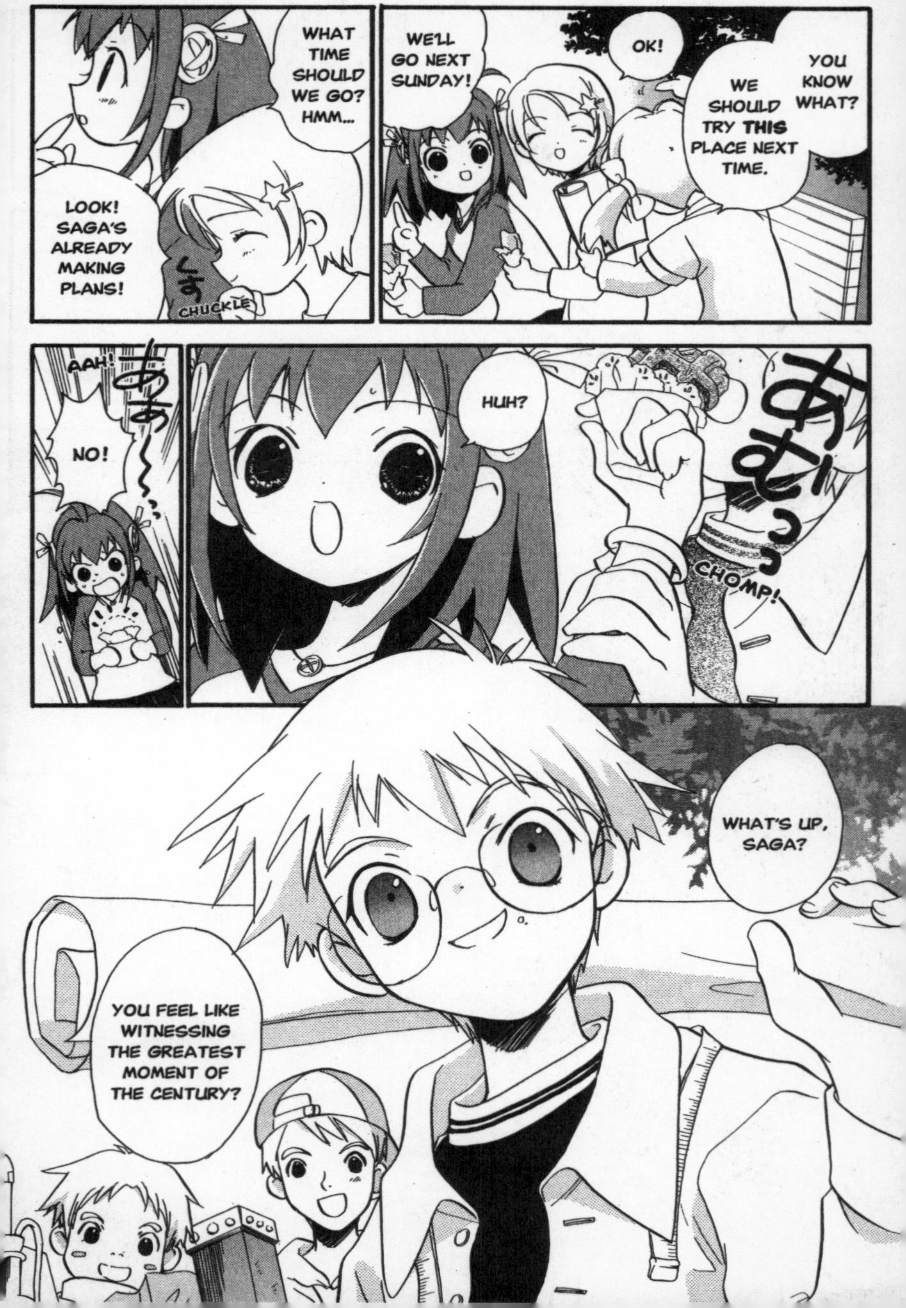
YOU KNOW WHAT?
WE SHOULD TRY THIS PLACE NEXT TIME.
OK!
WE'LL GO NEXT SUNDAY!
WHAT TIME SHOULD WE GO? HMM...
LOOK! SAGA'S ALREADY MAKING PLANS!
くす
CHUCKLE
あむっっ
CHOMP!
HUH?
AAH!
ああ〜〜
NO!
WHAT'S UP, SAGA?
YOU FEEL LIKE WITNESSING THE GREATEST MOMENT OF THE CENTURY?

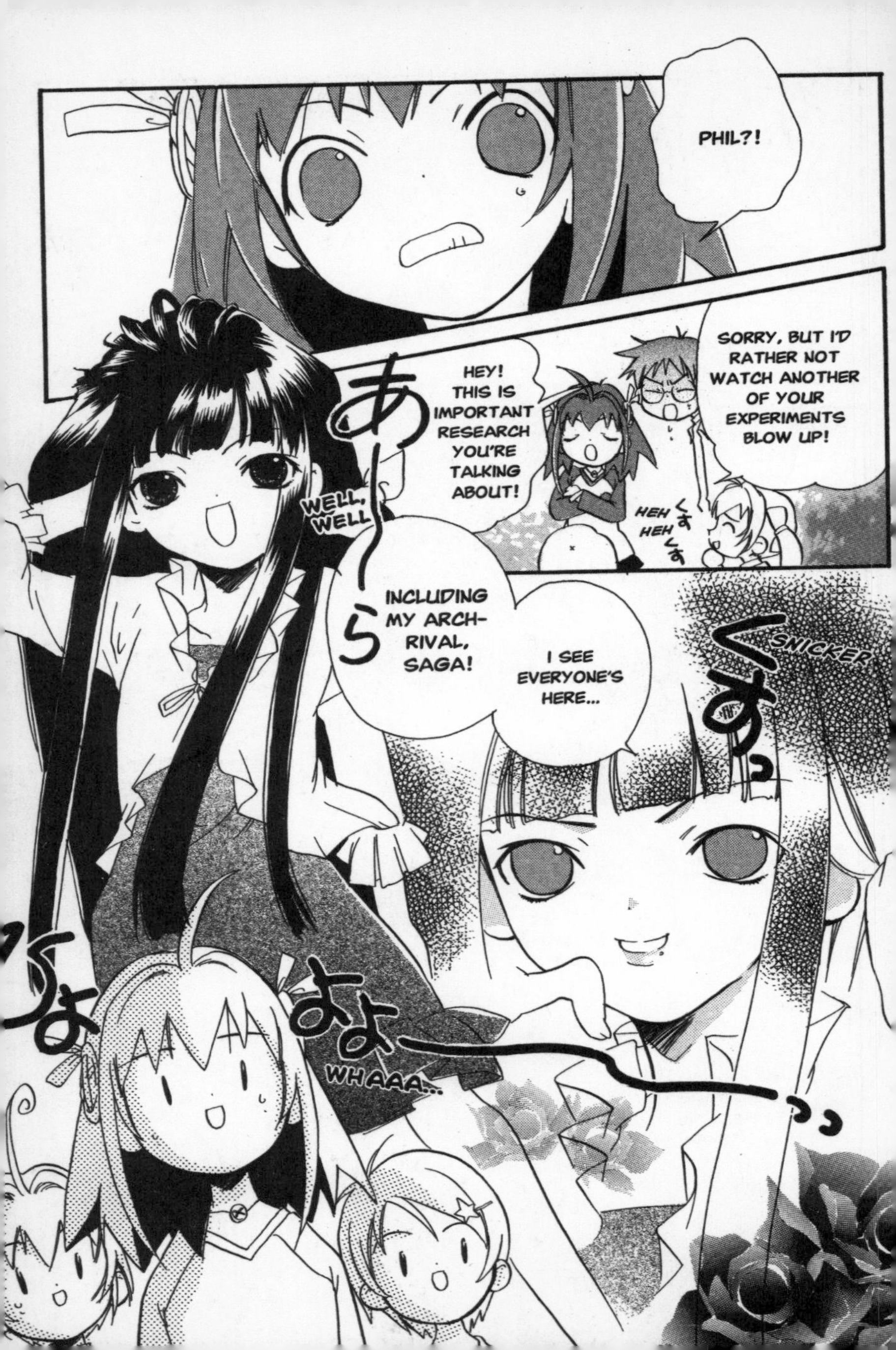
PHIL?!
SORRY, BUT I'D RATHER NOT WATCH ANOTHER OF YOUR EXPERIMENTS BLOW UP!
HEY! THIS IS IMPORTANT RESEARCH YOU'RE TALKING ABOUT!
くす くす
HEH HEH
くすっ
SNICKER
I SEE EVERYONE'S HERE...
INCLUDING MY ARCH-RIVAL, SAGA!
あーら
WELL, WELL
WHAAA...

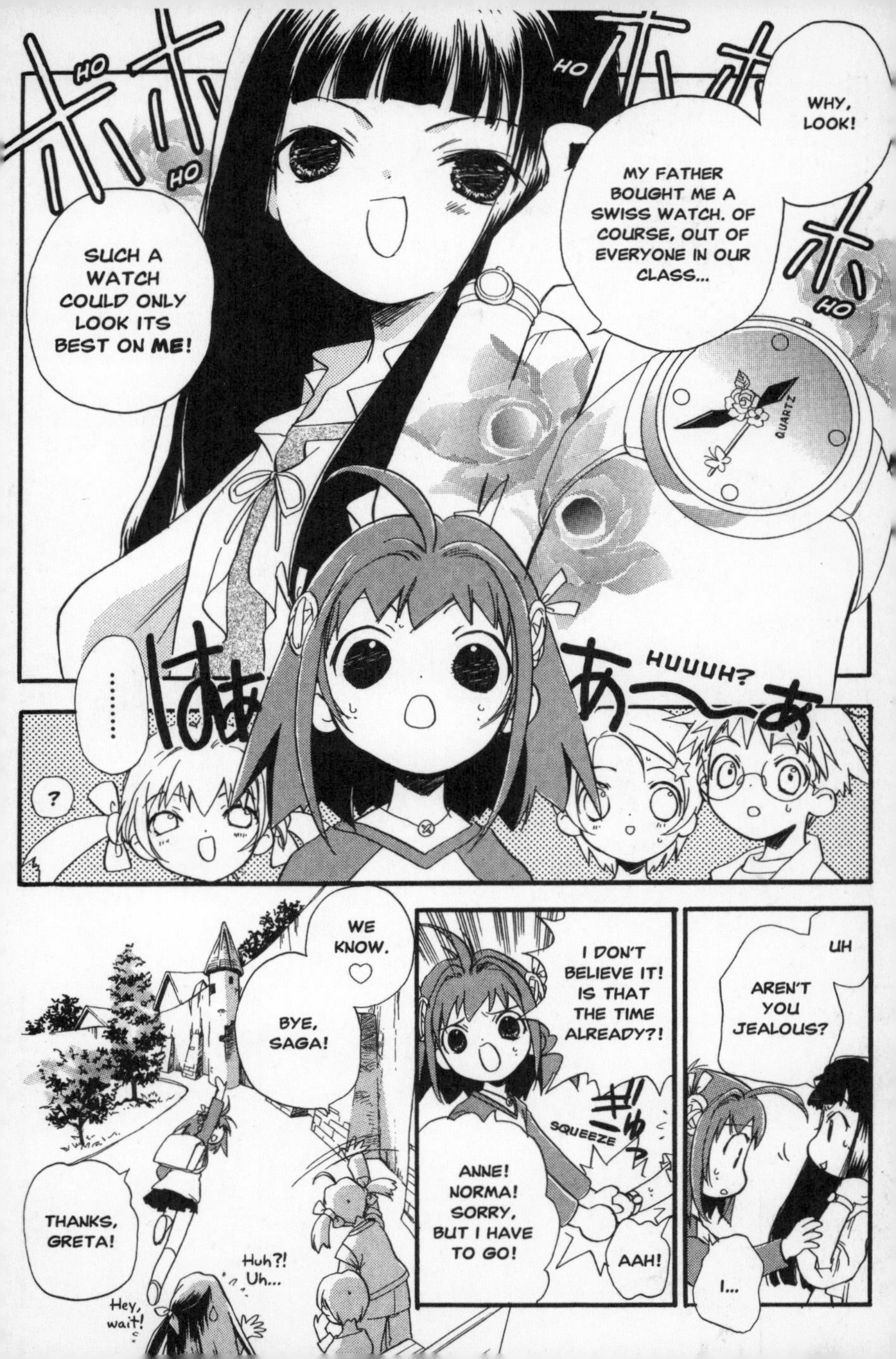
HO
HO
WHY, LOOK!
MY FATHER BOUGHT ME A SWISS WATCH. OF COURSE, OUT OF EVERYONE IN OUR CLASS...
HO
SUCH A WATCH COULD ONLY LOOK ITS BEST ON ME!
HO
HUUUH?
......
?
UH
AREN'T YOU JEALOUS?
I...
I DON'T BELIEVE IT! IS THAT THE TIME ALREADY?!
SQUEEZE
AAH!
ANNE! NORMA! SORRY, BUT I HAVE TO GO!
WE KNOW. ♡
BYE, SAGA!
THANKS, GRETA!
Huh?! Uh...
Hey, wait!

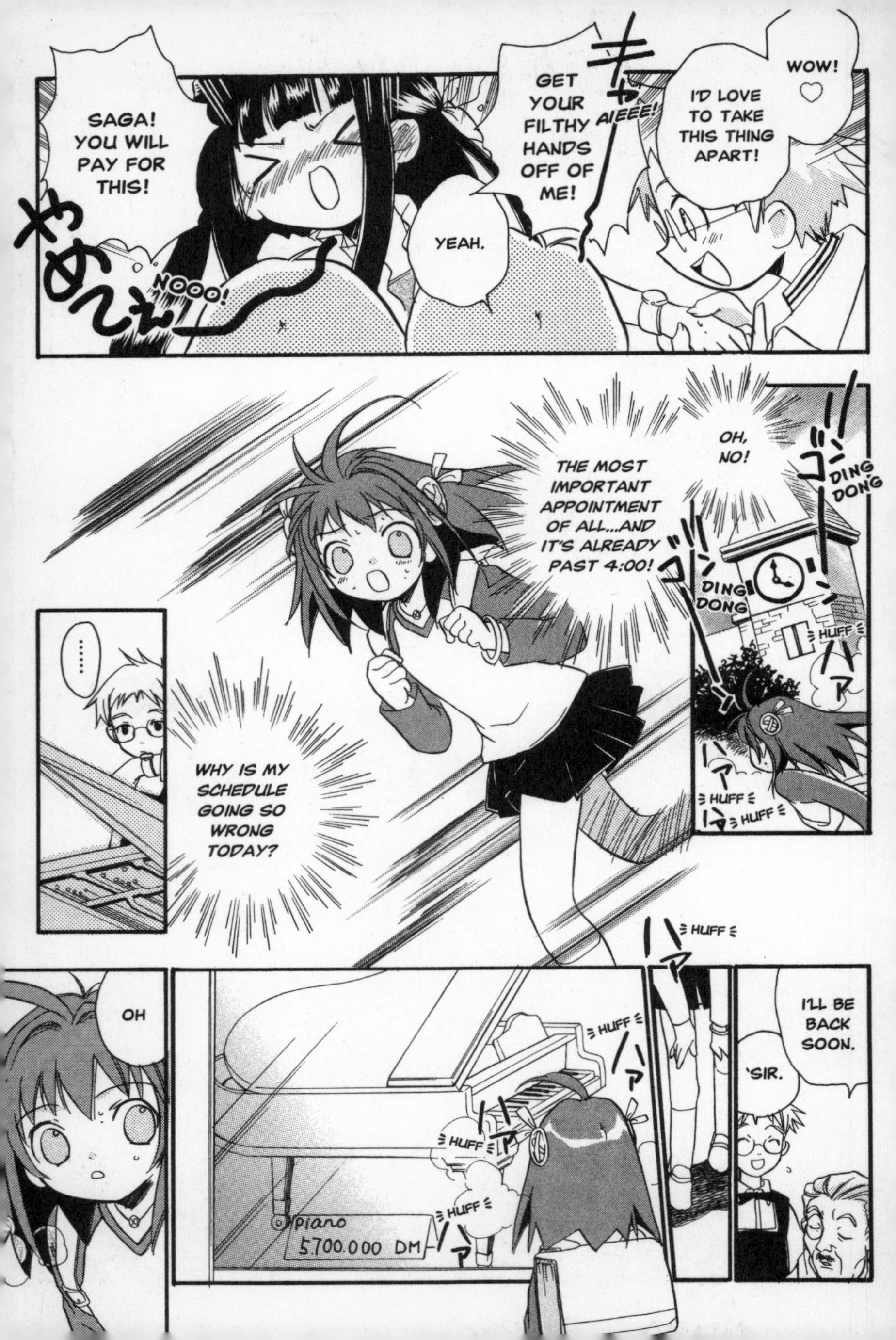
WOW! ♡
I'D LOVE TO TAKE THIS THING APART!
AIEEE!
GET YOUR FILTHY HANDS OFF OF ME!
YEAH.
SAGA! YOU WILL PAY FOR THIS!
NOOO!
DING DONG
DING DONG
HUFF
HUFF
HUFF
OH, NO!
THE MOST IMPORTANT APPOINTMENT OF ALL...AND IT'S ALREADY PAST 4:00!
WHY IS MY SCHEDULE GOING SO WRONG TODAY?
......
I'LL BE BACK SOON.
'SIR.
HUFF
HUFF
HUFF
HUFF
Piano
5700.000 DM
OH

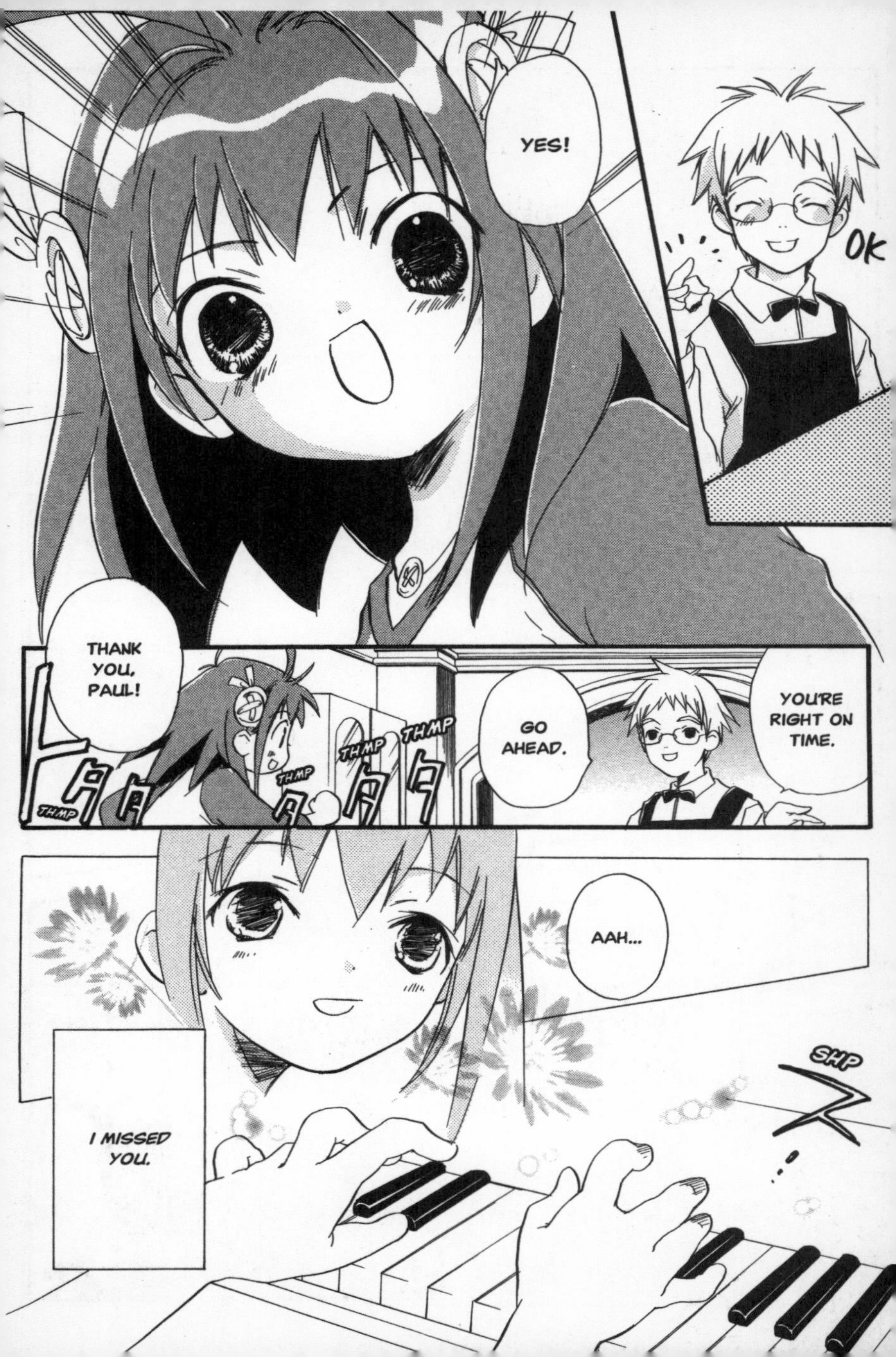
OK
YES!
THANK YOU, PAUL!
YOU'RE RIGHT ON TIME.
GO AHEAD.
THMP
THMP
THMP
THMP
AAH...
SHP
I MISSED YOU.

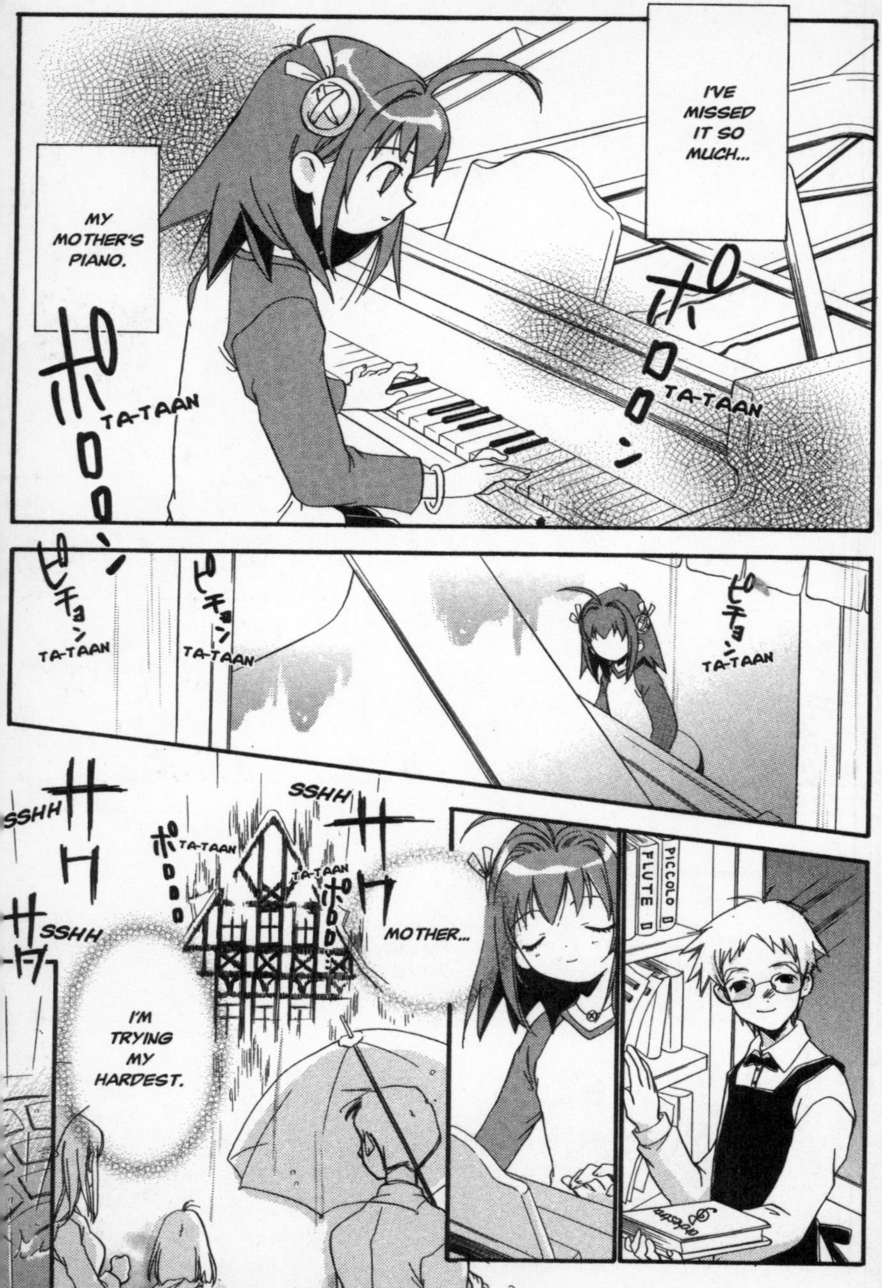

I'VE MISSED IT SO MUCH...
ポロロン
TA-TAAN
MY MOTHER'S PIANO.
ポロロン
TA-TAAN
ピチョン
TA-TAAN
ピチョン
TA-TAAN
ピチョン
TA-TAAN
PICCOLO
FLUTE
MOTHER...
サワ
SSHH
ポロロロ
TA-TAAN
ポロロロ
TA-TAAN
I'M TRYING MY HARDEST.
サワ
SSHH
サワサワ
SSHH

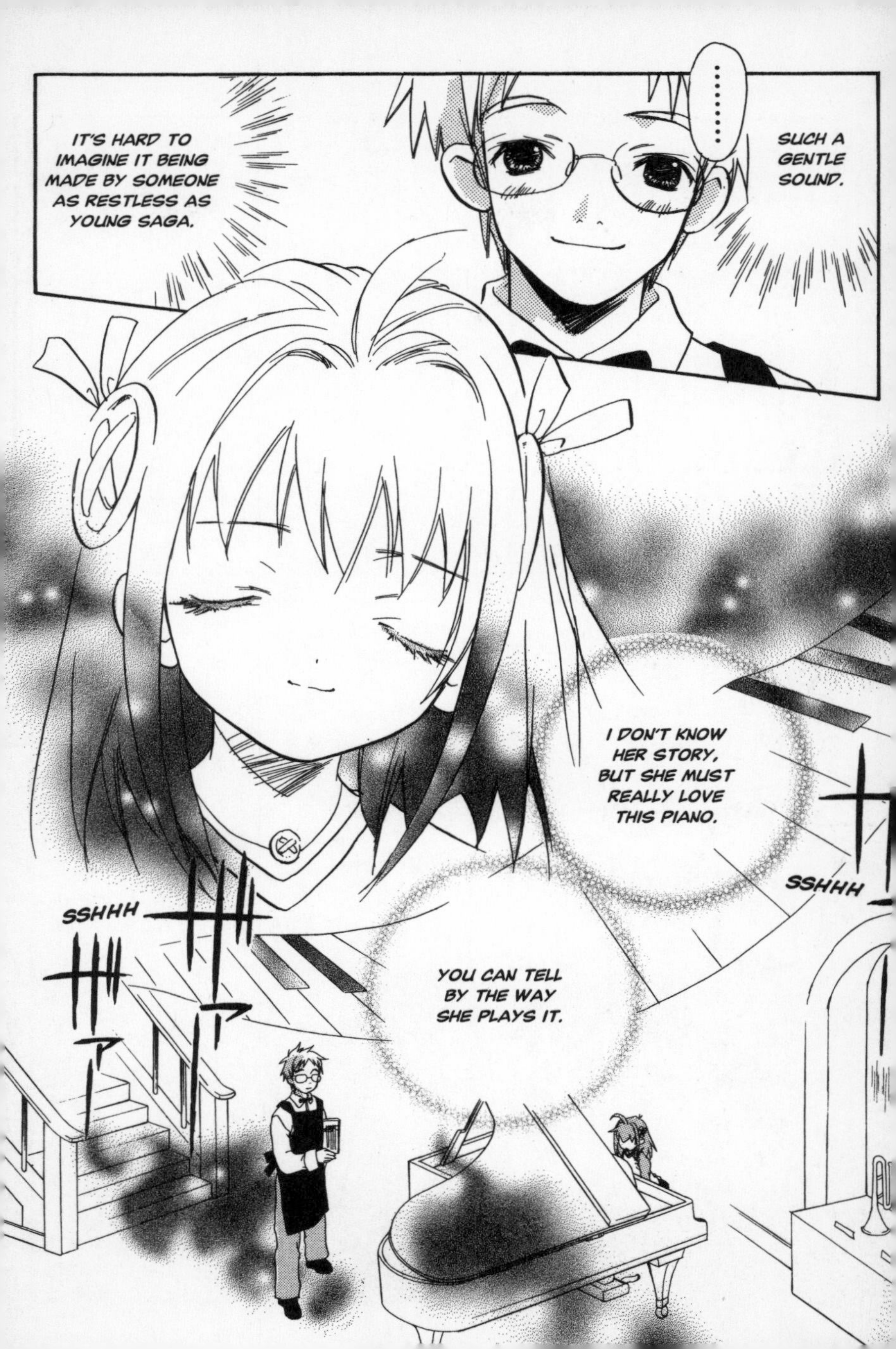
......
SUCH A GENTLE SOUND.
IT'S HARD TO IMAGINE IT BEING MADE BY SOMEONE AS RESTLESS AS YOUNG SAGA.
I DON'T KNOW HER STORY, BUT SHE MUST REALLY LOVE THIS PIANO.
SSHHH
YOU CAN TELL BY THE WAY SHE PLAYS IT.
SSHHH

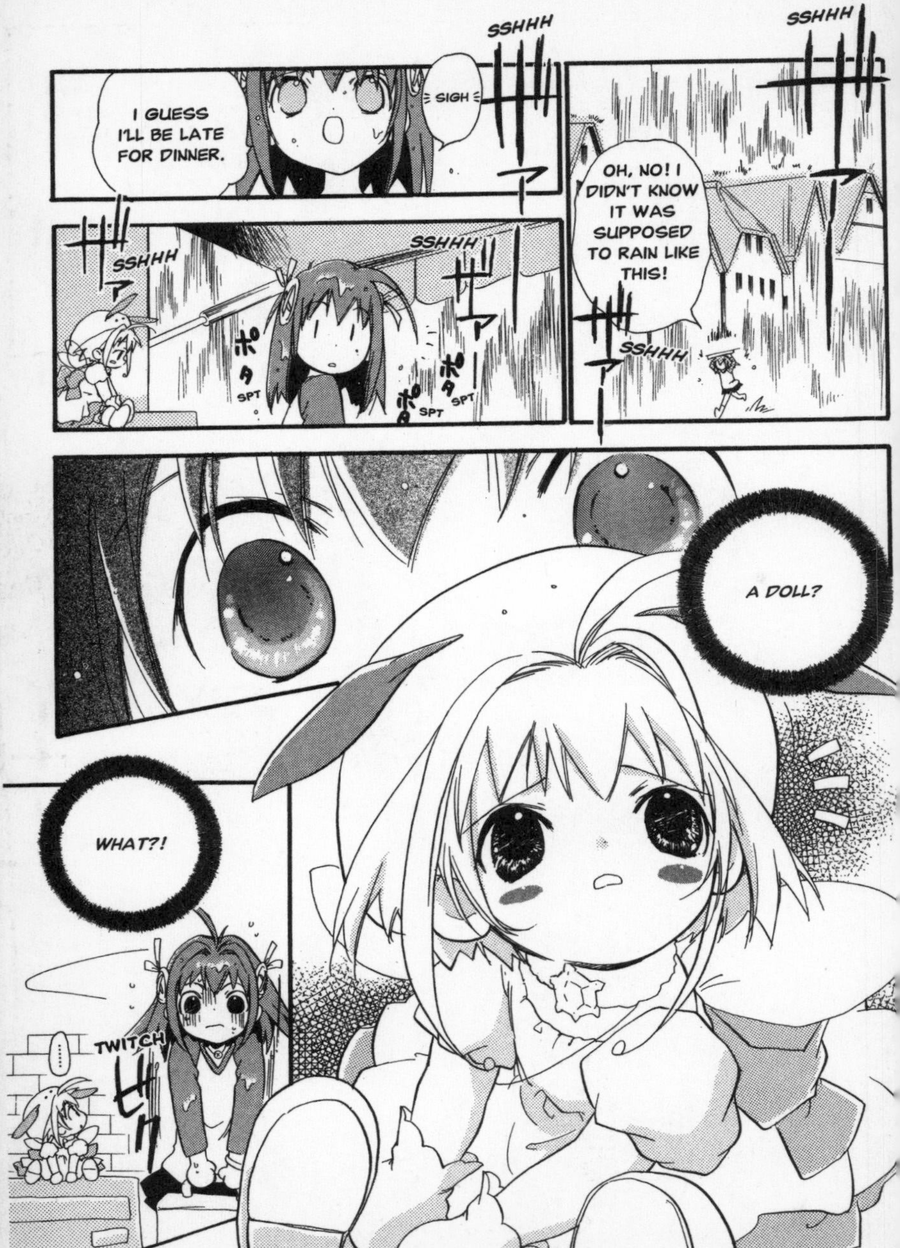
SSHHH
OH, NO! I DIDN'T KNOW IT WAS SUPPOSED TO RAIN LIKE THIS!
SSHHH
SSHHH
SIGH
I GUESS I'LL BE LATE FOR DINNER.
SSHHH
SSHHH
SPT
SPT
SPT
A DOLL?
WHAT?!
......
TWITCH

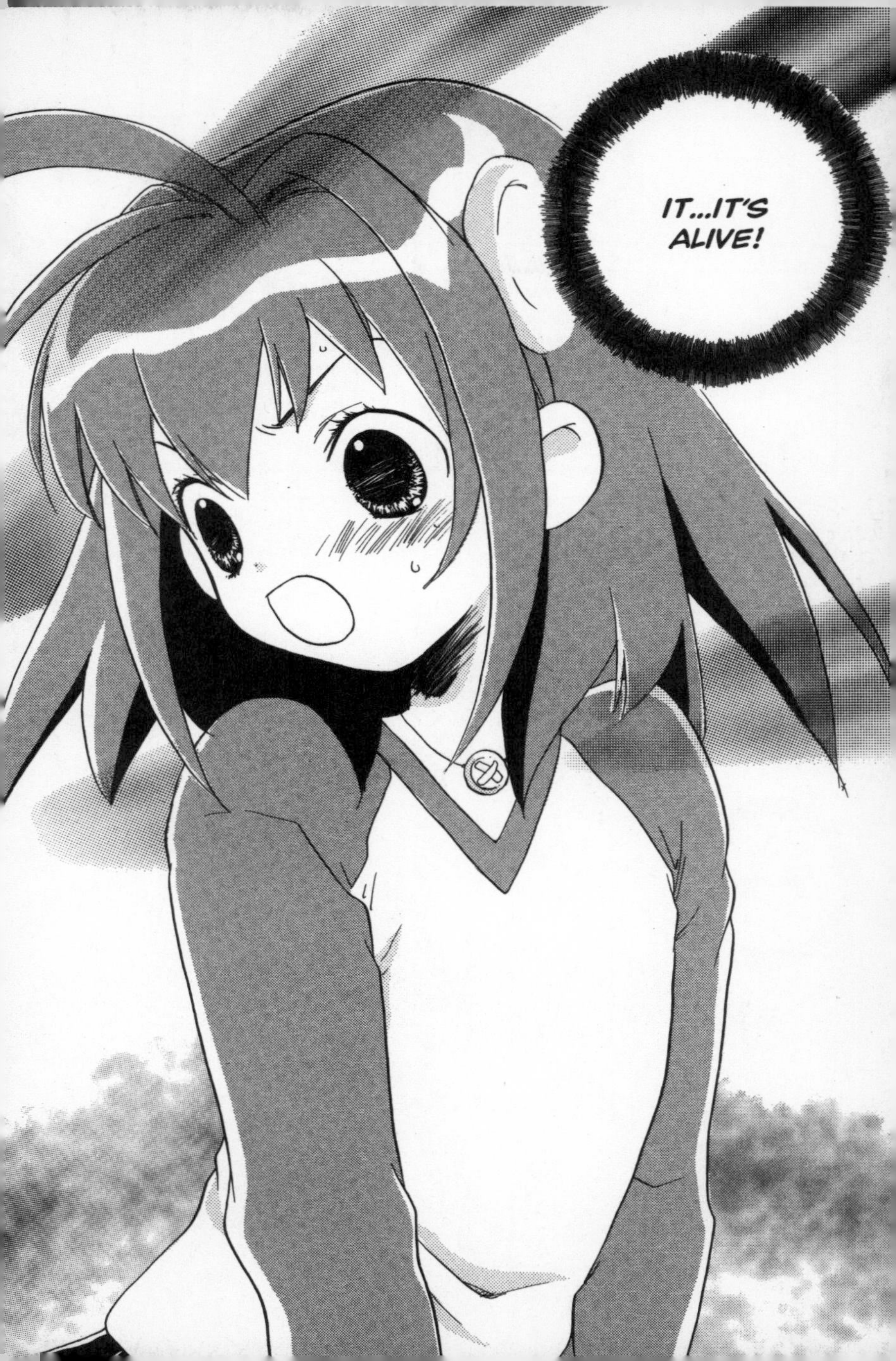
IT...IT'S ALIVE!

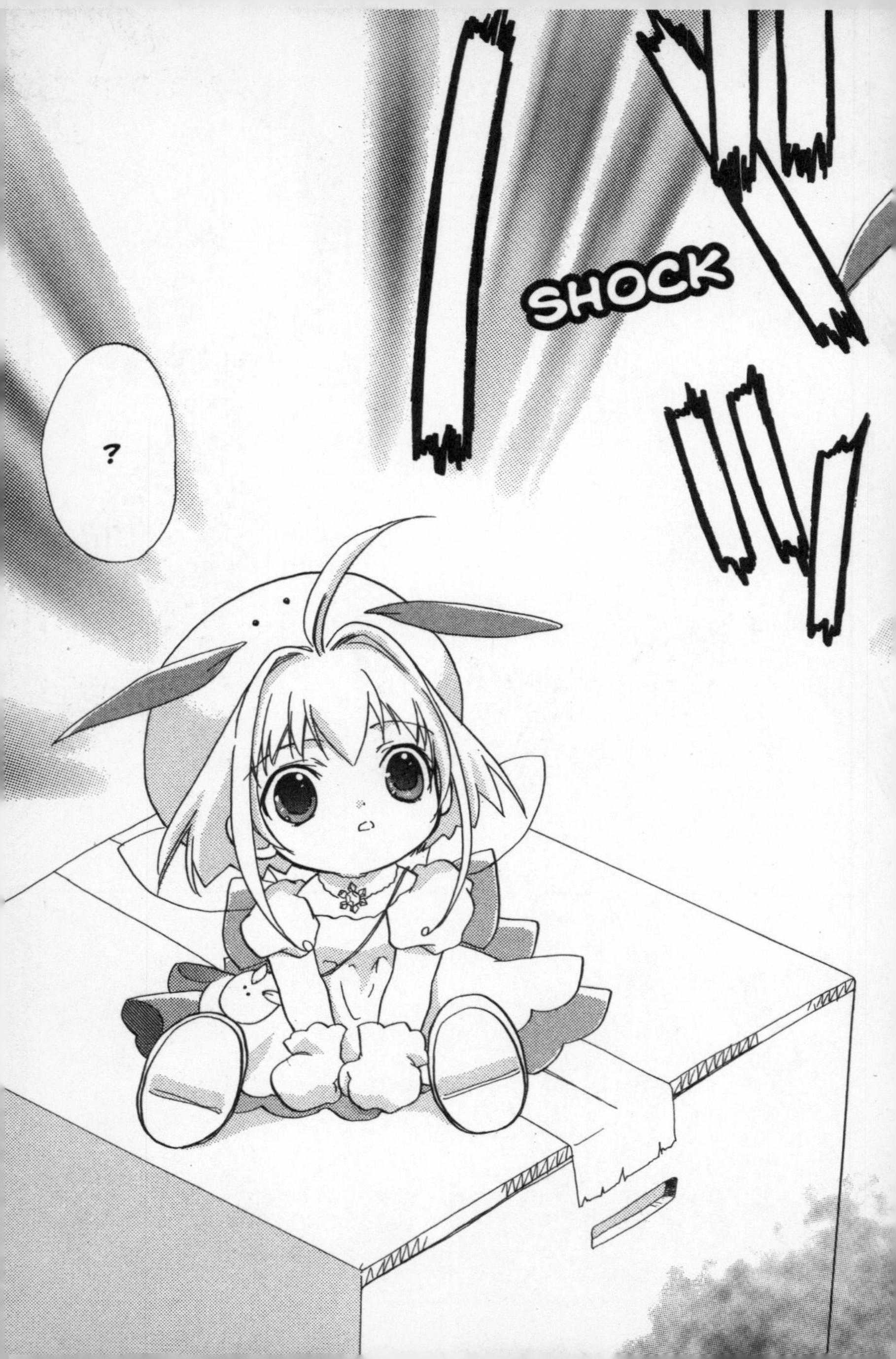
SHOCK
?

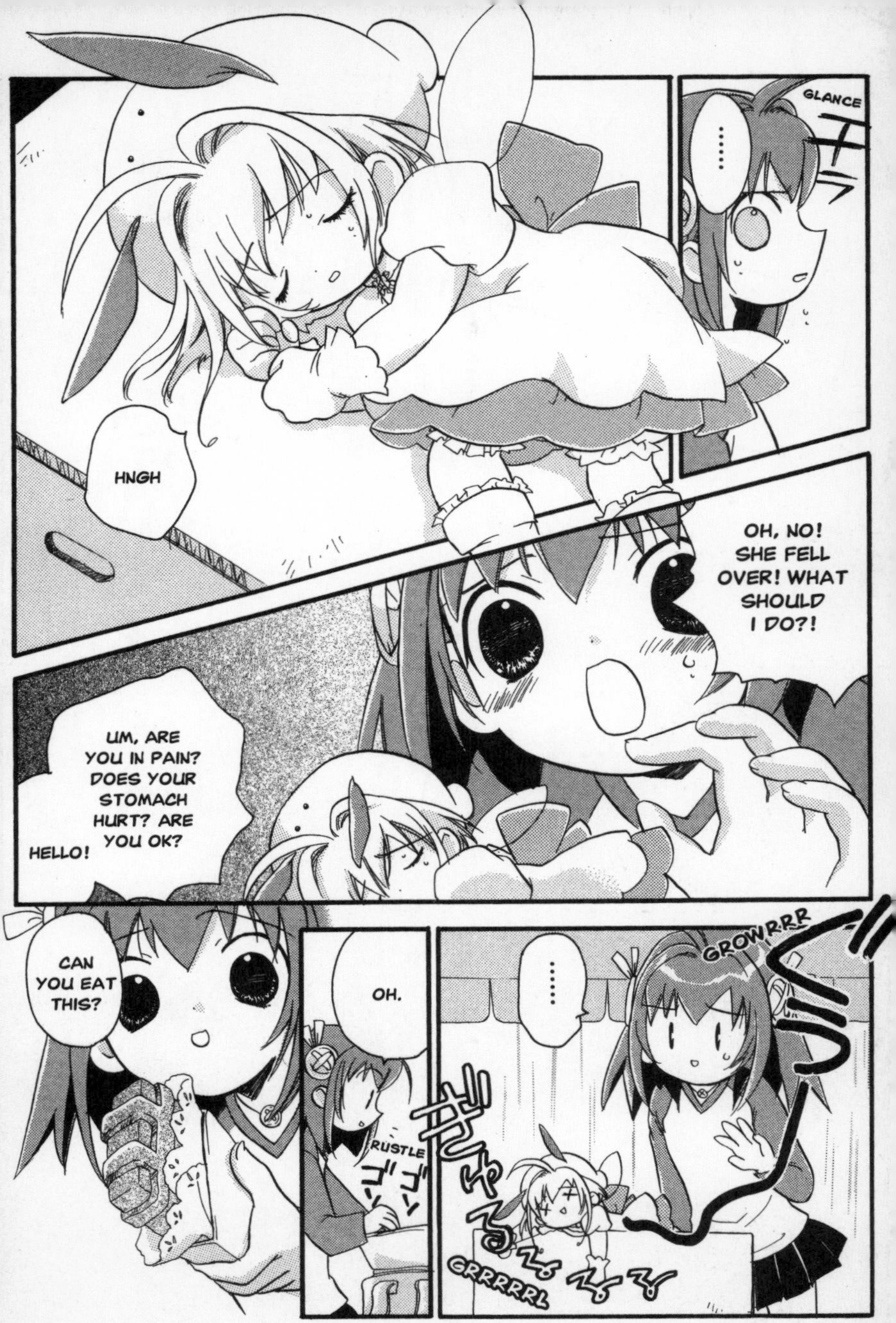
GLANCE
……
HNGH
OH, NO! SHE FELL OVER! WHAT SHOULD I DO?!
UM, ARE YOU IN PAIN? DOES YOUR STOMACH HURT? ARE YOU OK?
HELLO!
……
GROWRRR
GRRRRRL
OH.
RUSTLE
CAN YOU EAT THIS?

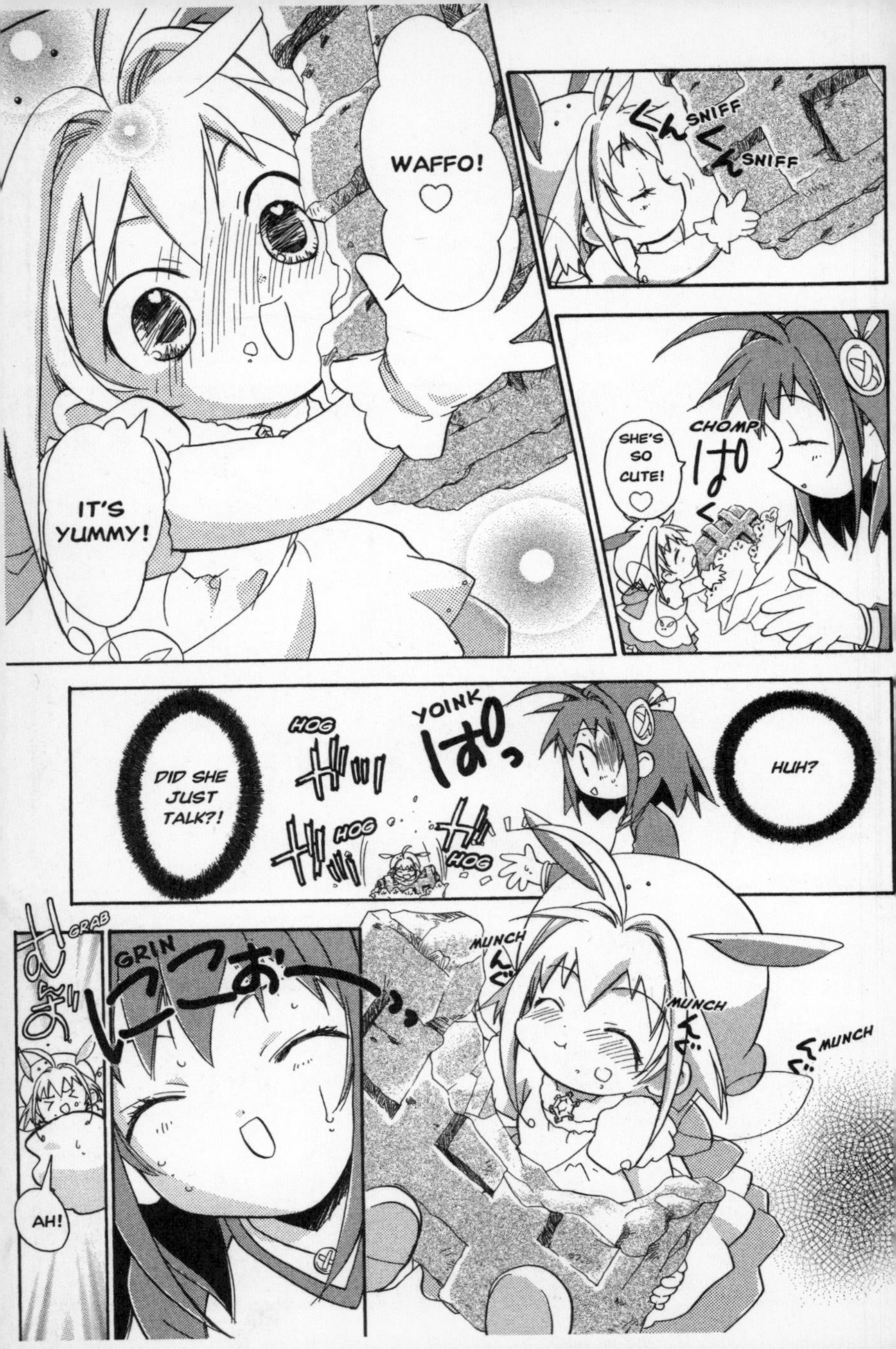

くんくん
SNIFF
SNIFF
SHE'S SO CUTE! ♡
ぱく
CHOMP
WAFFO! ♡
IT'S YUMMY!
HUH?
ぱっ
YOINK
HOG
HOG
HOG
DID SHE JUST TALK?!
MUNCH
MUNCH
MUNCH
GRIN
GRAB
AH!

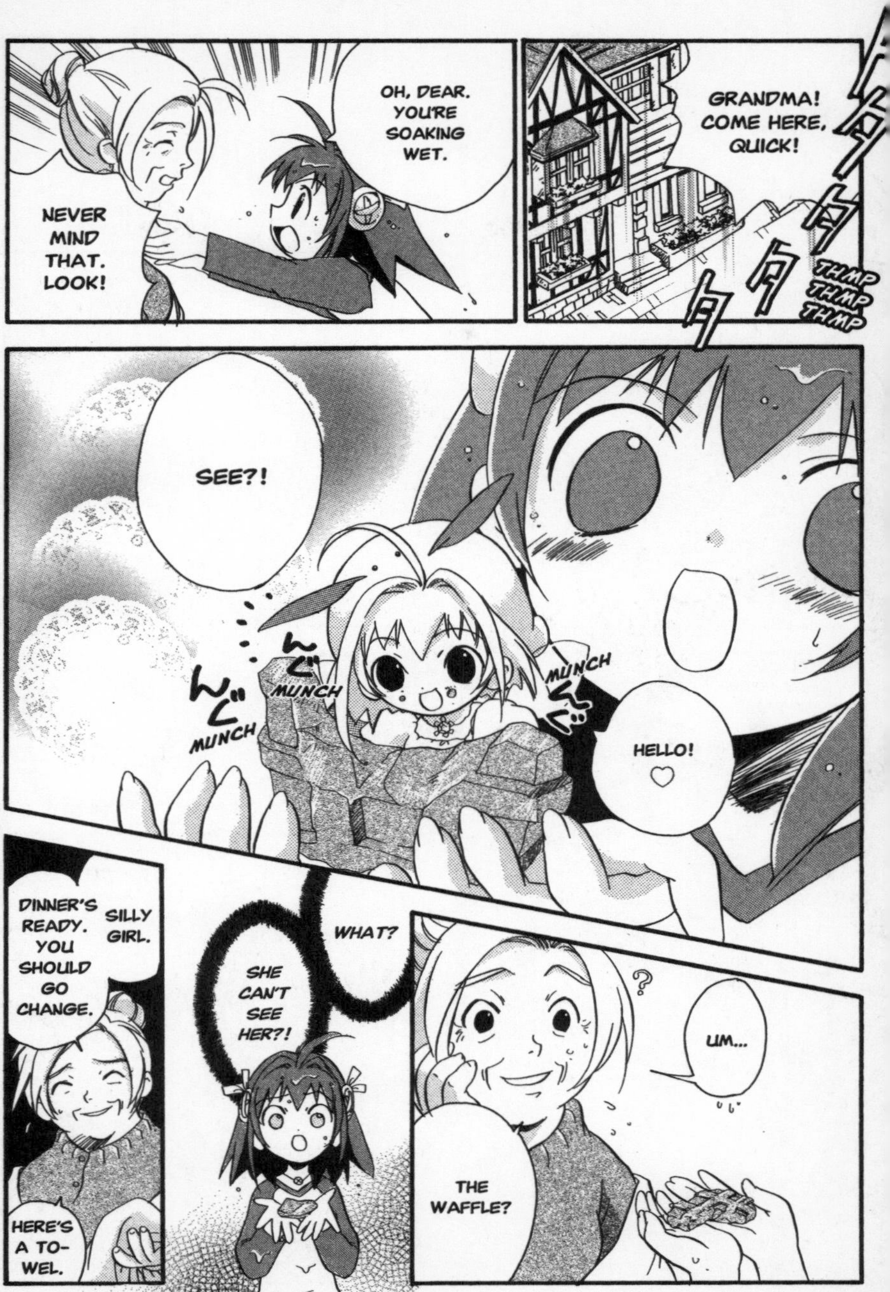

GRANDMA! COME HERE, QUICK!
タタタタ
THMP THMP THMP
OH, DEAR. YOU'RE SOAKING WET.
NEVER MIND THAT. LOOK!
SEE?!
HELLO! ♡
んぐ MUNCH
んぐ MUNCH
んぐ MUNCH
UM...
THE WAFFLE?
WHAT?
SHE CAN'T SEE HER?!
SILLY GIRL.
DINNER'S READY. YOU SHOULD GO CHANGE.
HERE'S A TO-WEL.

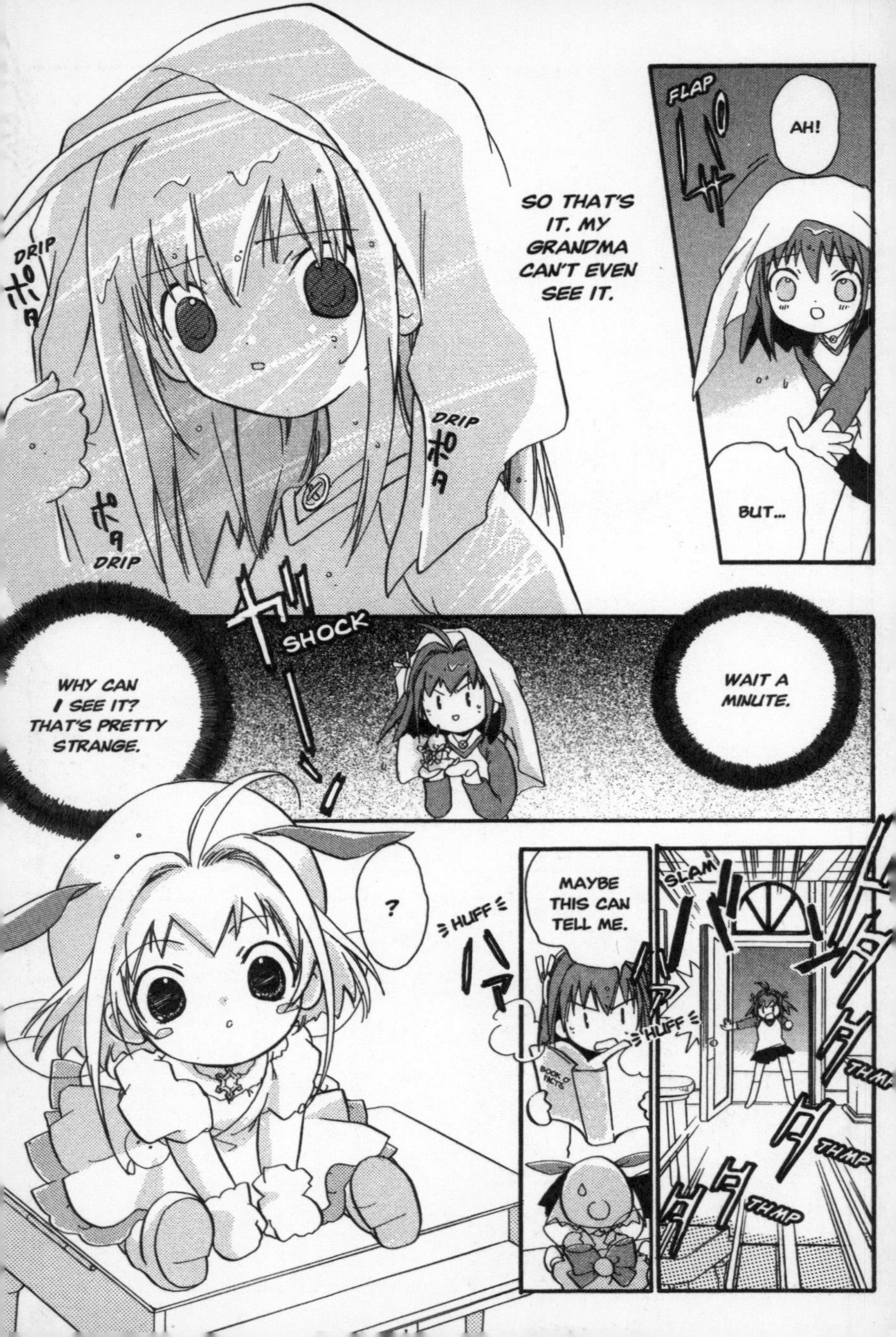
FLAP
AH!
BUT...
SO THAT'S IT. MY GRANDMA CAN'T EVEN SEE IT.
DRIP
DRIP
DRIP
WAIT A MINUTE.
SHOCK
WHY CAN I SEE IT? THAT'S PRETTY STRANGE.
SLAM
THMP
THMP
THMP
MAYBE THIS CAN TELL ME.
HUFF
HUFF
BOOK O' FACTS
?

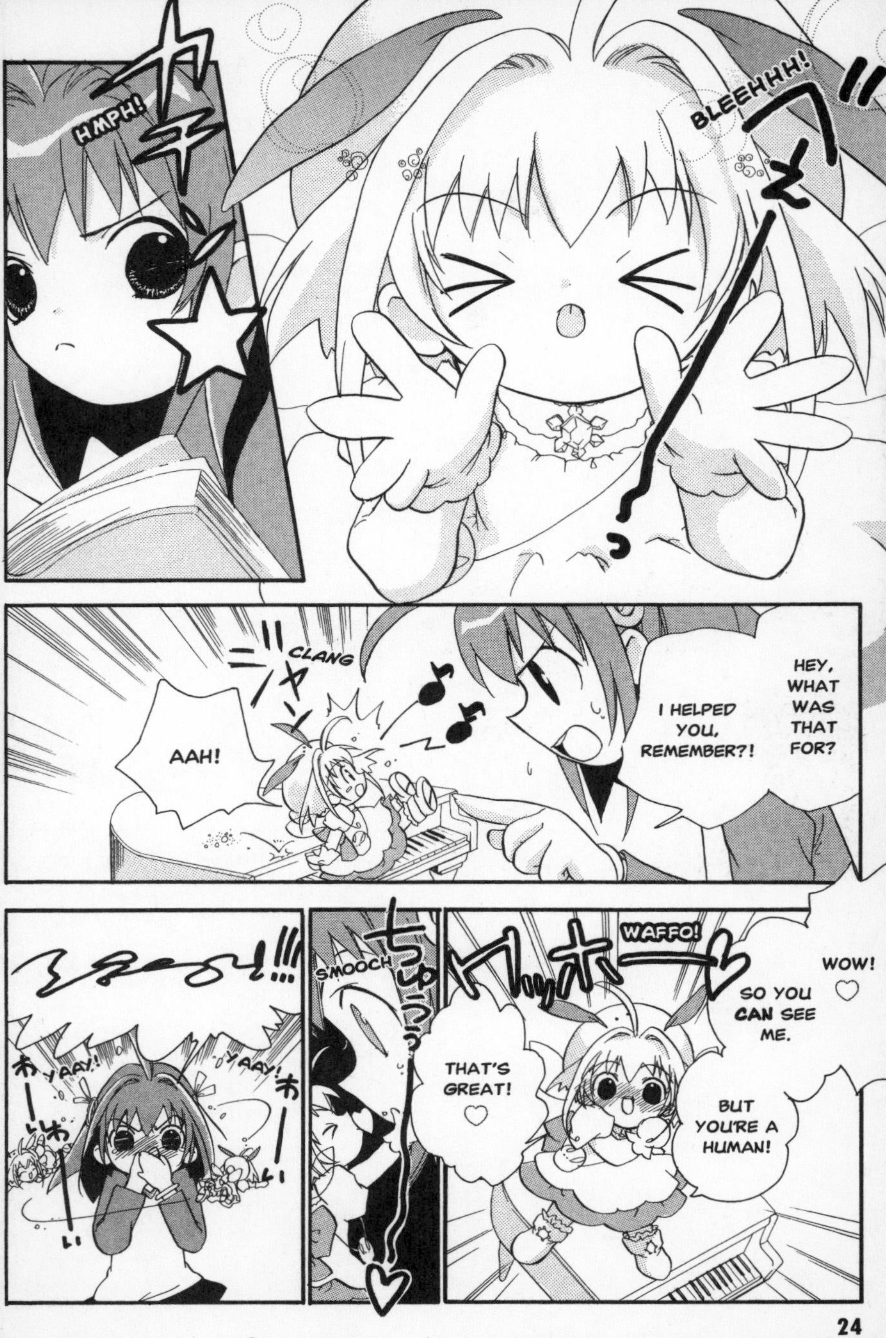

BLEEHHH!
HMPH!
HEY, WHAT WAS THAT FOR?
I HELPED YOU, REMEMBER?!
CLANG
AAH!
WAFFO!
WOW! ♡
SO YOU CAN SEE ME.
BUT YOU'RE A HUMAN!
THAT'S GREAT! ♡
SMOOCH
YAAY!
YAAY!

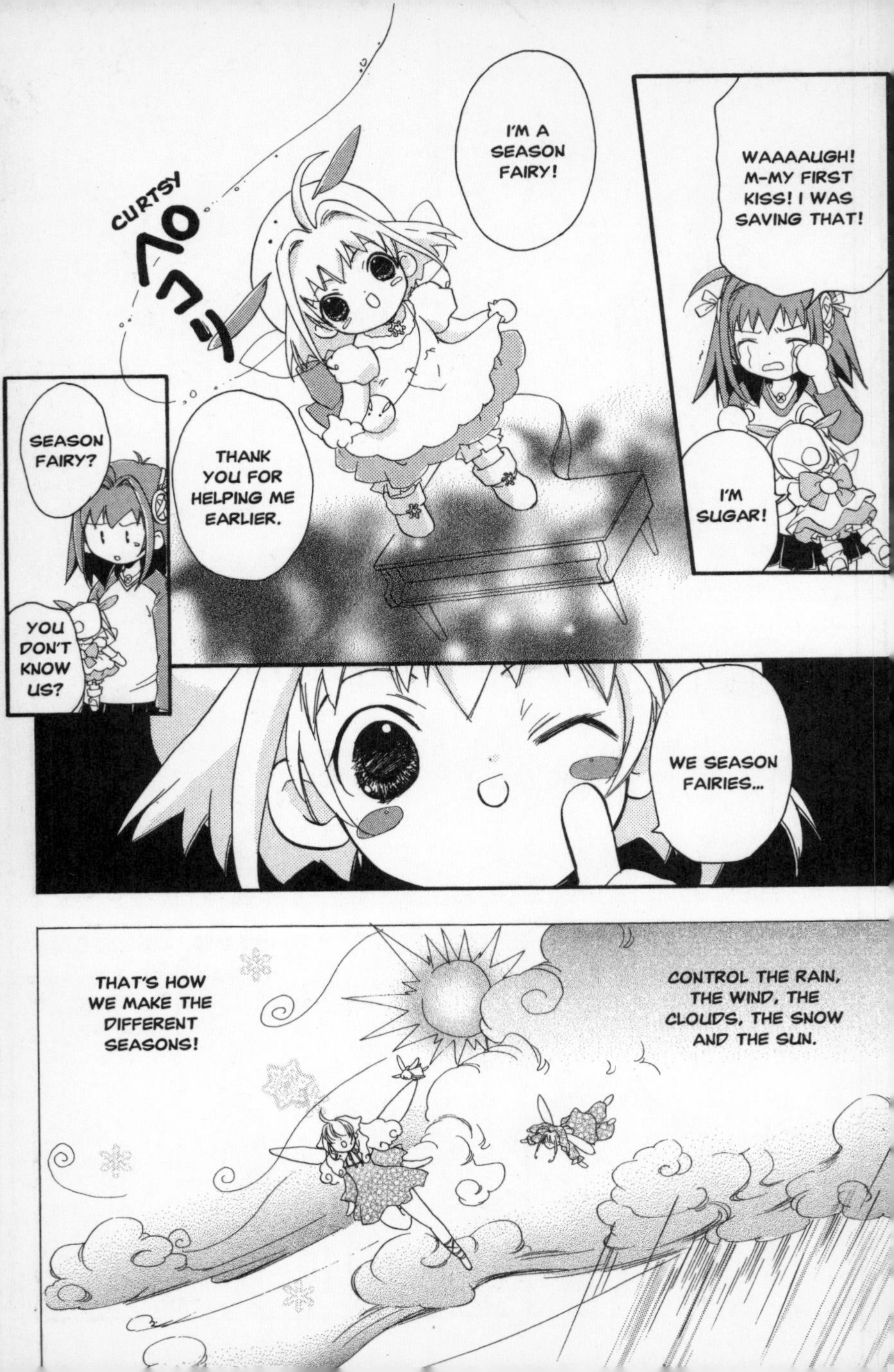
WAAAAUGH! M-MY FIRST KISS! I WAS SAVING THAT!
I'M SUGAR!
I'M A SEASON FAIRY!
CURTSY
THANK YOU FOR HELPING ME EARLIER.
SEASON FAIRY?
YOU DON'T KNOW US?
WE SEASON FAIRIES...
CONTROL THE RAIN, THE WIND, THE CLOUDS, THE SNOW AND THE SUN.
THAT'S HOW WE MAKE THE DIFFERENT SEASONS!

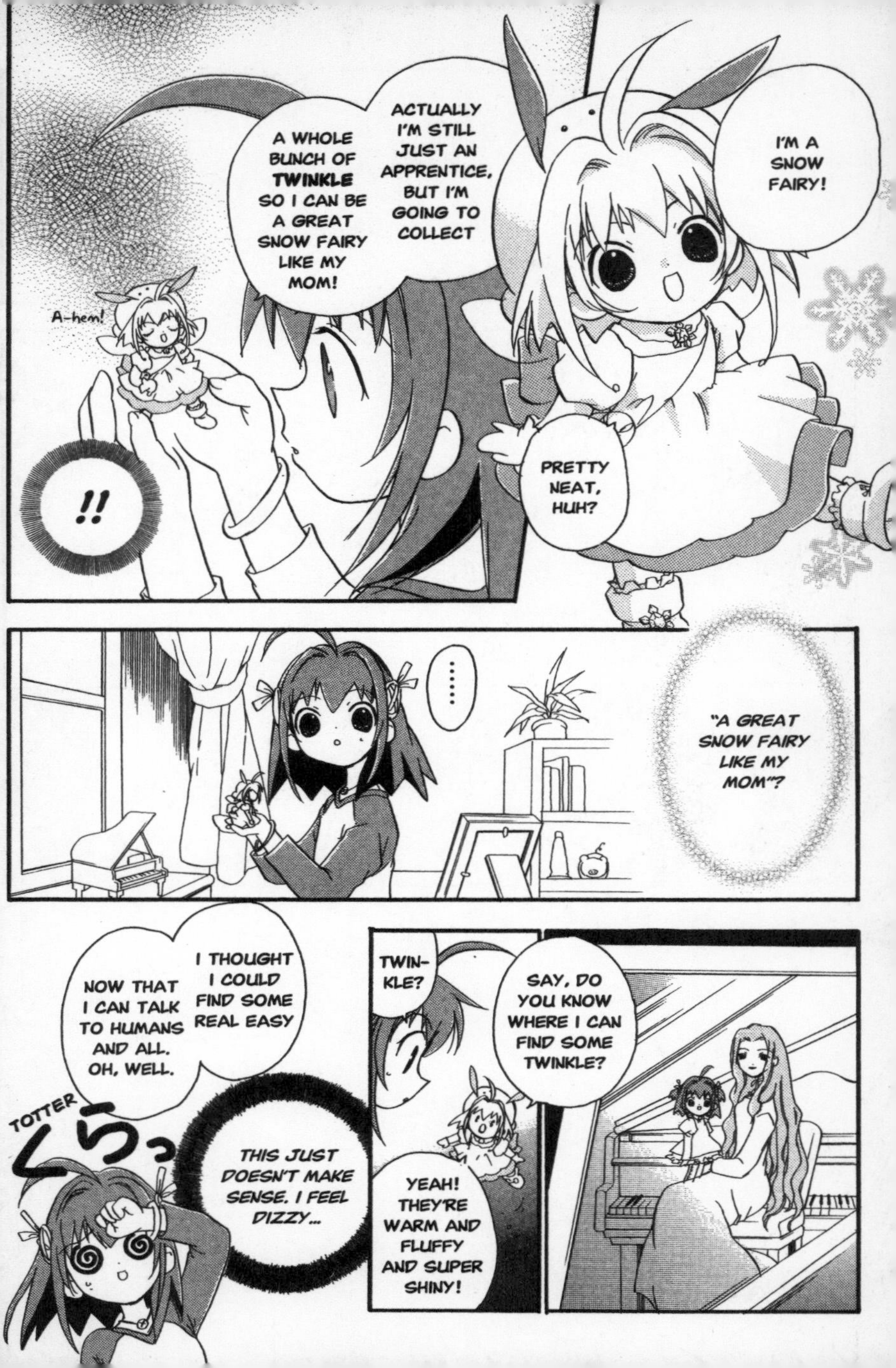
I'M A SNOW FAIRY!
ACTUALLY I'M STILL JUST AN APPRENTICE, BUT I'M GOING TO COLLECT
A WHOLE BUNCH OF **TWINKLE** SO I CAN BE A GREAT SNOW FAIRY LIKE MY MOM!
PRETTY NEAT, HUH?
A-hem!
!!
"A GREAT SNOW FAIRY LIKE MY MOM"?
......
SAY, DO YOU KNOW WHERE I CAN FIND SOME TWINKLE?
TWIN-KLE?
YEAH! THEY'RE WARM AND FLUFFY AND SUPER SHINY!
I THOUGHT I COULD FIND SOME REAL EASY
NOW THAT I CAN TALK TO HUMANS AND ALL. OH, WELL.
TOTTER
くらっ
THIS JUST DOESN'T MAKE SENSE. I FEEL DIZZY...

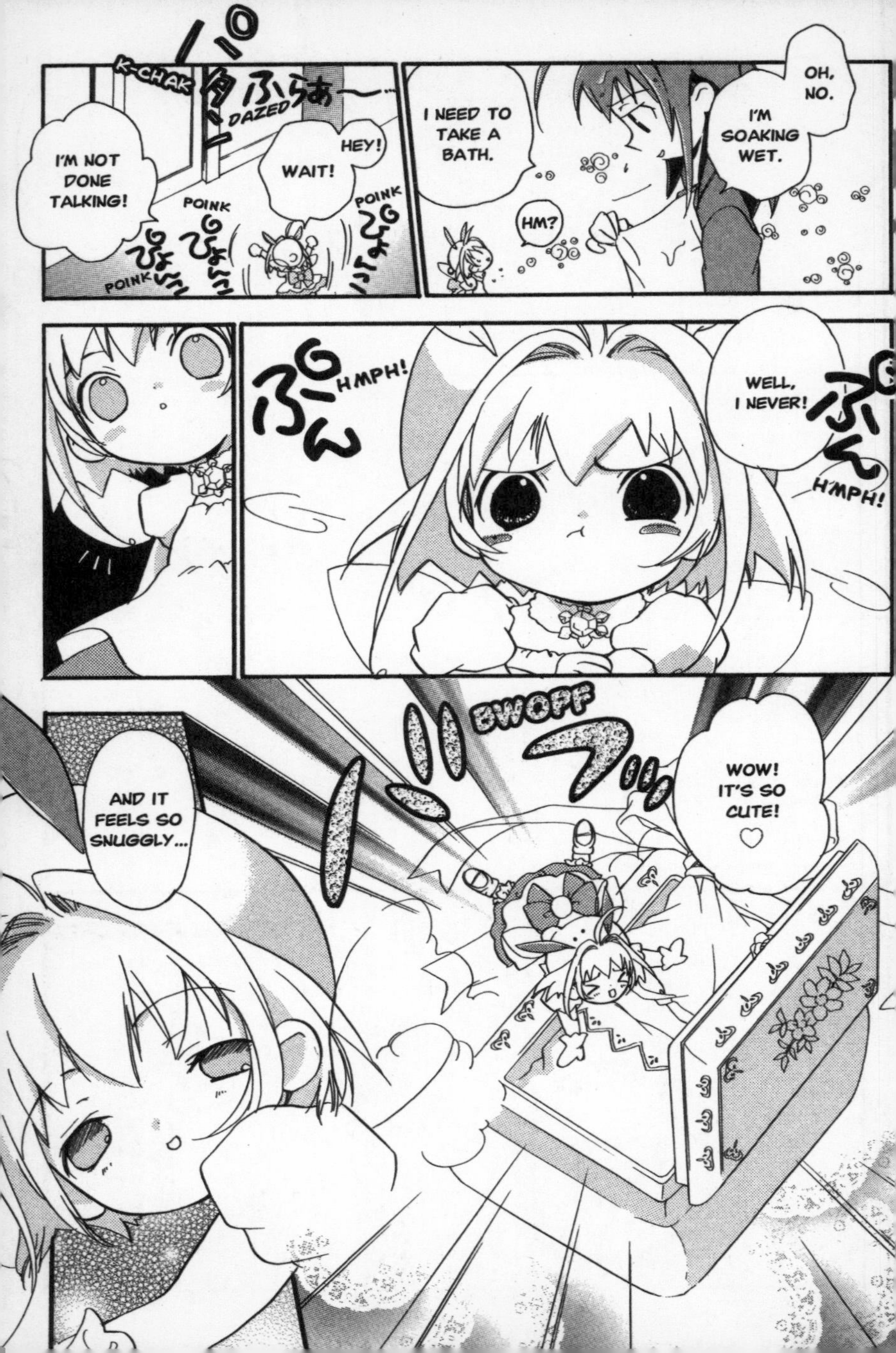
OH, NO.
I'M SOAKING WET.
I NEED TO TAKE A BATH.
HM?
K-CHAK
ふらぁ〜
DAZED
HEY!
WAIT!
I'M NOT DONE TALKING!
POINK
POINK
POINK
WELL, I NEVER!
ぷん
H'MPH!
ぷん
HMPH!
WOW! IT'S SO CUTE! ♡
BWOFF
AND IT FEELS SO SNUGGLY...

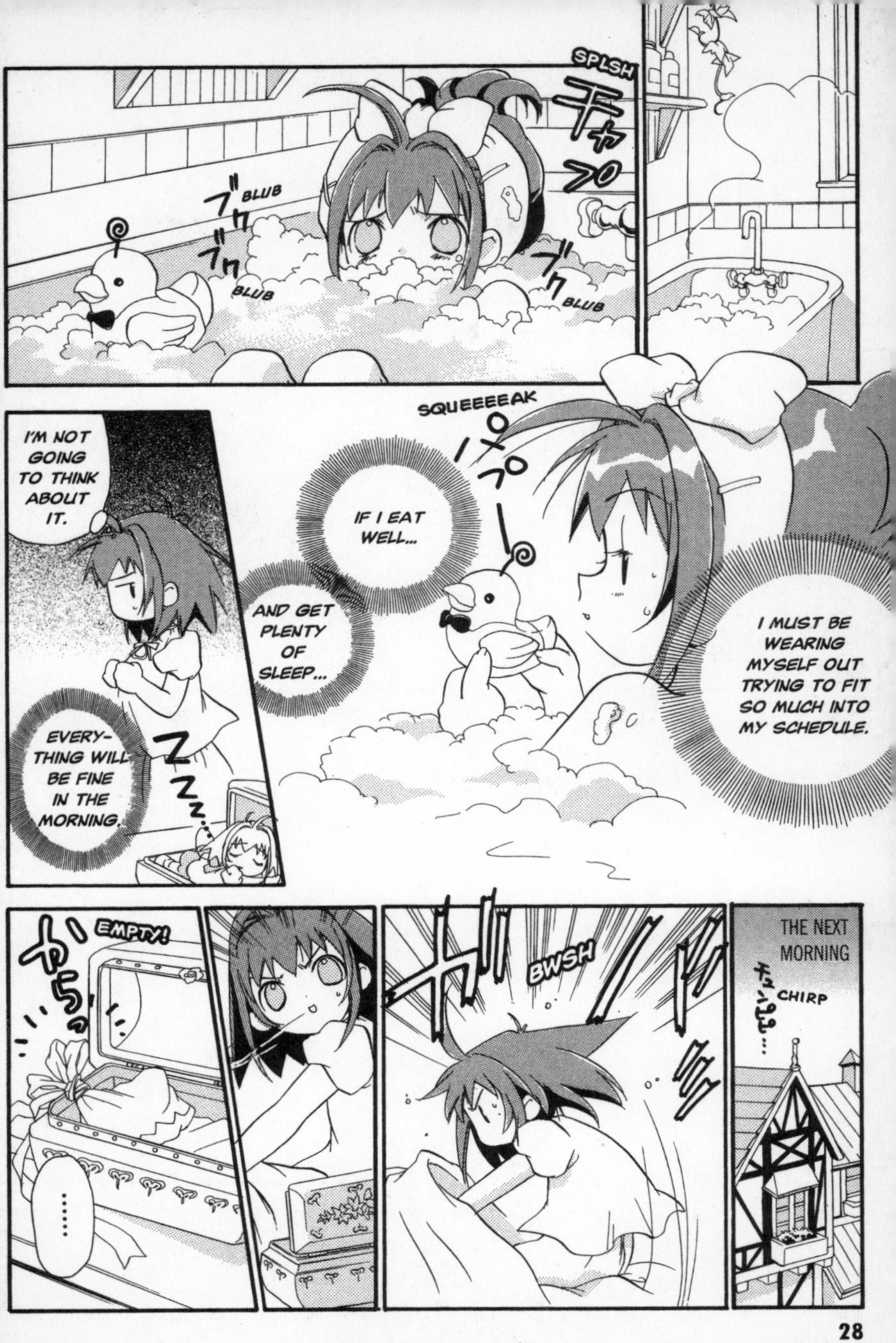
SPLSH
BLUB
BLUB
BLUB
SQUEEEEAK
I MUST BE WEARING MYSELF OUT TRYING TO FIT SO MUCH INTO MY SCHEDULE.
IF I EAT WELL...
AND GET PLENTY OF SLEEP...
I'M NOT GOING TO THINK ABOUT IT.
EVERY-THING WILL BE FINE IN THE MORNING.
ZZZ...
THE NEXT MORNING
CHIRP
BWSH
EMPTY!
......

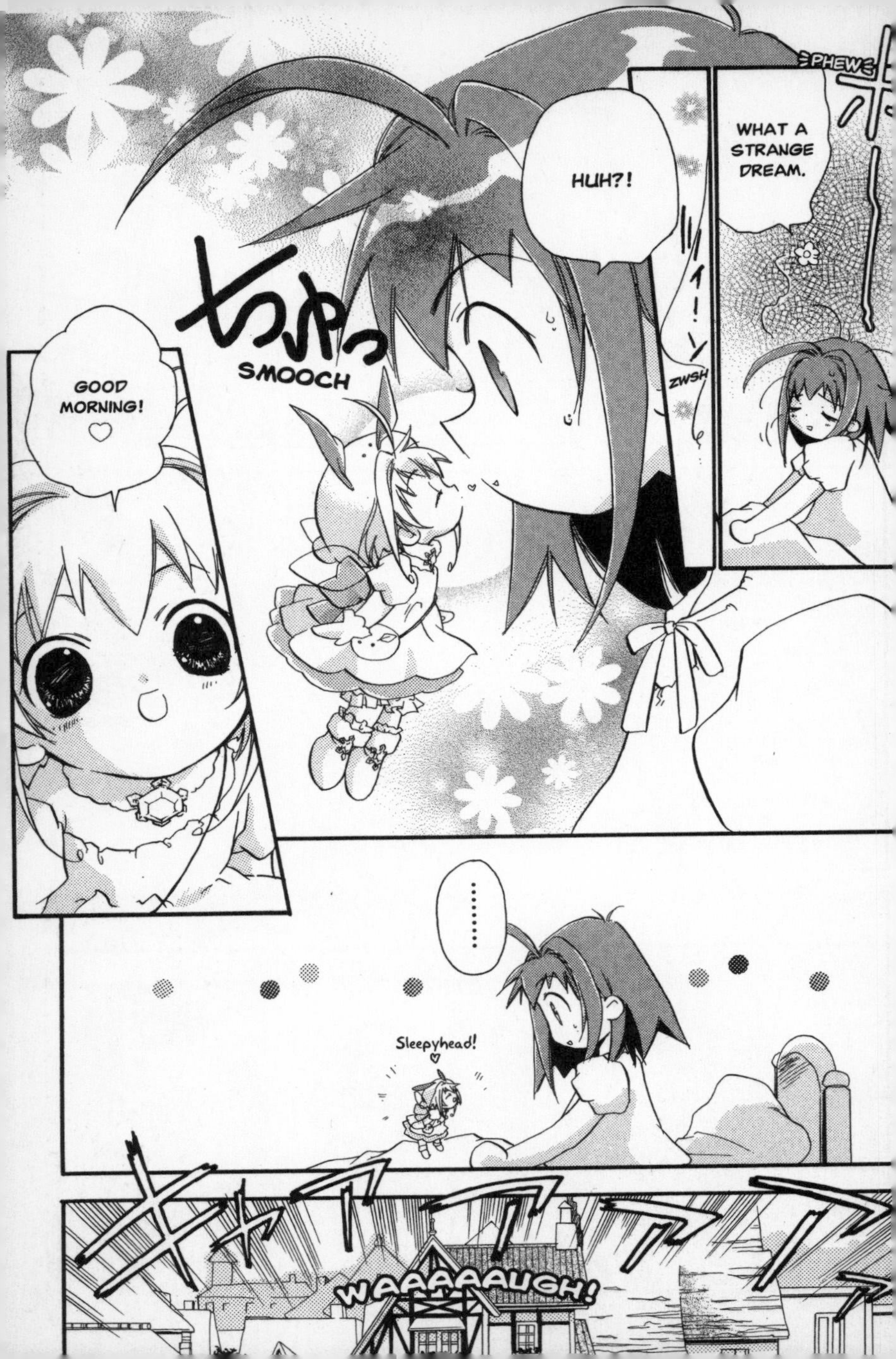
PHEW
WHAT A STRANGE DREAM.
HUH?!
ZWSH
ちゅっ
SMOOCH
GOOD MORNING! ♡
......
Sleepyhead! ♡
WAAAAAAUGH!

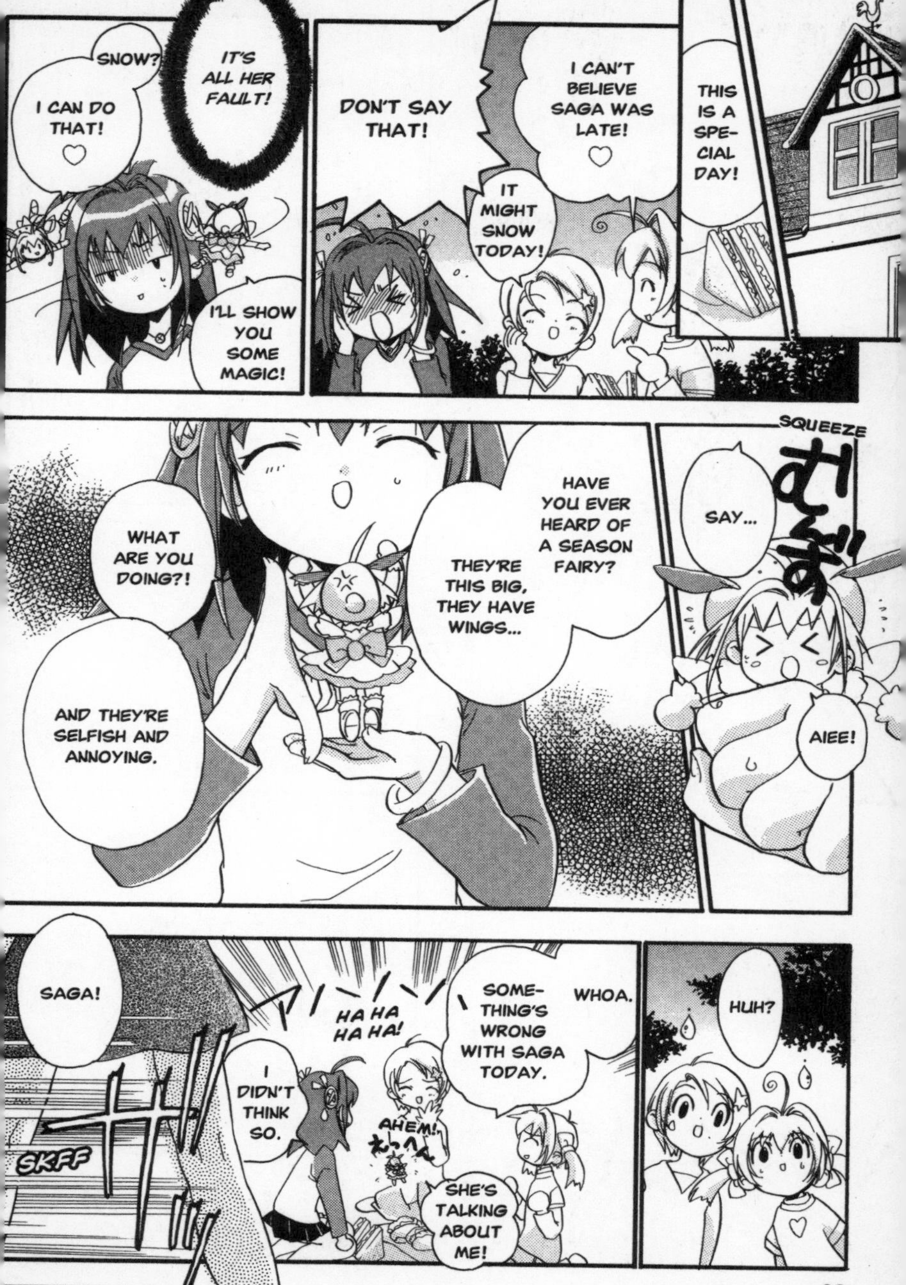
THIS IS A SPE-CIAL DAY!
I CAN'T BELIEVE SAGA WAS LATE! ♡
IT MIGHT SNOW TODAY!
DON'T SAY THAT!
IT'S ALL HER FAULT!
SNOW?
I CAN DO THAT! ♡
I'LL SHOW YOU SOME MAGIC!
SQUEEZE
SAY...
AIEE!
HAVE YOU EVER HEARD OF A SEASON FAIRY?
THEY'RE THIS BIG, THEY HAVE WINGS...
WHAT ARE YOU DOING?!
AND THEY'RE SELFISH AND ANNOYING.
HUH?
WHOA.
SOME-THING'S WRONG WITH SAGA TODAY.
HA HA HA HA!
I DIDN'T THINK SO.
AHEM!
SHE'S TALKING ABOUT ME!
SAGA!
SKFF

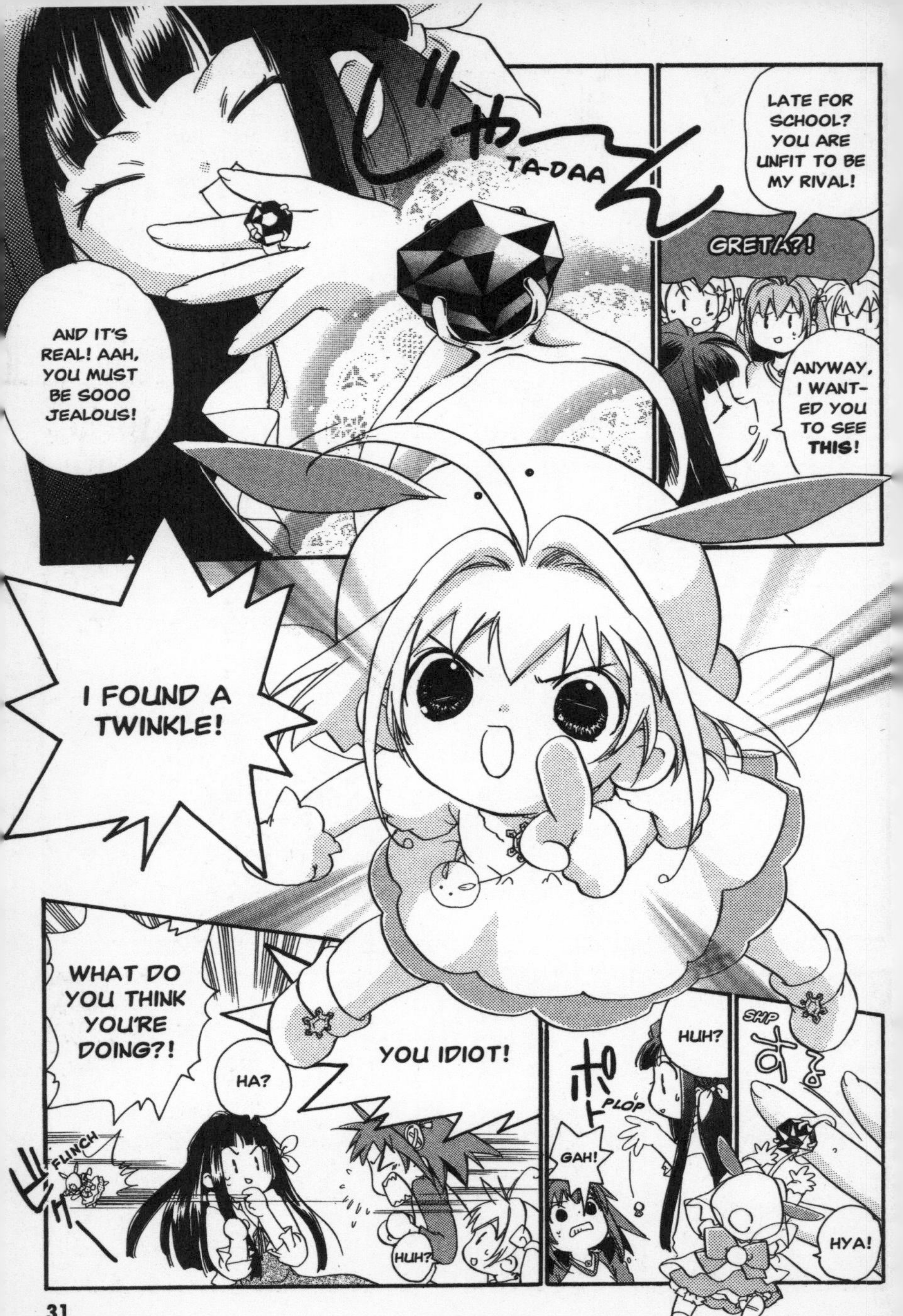
LATE FOR SCHOOL? YOU ARE UNFIT TO BE MY RIVAL!
GRETA?!
ANYWAY, I WANTED YOU TO SEE THIS!
じゃーん
TA-DAA
AND IT'S REAL! AAH, YOU MUST BE SOOO JEALOUS!
I FOUND A TWINKLE!
SHP
する
HUH?
HYA!
ポト
PLOP
GAH!
WHAT DO YOU THINK YOU'RE DOING?!
YOU IDIOT!
HA?
FLINCH
HUH?

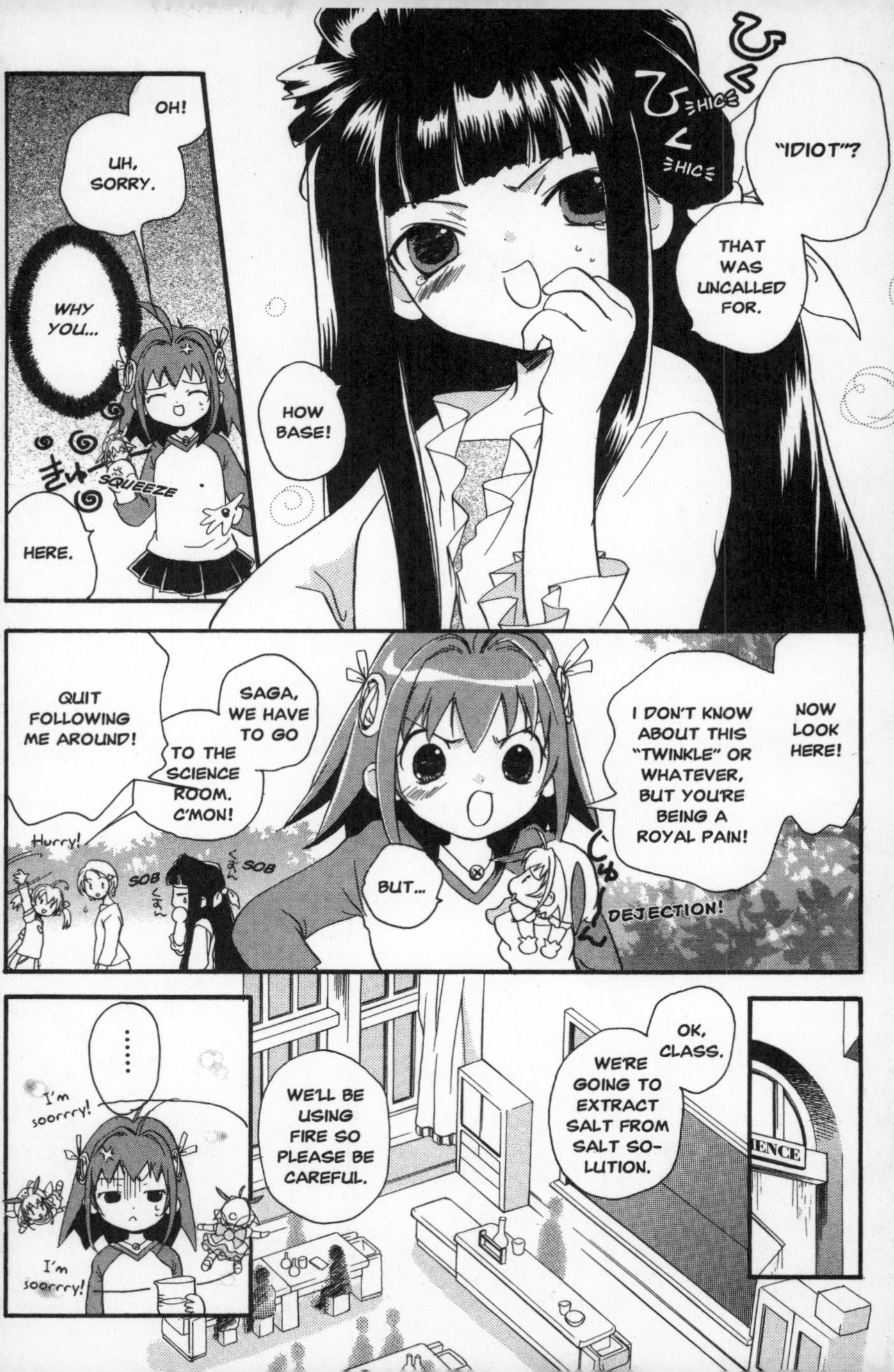
HIC
HIC
"IDIOT"?
THAT WAS UNCALLED FOR.
HOW BASE!
OH!
UH, SORRY.
WHY YOU...
SQUEEZE
HERE.
NOW LOOK HERE!
I DON'T KNOW ABOUT THIS "TWINKLE" OR WHATEVER, BUT YOU'RE BEING A ROYAL PAIN!
DEJECTION!
BUT...
SAGA, WE HAVE TO GO
TO THE SCIENCE ROOM. C'MON!
QUIT FOLLOWING ME AROUND!
SOB
SOB
Hurry!
OK, CLASS.
WE'RE GOING TO EXTRACT SALT FROM SALT SO-LUTION.
WE'LL BE USING FIRE SO PLEASE BE CAREFUL.
......
I'm soorrry!
I'm soorrry!

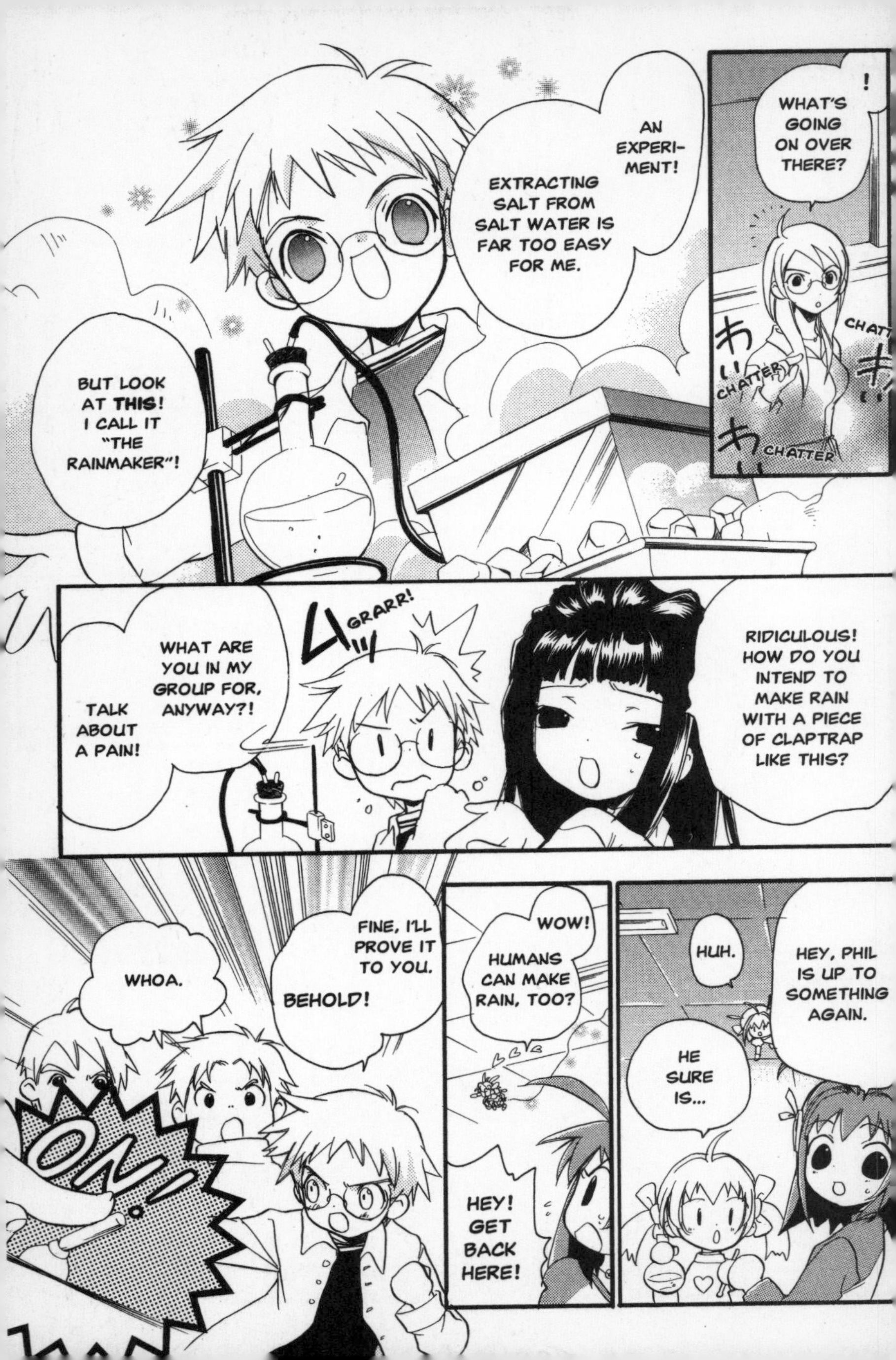
!
WHAT'S GOING ON OVER THERE?
CHATTER
CHATTER
CHATTER
AN EXPERIMENT!
EXTRACTING SALT FROM SALT WATER IS FAR TOO EASY FOR ME.
BUT LOOK AT **THIS**! I CALL IT "THE RAINMAKER"!
RIDICULOUS! HOW DO YOU INTEND TO MAKE RAIN WITH A PIECE OF CLAPTRAP LIKE THIS?
GRARR!
WHAT ARE YOU IN MY GROUP FOR, ANYWAY?!
TALK ABOUT A PAIN!
HEY, PHIL IS UP TO SOMETHING AGAIN.
HUH.
HE SURE IS...
WOW!
HUMANS CAN MAKE RAIN, TOO?
HEY! GET BACK HERE!
FINE, I'LL PROVE IT TO YOU.
BEHOLD!
WHOA.
ON!

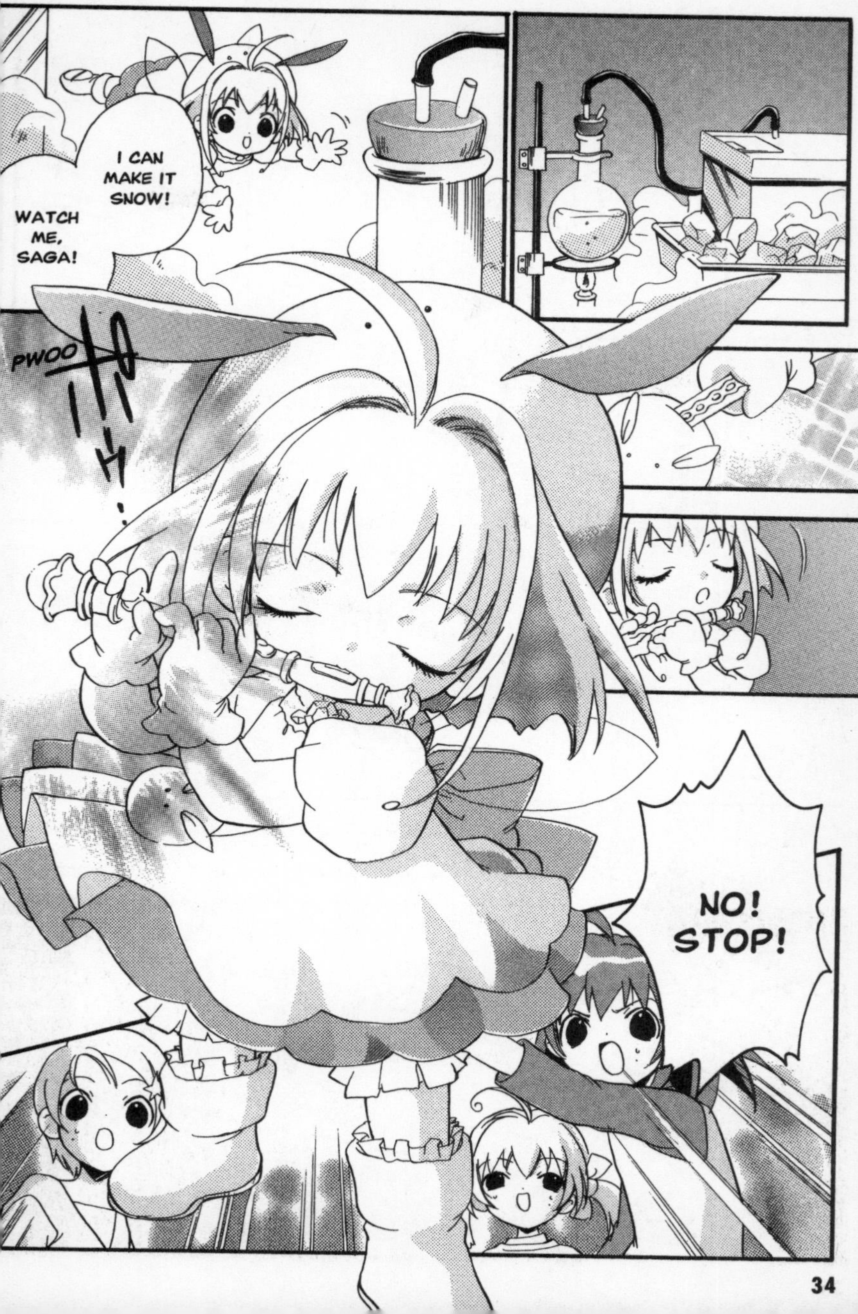
I CAN MAKE IT SNOW!
WATCH ME, SAGA!
PWOO
NO! STOP!

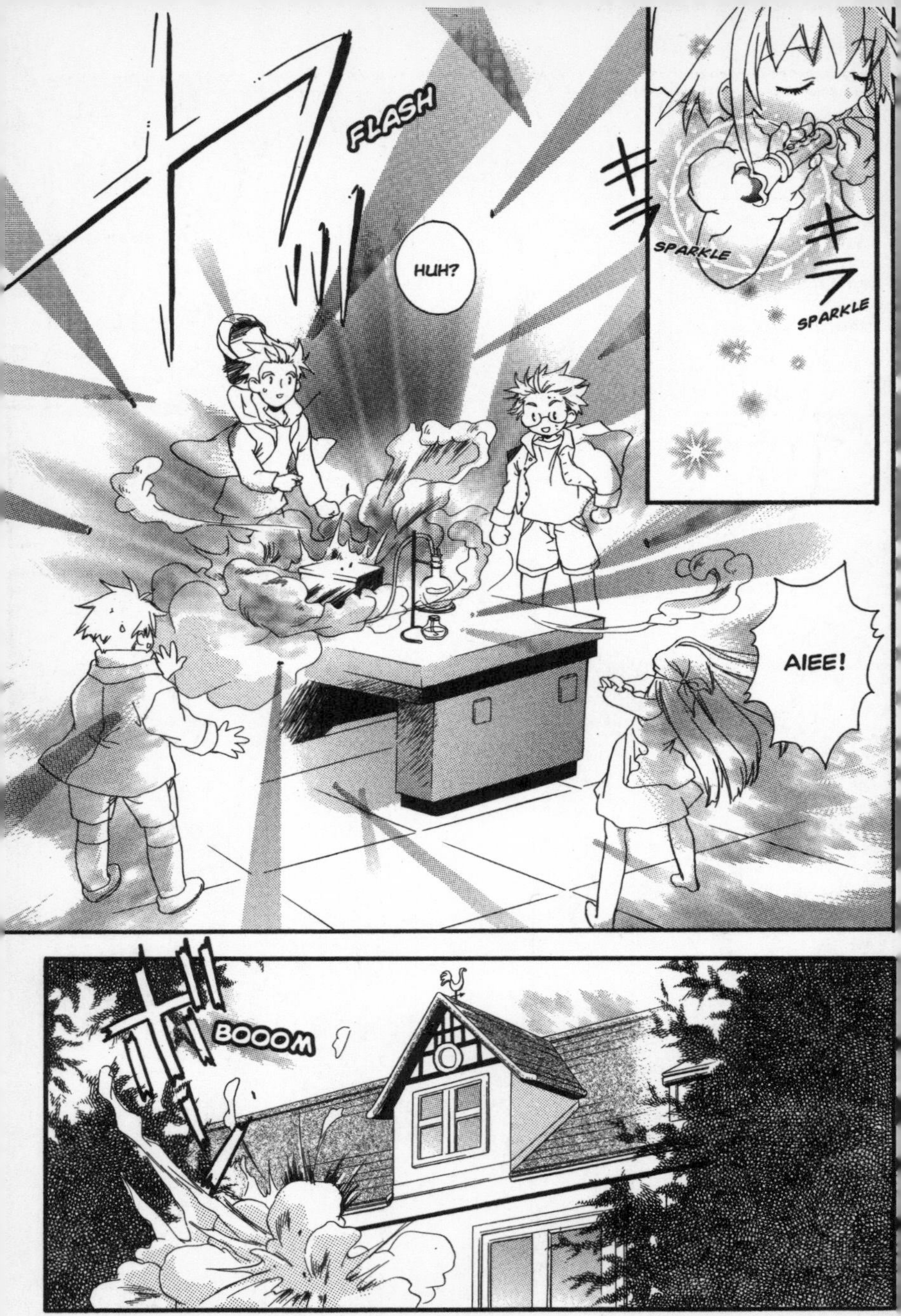

キラ
SPARKLE
キラ
SPARKLE
FLASH
HUH?
AIEE!
BOOOM

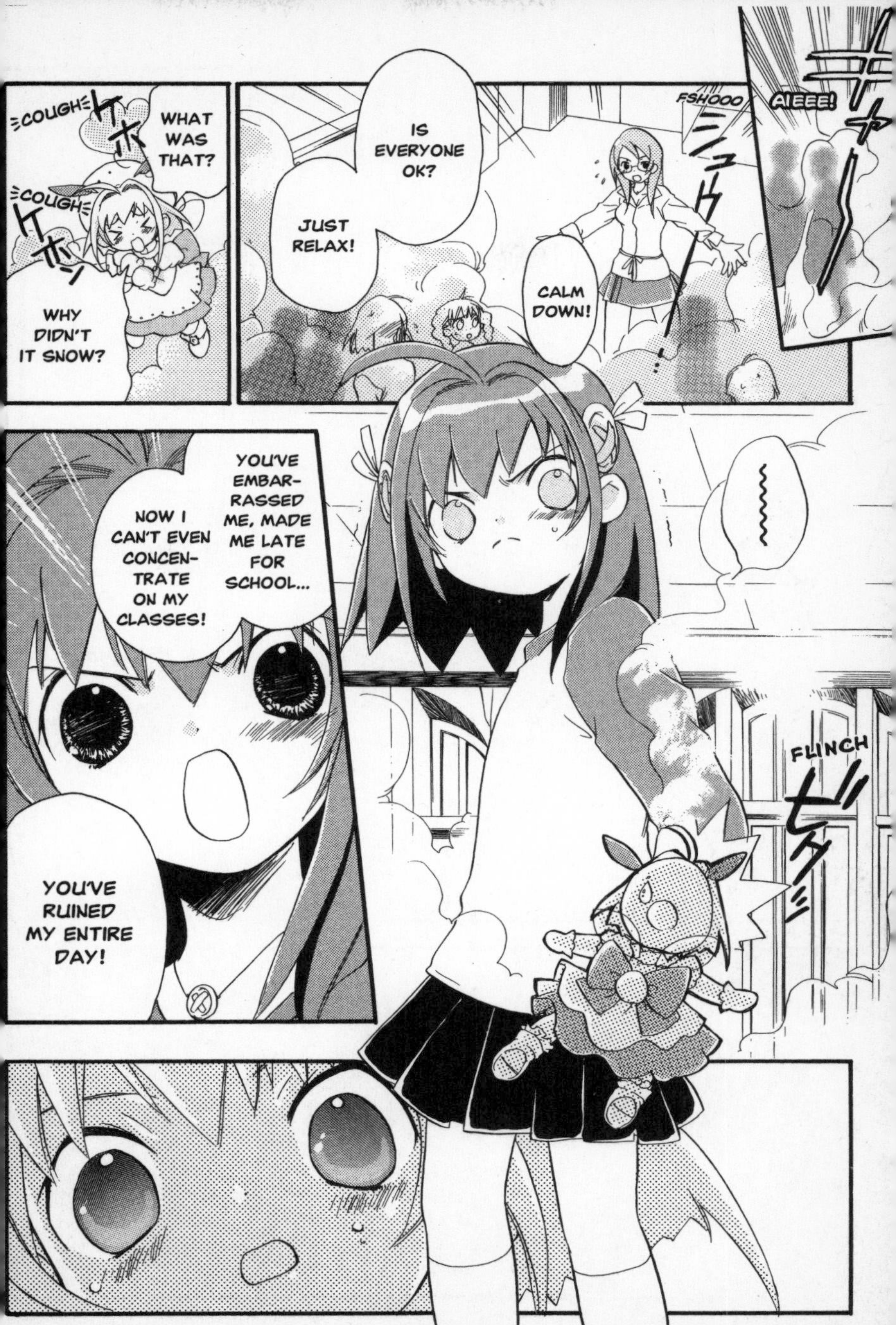
AIEEE!
FSHOOO
IS EVERYONE OK?
CALM DOWN!
JUST RELAX!
COUGH
WHAT WAS THAT?
COUGH
WHY DIDN'T IT SNOW?
FLINCH
YOU'VE EMBARRASSED ME, MADE ME LATE FOR SCHOOL...
NOW I CAN'T EVEN CONCENTRATE ON MY CLASSES!
YOU'VE RUINED MY ENTIRE DAY!

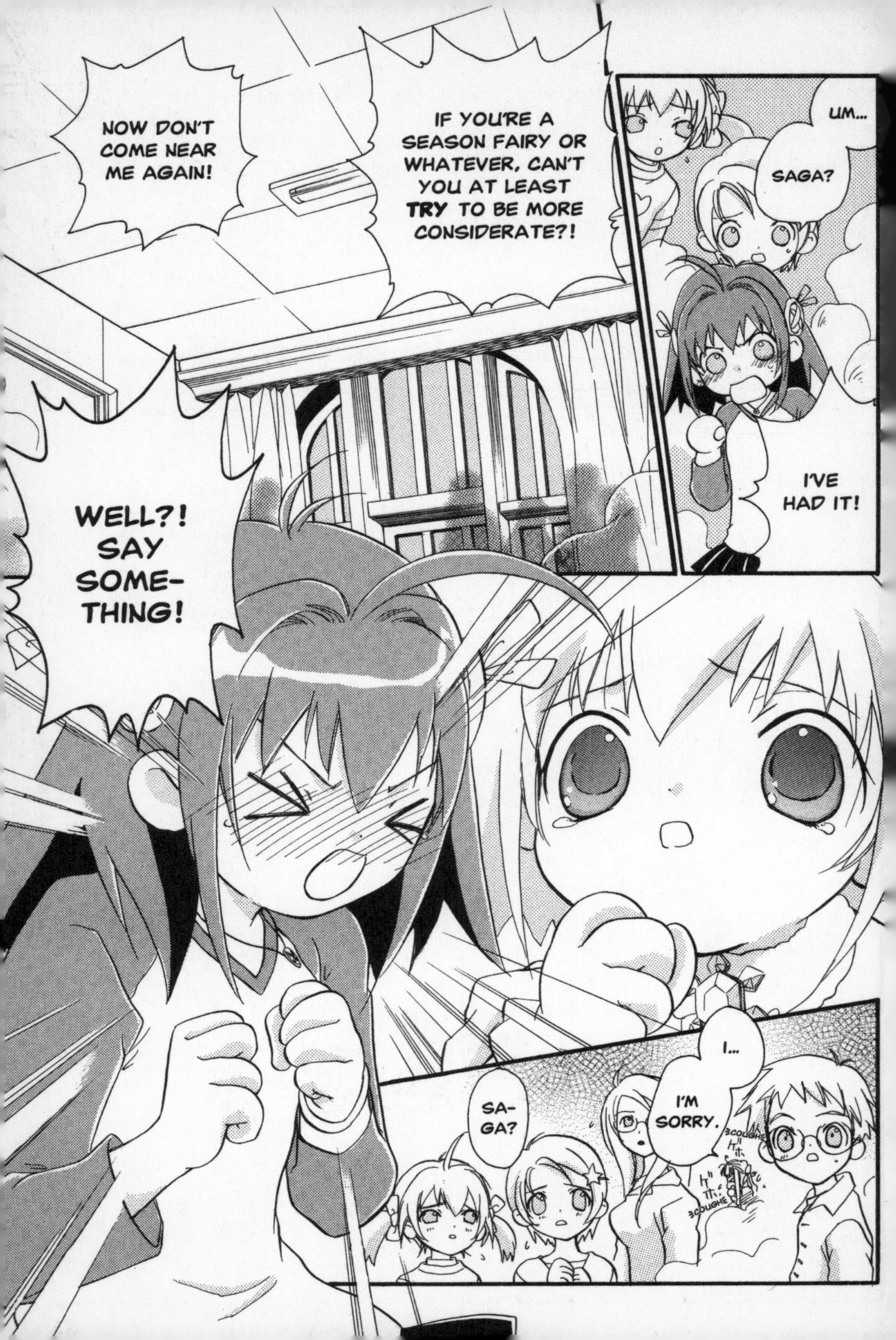
UM...
SAGA?
I'VE HAD IT!
IF YOU'RE A SEASON FAIRY OR WHATEVER, CAN'T YOU AT LEAST TRY TO BE MORE CONSIDERATE?!
NOW DON'T COME NEAR ME AGAIN!
WELL?! SAY SOME-THING!
I...
I'M SORRY.
SA-GA?
COUGH
COUGH

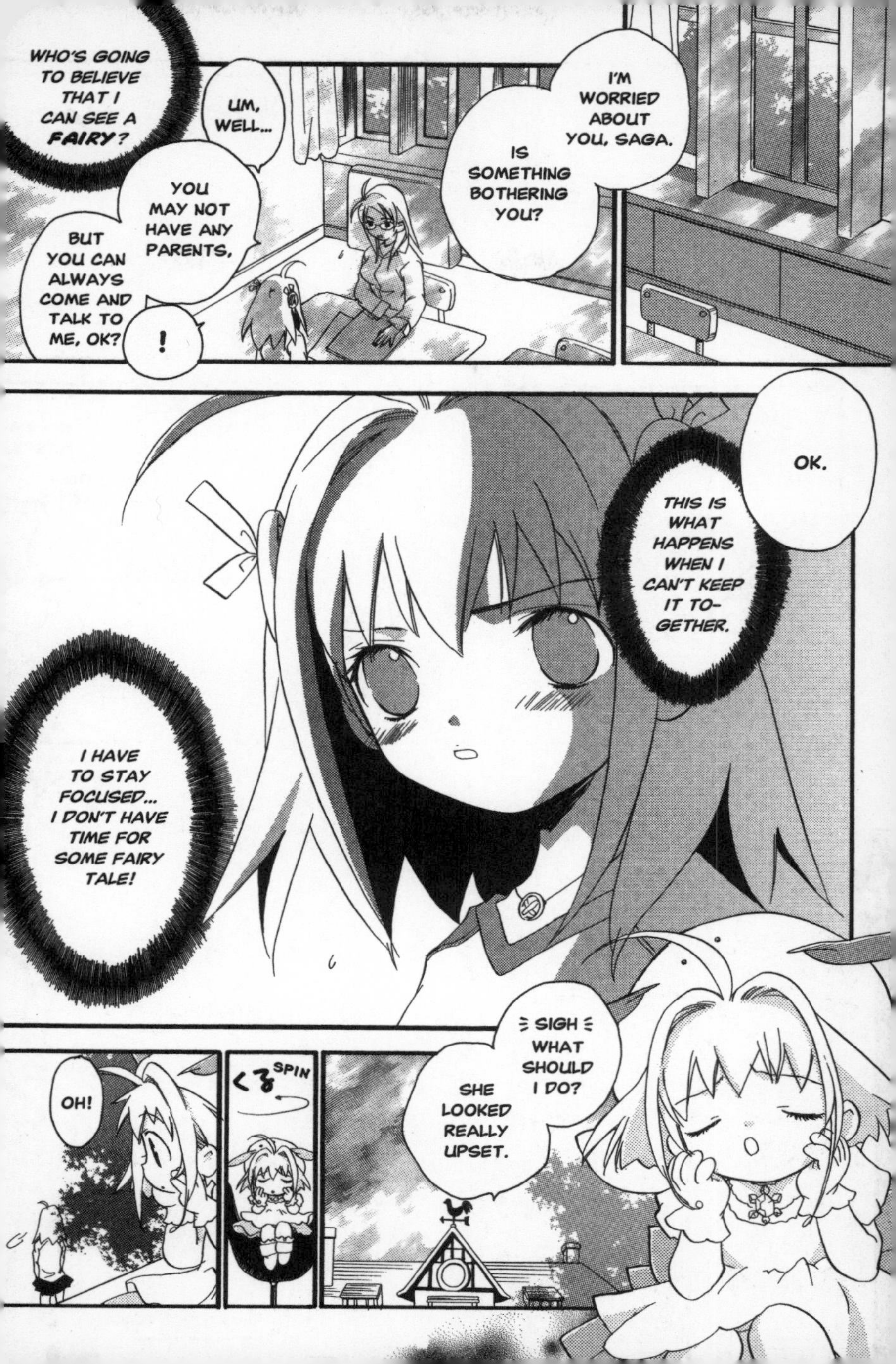
I'M WORRIED ABOUT YOU, SAGA.
IS SOMETHING BOTHERING YOU?
UM, WELL...
WHO'S GOING TO BELIEVE THAT I CAN SEE A FAIRY?
YOU MAY NOT HAVE ANY PARENTS,
BUT YOU CAN ALWAYS COME AND TALK TO ME, OK?
!
OK.
THIS IS WHAT HAPPENS WHEN I CAN'T KEEP IT TO-GETHER.
I HAVE TO STAY FOCUSED... I DON'T HAVE TIME FOR SOME FAIRY TALE!
≡SIGH≡ WHAT SHOULD I DO?
SHE LOOKED REALLY UPSET.
くる SPIN
OH!

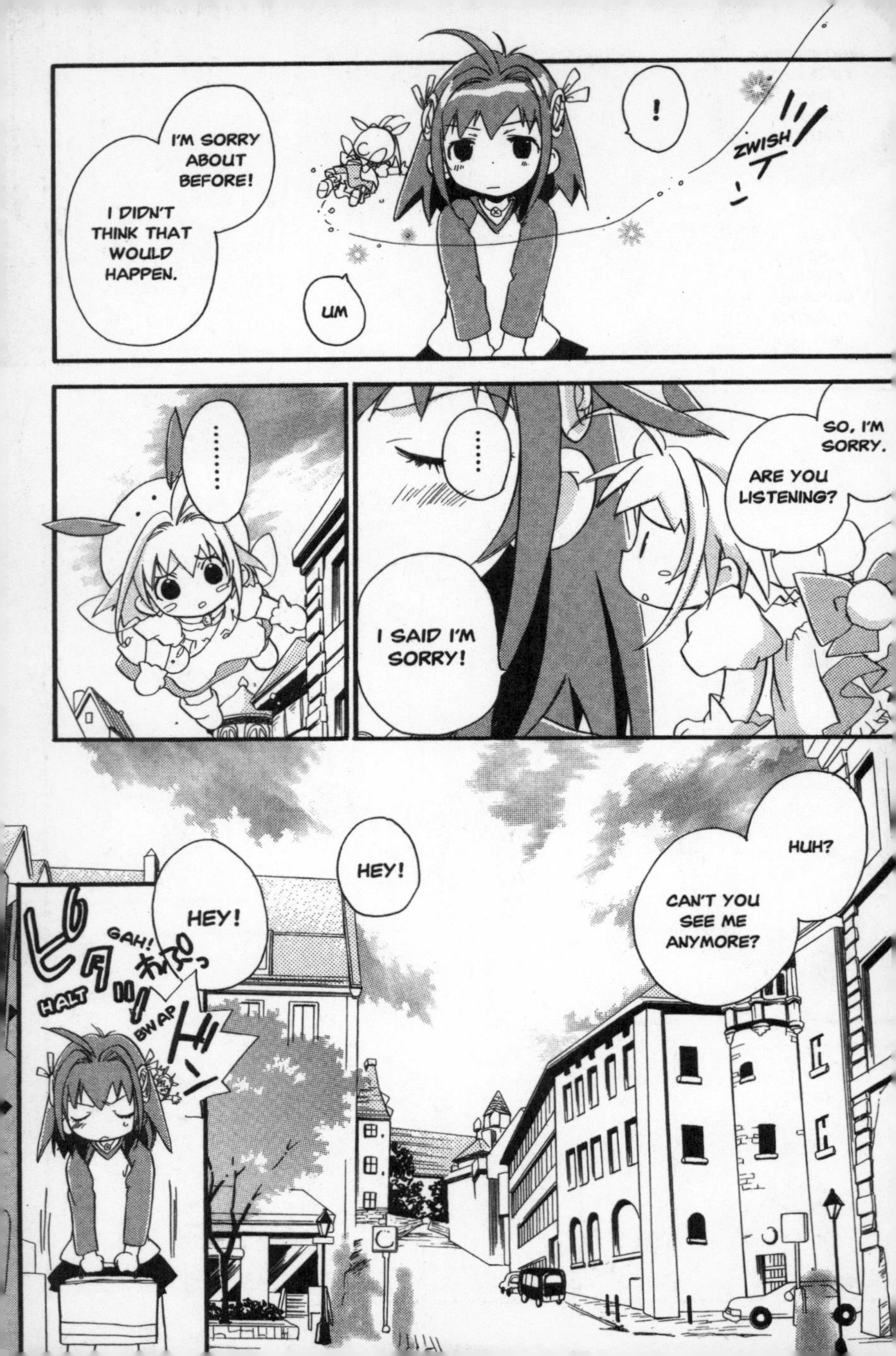
ZWISH
!
I'M SORRY ABOUT BEFORE!
I DIDN'T THINK THAT WOULD HAPPEN.
UM
SO, I'M SORRY.
ARE YOU LISTENING?
......
I SAID I'M SORRY!
......
HUH?
CAN'T YOU SEE ME ANYMORE?
HEY!
HEY!
GAH!
HALT
BWAP

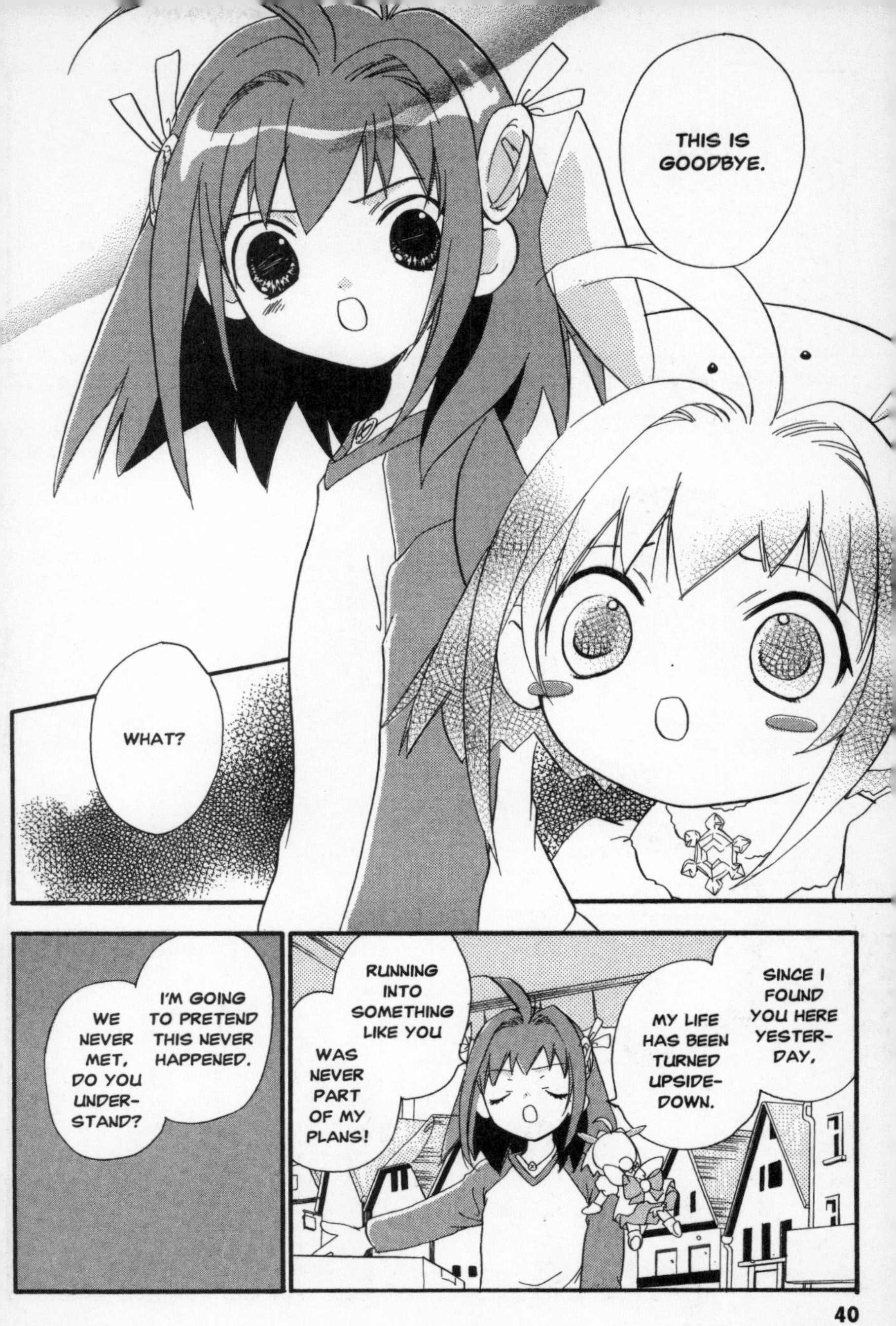
THIS IS GOODBYE.
WHAT?
SINCE I FOUND YOU HERE YESTER-DAY,
MY LIFE HAS BEEN TURNED UPSIDE-DOWN.
RUNNING INTO SOMETHING LIKE YOU
WAS NEVER PART OF MY PLANS!
I'M GOING TO PRETEND THIS NEVER HAPPENED.
WE NEVER MET, DO YOU UNDER-STAND?

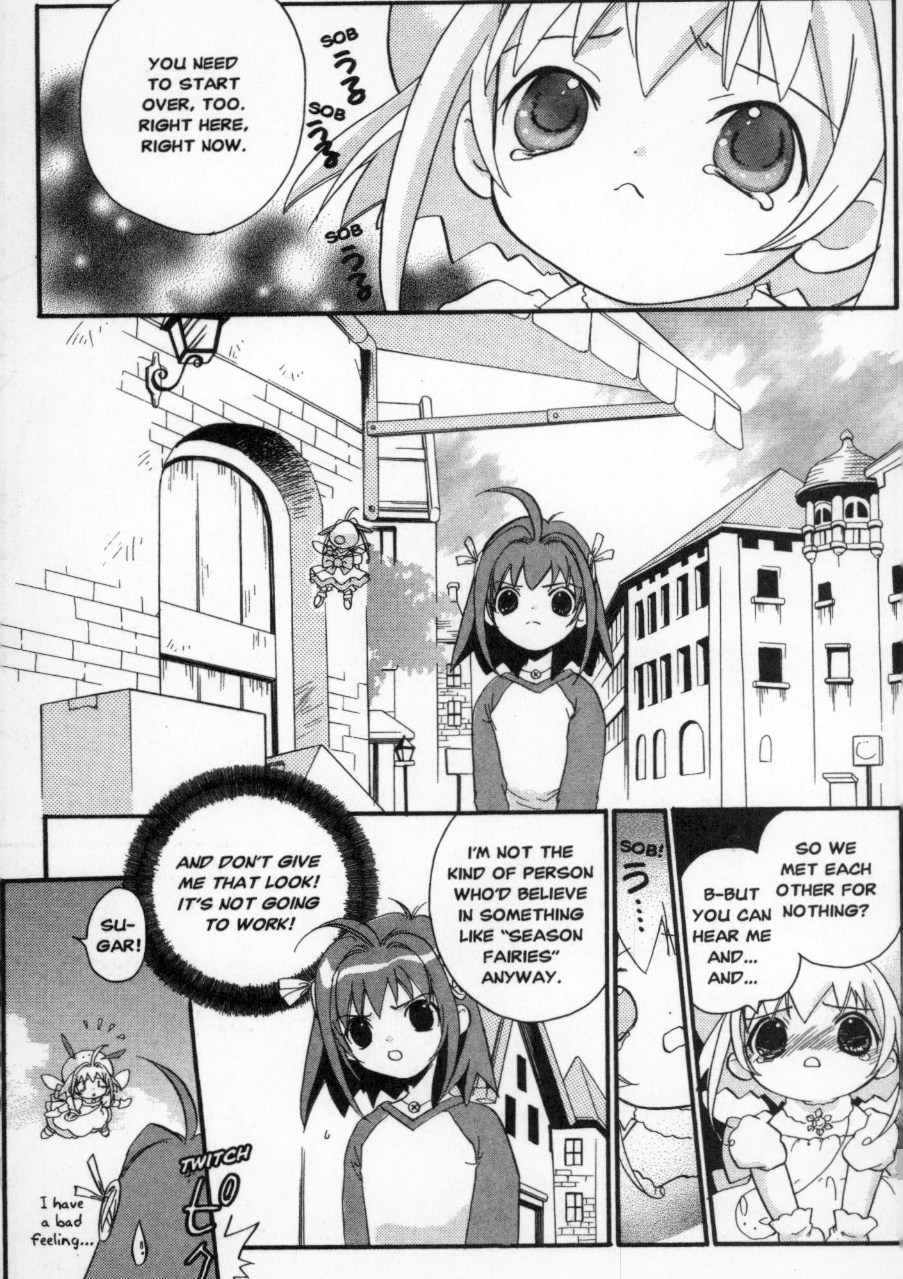
YOU NEED TO START OVER, TOO. RIGHT HERE, RIGHT NOW.
SOB
SOB
SOB
SO WE MET EACH OTHER FOR NOTHING?
B-BUT YOU CAN HEAR ME AND... AND...
SOB!
I'M NOT THE KIND OF PERSON WHO'D BELIEVE IN SOMETHING LIKE "SEASON FAIRIES" ANYWAY.
AND DON'T GIVE ME THAT LOOK! IT'S NOT GOING TO WORK!
SU-GAR!
TWITCH
I have a bad feeling...

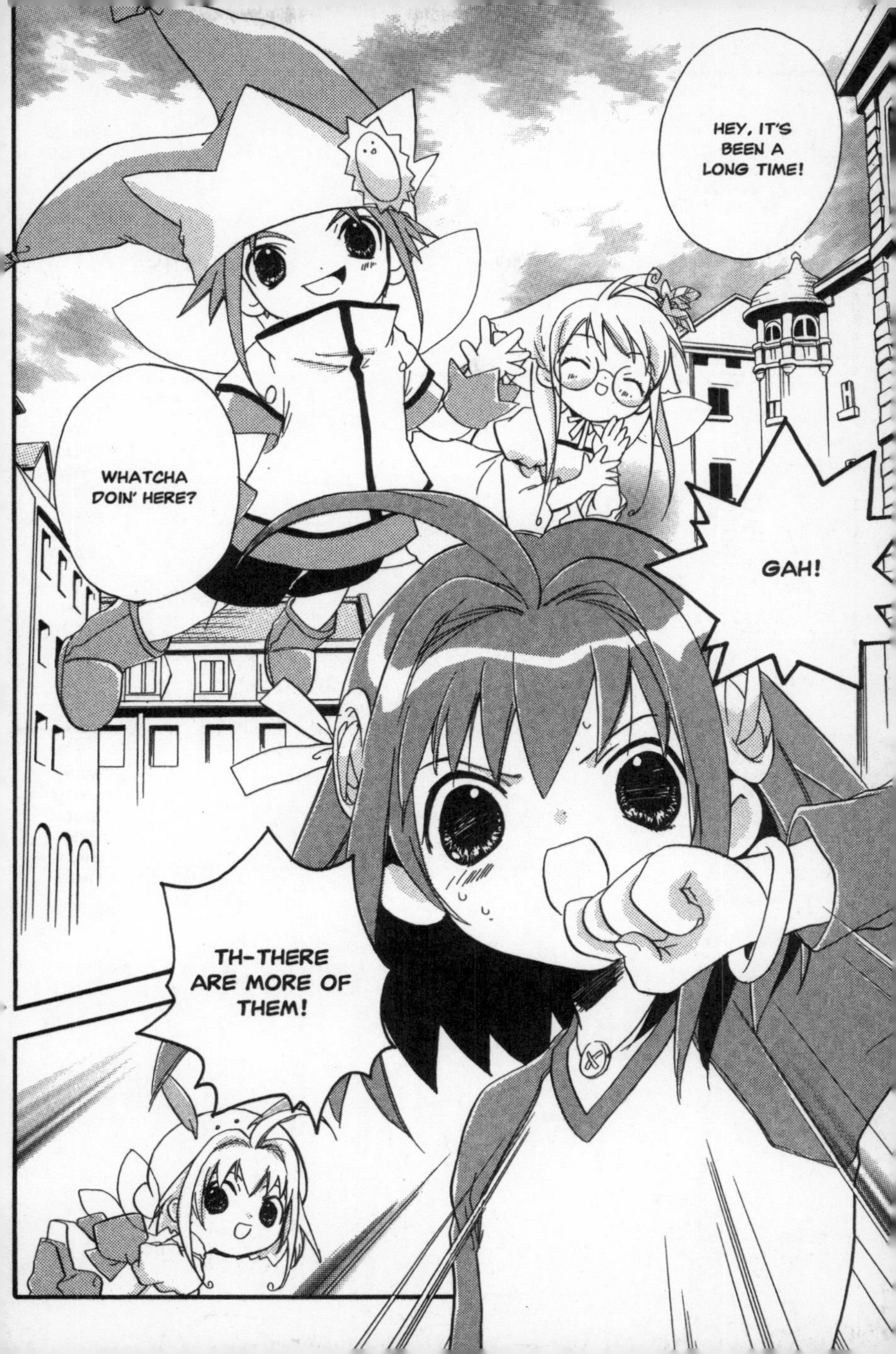
HEY, IT'S BEEN A LONG TIME!
WHATCHA DOIN' HERE?
GAH!
TH-THERE ARE MORE OF THEM!

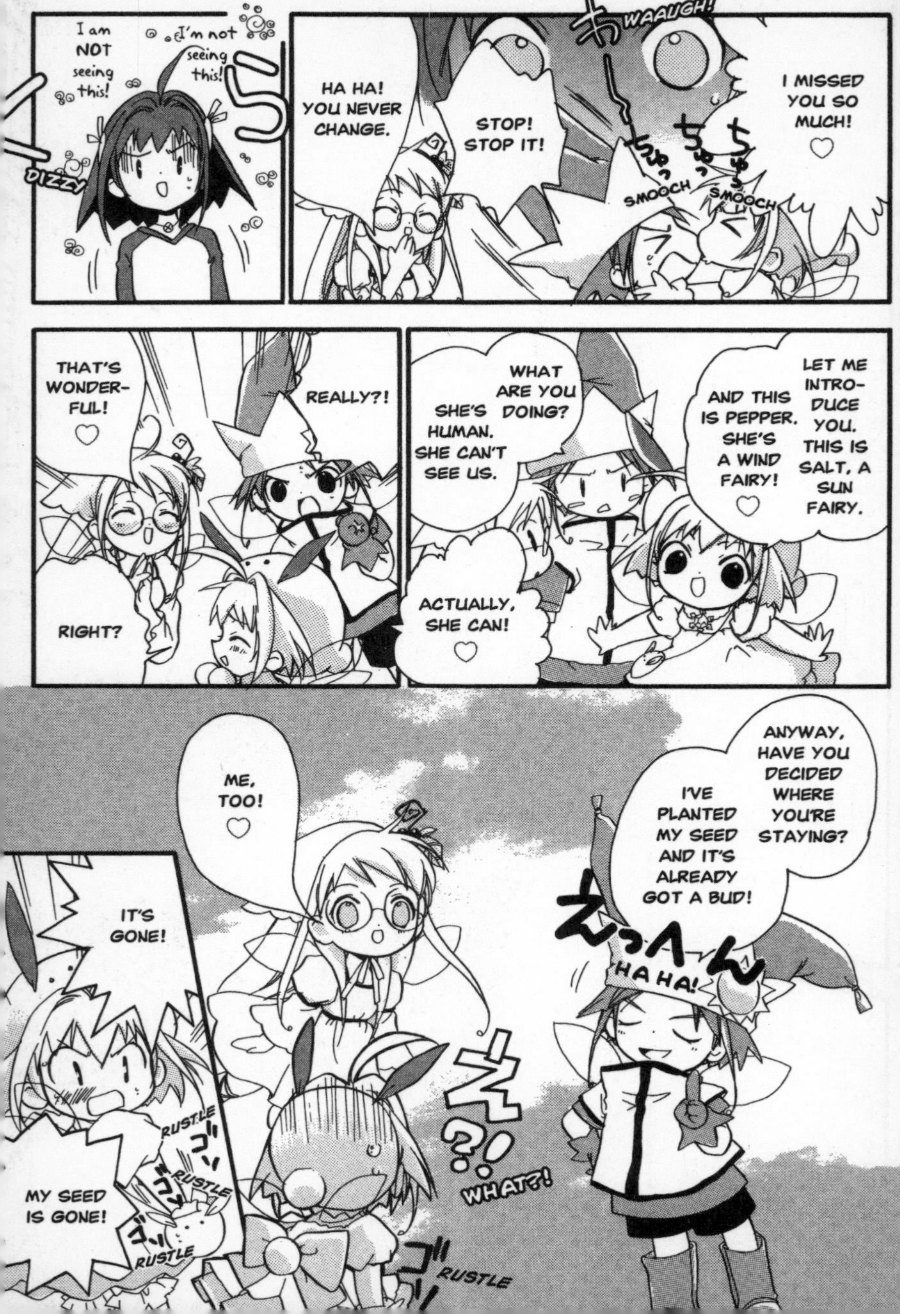
WAAUGH!
I MISSED YOU SO MUCH! ♡
SMOOCH
SMOOCH
STOP! STOP IT!
HA HA! YOU NEVER CHANGE.
I'm not seeing this!
I am NOT seeing this!
DIZZY
LET ME INTRODUCE YOU. THIS IS SALT, A SUN FAIRY.
AND THIS IS PEPPER. SHE'S A WIND FAIRY! ♡
WHAT ARE YOU DOING?
SHE'S HUMAN. SHE CAN'T SEE US.
ACTUALLY, SHE CAN! ♡
REALLY?!
THAT'S WONDERFUL! ♡
RIGHT?
ANYWAY, HAVE YOU DECIDED WHERE YOU'RE STAYING?
I'VE PLANTED MY SEED AND IT'S ALREADY GOT A BUD!
HA HA!
ME, TOO! ♡
?!
WHAT?!
RUSTLE
IT'S GONE!
RUSTLE
RUSTLE
MY SEED IS GONE!
RUSTLE

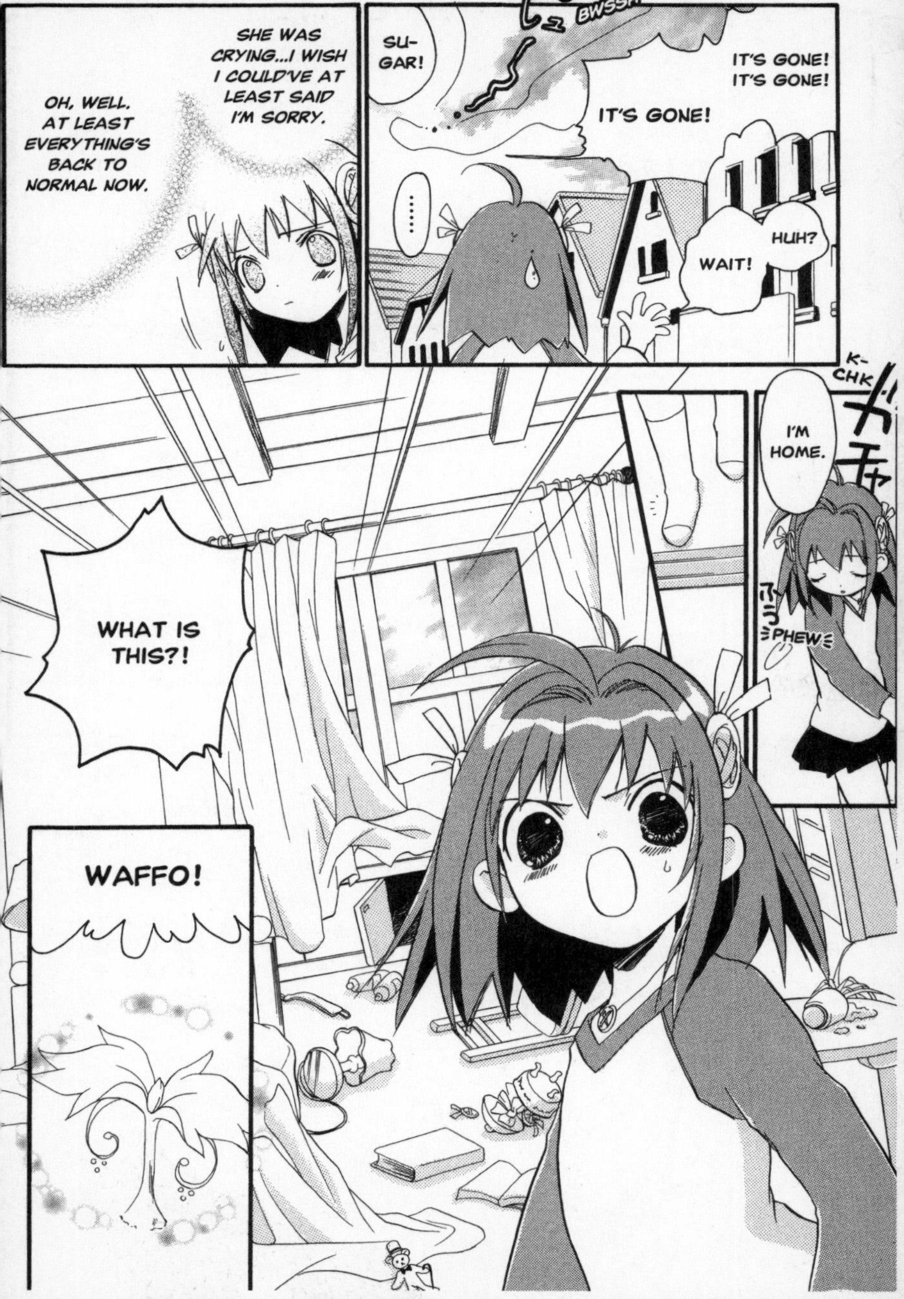
BWSSH
IT'S GONE! IT'S GONE!
SU-GAR!
IT'S GONE!
......
HUH?
WAIT!
SHE WAS CRYING...I WISH I COULD'VE AT LEAST SAID I'M SORRY.
OH, WELL. AT LEAST EVERYTHING'S BACK TO NORMAL NOW.
K-CHK
I'M HOME.
PHEW
WHAT IS THIS?!
WAFFO!

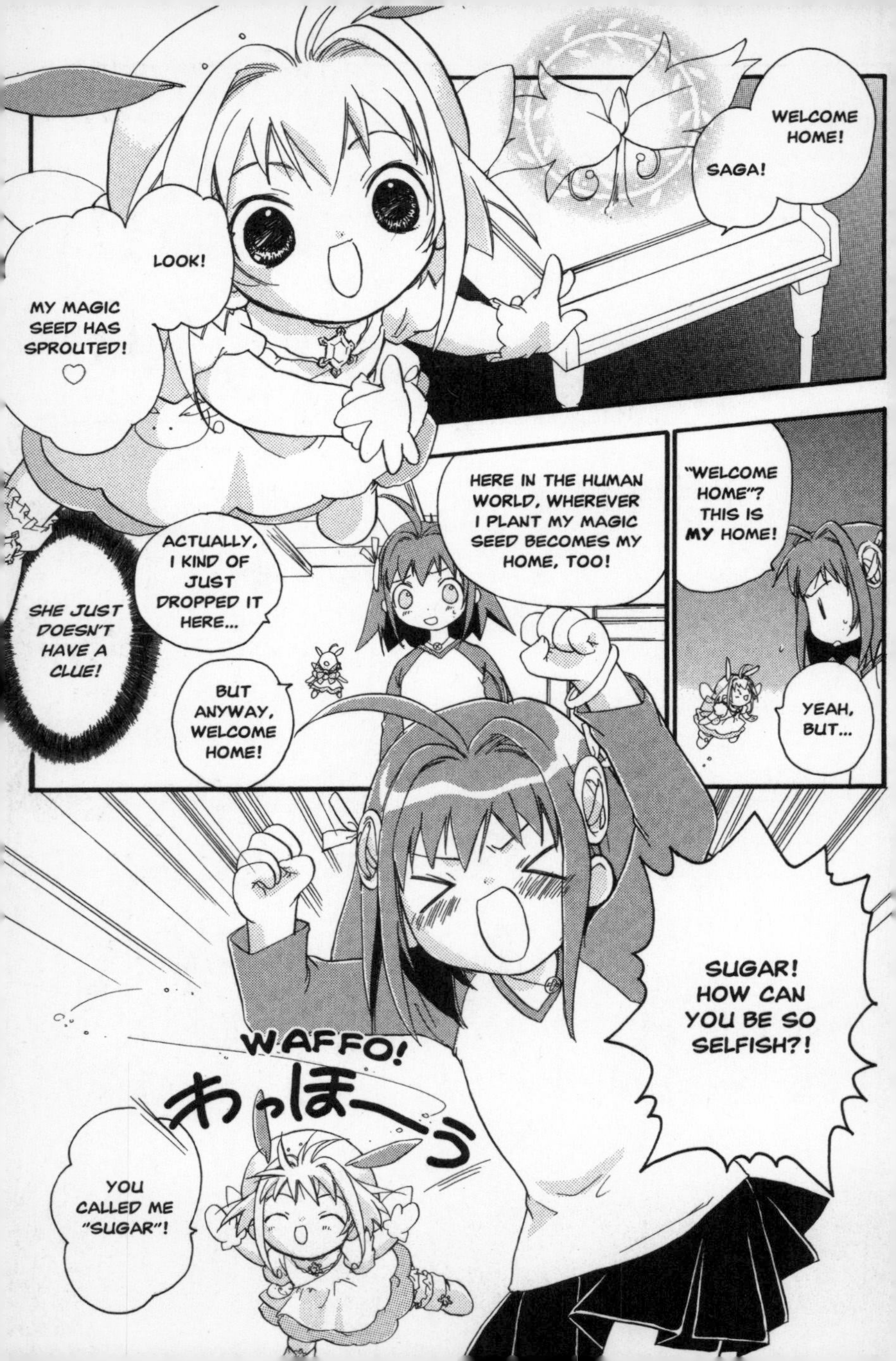
WELCOME HOME!
SAGA!
LOOK!
MY MAGIC SEED HAS SPROUTED! ♡
"WELCOME HOME"? THIS IS MY HOME!
YEAH, BUT...
HERE IN THE HUMAN WORLD, WHEREVER I PLANT MY MAGIC SEED BECOMES MY HOME, TOO!
ACTUALLY, I KIND OF JUST DROPPED IT HERE...
BUT ANYWAY, WELCOME HOME!
SHE JUST DOESN'T HAVE A CLUE!
SUGAR! HOW CAN YOU BE SO SELFISH?!
WAFFO!
わっほ〜う
YOU CALLED ME "SUGAR"!

THE STORY OF A FAIRY ONLY YOU CAN SEE. A FAIRY
THAT ANY YOUNG GIRL WOULD FALL IN LOVE WITH...
BUT FOR ONE GIRL IN PARTICULAR, THIS FAIRY
MEANS NOTHING BUT TROUBLE.

THIS IS WHAT HAPPENS WHEN THE DOWN-TO-EARTH,
NO-NONSENSE SAGA MEETS AN APPRENTICE SEASON
FAIRY NAMED SUGAR.

THEY FIGHT A LOT, BUT THEY APOLOGIZE JUST
AS MUCH. AND SOMEWHERE ALONG THE WAY, THEY
SLOWLY MATURE INTO ADULTS.

THIS STORY IS BEING WRITTEN WITH THE
CHARACTERS' EMOTIONS VERY MUCH IN MIND. FEEL
FREE TO LET US KNOW HOW WE'RE DOING! ♡

BH SNOW ✚ CLINIC

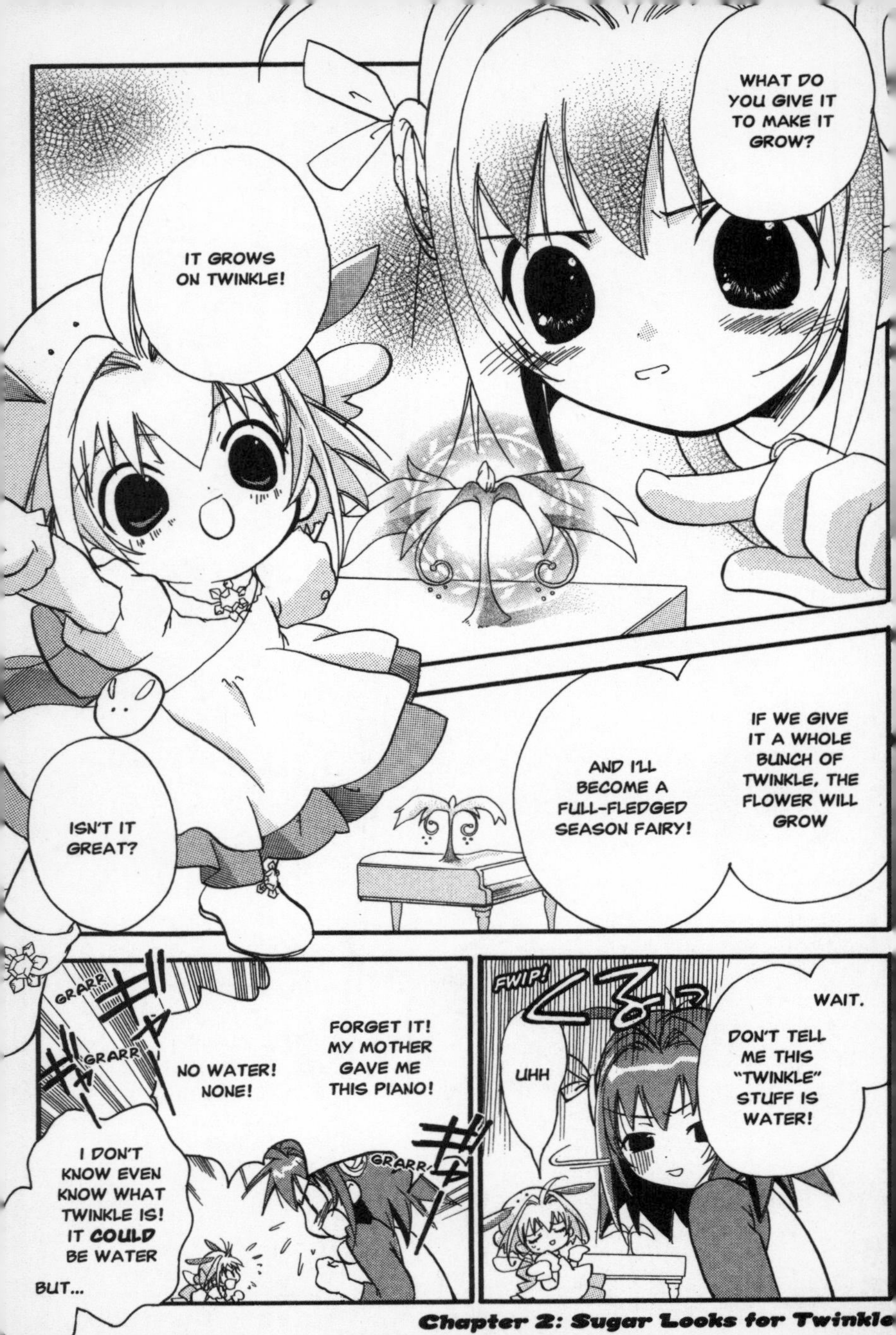
WHAT DO YOU GIVE IT TO MAKE IT GROW?
IT GROWS ON TWINKLE!
IF WE GIVE IT A WHOLE BUNCH OF TWINKLE, THE FLOWER WILL GROW
AND I'LL BECOME A FULL-FLEDGED SEASON FAIRY!
ISN'T IT GREAT?
FWIP!
WAIT.
DON'T TELL ME THIS "TWINKLE" STUFF IS WATER!
UHH
FORGET IT! MY MOTHER GAVE ME THIS PIANO!
NO WATER! NONE!
GRARR
GRARR
GRARR
I DON'T KNOW EVEN KNOW WHAT TWINKLE IS! IT **COULD** BE WATER
BUT...

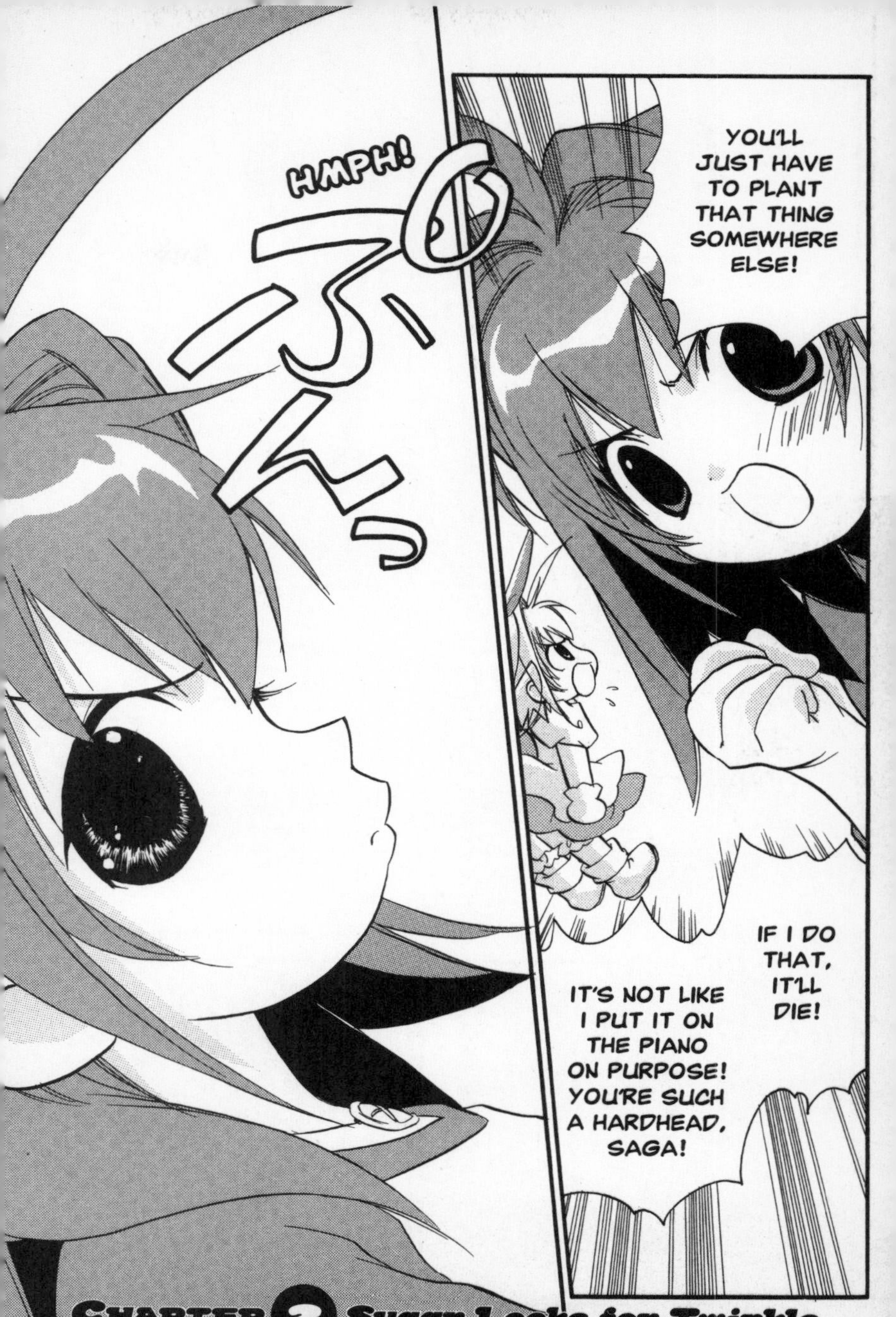
YOU'LL JUST HAVE TO PLANT THAT THING SOMEWHERE ELSE!
IF I DO THAT, IT'LL DIE!
IT'S NOT LIKE I PUT IT ON THE PIANO ON PURPOSE! YOU'RE SUCH A HARDHEAD, SAGA!
HMPH!
ふーんっ

CHAPTER 2 Sugar Looks for Twinkle

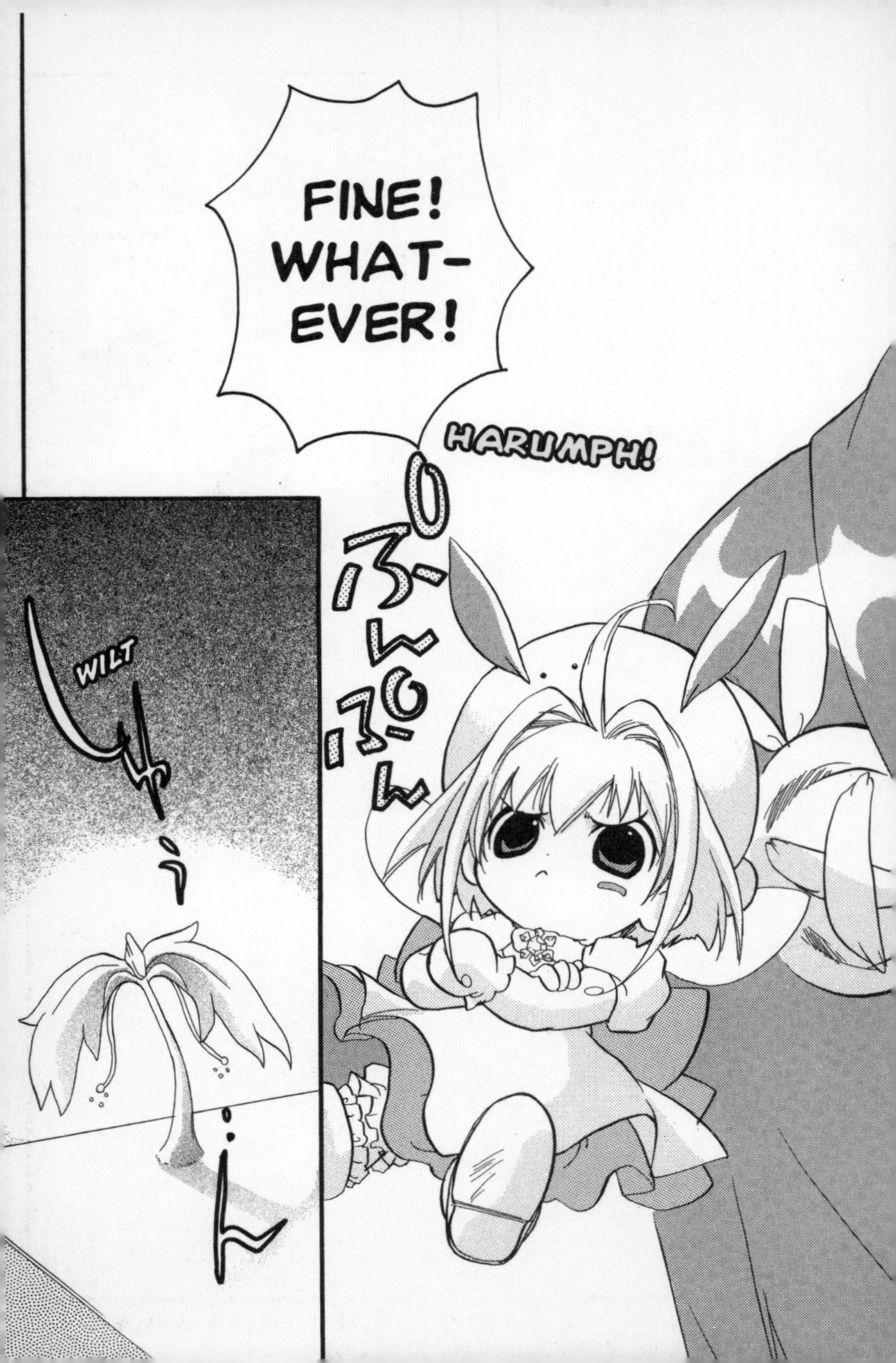

FINE! WHAT-EVER!
HARUMPH!
ぷーんぷーん
WILT

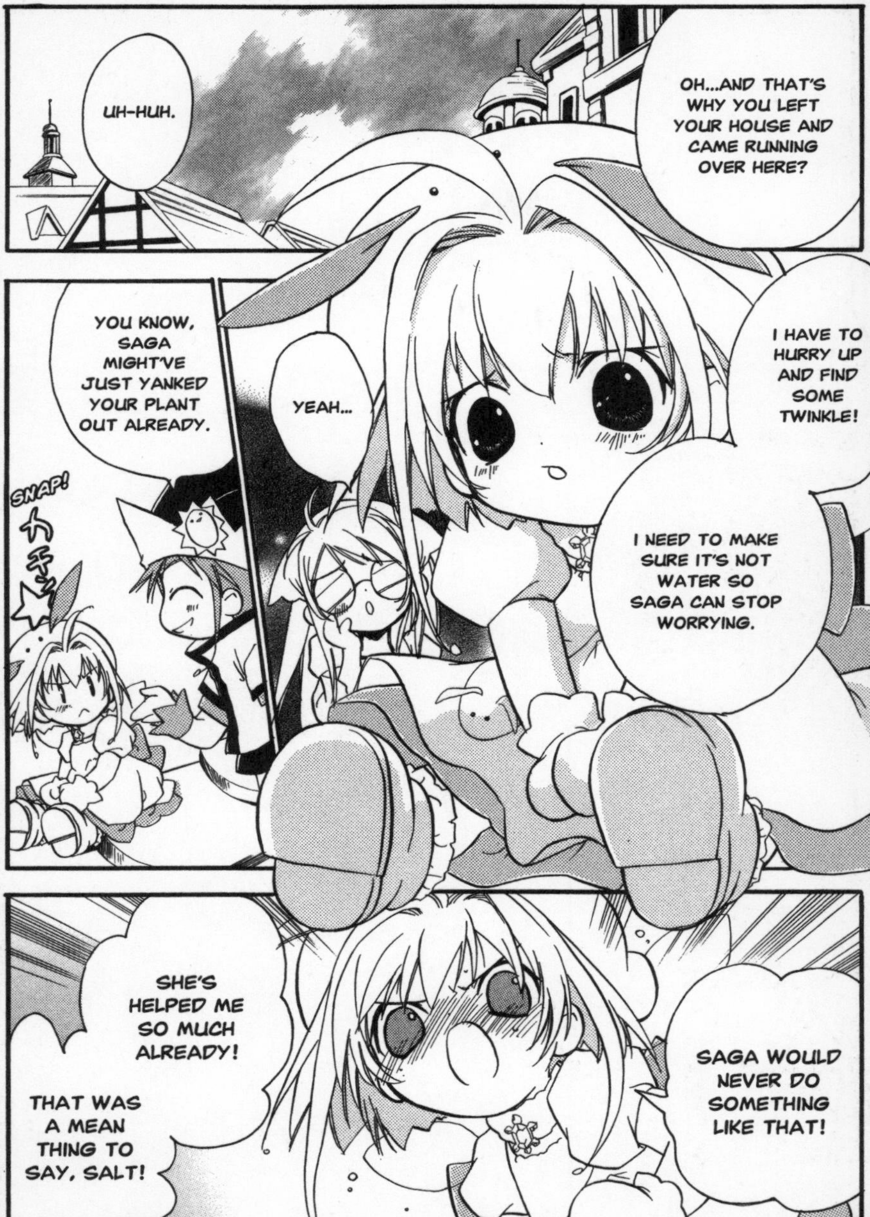
OH...AND THAT'S WHY YOU LEFT YOUR HOUSE AND CAME RUNNING OVER HERE?
UH-HUH.
I HAVE TO HURRY UP AND FIND SOME TWINKLE!
YEAH...
I NEED TO MAKE SURE IT'S NOT WATER SO SAGA CAN STOP WORRYING.
YOU KNOW, SAGA MIGHT'VE JUST YANKED YOUR PLANT OUT ALREADY.
SNAP!
SAGA WOULD NEVER DO SOMETHING LIKE THAT!
SHE'S HELPED ME SO MUCH ALREADY!
THAT WAS A MEAN THING TO SAY, SALT!

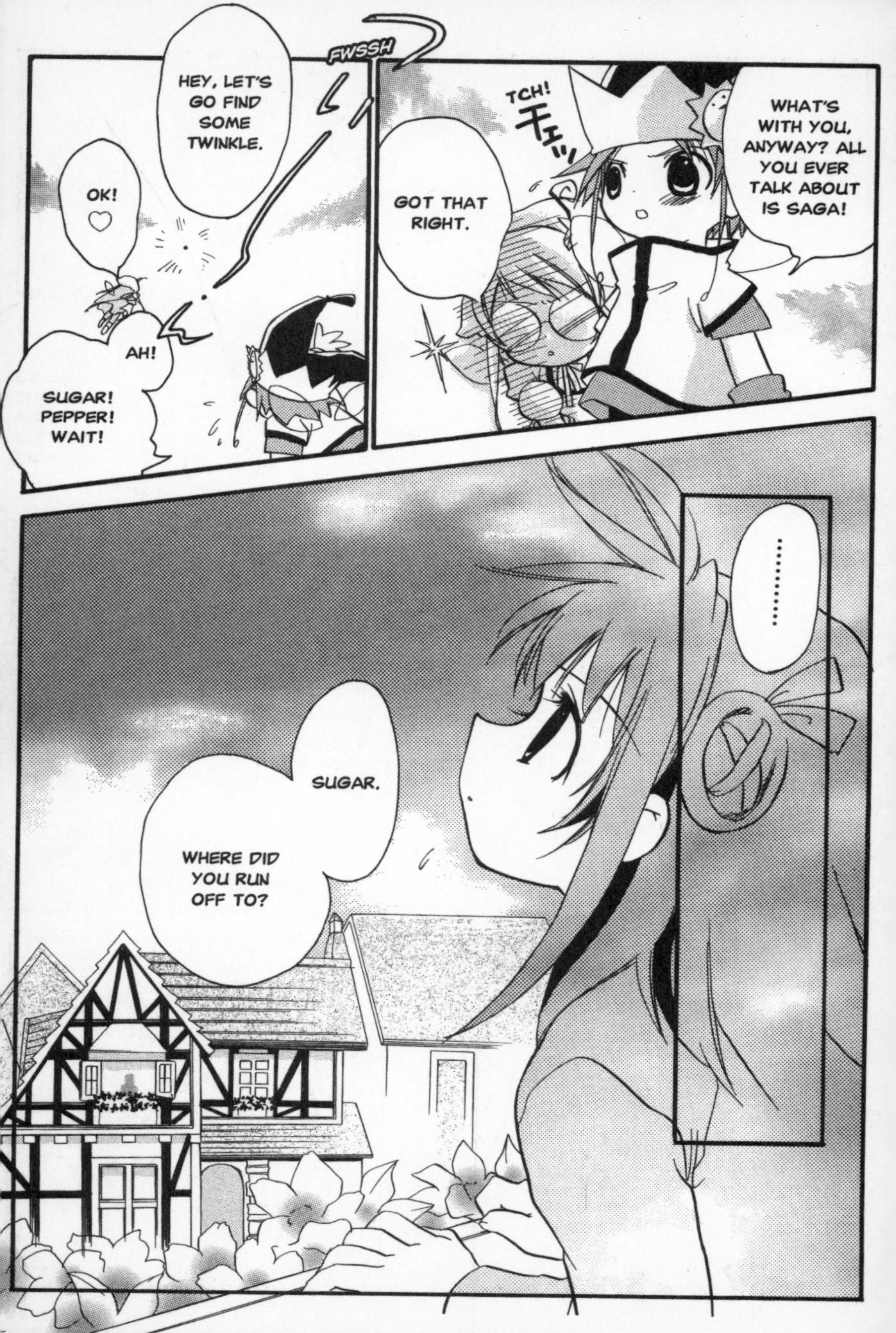
WHAT'S WITH YOU, ANYWAY? ALL YOU EVER TALK ABOUT IS SAGA!
TCH!
チェッ
GOT THAT RIGHT.
FWSSH
HEY, LET'S GO FIND SOME TWINKLE.
OK! ♡
AH!
SUGAR! PEPPER! WAIT!
......
SUGAR.
WHERE DID YOU RUN OFF TO?

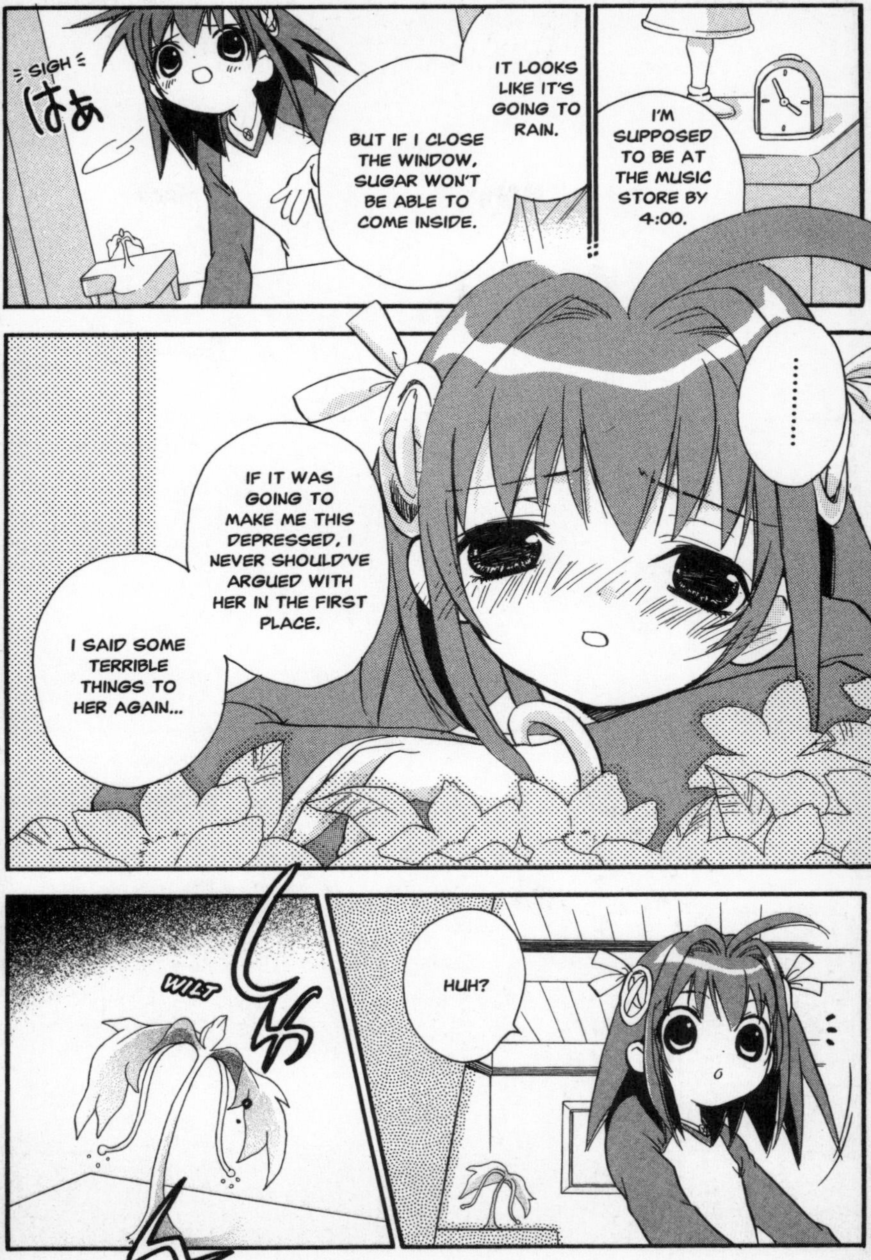
I'M SUPPOSED TO BE AT THE MUSIC STORE BY 4:00.
IT LOOKS LIKE IT'S GOING TO RAIN.
BUT IF I CLOSE THE WINDOW, SUGAR WON'T BE ABLE TO COME INSIDE.
SIGH
はぁ
......
IF IT WAS GOING TO MAKE ME THIS DEPRESSED, I NEVER SHOULD'VE ARGUED WITH HER IN THE FIRST PLACE.
I SAID SOME TERRIBLE THINGS TO HER AGAIN...
HUH?
WILT

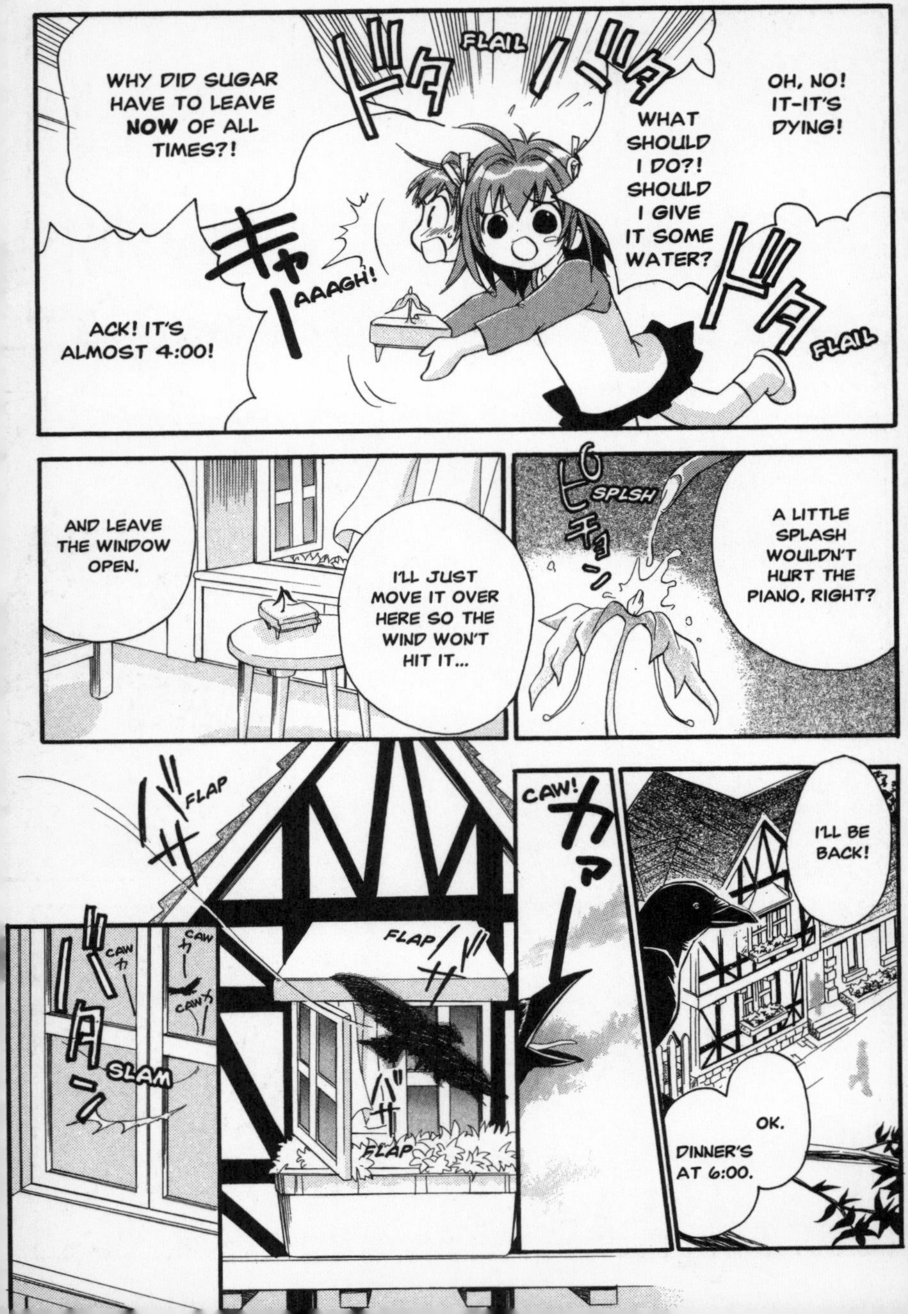
FLAIL
OH, NO! IT-IT'S DYING!
WHAT SHOULD I DO?! SHOULD I GIVE IT SOME WATER?
FLAIL
WHY DID SUGAR HAVE TO LEAVE NOW OF ALL TIMES?!
AAAGH!
ACK! IT'S ALMOST 4:00!
SPLSH
A LITTLE SPLASH WOULDN'T HURT THE PIANO, RIGHT?
I'LL JUST MOVE IT OVER HERE SO THE WIND WON'T HIT IT...
AND LEAVE THE WINDOW OPEN.
I'LL BE BACK!
OK.
DINNER'S AT 6:00.
CAW!
FLAP
FLAP
FLAP
CAW
CAW
CAW
SLAM

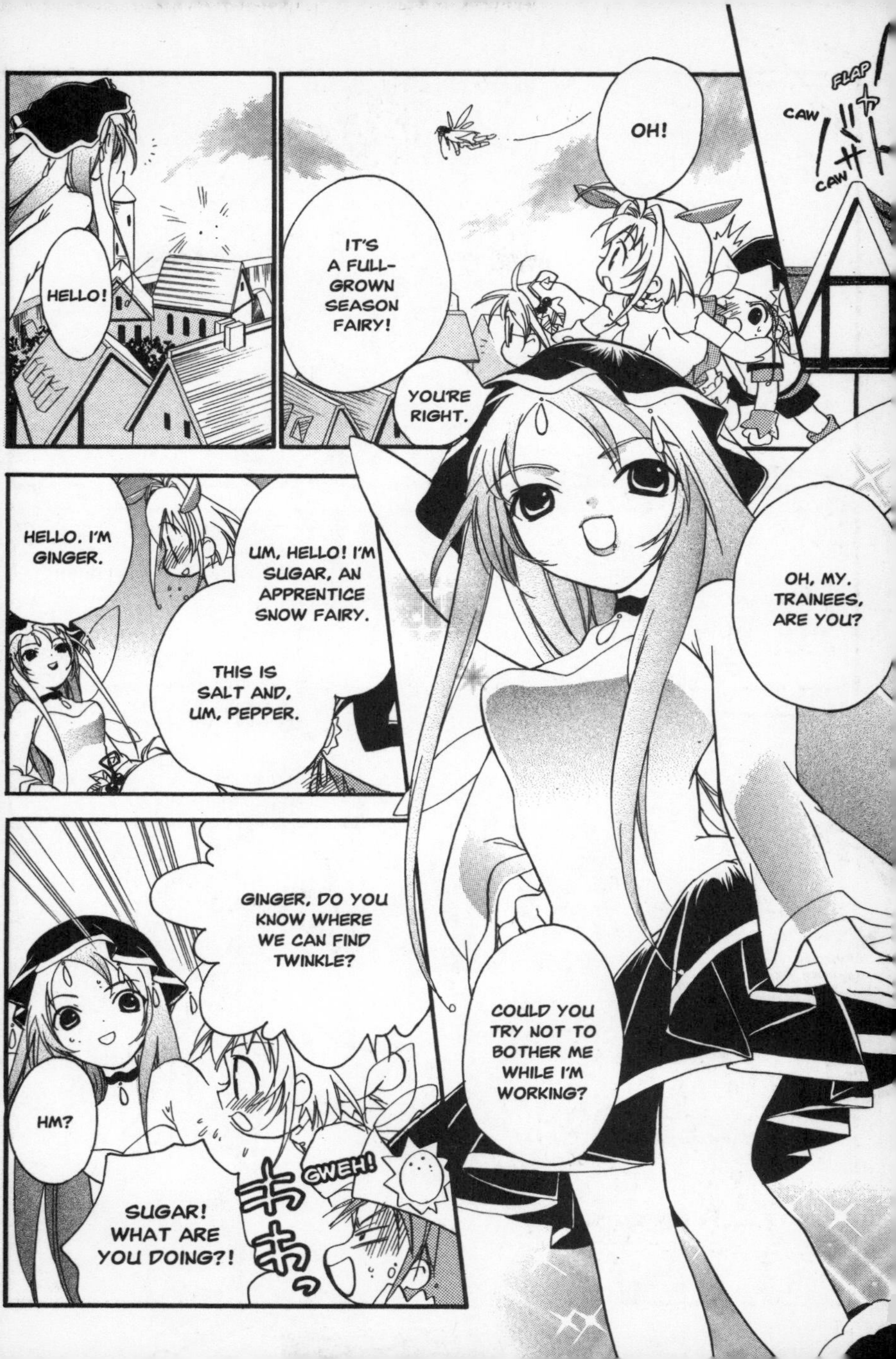
FLAP
CAW
CAW
OH!
IT'S A FULL-GROWN SEASON FAIRY!
YOU'RE RIGHT.
HELLO!
OH, MY. TRAINEES, ARE YOU?
COULD YOU TRY NOT TO BOTHER ME WHILE I'M WORKING?
UM, HELLO! I'M SUGAR, AN APPRENTICE SNOW FAIRY.
THIS IS SALT AND, UM, PEPPER.
HELLO. I'M GINGER.
GINGER, DO YOU KNOW WHERE WE CAN FIND TWINKLE?
HM?
GWEH!
SUGAR! WHAT ARE YOU DOING?!

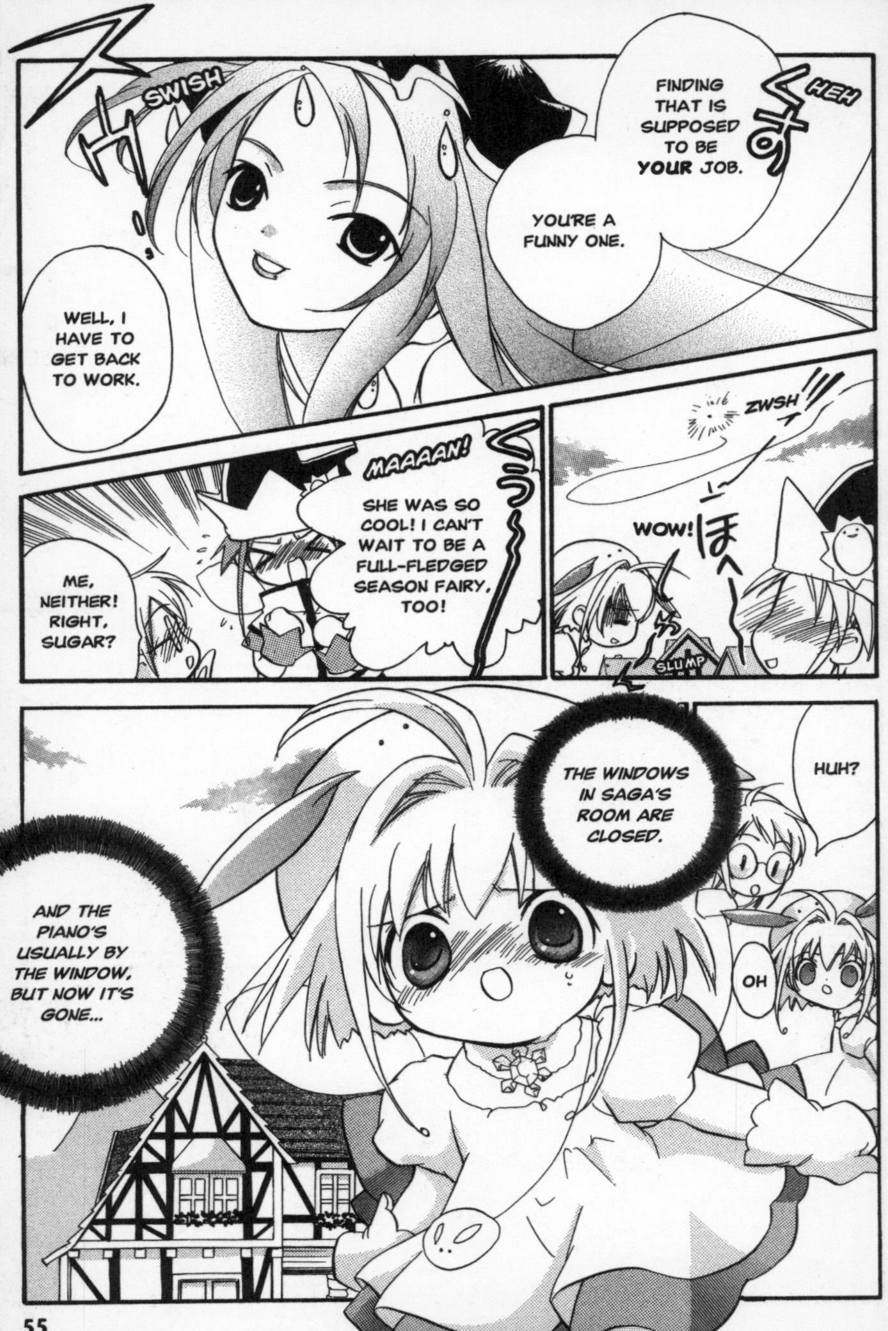
FINDING THAT IS SUPPOSED TO BE YOUR JOB.
HEH
くす
YOU'RE A FUNNY ONE.
SWISH
WELL, I HAVE TO GET BACK TO WORK.
ZWSH
WOW!
ほへ〜
SLUMP
MAAAAN!
くぅ〜
SHE WAS SO COOL! I CAN'T WAIT TO BE A FULL-FLEDGED SEASON FAIRY, TOO!
ME, NEITHER! RIGHT, SUGAR?
HUH?
OH
THE WINDOWS IN SAGA'S ROOM ARE CLOSED.
AND THE PIANO'S USUALLY BY THE WINDOW, BUT NOW IT'S GONE...

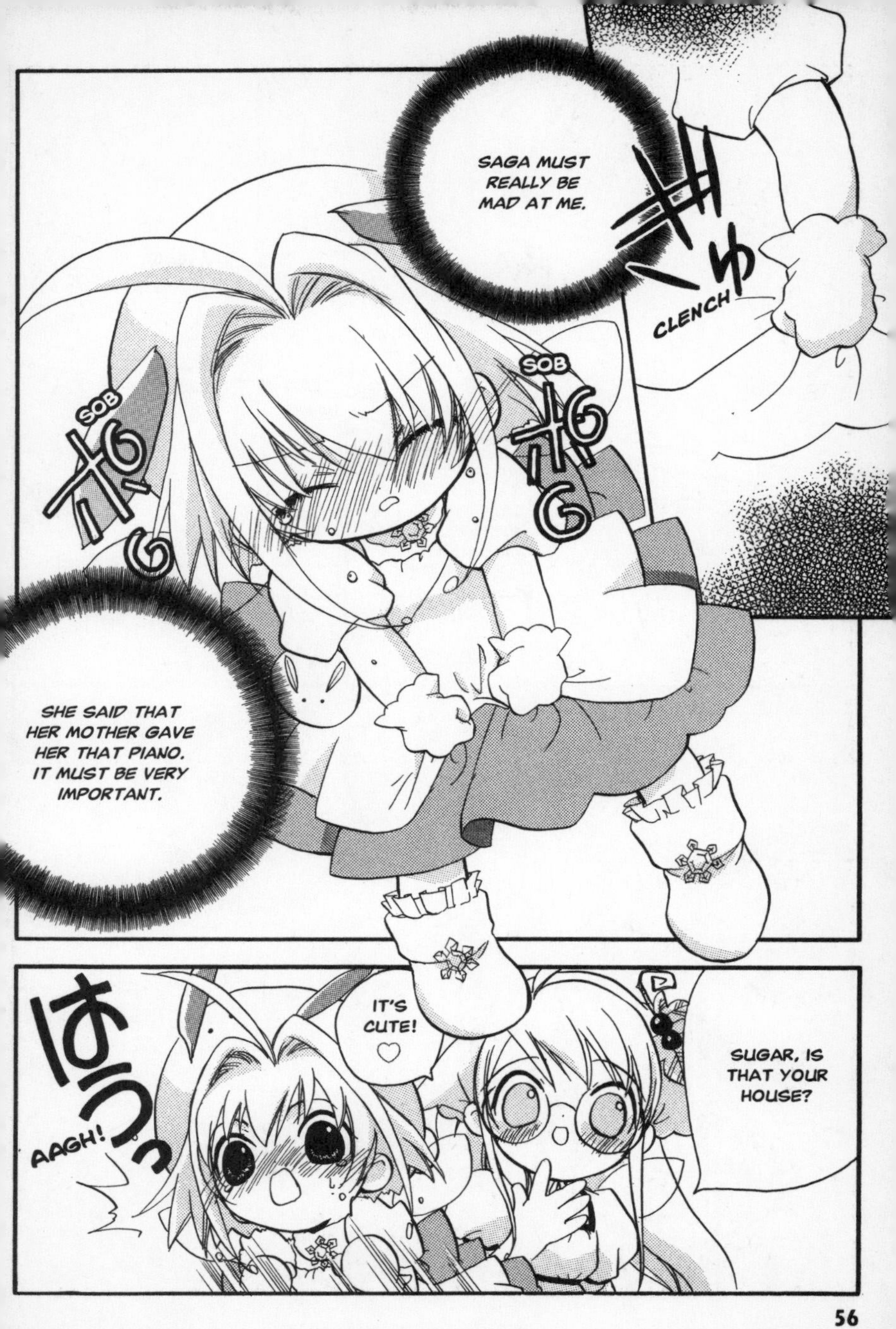

SAGA MUST REALLY BE MAD AT ME.
CLENCH
SOB
SOB
SHE SAID THAT HER MOTHER GAVE HER THAT PIANO. IT MUST BE VERY IMPORTANT.
SUGAR, IS THAT YOUR HOUSE?
IT'S CUTE!
はうっ
AAGH!

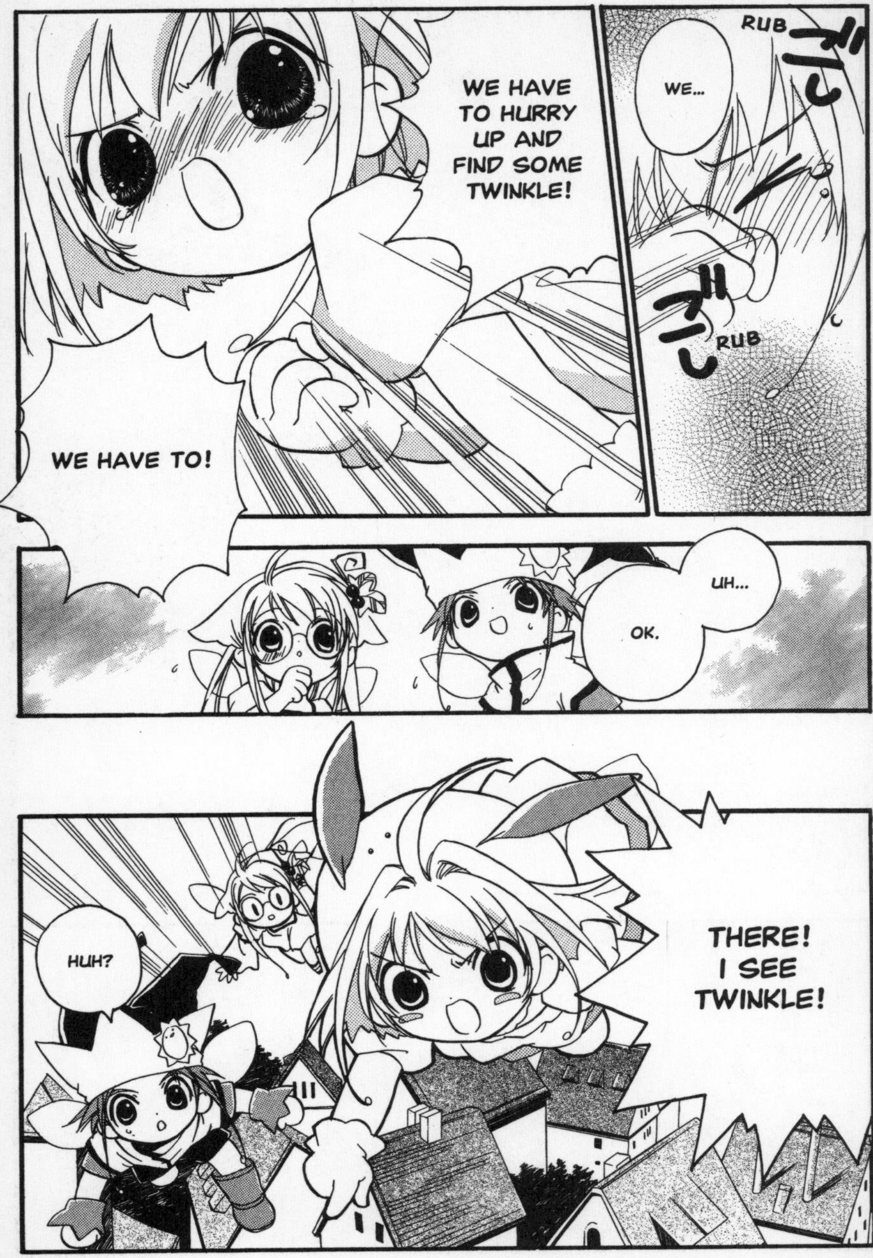
RUB
WE...
RUB
WE HAVE TO HURRY UP AND FIND SOME TWINKLE!
WE HAVE TO!
UH... OK.
THERE! I SEE TWINKLE!
HUH?

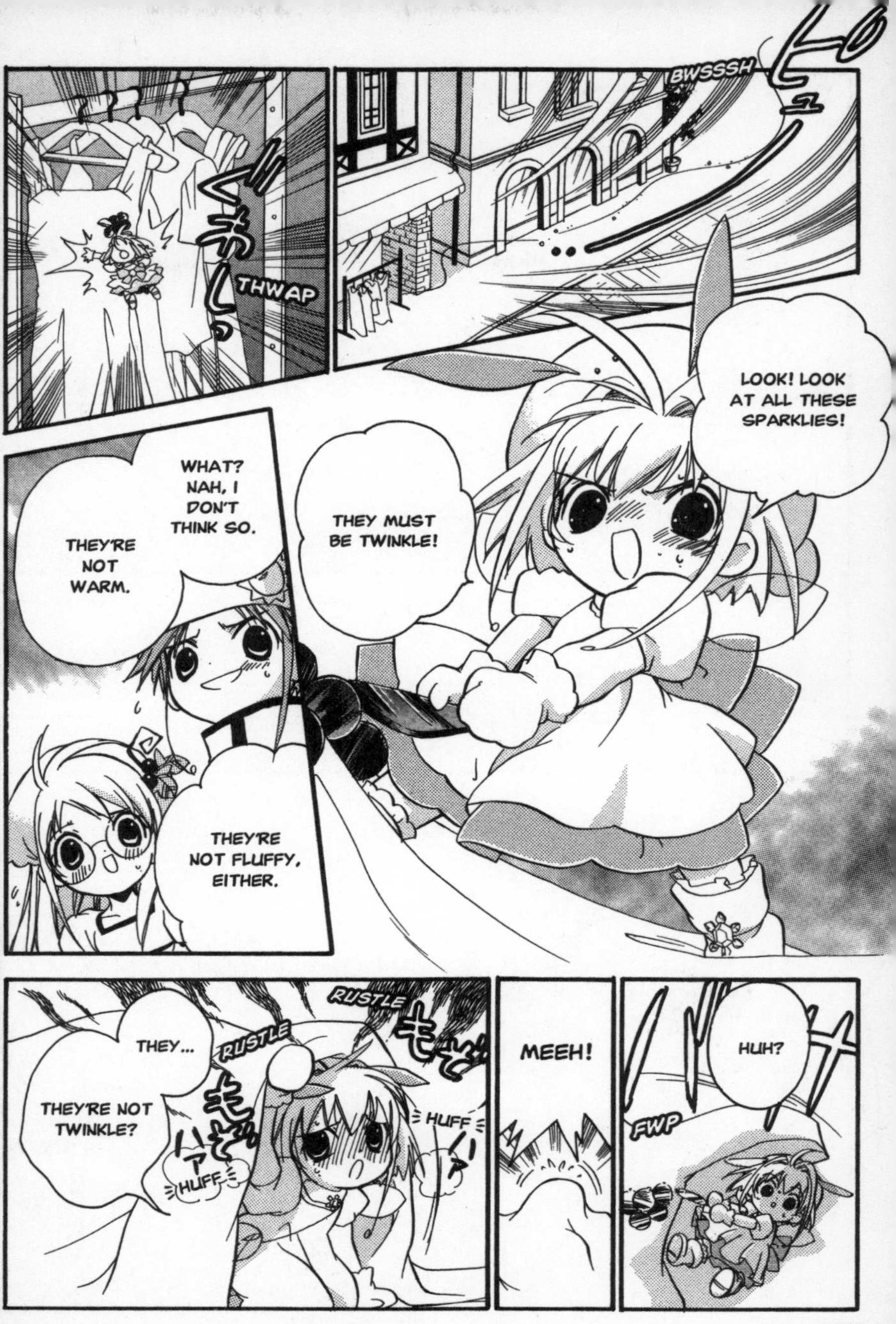
BWSSSH
THWAP
LOOK! LOOK AT ALL THESE SPARKLIES!
THEY MUST BE TWINKLE!
WHAT? NAH, I DON'T THINK SO.
THEY'RE NOT WARM.
THEY'RE NOT FLUFFY, EITHER.
HUH?
FWP
MEEH!
RUSTLE
RUSTLE
HUFF
HUFF
THEY...
THEY'RE NOT TWINKLE?

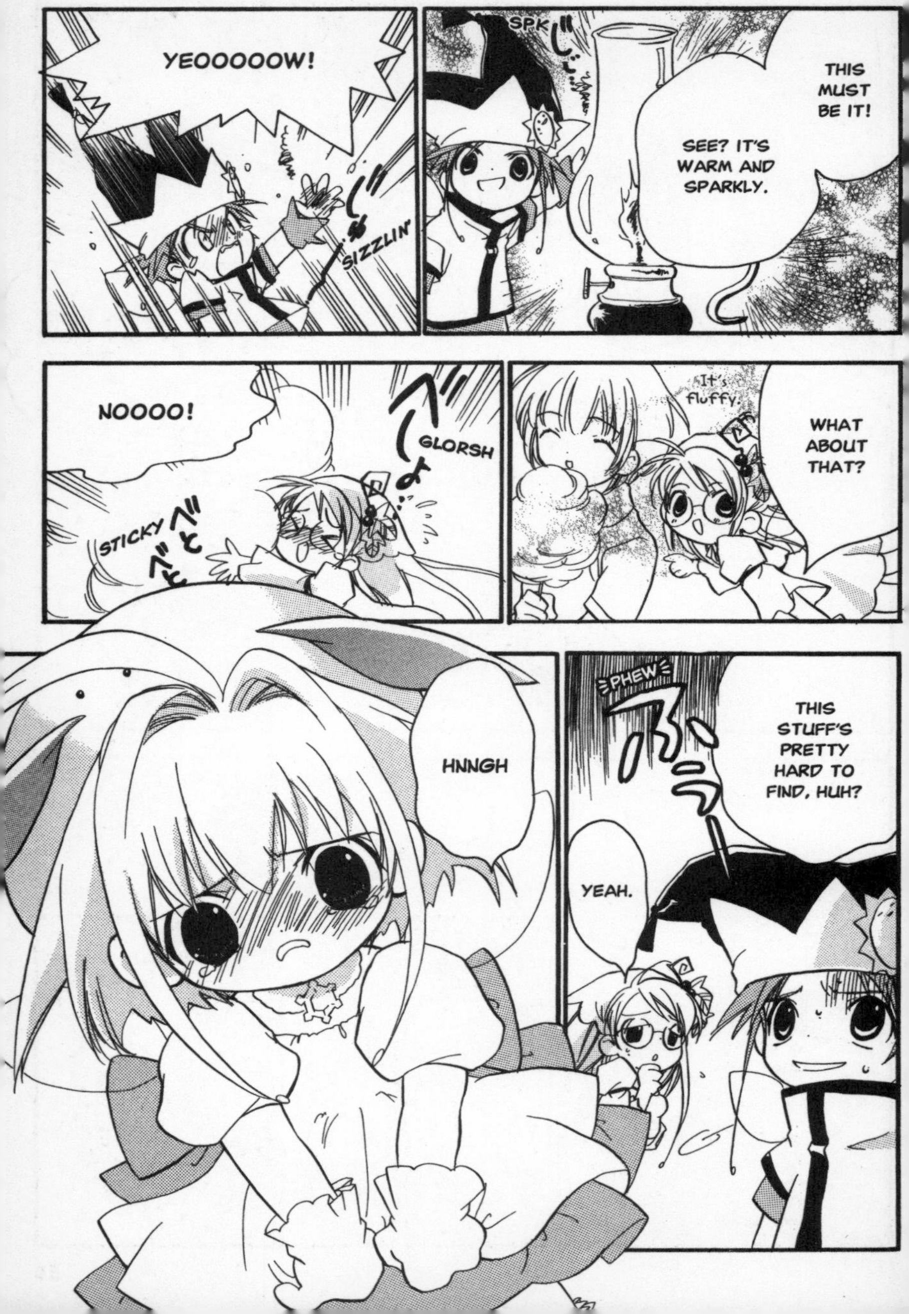
SPK
THIS MUST BE IT!
SEE? IT'S WARM AND SPARKLY.
YEOOOOOW!
SIZZLIN'
It's fluffy.
WHAT ABOUT THAT?
NOOOO!
GLORSH
STICKY
PHEW
THIS STUFF'S PRETTY HARD TO FIND, HUH?
YEAH.
HNNGH

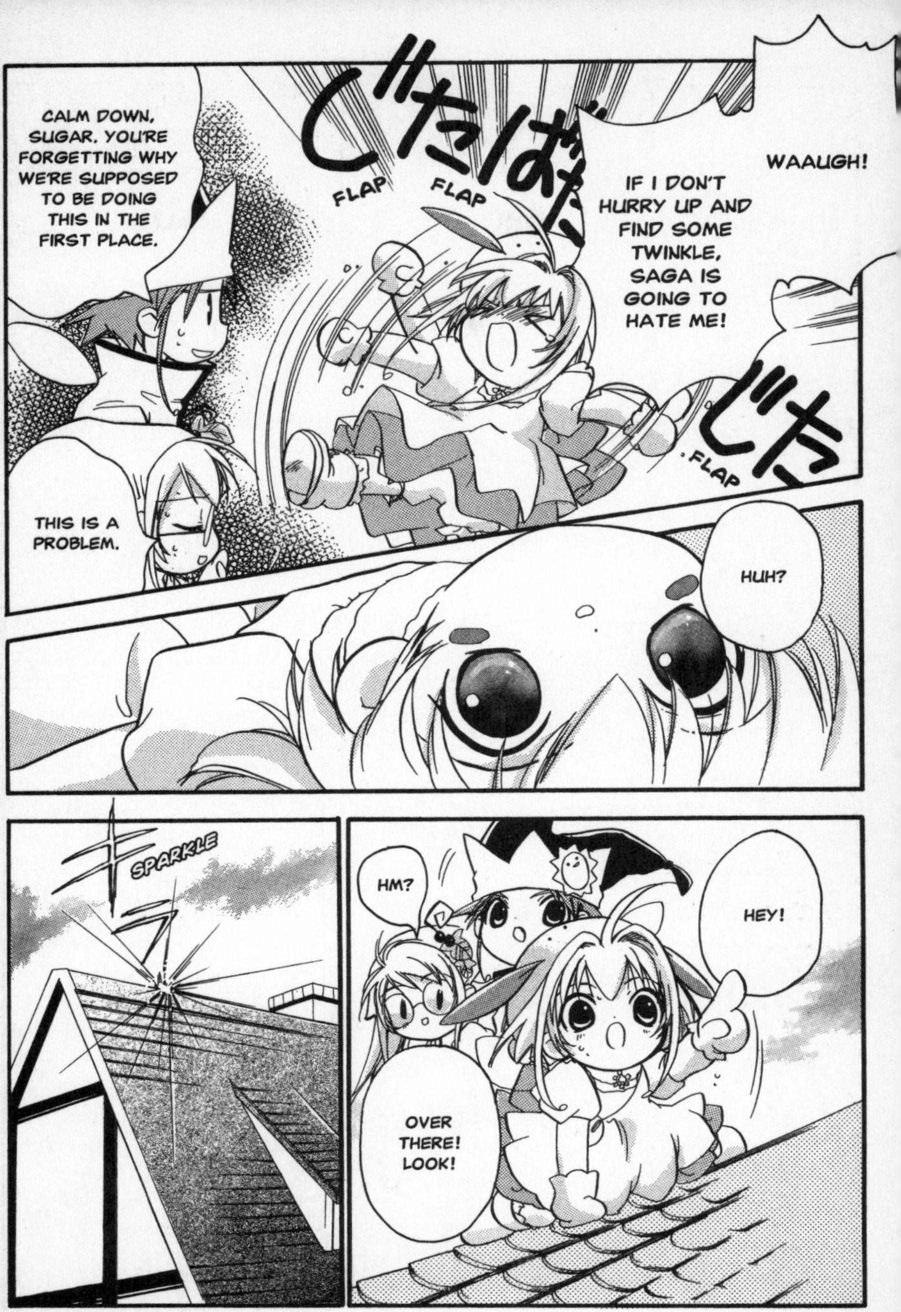
WAAUGH!
IF I DON'T HURRY UP AND FIND SOME TWINKLE, SAGA IS GOING TO HATE ME!
FLAP FLAP
FLAP
CALM DOWN, SUGAR. YOU'RE FORGETTING WHY WE'RE SUPPOSED TO BE DOING THIS IN THE FIRST PLACE.
THIS IS A PROBLEM.
HUH?
HEY!
HM?
OVER THERE! LOOK!
SPARKLE

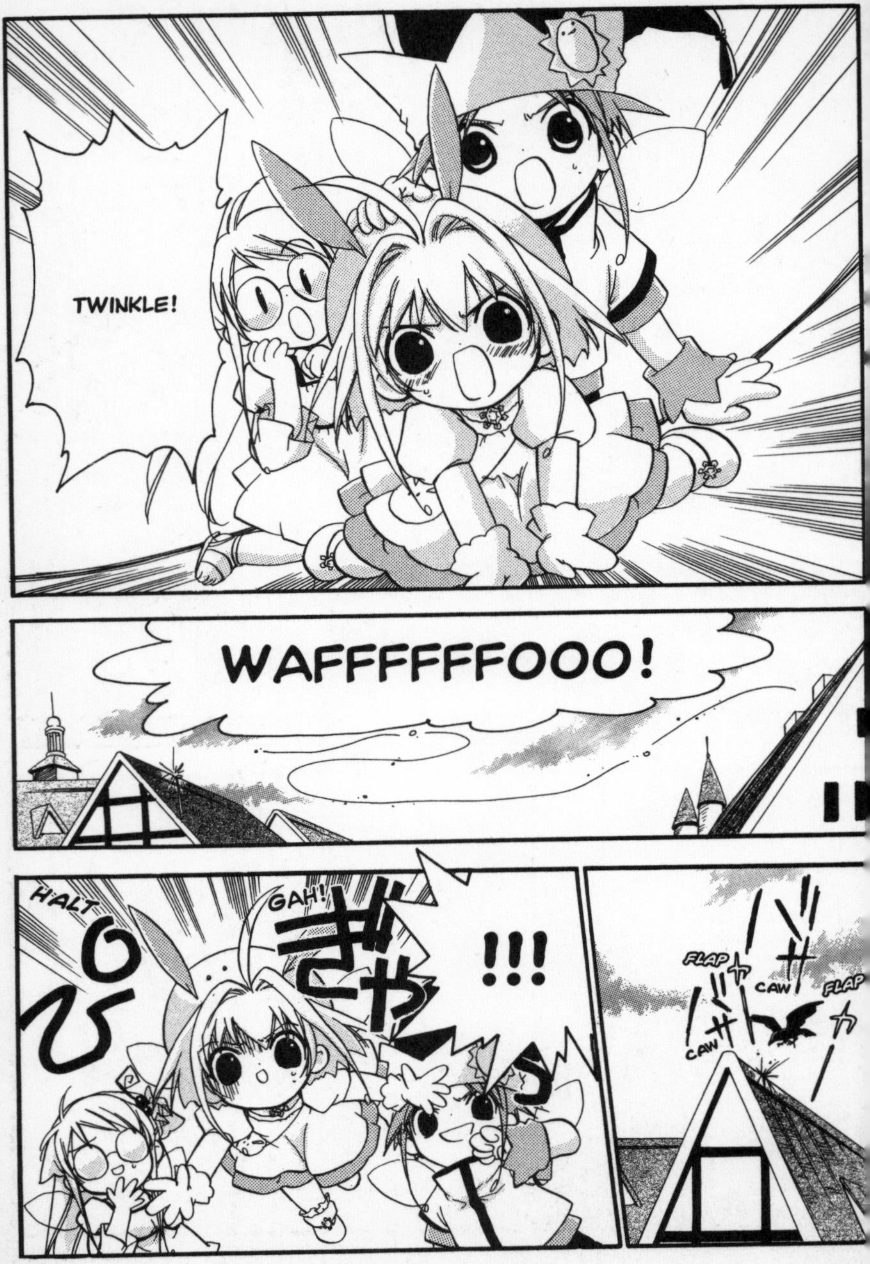
TWINKLE!
WAFFFFFFOOO!
FLAP
CAW
FLAP
CAW
HALT
GAH!
!!!

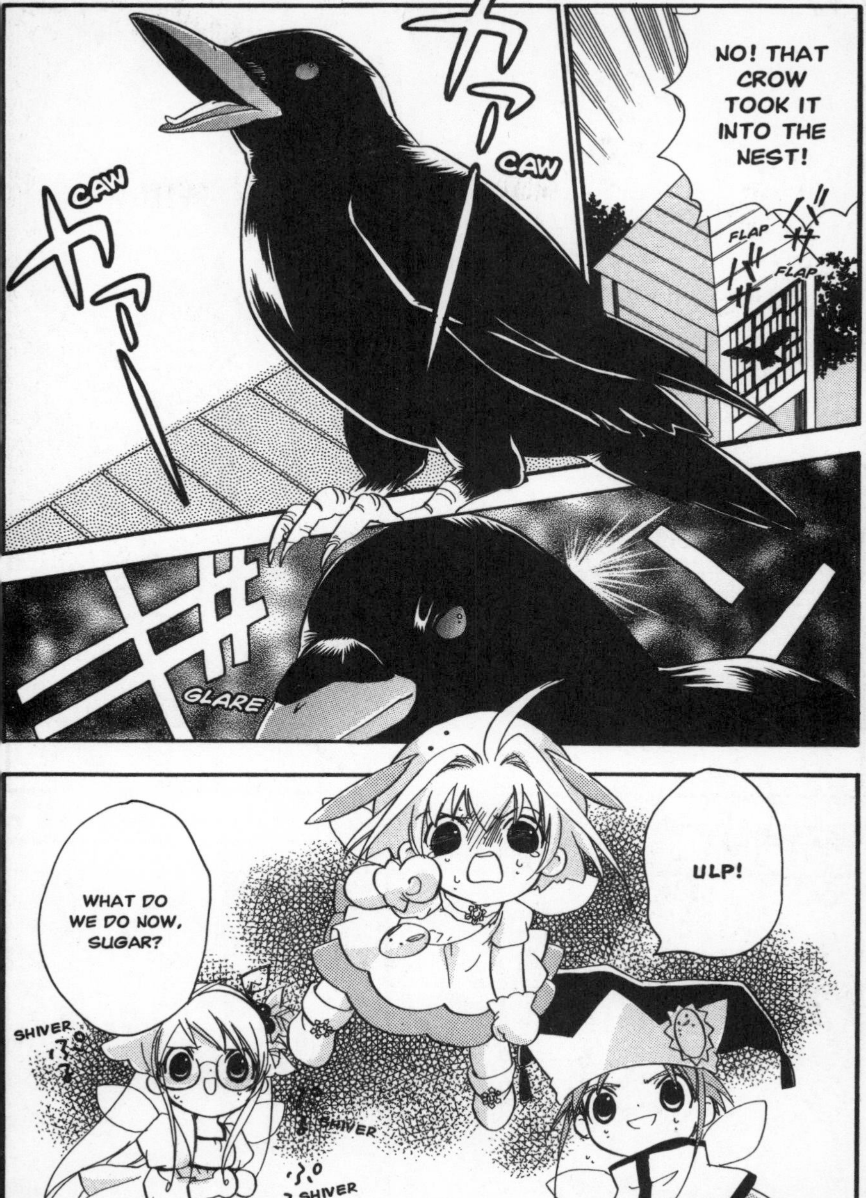
NO! THAT CROW TOOK IT INTO THE NEST!
FLAP
FLAP
カァー
CAW
カァー
CAW
GLARE
ULP!
WHAT DO WE DO NOW, SUGAR?
SHIVER
SHIVER
SHIVER

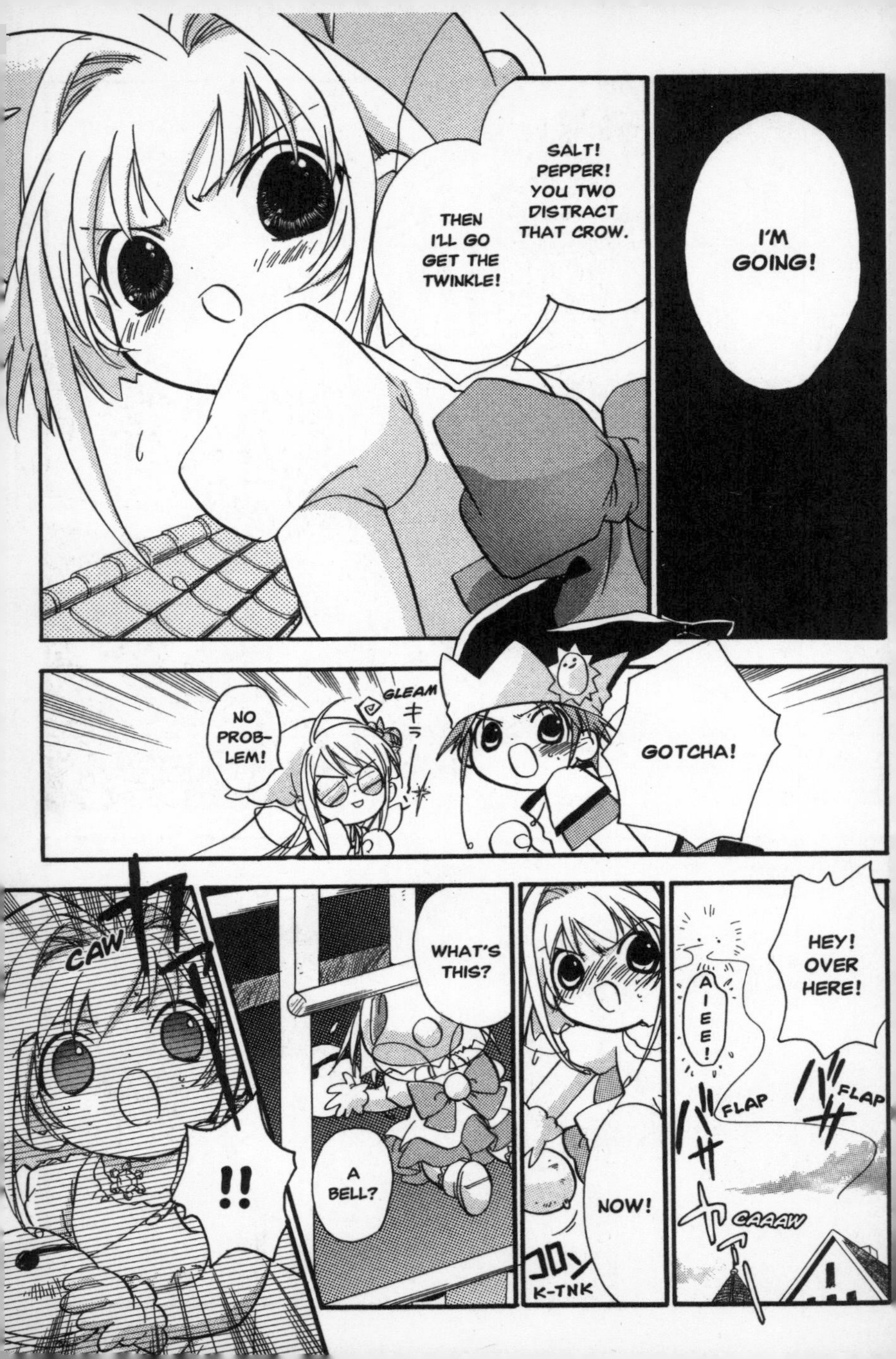
I'M GOING!
SALT! PEPPER! YOU TWO DISTRACT THAT CROW.
THEN I'LL GO GET THE TWINKLE!
GOTCHA!
GLEAM
キラ
NO PROB-LEM!
HEY! OVER HERE!
AIEE!
FLAP
FLAP
CAAAW
NOW!
コロン
K-TNK
WHAT'S THIS?
A BELL?
CAW
!!

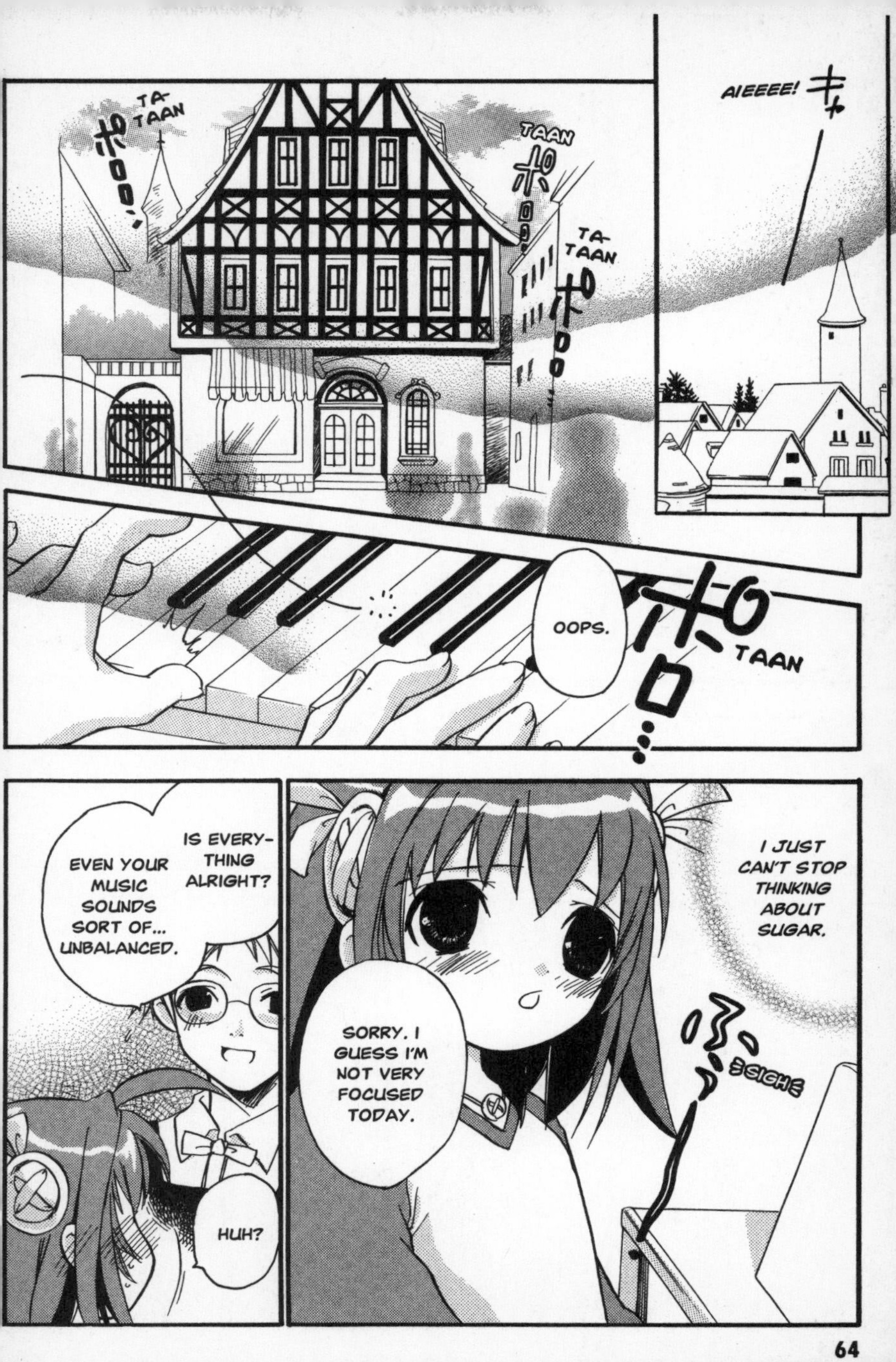
AIEEEE!
TAAN
TA TAAN
TA TAAN
OOPS.
TAAN
I JUST CAN'T STOP THINKING ABOUT SUGAR.
SIGH
SORRY. I GUESS I'M NOT VERY FOCUSED TODAY.
IS EVERY-THING ALRIGHT?
EVEN YOUR MUSIC SOUNDS SORT OF... UNBALANCED.
HUH?

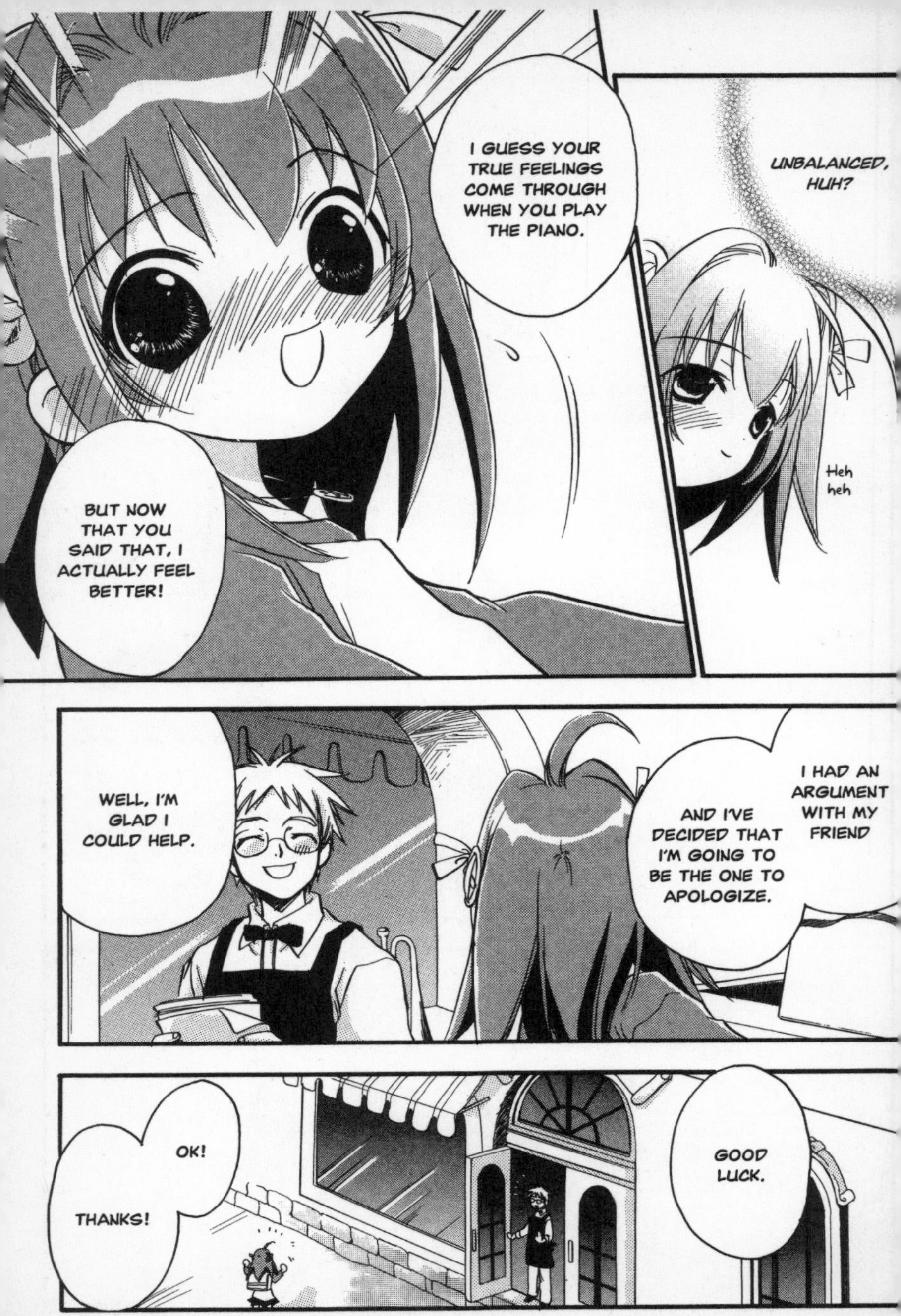
UNBALANCED, HUH?
Heh heh
I GUESS YOUR TRUE FEELINGS COME THROUGH WHEN YOU PLAY THE PIANO.
BUT NOW THAT YOU SAID THAT, I ACTUALLY FEEL BETTER!
I HAD AN ARGUMENT WITH MY FRIEND
AND I'VE DECIDED THAT I'M GOING TO BE THE ONE TO APOLOGIZE.
WELL, I'M GLAD I COULD HELP.
GOOD LUCK.
OK!
THANKS!

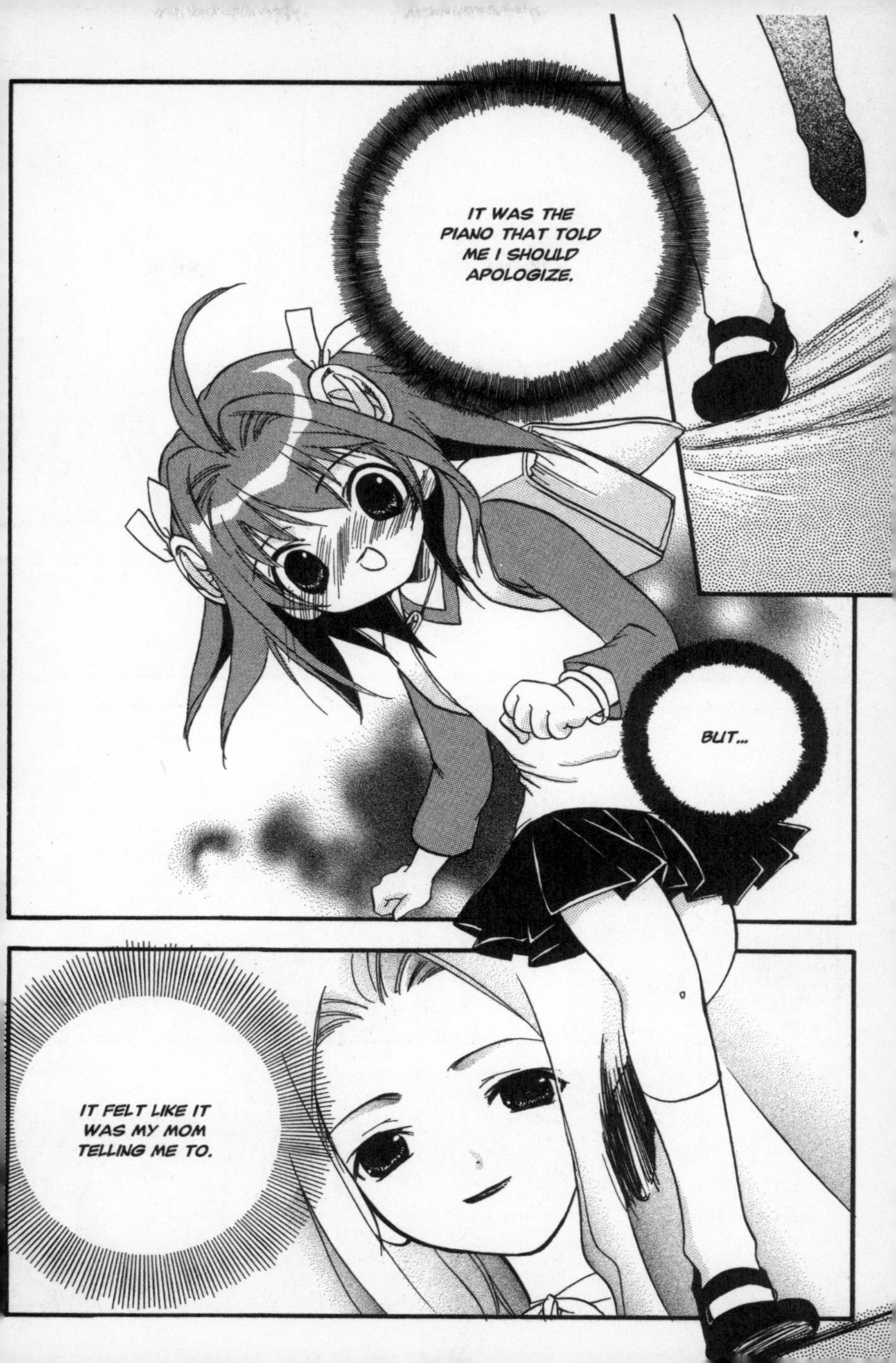
IT WAS THE PIANO THAT TOLD ME I SHOULD APOLOGIZE.
BUT...
IT FELT LIKE IT WAS MY MOM TELLING ME TO.

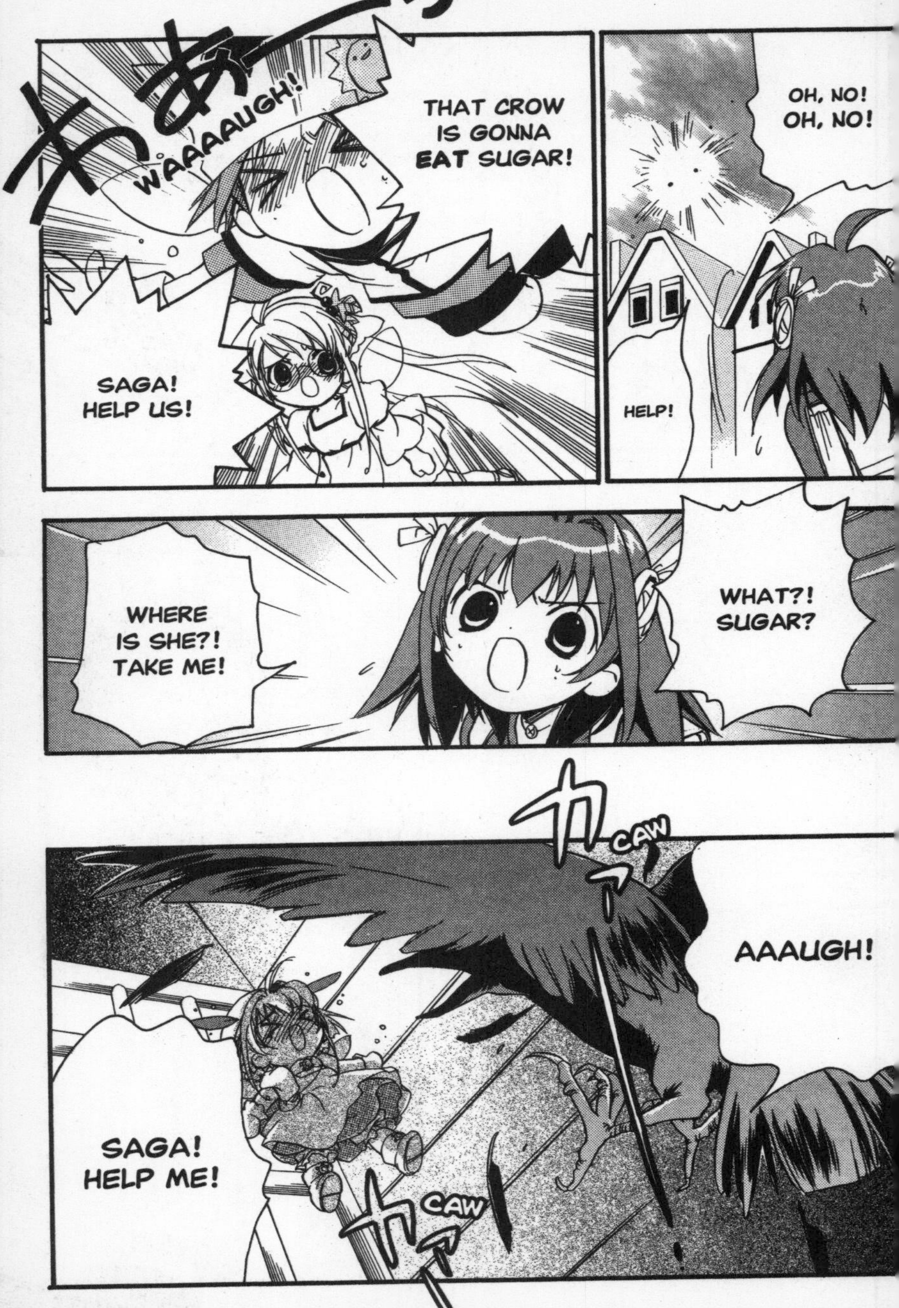
OH, NO! OH, NO!
HELP!
WAAAAUGH!
THAT CROW IS GONNA EAT SUGAR!
SAGA! HELP US!
WHAT?! SUGAR?
WHERE IS SHE?! TAKE ME!
CAW
AAAUGH!
SAGA! HELP ME!
CAW

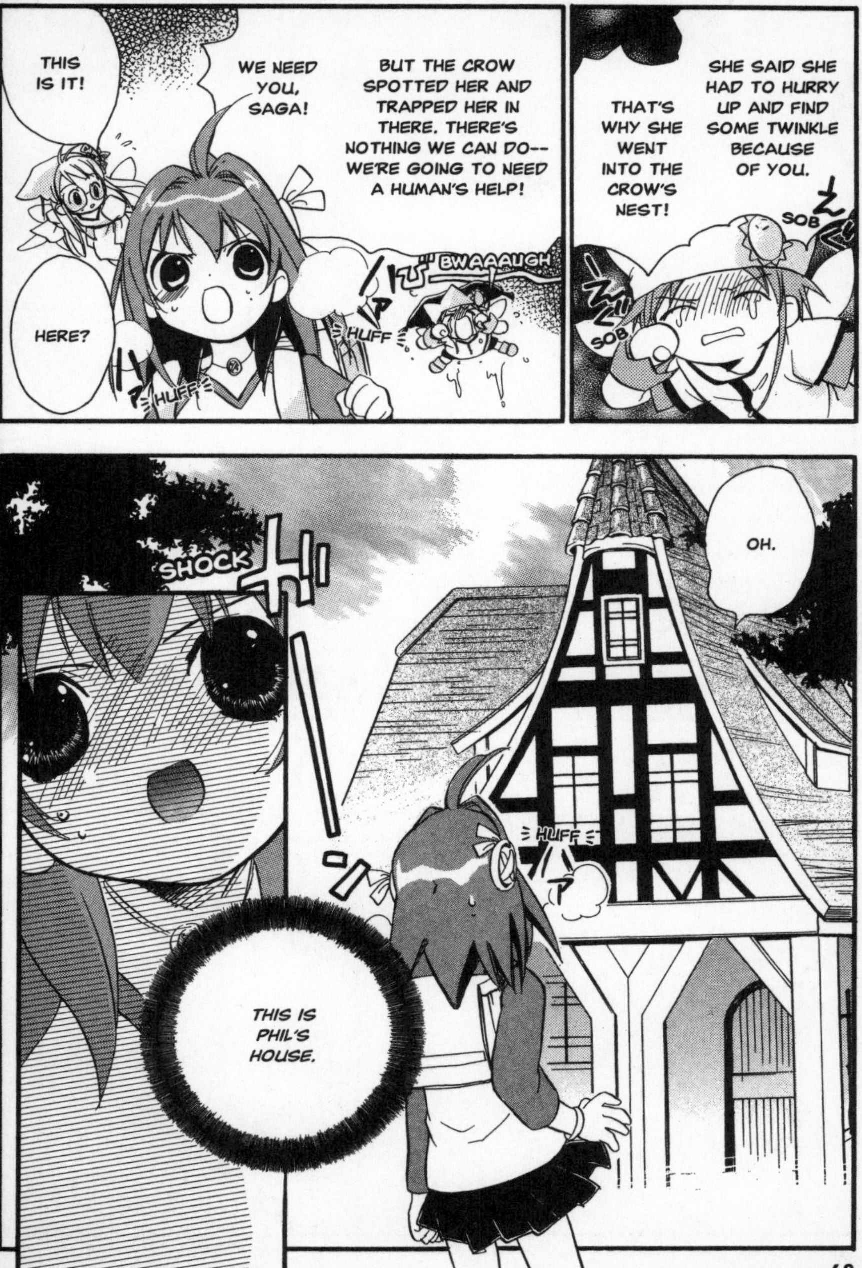
SHE SAID SHE HAD TO HURRY UP AND FIND SOME TWINKLE BECAUSE OF YOU.
THAT'S WHY SHE WENT INTO THE CROW'S NEST!
SOB
SOB
BUT THE CROW SPOTTED HER AND TRAPPED HER IN THERE. THERE'S NOTHING WE CAN DO-- WE'RE GOING TO NEED A HUMAN'S HELP!
WE NEED YOU, SAGA!
BWAAAUGH
HUFF
THIS IS IT!
HERE?
HUFF
OH.
SHOCK
HUFF
THIS IS PHIL'S HOUSE.

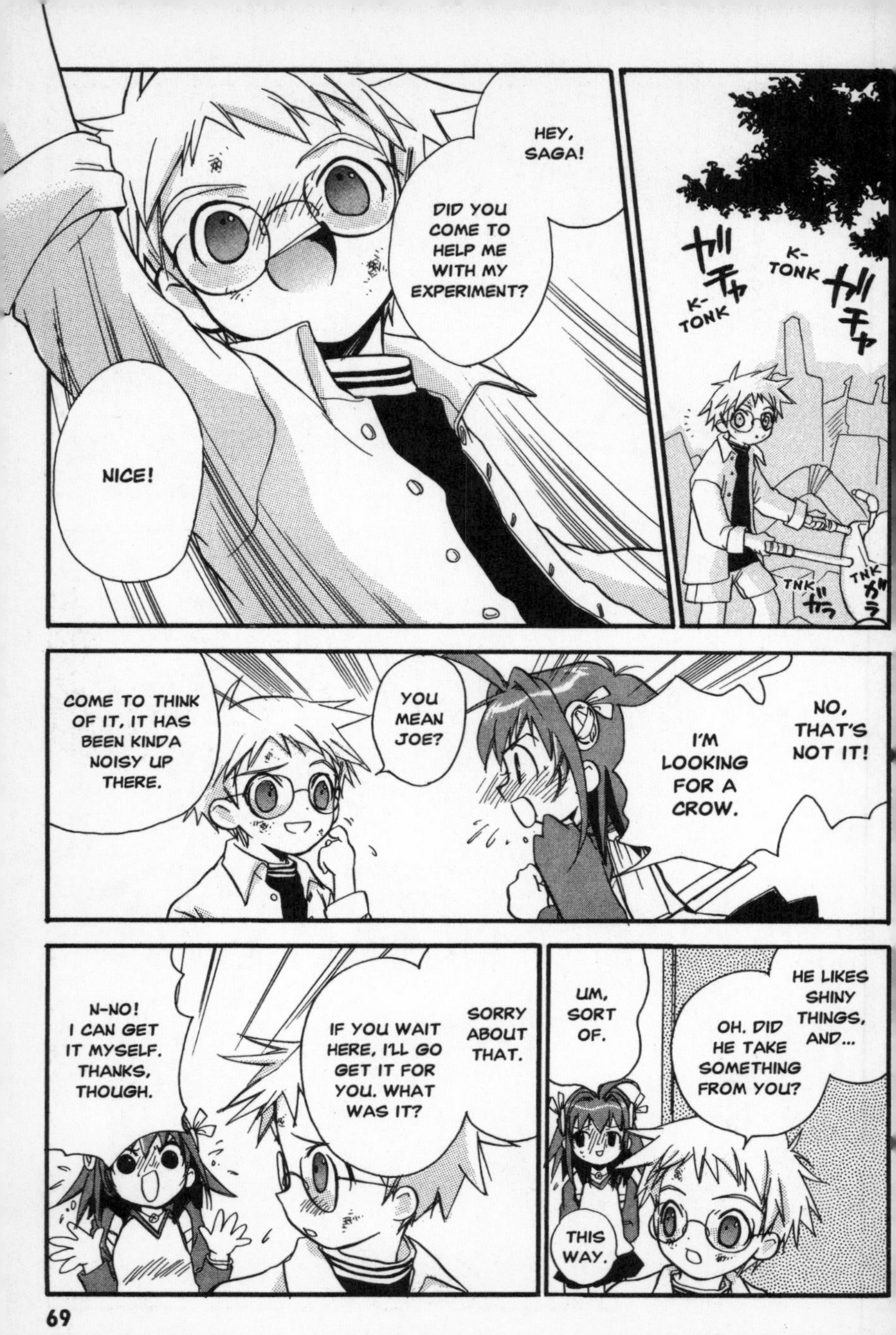
ガチャ
K-TONK
K-TONK
ガチャ
TNK
ガラ
TNK
ガラ
HEY, SAGA!
DID YOU COME TO HELP ME WITH MY EXPERIMENT?
NICE!
NO, THAT'S NOT IT!
I'M LOOKING FOR A CROW.
YOU MEAN JOE?
COME TO THINK OF IT, IT HAS BEEN KINDA NOISY UP THERE.
HE LIKES SHINY THINGS, AND...
OH. DID HE TAKE SOMETHING FROM YOU?
UM, SORT OF.
THIS WAY.
SORRY ABOUT THAT.
IF YOU WAIT HERE, I'LL GO GET IT FOR YOU. WHAT WAS IT?
N-NO! I CAN GET IT MYSELF. THANKS, THOUGH.

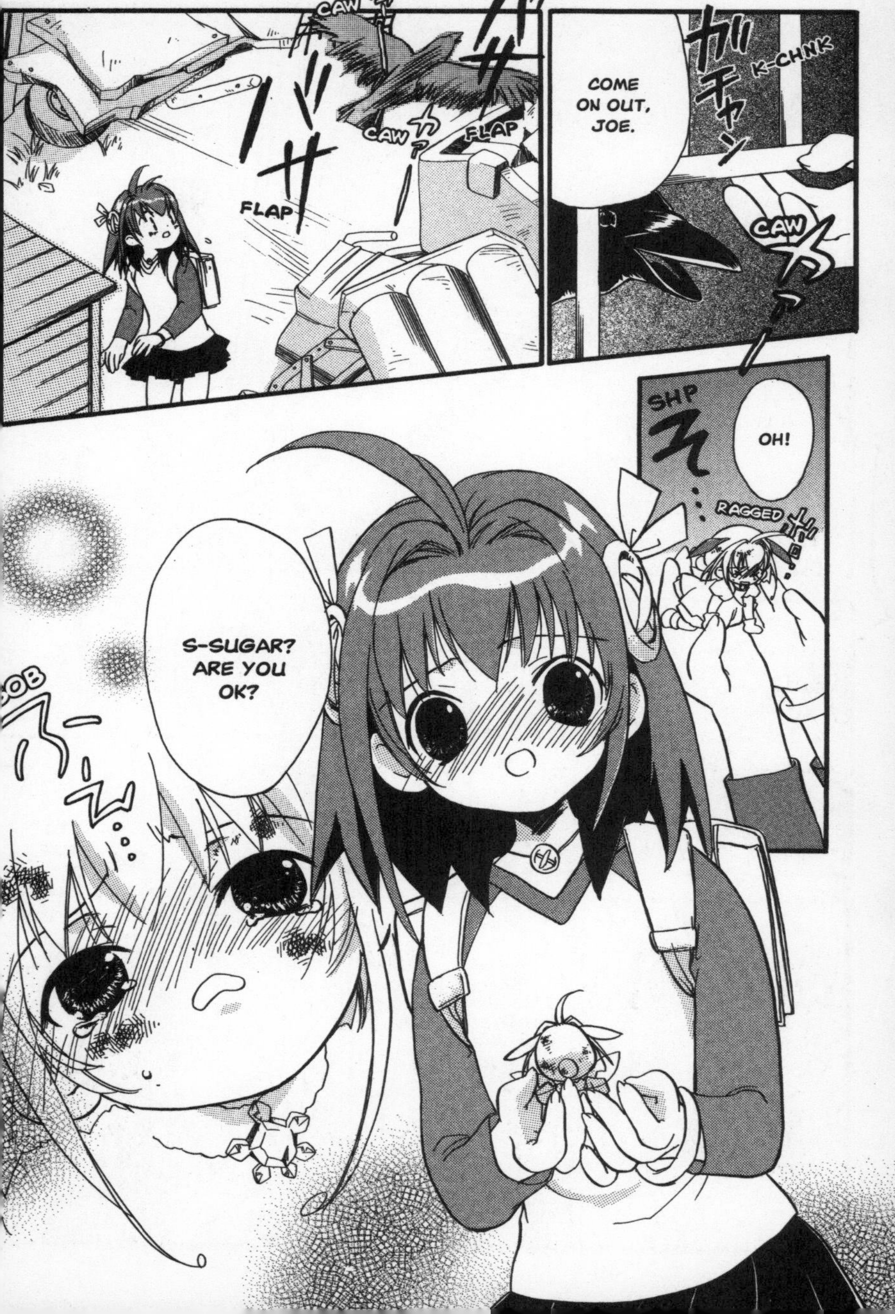
K-CHNK
COME ON OUT, JOE.
CAW
CAW
FLAP
CAW
FLAP
SHP
OH!
RAGGED
S-SUGAR? ARE YOU OK?

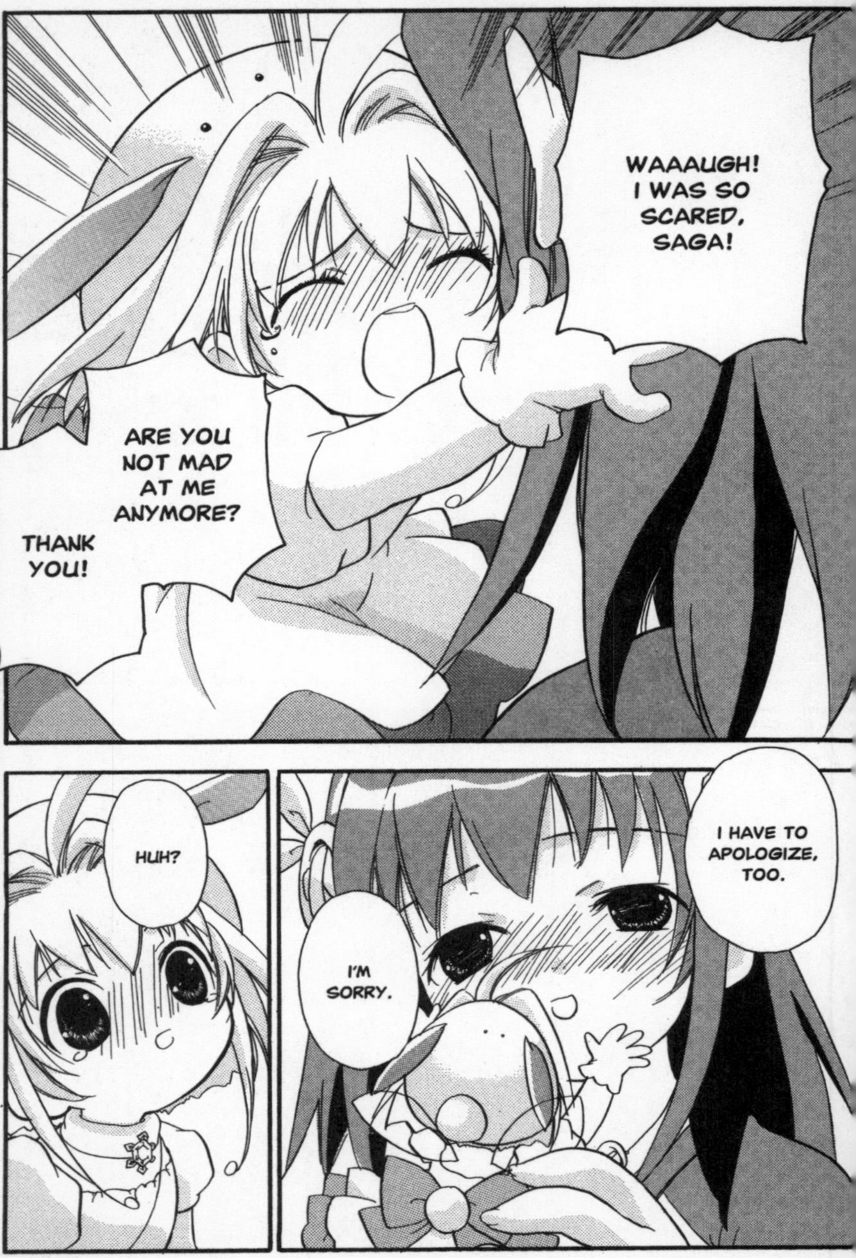
WAAAUGH! I WAS SO SCARED, SAGA!
ARE YOU NOT MAD AT ME ANYMORE?
THANK YOU!
I HAVE TO APOLOGIZE, TOO.
I'M SORRY.
HUH?

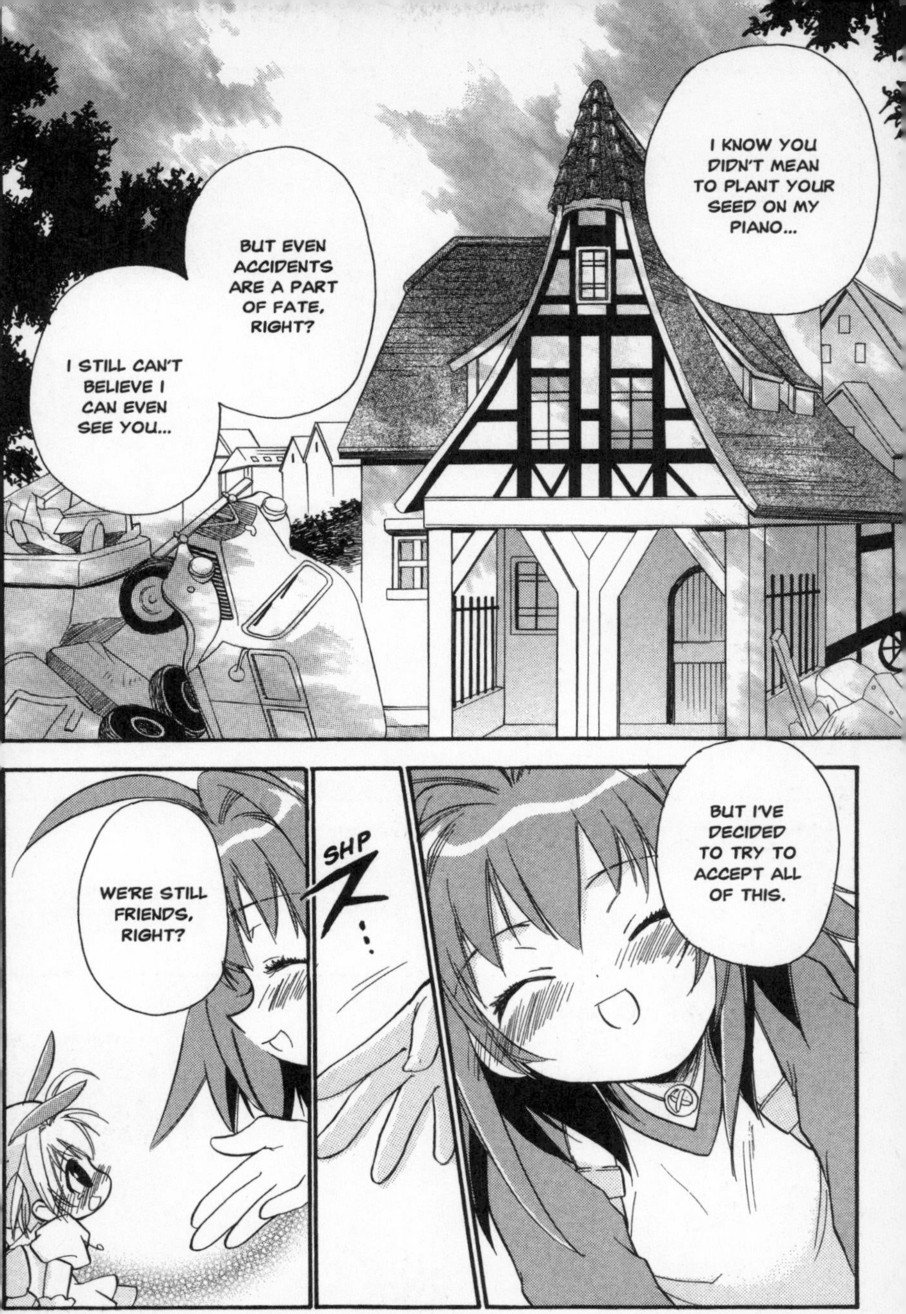
I KNOW YOU DIDN'T MEAN TO PLANT YOUR SEED ON MY PIANO...
BUT EVEN ACCIDENTS ARE A PART OF FATE, RIGHT?
I STILL CAN'T BELIEVE I CAN EVEN SEE YOU...
BUT I'VE DECIDED TO TRY TO ACCEPT ALL OF THIS.
SHP
...
WE'RE STILL FRIENDS, RIGHT?

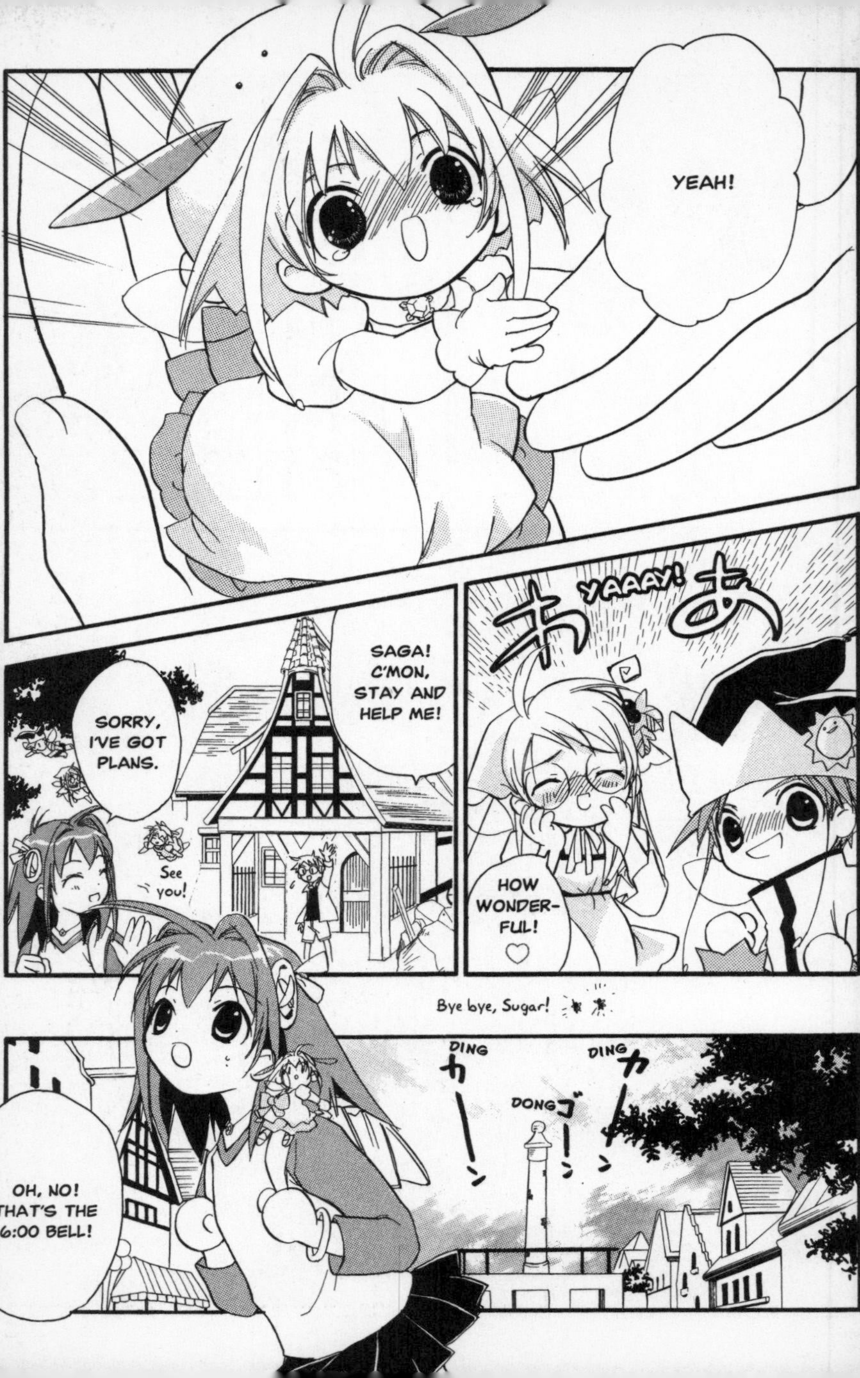
YEAH!
YAAAY!
あ あ
HOW WONDER-FUL!
SAGA! C'MON, STAY AND HELP ME!
SORRY, I'VE GOT PLANS.
See you!
Bye bye, Sugar!
DING
カーン
DING
カーン
DONG
ゴーン
OH, NO! THAT'S THE 6:00 BELL!

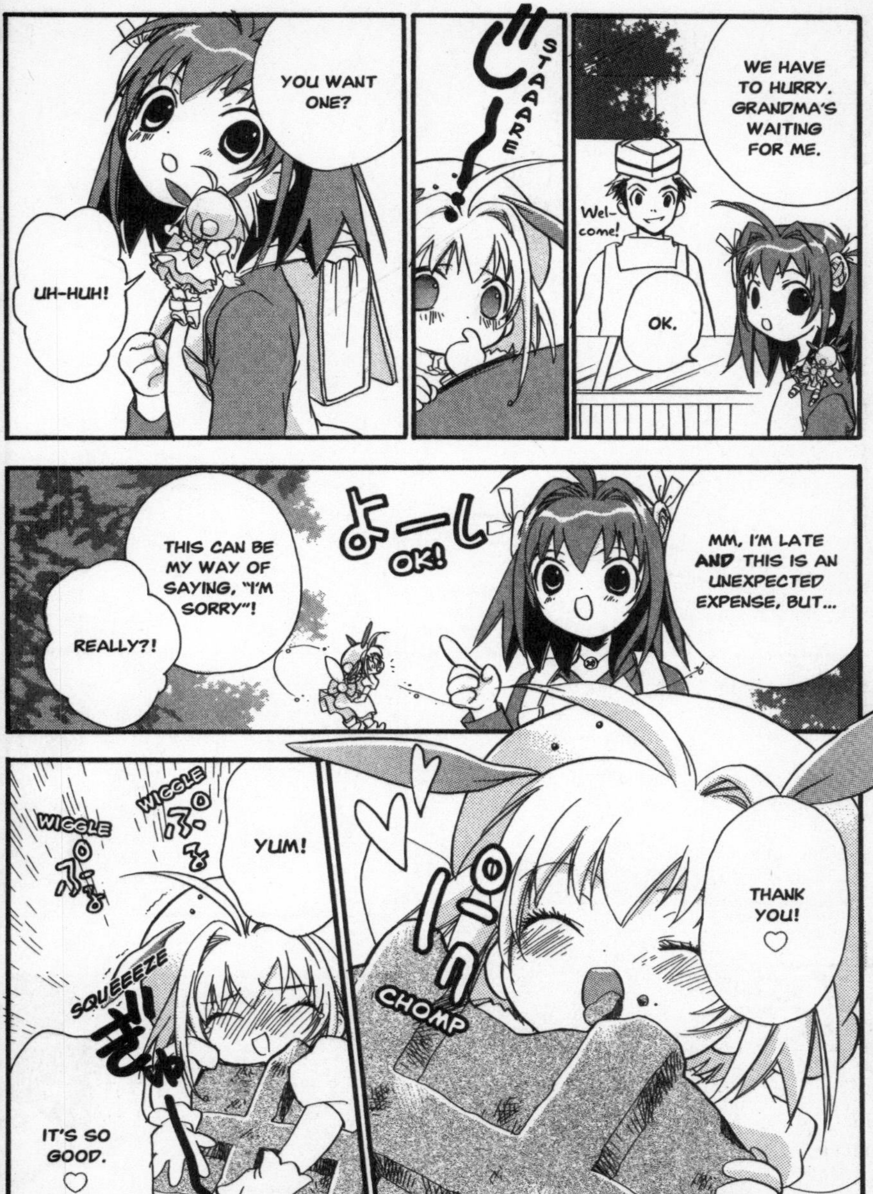

WE HAVE TO HURRY. GRANDMA'S WAITING FOR ME.
Wel-come!
OK.
STAAARE
YOU WANT ONE?
UH-HUH!
MM, I'M LATE AND THIS IS AN UNEXPECTED EXPENSE, BUT...
よーし
OK!
THIS CAN BE MY WAY OF SAYING, "I'M SORRY"!
REALLY?!
THANK YOU! ♡
CHOMP
YUM!
WIGGLE
WIGGLE
SQUEEEZE
IT'S SO GOOD. ♡

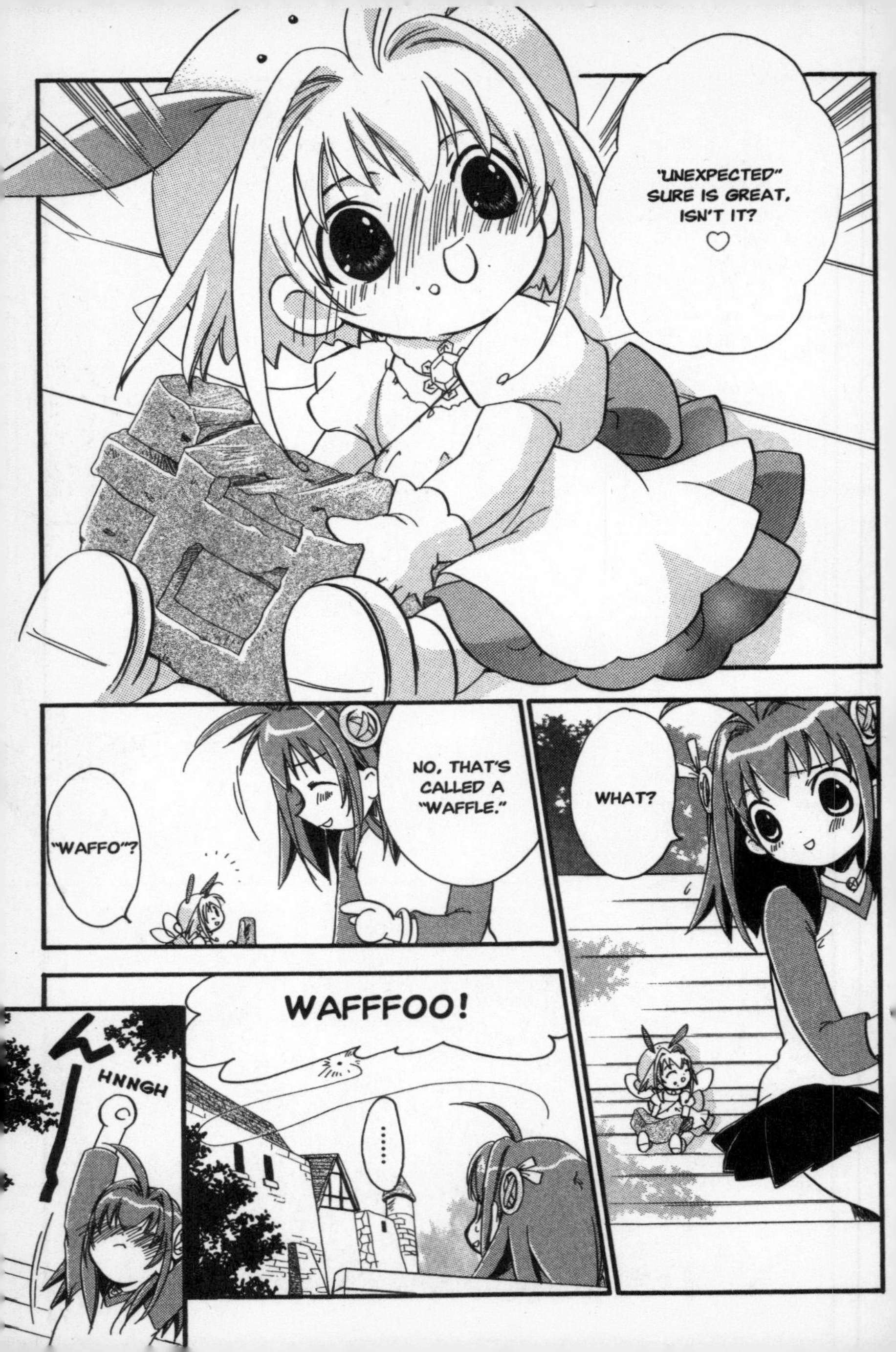
"UNEXPECTED" SURE IS GREAT, ISN'T IT? ♡
WHAT?
NO, THAT'S CALLED A "WAFFLE."
"WAFFO"?
WAFFFOO!
......
ん
HNNGH

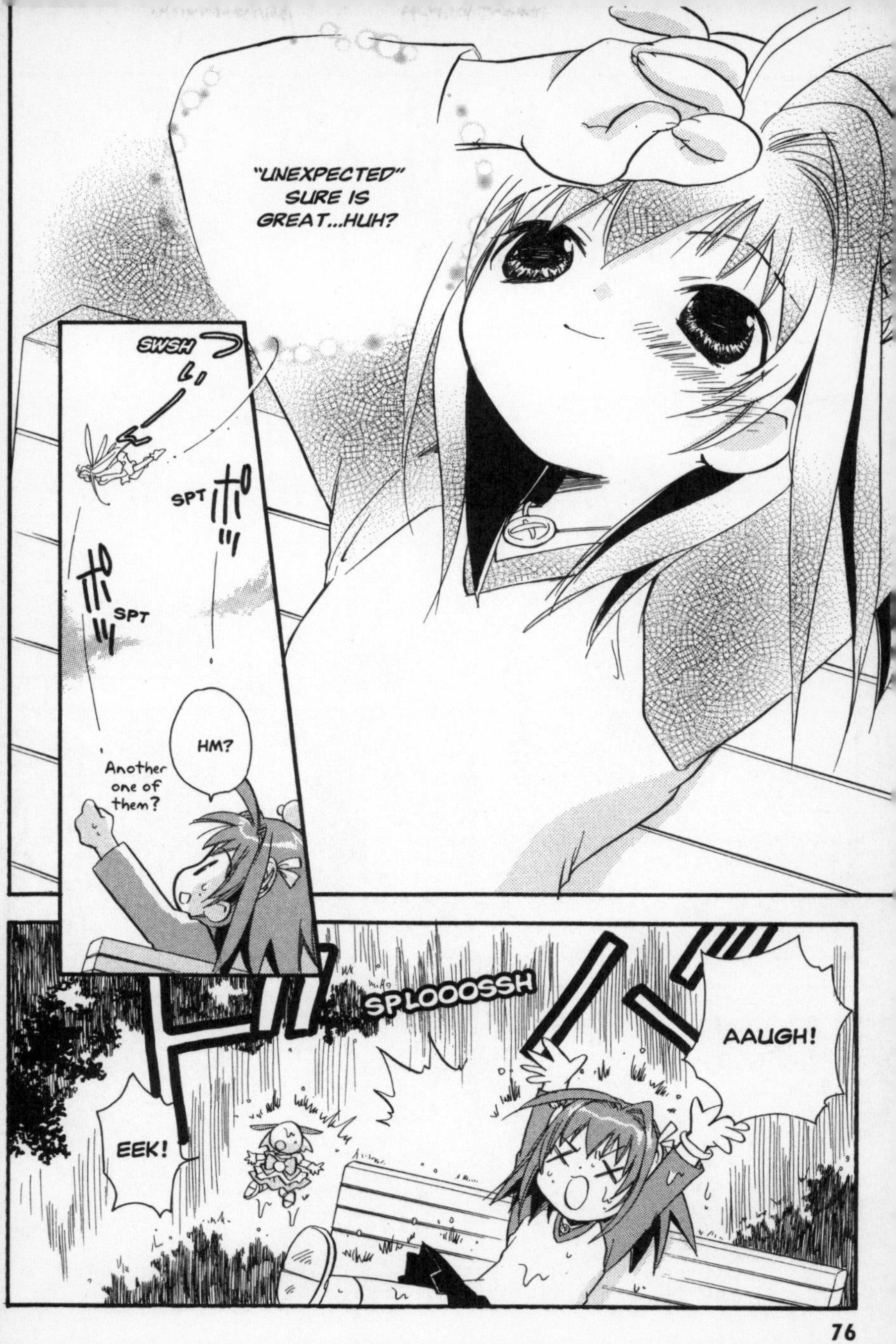

"UNEXPECTED" SURE IS GREAT...HUH?
SWSH
SPT
SPT
HM?
Another one of them?
SPLOOOSSH
AAUGH!
EEK!

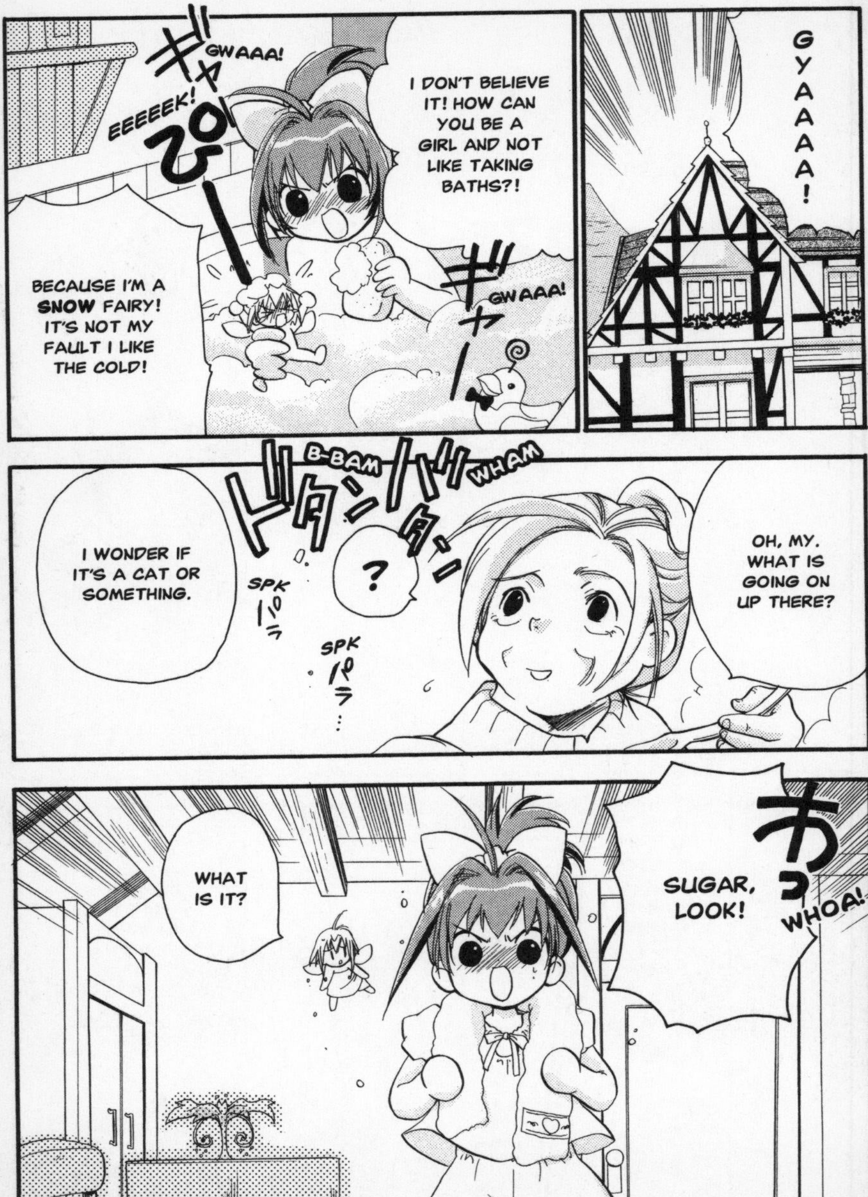

GYAAAAA!
GWAAA!
EEEEEK!
I DON'T BELIEVE IT! HOW CAN YOU BE A GIRL AND NOT LIKE TAKING BATHS?!
BECAUSE I'M A **SNOW** FAIRY! IT'S NOT MY FAULT I LIKE THE COLD!
GWAAA!
B-BAM
WHAM
OH, MY. WHAT IS GOING ON UP THERE?
?
SPK
I WONDER IF IT'S A CAT OR SOMETHING.
SPK
WHOA!
SUGAR, LOOK!
WHAT IS IT?

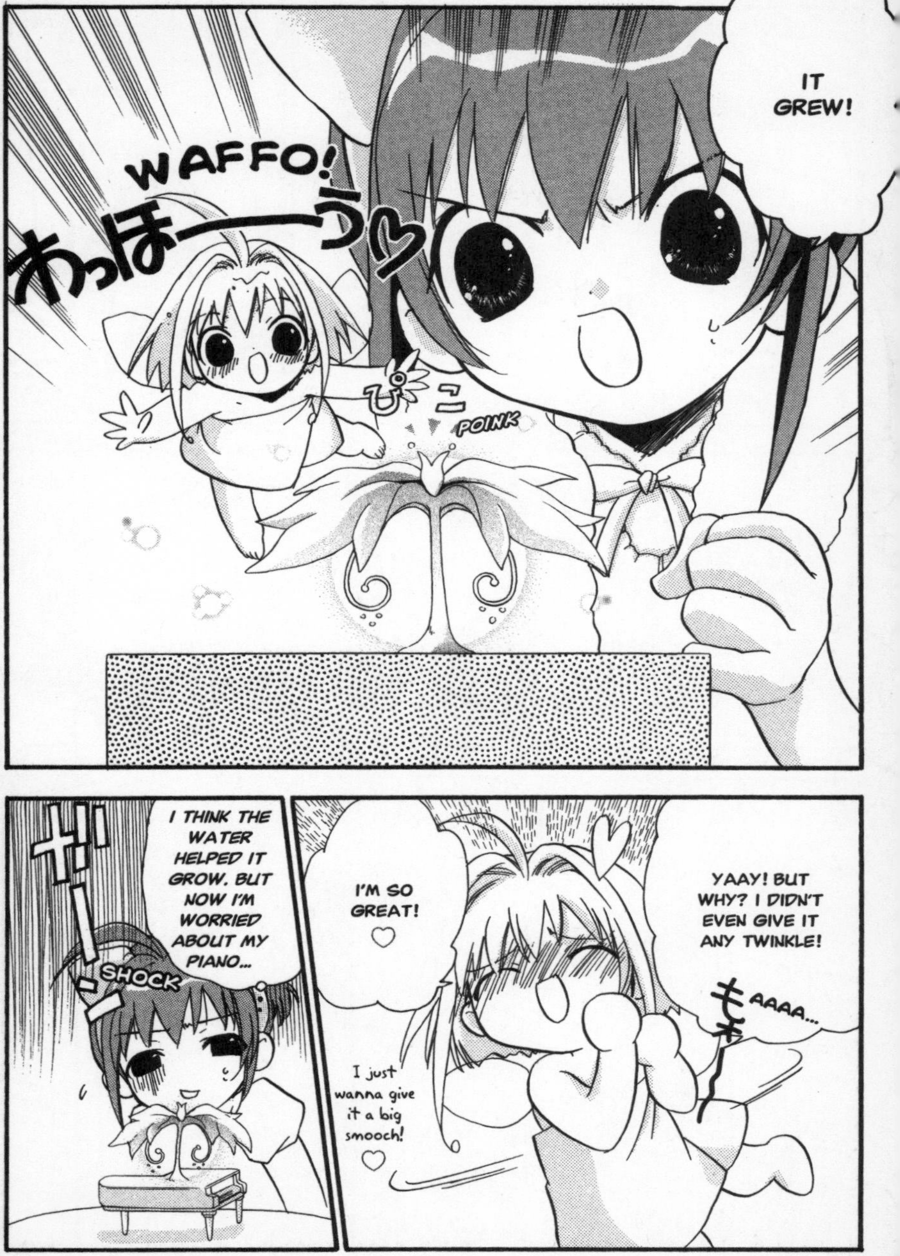
IT GREW!
わっほーーう
WAFFO!
ぴこ
POINK
YAAY! BUT WHY? I DIDN'T EVEN GIVE IT ANY TWINKLE!
I'M SO GREAT!
I just wanna give it a big smooch!
AAAA...
I THINK THE WATER HELPED IT GROW. BUT NOW I'M WORRIED ABOUT MY PIANO...
SHOCK

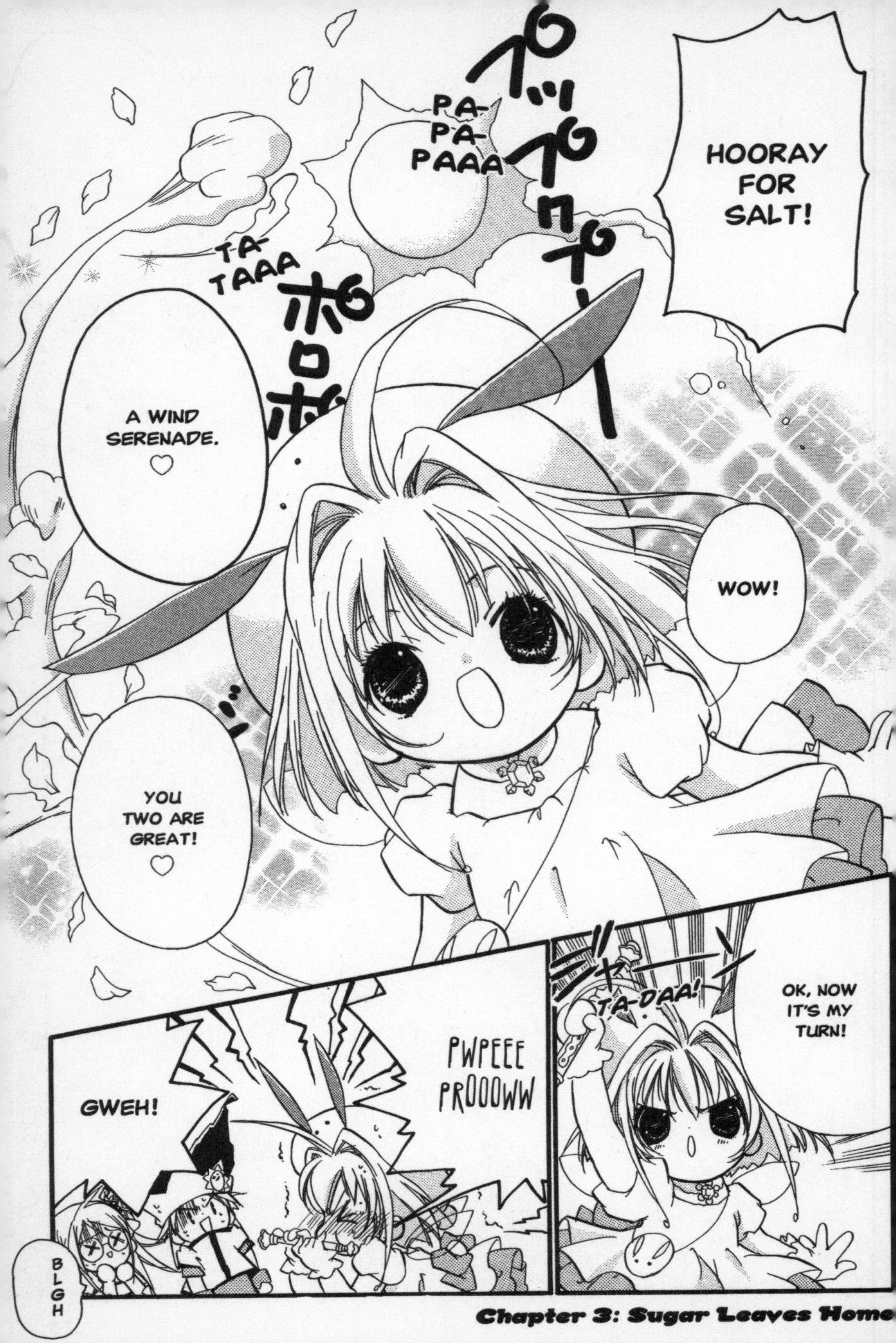
HOORAY FOR SALT!
PA-PA-PAAA
TA-TAAA
WOW!
A WIND SERENADE. ♡
YOU TWO ARE GREAT! ♡
OK, NOW IT'S MY TURN!
TA-DAA!
PWPEEE PROOOWW
GWEH!
BLGH

Chapter 3: Sugar Leaves Home

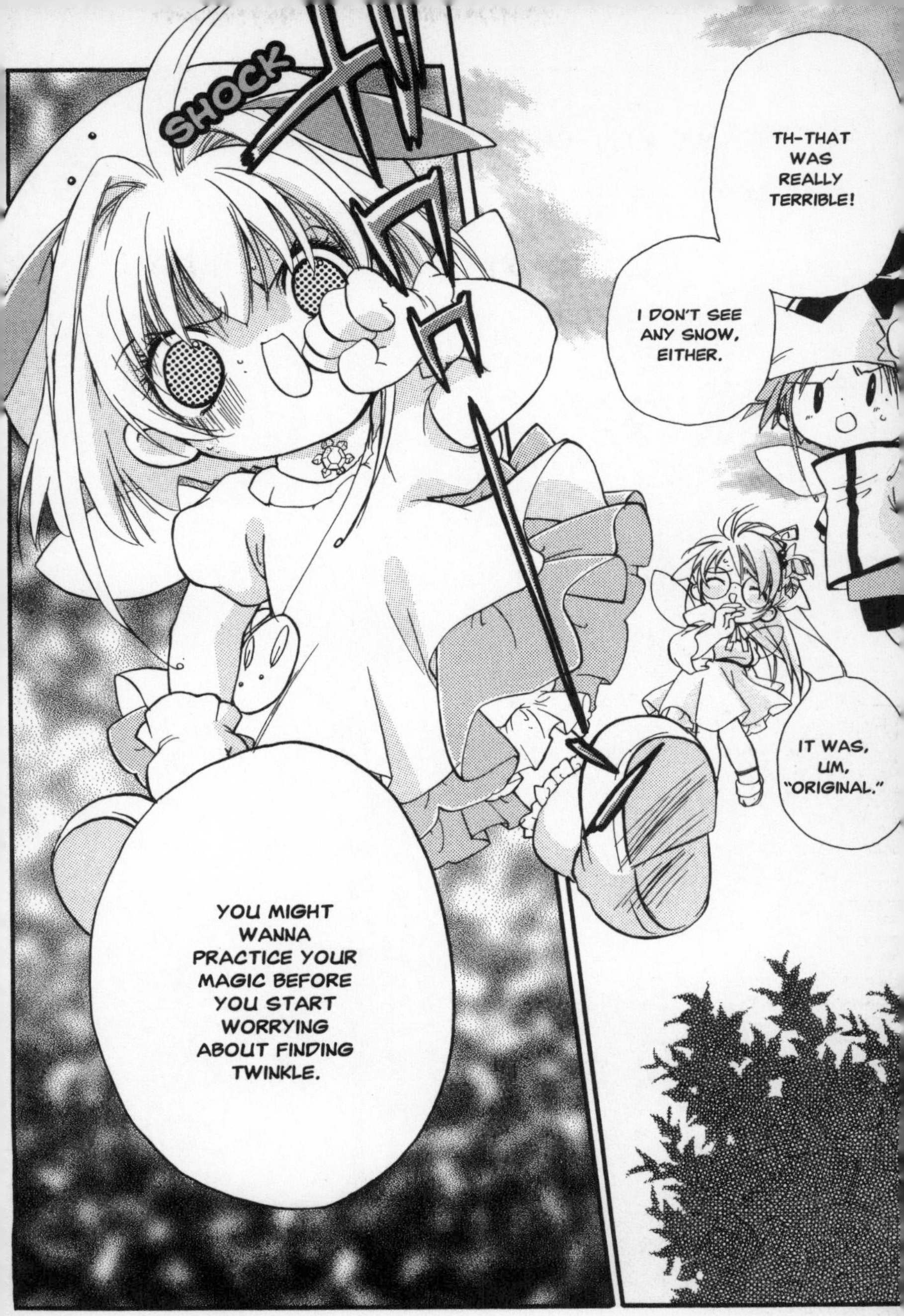
TH-THAT WAS REALLY TERRIBLE!
I DON'T SEE ANY SNOW, EITHER.
IT WAS, UM, "ORIGINAL."
SHOCK
YOU MIGHT WANNA PRACTICE YOUR MAGIC BEFORE YOU START WORRYING ABOUT FINDING TWINKLE.

CHAPTER 3 Sugar Leaves Home

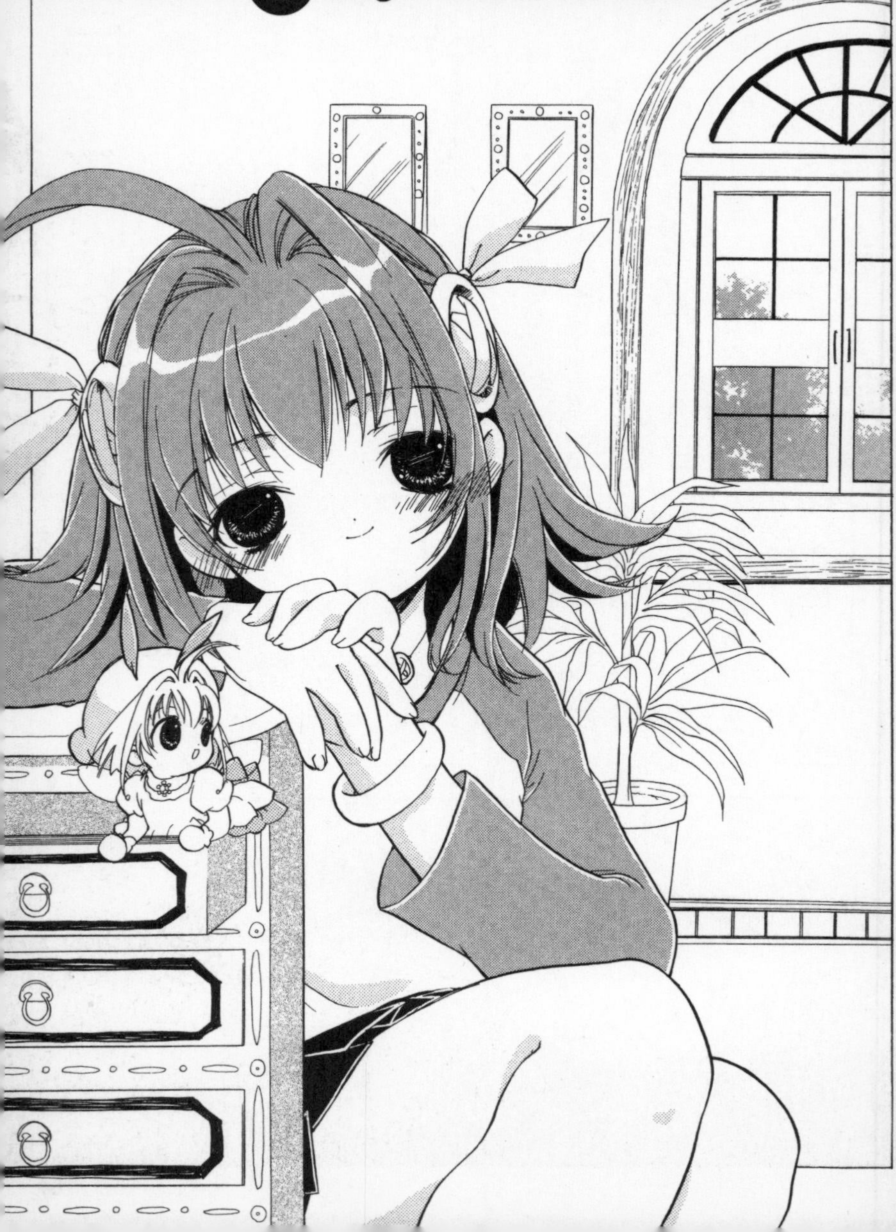

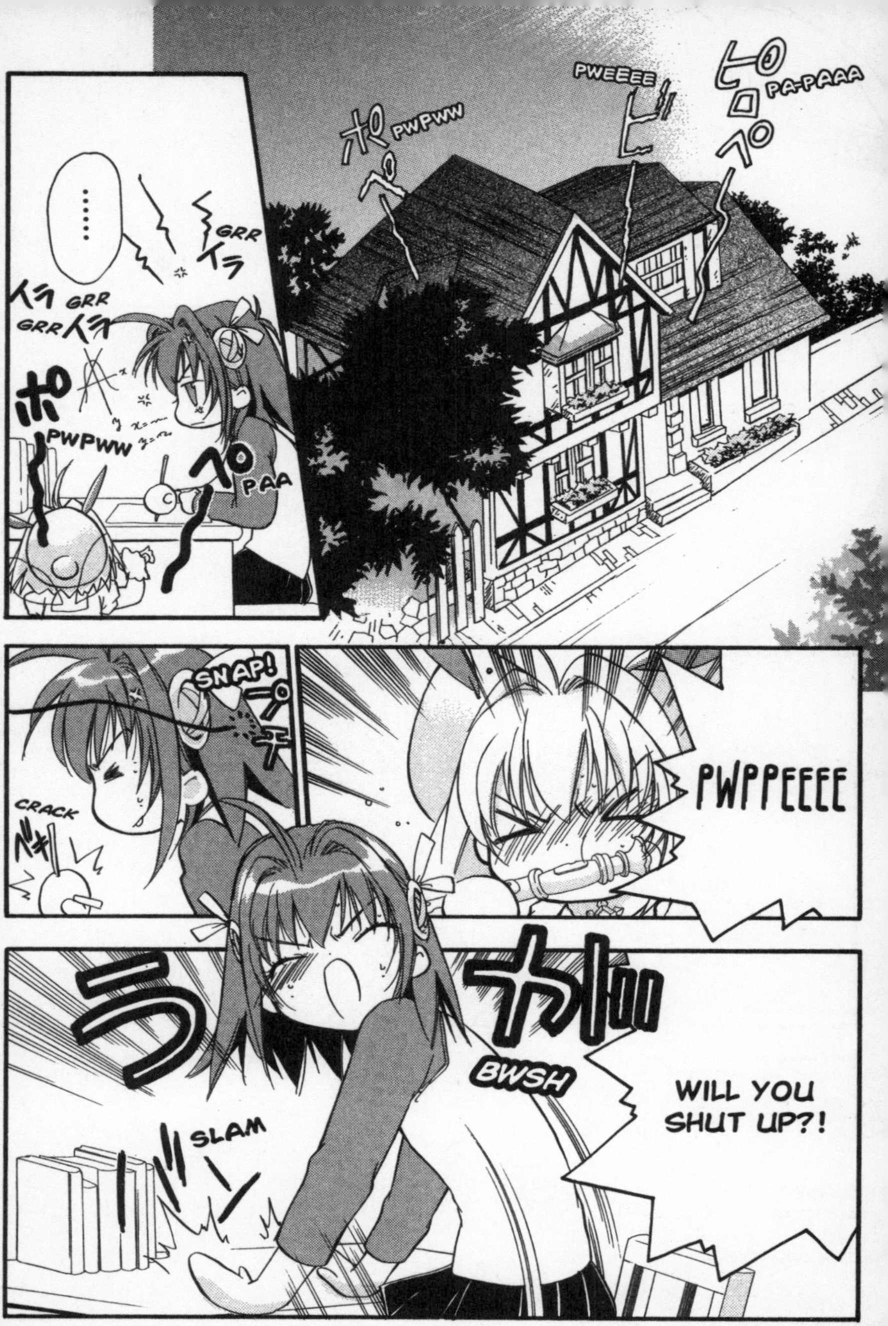
PA-PAAA
PWEEEE
PWPWW
……
GRR
GRR
GRR
PWPWW
PAA
PWPPEEEE
SNAP!
CRACK
BWSH
WILL YOU SHUT UP?!
SLAM

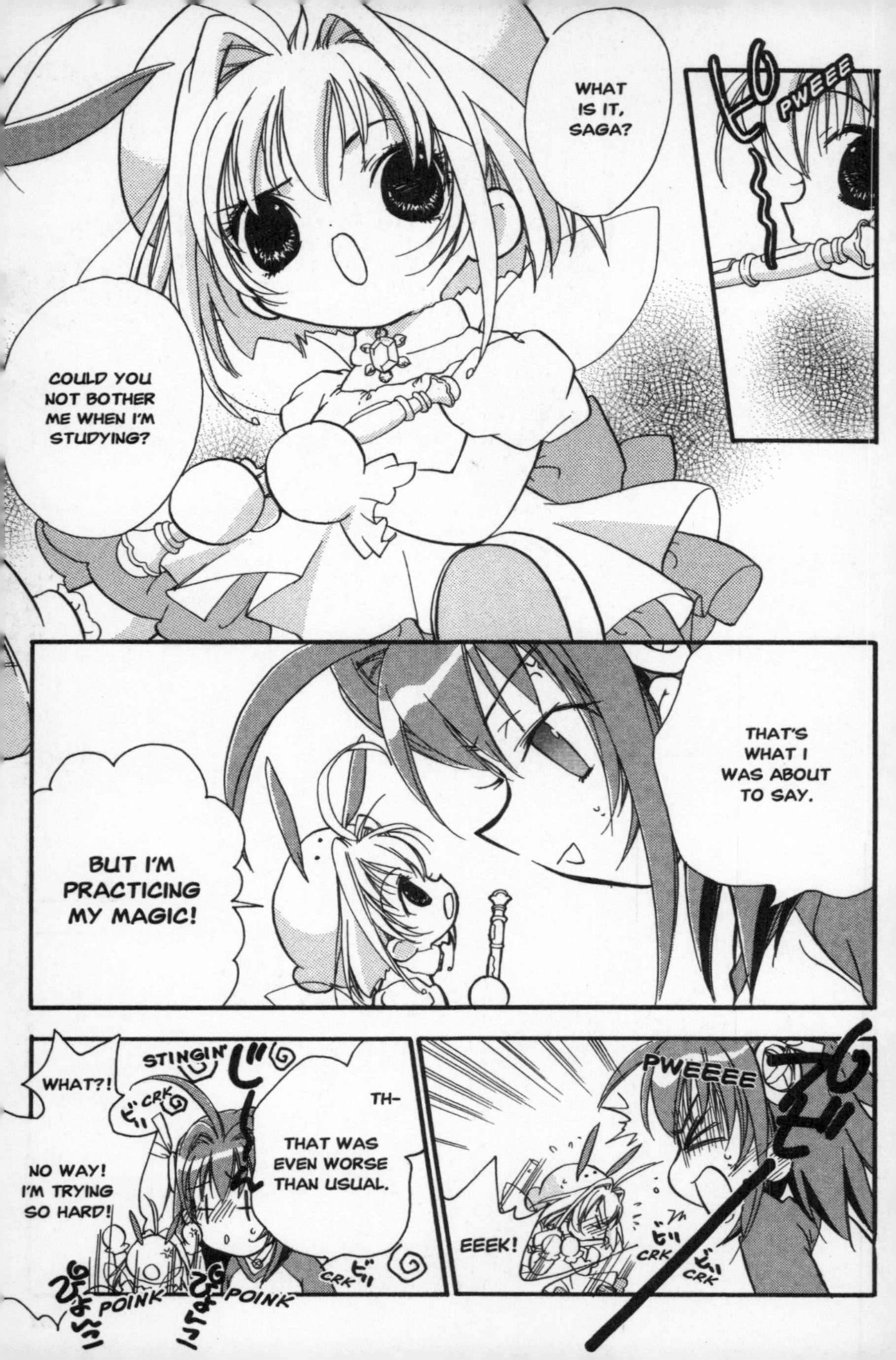
PWEEE
WHAT IS IT, SAGA?
COULD YOU NOT BOTHER ME WHEN I'M STUDYING?
THAT'S WHAT I WAS ABOUT TO SAY.
BUT I'M PRACTICING MY MAGIC!
PWEEEEE
EEEK!
CRK
CRK
TH-
THAT WAS EVEN WORSE THAN USUAL.
STINGIN'
WHAT?!
CRK
CRK
NO WAY! I'M TRYING SO HARD!
POINK
POINK

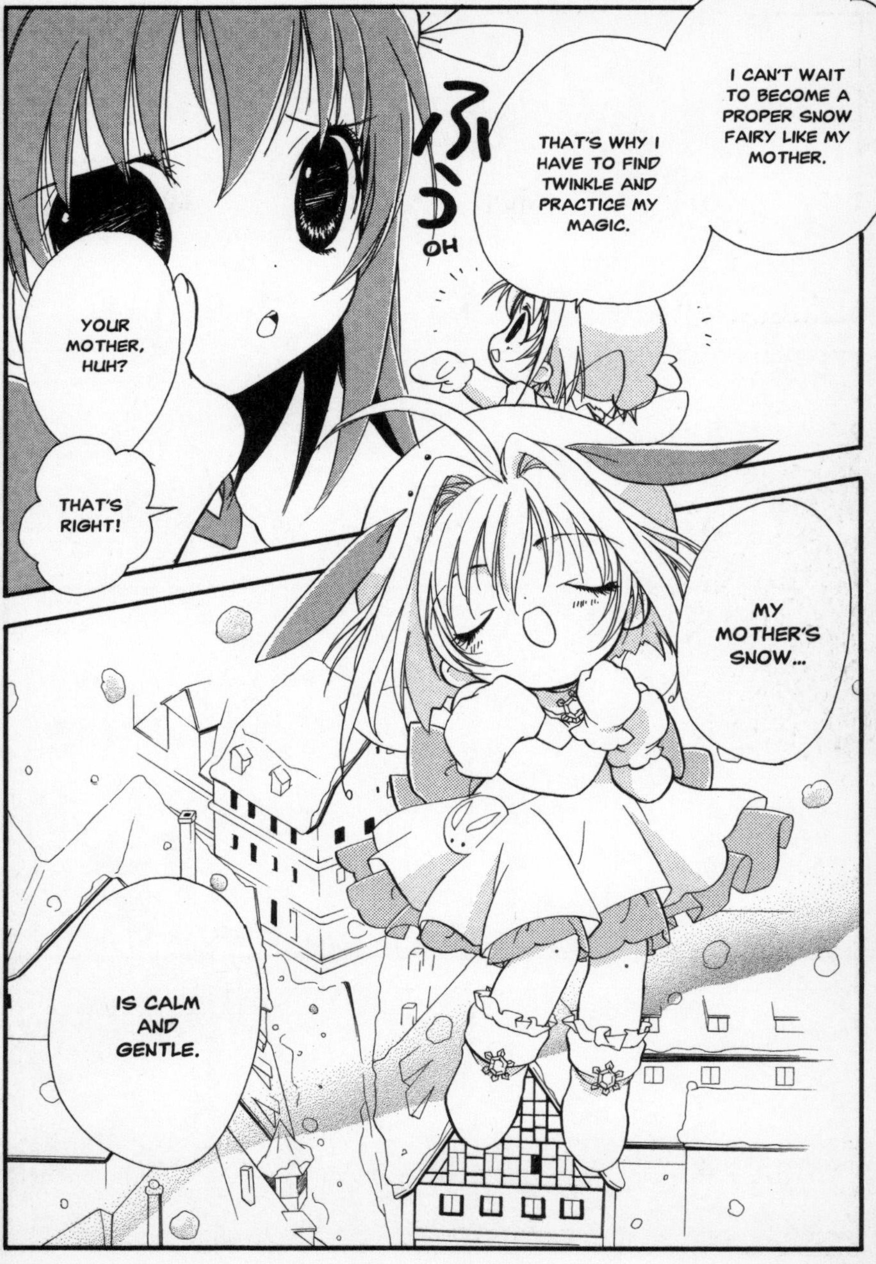
I CAN'T WAIT TO BECOME A PROPER SNOW FAIRY LIKE MY MOTHER.
THAT'S WHY I HAVE TO FIND TWINKLE AND PRACTICE MY MAGIC.
ふっ
OH
YOUR MOTHER, HUH?
THAT'S RIGHT!
MY MOTHER'S SNOW...
IS CALM AND GENTLE.

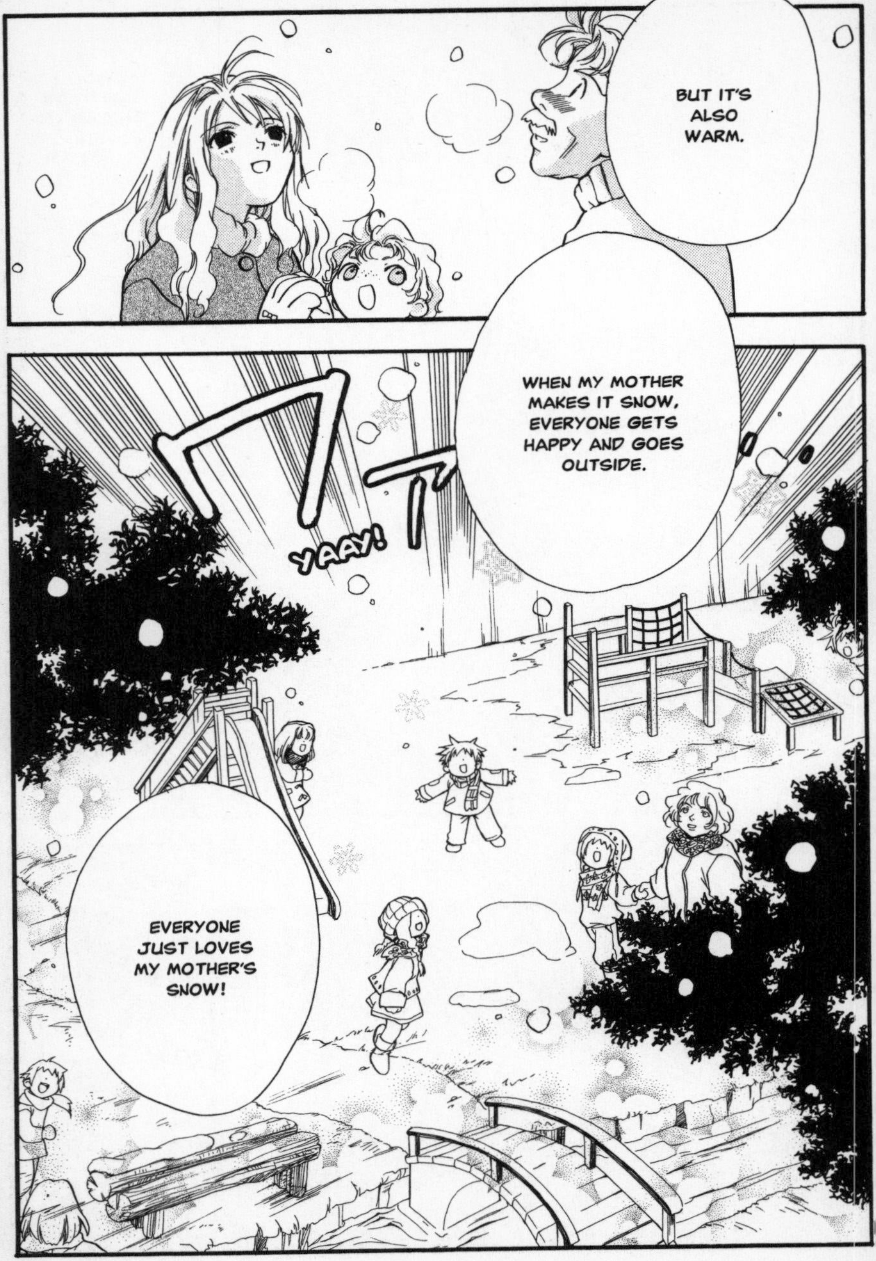
BUT IT'S ALSO WARM.
WHEN MY MOTHER MAKES IT SNOW, EVERYONE GETS HAPPY AND GOES OUTSIDE.
YAAY!
EVERYONE JUST LOVES MY MOTHER'S SNOW!

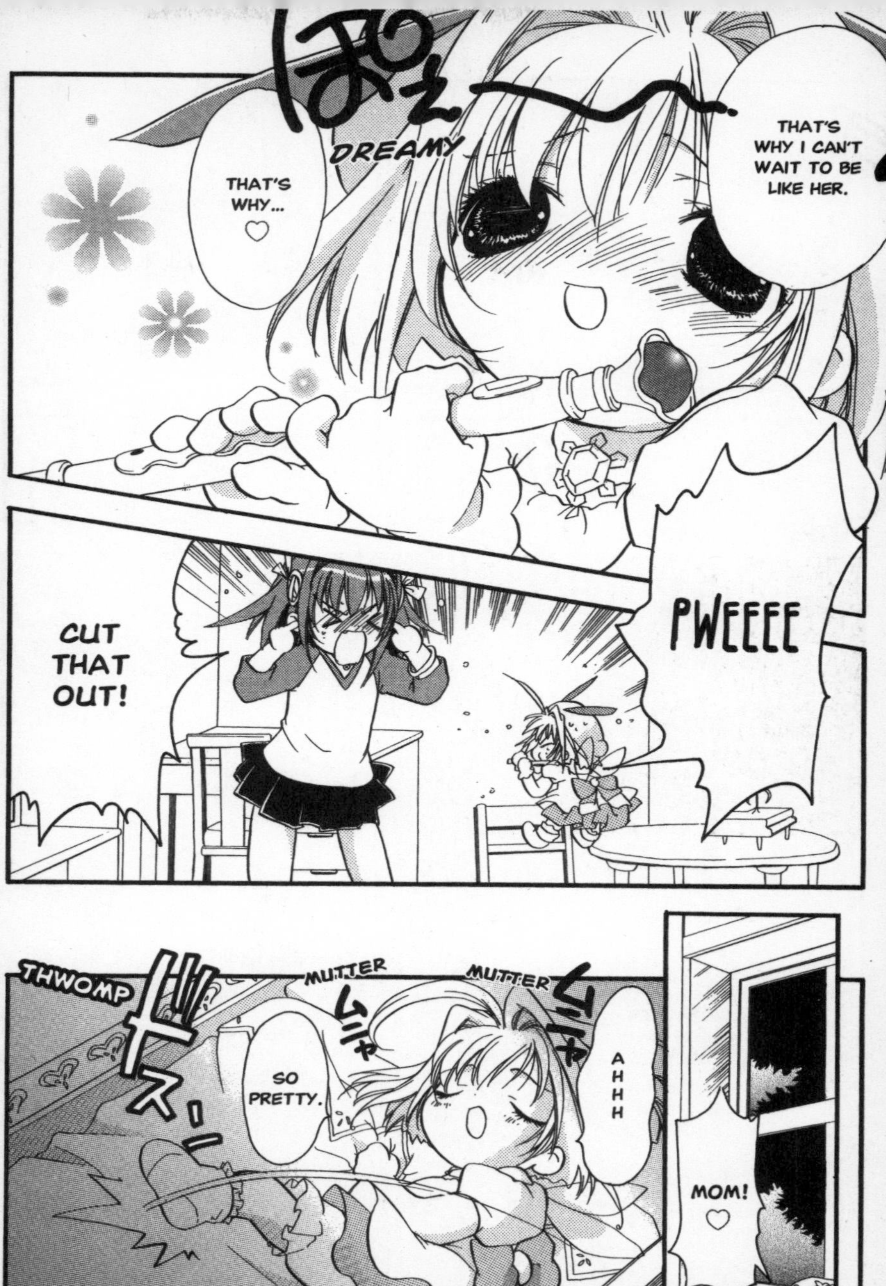
THAT'S WHY I CAN'T WAIT TO BE LIKE HER.
DREAMY
THAT'S WHY... ♡
PWEEEE
CUT THAT OUT!
MOM! ♡
MUTTER
AHHH
MUTTER
SO PRETTY.
THWOMP

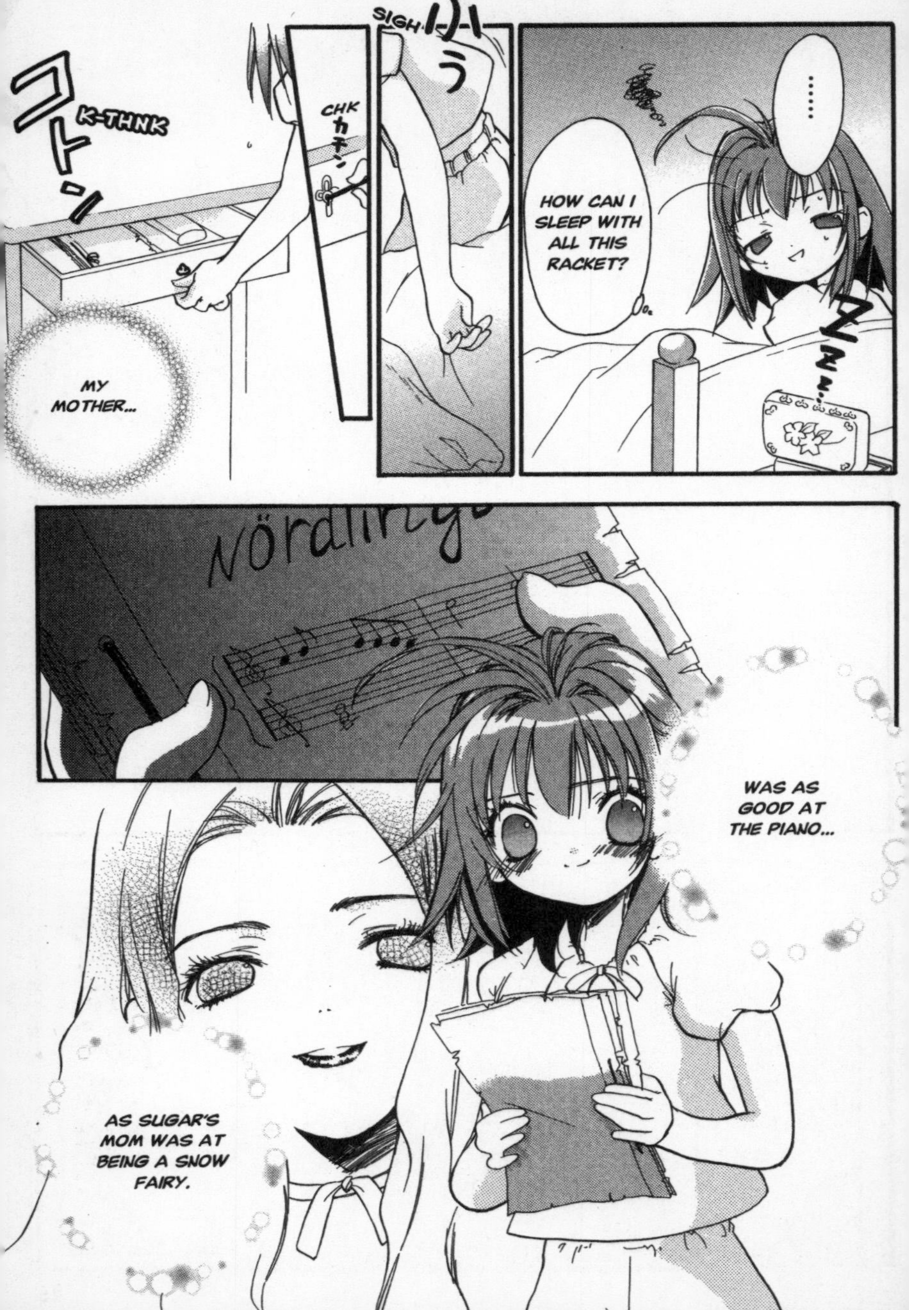

……
HOW CAN I SLEEP WITH ALL THIS RACKET?
ZZZ...
SIGH
ふう
CHK
カチン
K-THNK
コトッ
MY MOTHER...
WAS AS GOOD AT THE PIANO...
AS SUGAR'S MOM WAS AT BEING A SNOW FAIRY.

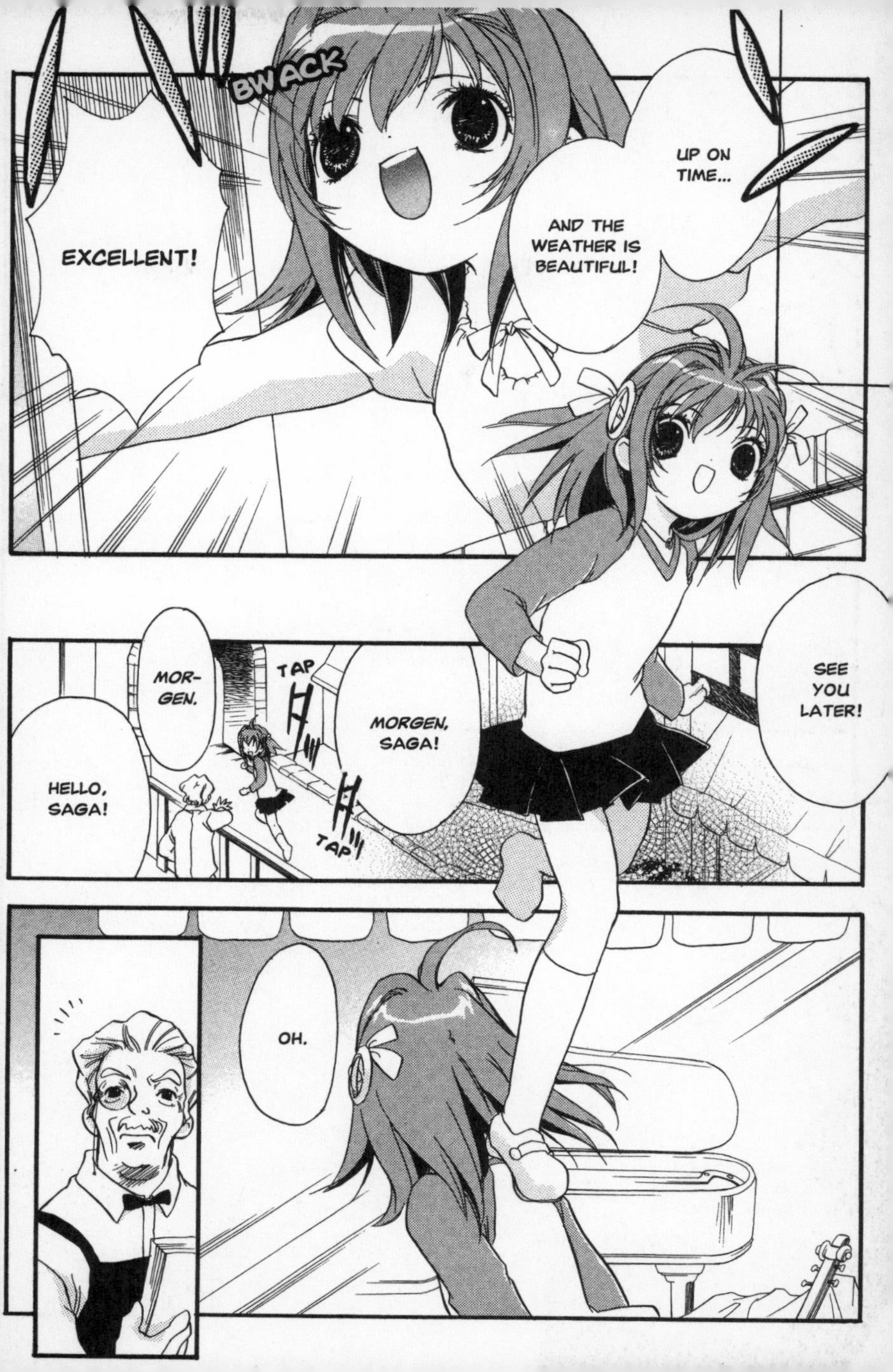
BWACK
UP ON TIME...
AND THE WEATHER IS BEAUTIFUL!
EXCELLENT!
SEE YOU LATER!
MORGEN, SAGA!
TAP
MOR-GEN.
TAP
HELLO, SAGA!
OH.

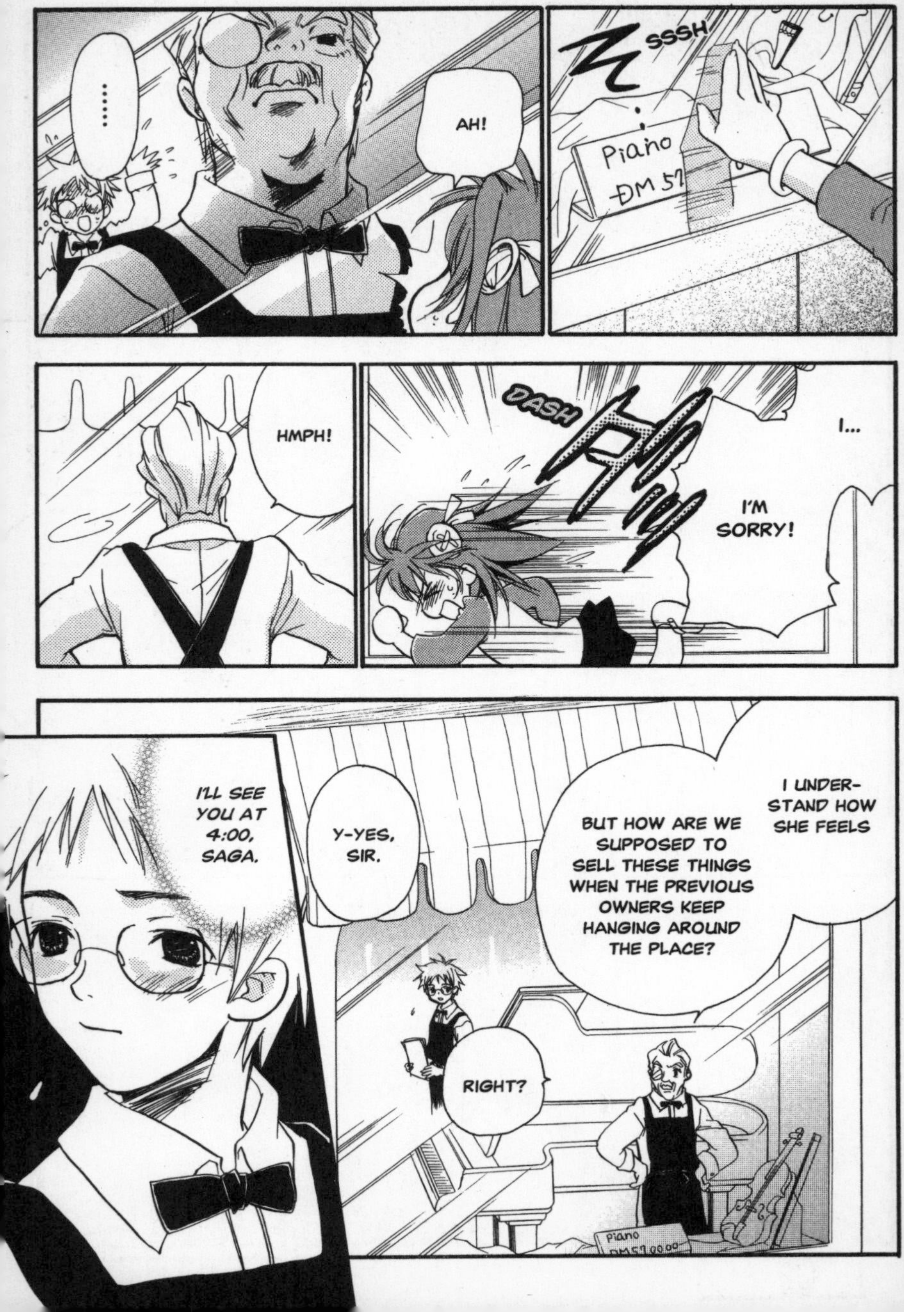
SSSH
Piano
DM 57
AH!
......
DASH
I...
I'M SORRY!
HMPH!
I UNDER-STAND HOW SHE FEELS
BUT HOW ARE WE SUPPOSED TO SELL THESE THINGS WHEN THE PREVIOUS OWNERS KEEP HANGING AROUND THE PLACE?
RIGHT?
Y-YES, SIR.
I'LL SEE YOU AT 4:00, SAGA.

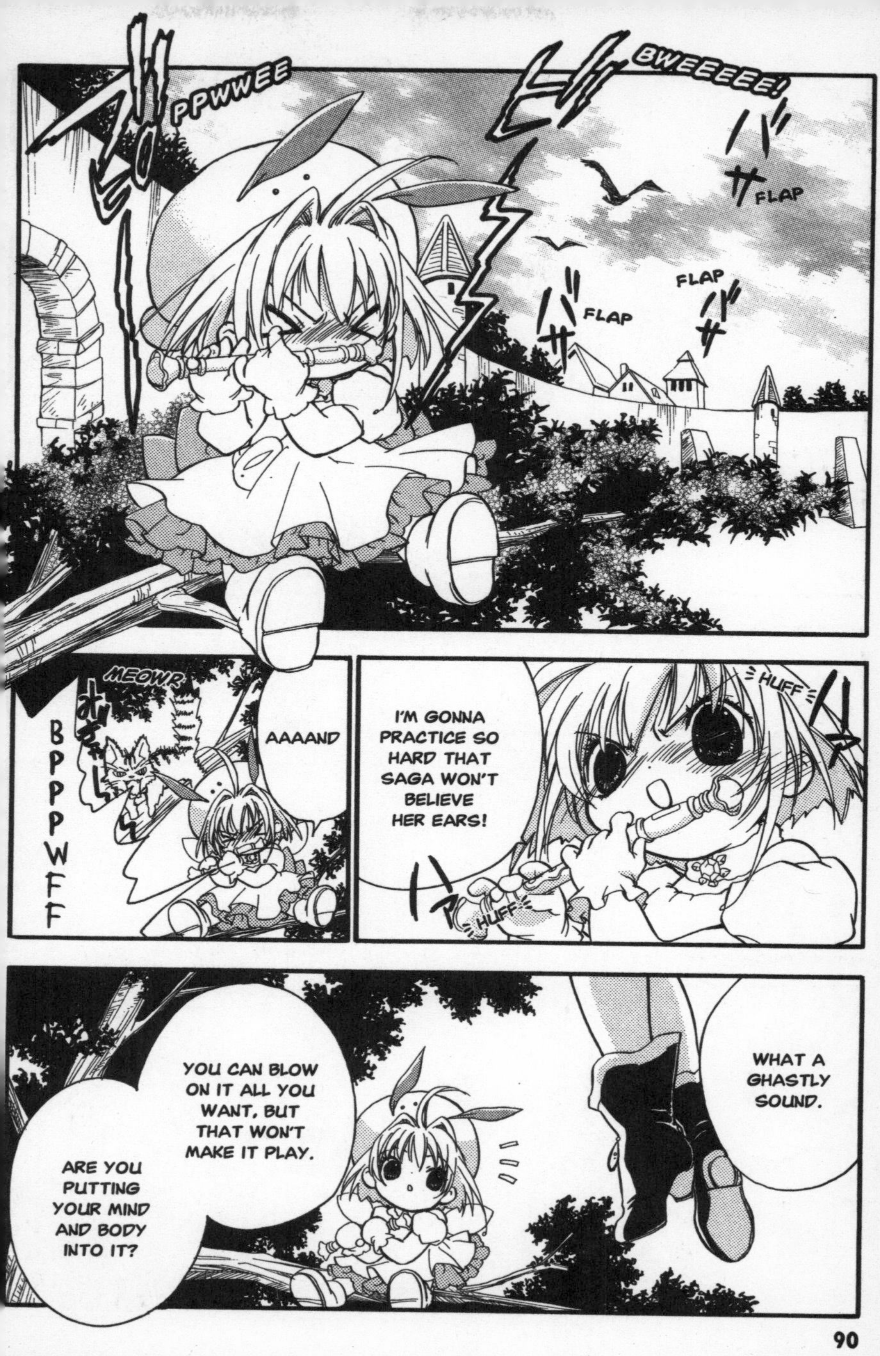
PPWWEE
BWEEEEEE!
FLAP
FLAP
FLAP
HUFF
I'M GONNA PRACTICE SO HARD THAT SAGA WON'T BELIEVE HER EARS!
HUFF
AAAAND
MEOWR
BPPPWFF
WHAT A GHASTLY SOUND.
YOU CAN BLOW ON IT ALL YOU WANT, BUT THAT WON'T MAKE IT PLAY.
ARE YOU PUTTING YOUR MIND AND BODY INTO IT?

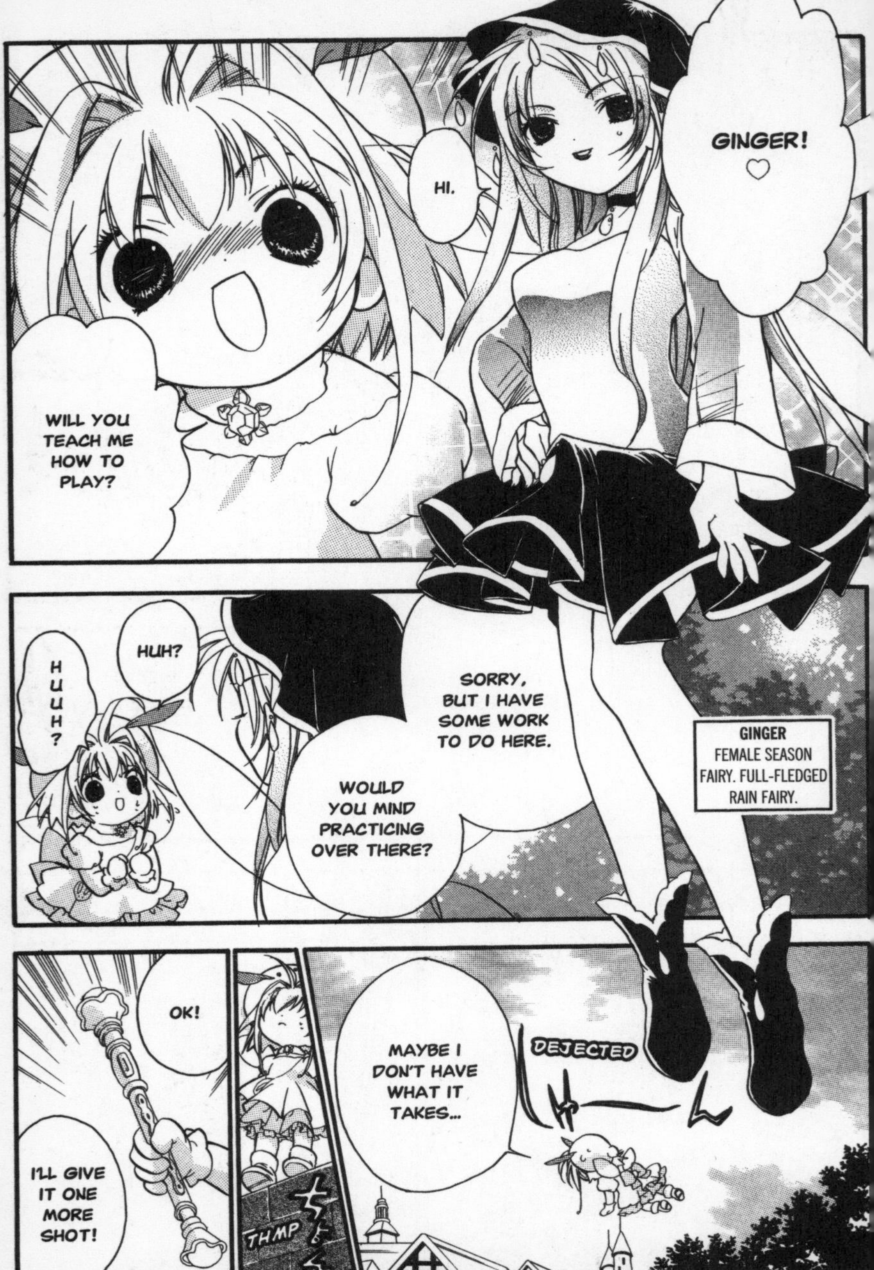
GINGER! ♡
HI.
WILL YOU TEACH ME HOW TO PLAY?
GINGER
FEMALE SEASON FAIRY. FULL-FLEDGED RAIN FAIRY.
SORRY, BUT I HAVE SOME WORK TO DO HERE.
WOULD YOU MIND PRACTICING OVER THERE?
HUH?
HUUUH?
DEJECTED
MAYBE I DON'T HAVE WHAT IT TAKES...
THMP
OK!
I'LL GIVE IT ONE MORE SHOT!

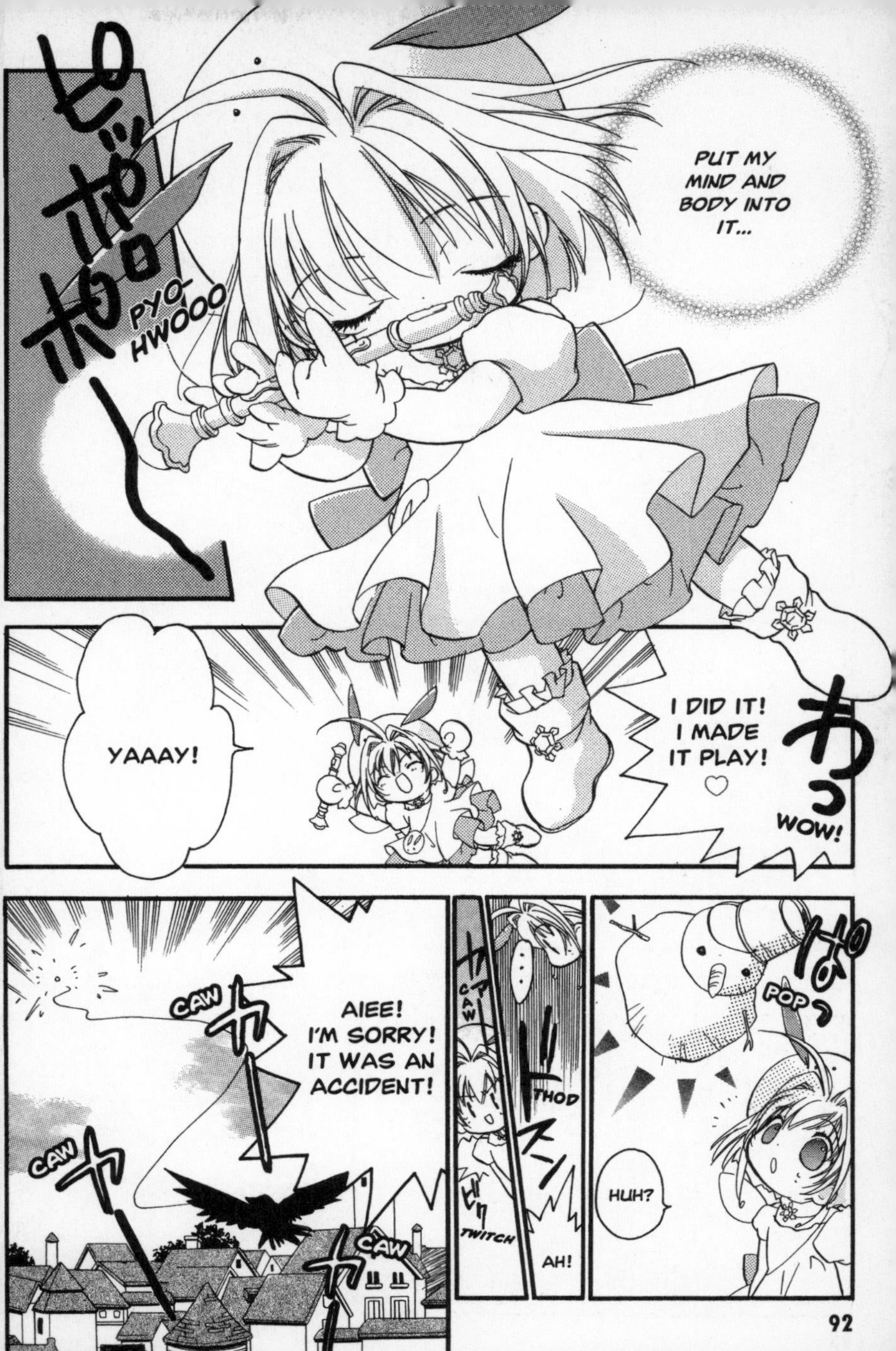
PUT MY MIND AND BODY INTO IT...
PYO-HWOOO
WOW!
I DID IT! I MADE IT PLAY!
YAAAY!
POP
HUH?
CAW
THOD
TWITCH
AH!
AIEE! I'M SORRY! IT WAS AN ACCIDENT!
CAW
CAW
CAW

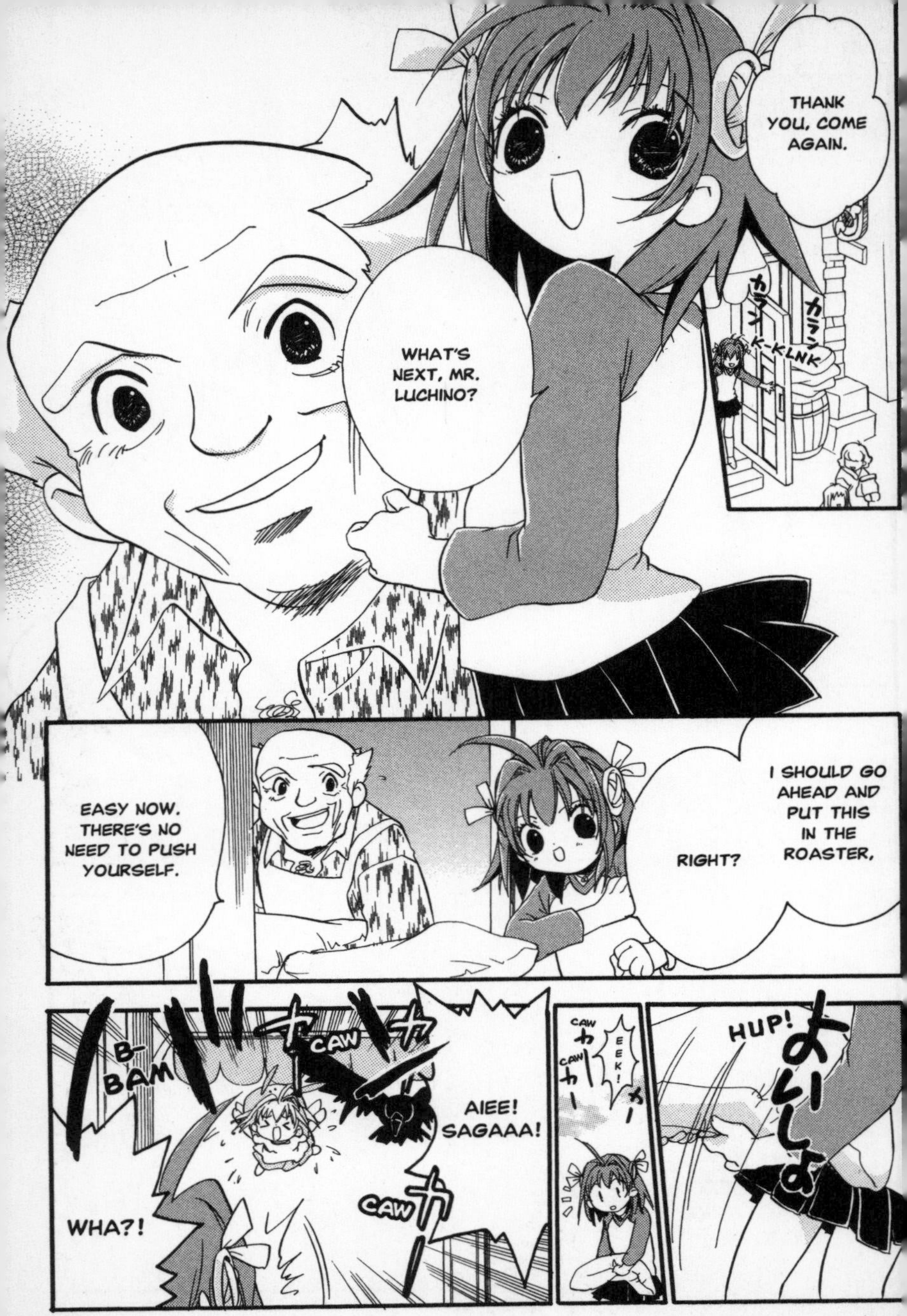
THANK YOU, COME AGAIN.
カラン
カラン
K-KLNK
WHAT'S NEXT, MR. LUCHINO?
I SHOULD GO AHEAD AND PUT THIS IN THE ROASTER,
RIGHT?
EASY NOW. THERE'S NO NEED TO PUSH YOURSELF.
HUP!
よいしょ
CAW
カー
CAW
カー
EEK!
B-BAM
CAW
AIEE! SAGAAA!
CAW
WHA?!

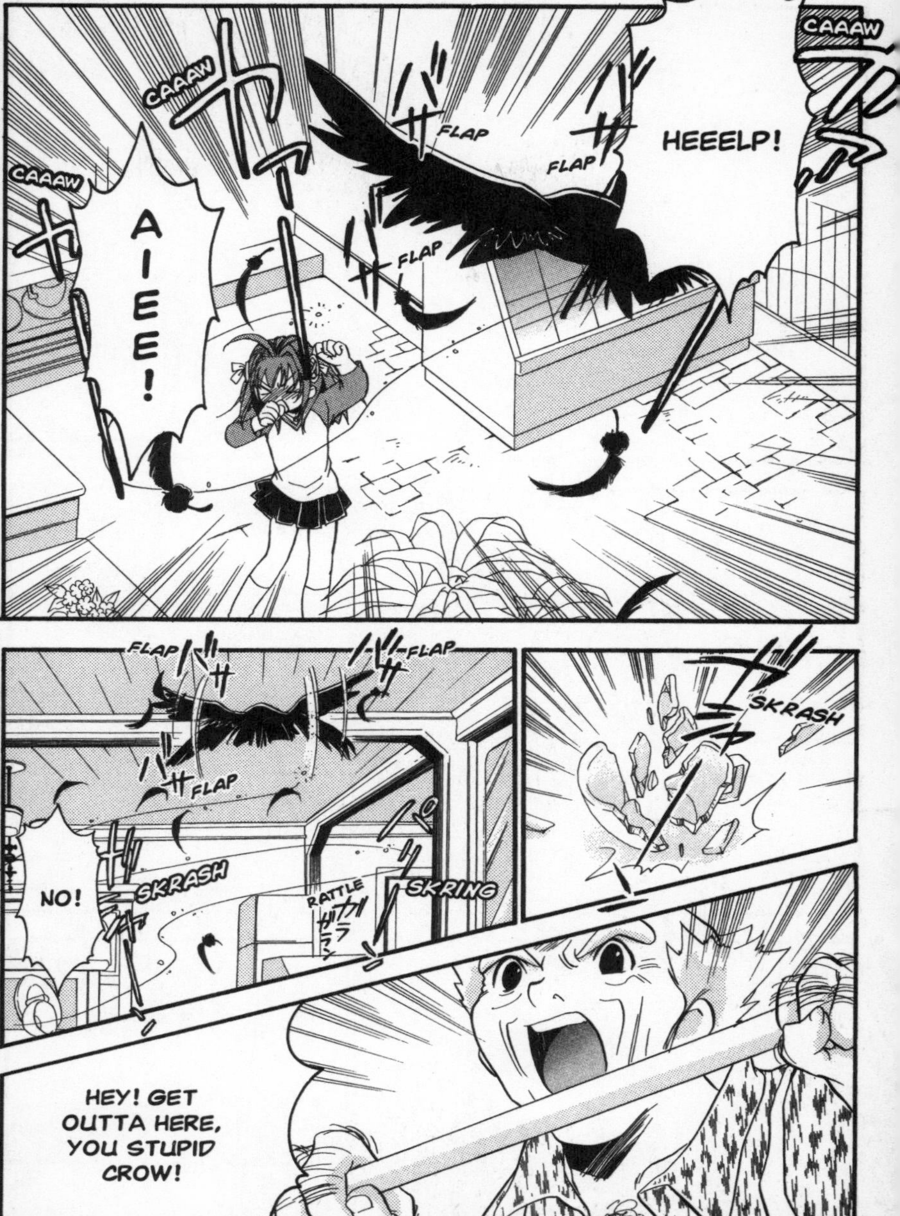
CAAAW
HEEELP!
FLAP
FLAP
FLAP
CAAAW
AIEE!
CAAAW
SKRASH
FLAP
FLAP
FLAP
SKRING
RATTLE
SKRASH
NO!
HEY! GET OUTTA HERE, YOU STUPID CROW!

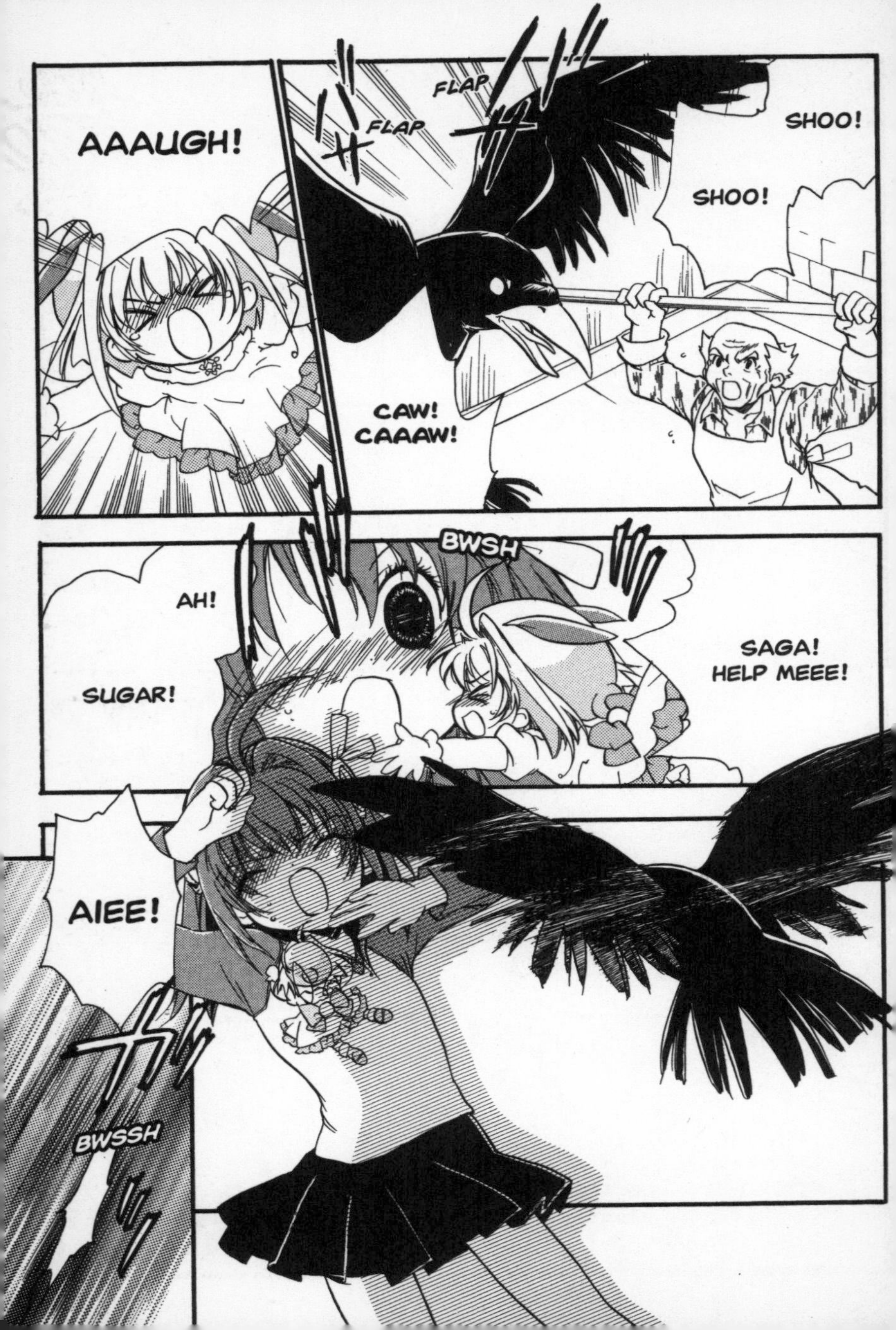
SHOO!
SHOO!
FLAP
FLAP
CAW! CAAAW!
AAAUGH!
BWSH
SAGA! HELP MEEE!
AH!
SUGAR!
AIEE!
BWSSH

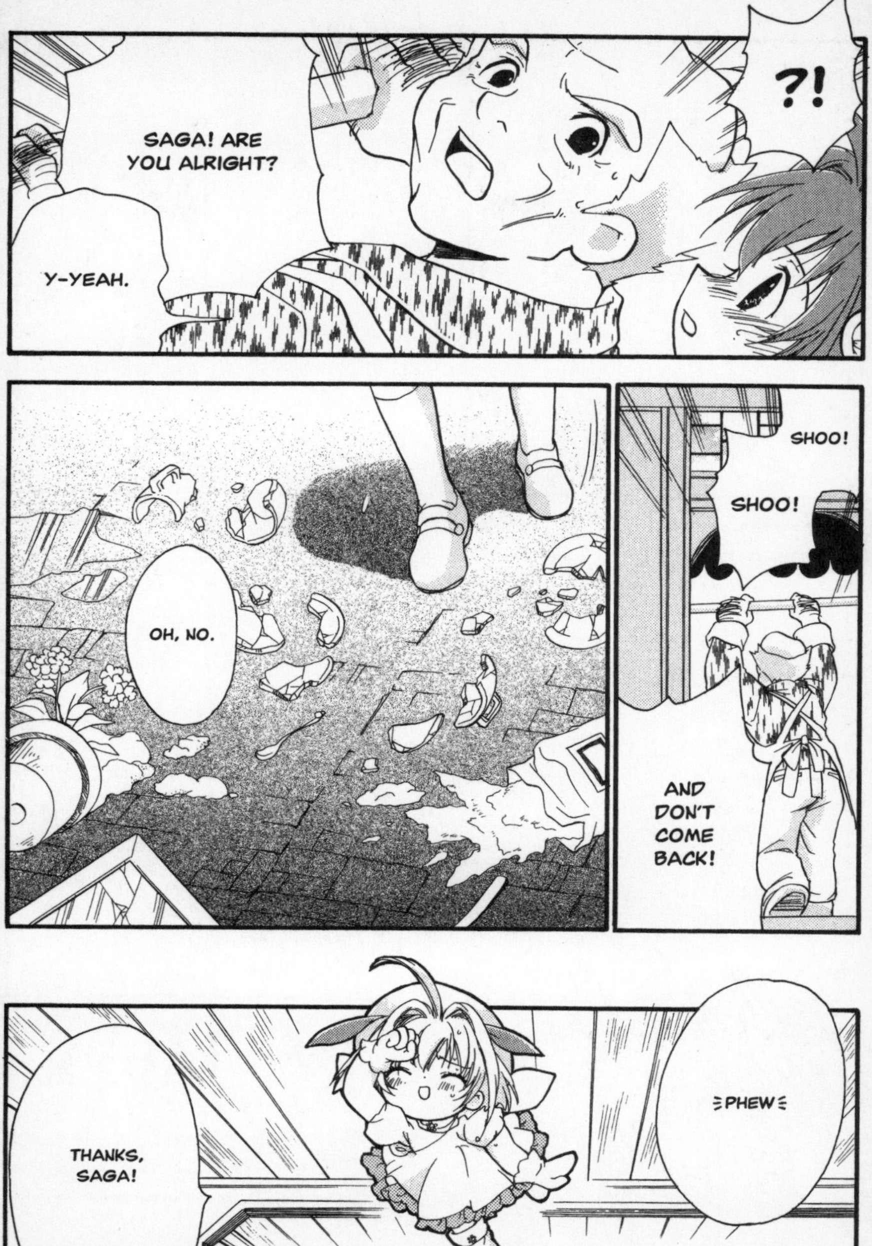
?!
SAGA! ARE YOU ALRIGHT?
Y-YEAH.
SHOO!
SHOO!
AND DON'T COME BACK!
OH, NO.
≡PHEW≡
THANKS, SAGA!

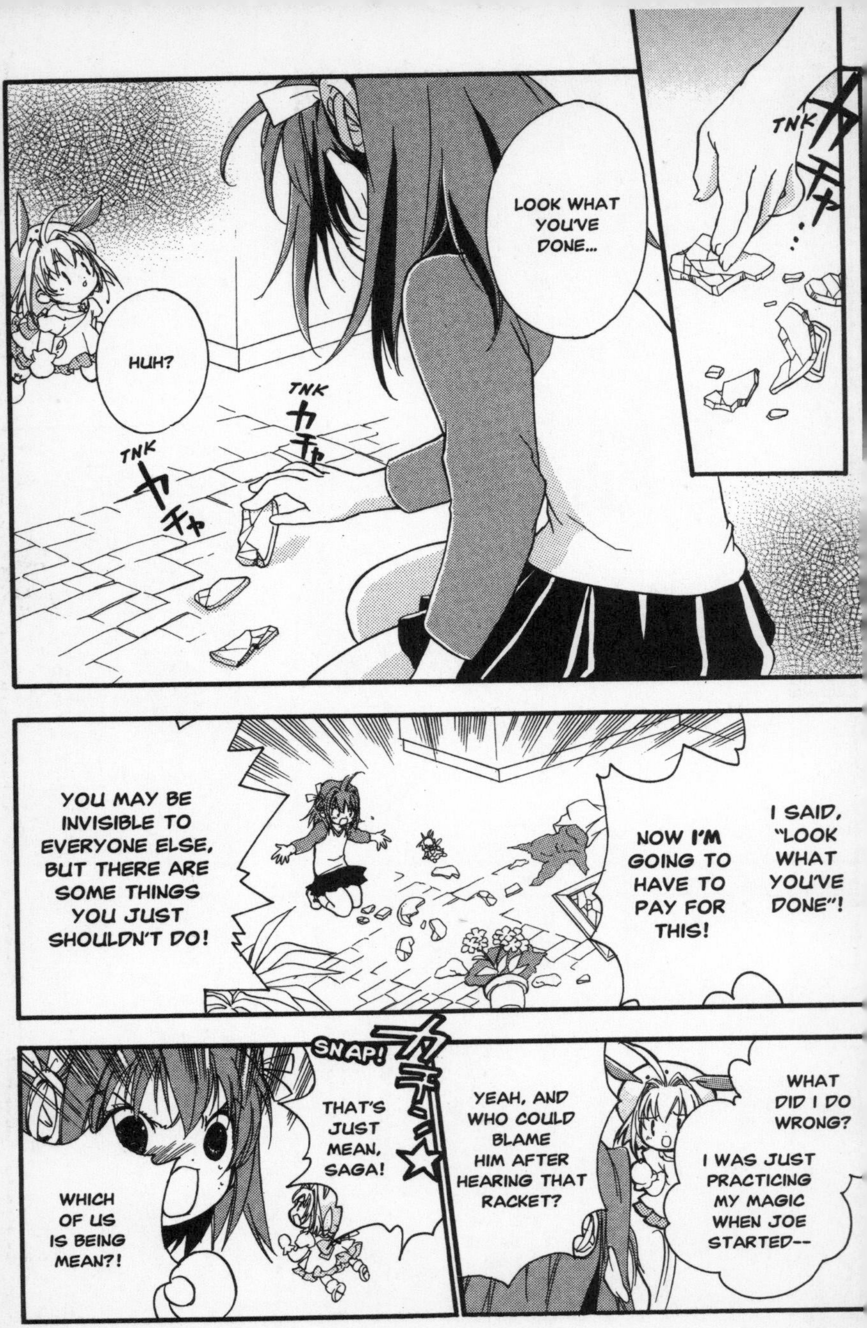
TNK
カチャ...
LOOK WHAT YOU'VE DONE...
HUH?
TNK
カチャ
TNK
カチャ
I SAID, "LOOK WHAT YOU'VE DONE"!
NOW I'M GOING TO HAVE TO PAY FOR THIS!
YOU MAY BE INVISIBLE TO EVERYONE ELSE, BUT THERE ARE SOME THINGS YOU JUST SHOULDN'T DO!
WHAT DID I DO WRONG?
I WAS JUST PRACTICING MY MAGIC WHEN JOE STARTED--
YEAH, AND WHO COULD BLAME HIM AFTER HEARING THAT RACKET?
SNAP!
THAT'S JUST MEAN, SAGA!
WHICH OF US IS BEING MEAN?!

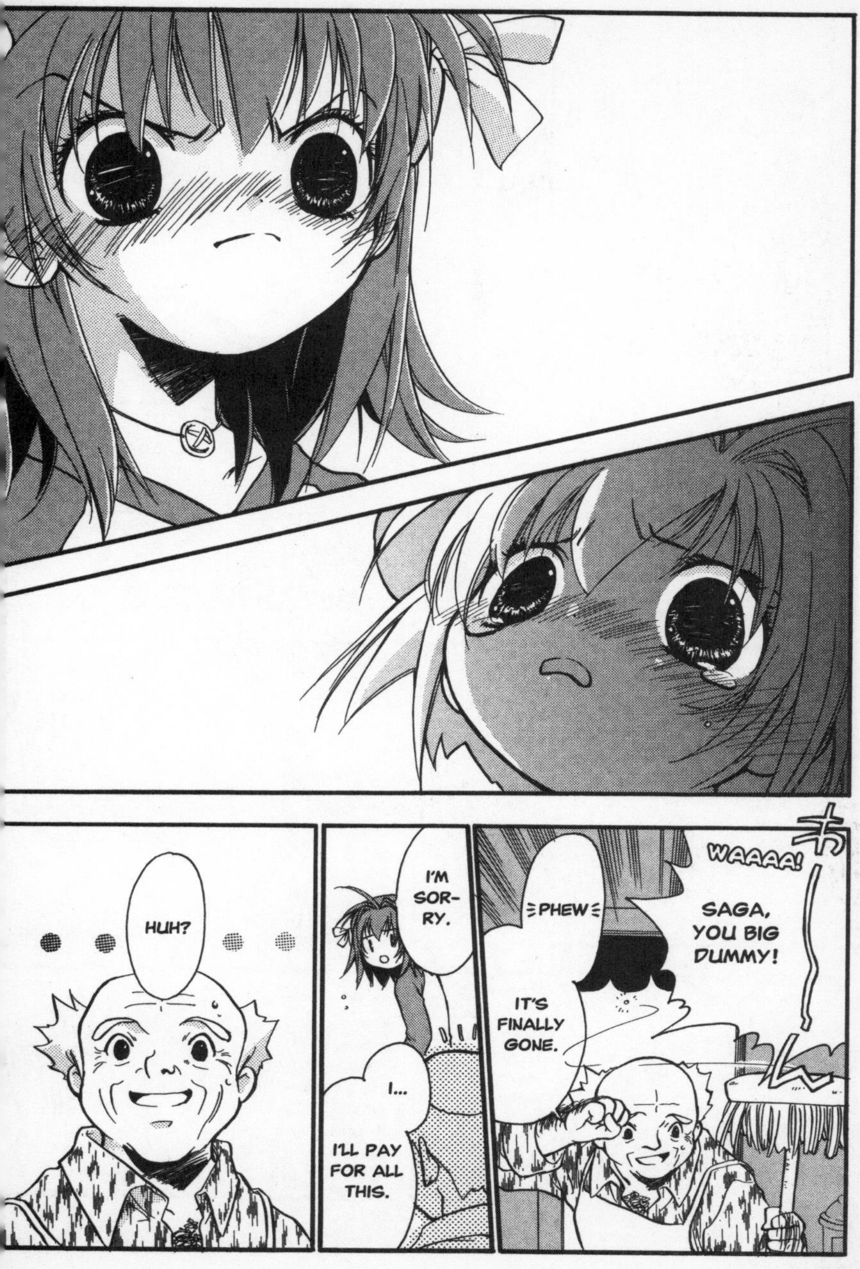
WAAAA!
SAGA, YOU BIG DUMMY!
≡PHEW≡
IT'S FINALLY GONE.
I'M SOR-RY.
I...
I'LL PAY FOR ALL THIS.
HUH?

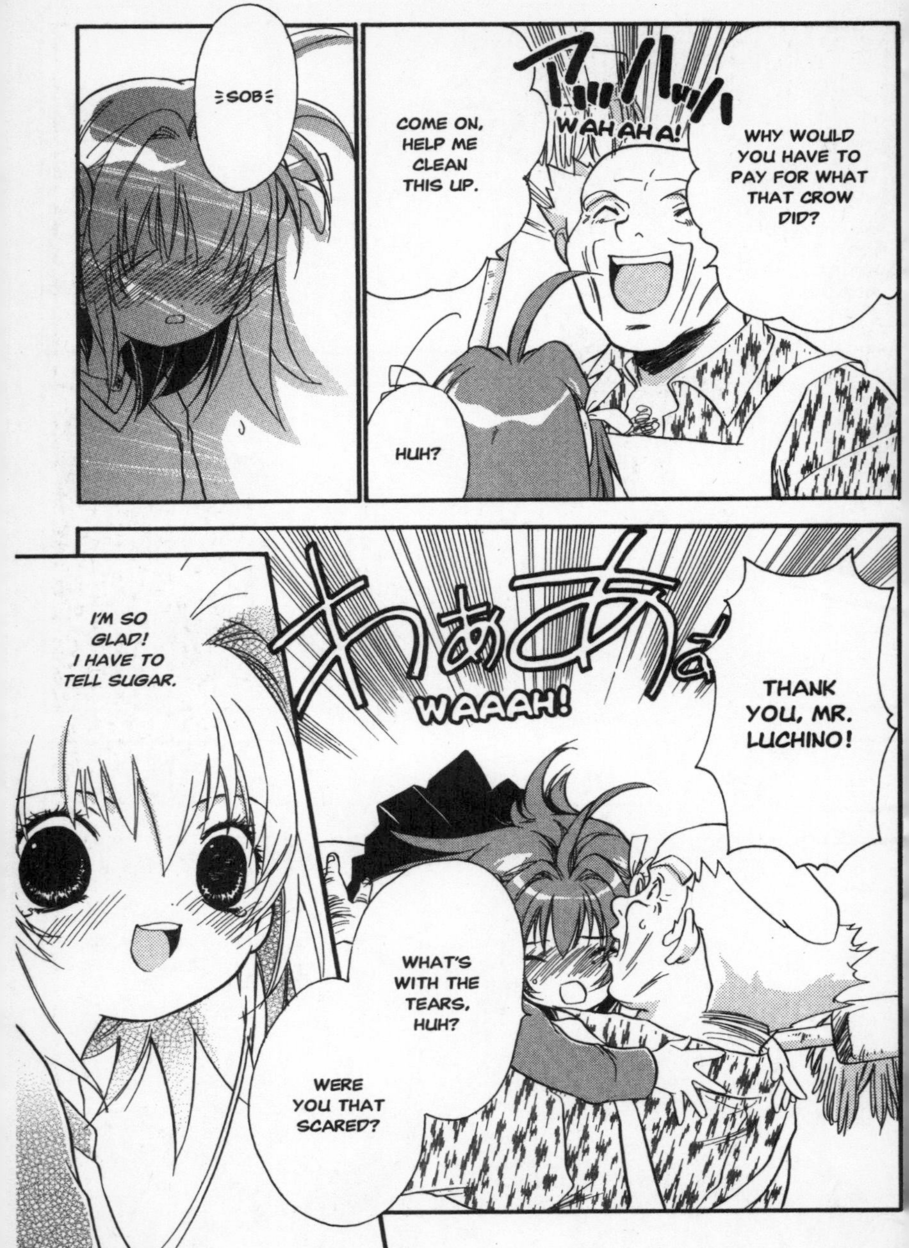
WHY WOULD YOU HAVE TO PAY FOR WHAT THAT CROW DID?
WAHAHA!
COME ON, HELP ME CLEAN THIS UP.
HUH?
SOB
THANK YOU, MR. LUCHINO!
WAAAH!
WHAT'S WITH THE TEARS, HUH?
WERE YOU THAT SCARED?
I'M SO GLAD! I HAVE TO TELL SUGAR.

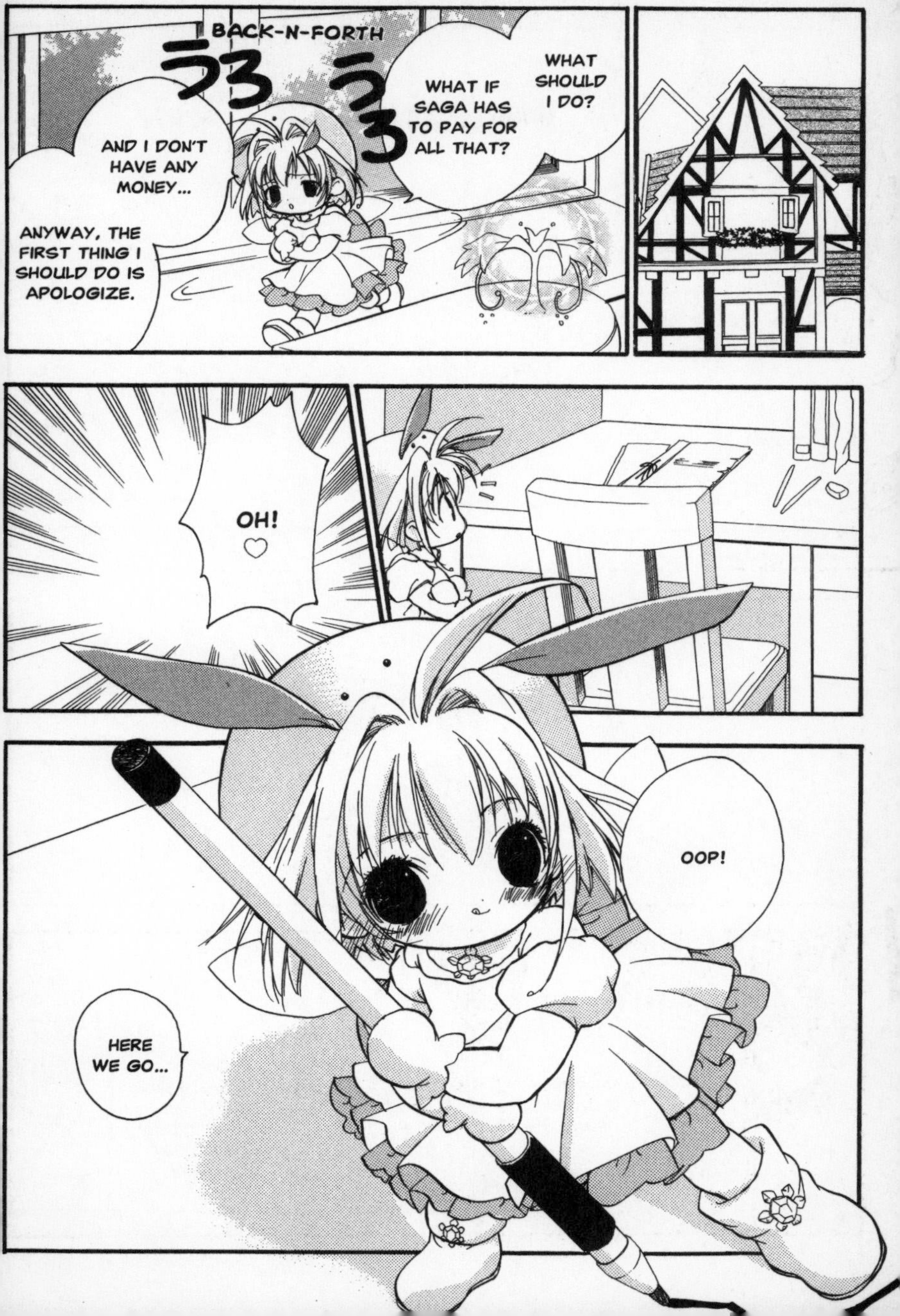
WHAT SHOULD I DO?
WHAT IF SAGA HAS TO PAY FOR ALL THAT?
BACK-N-FORTH
うろ うろ
AND I DON'T HAVE ANY MONEY...
ANYWAY, THE FIRST THING I SHOULD DO IS APOLOGIZE.
OH! ♡
OOP!
HERE WE GO...

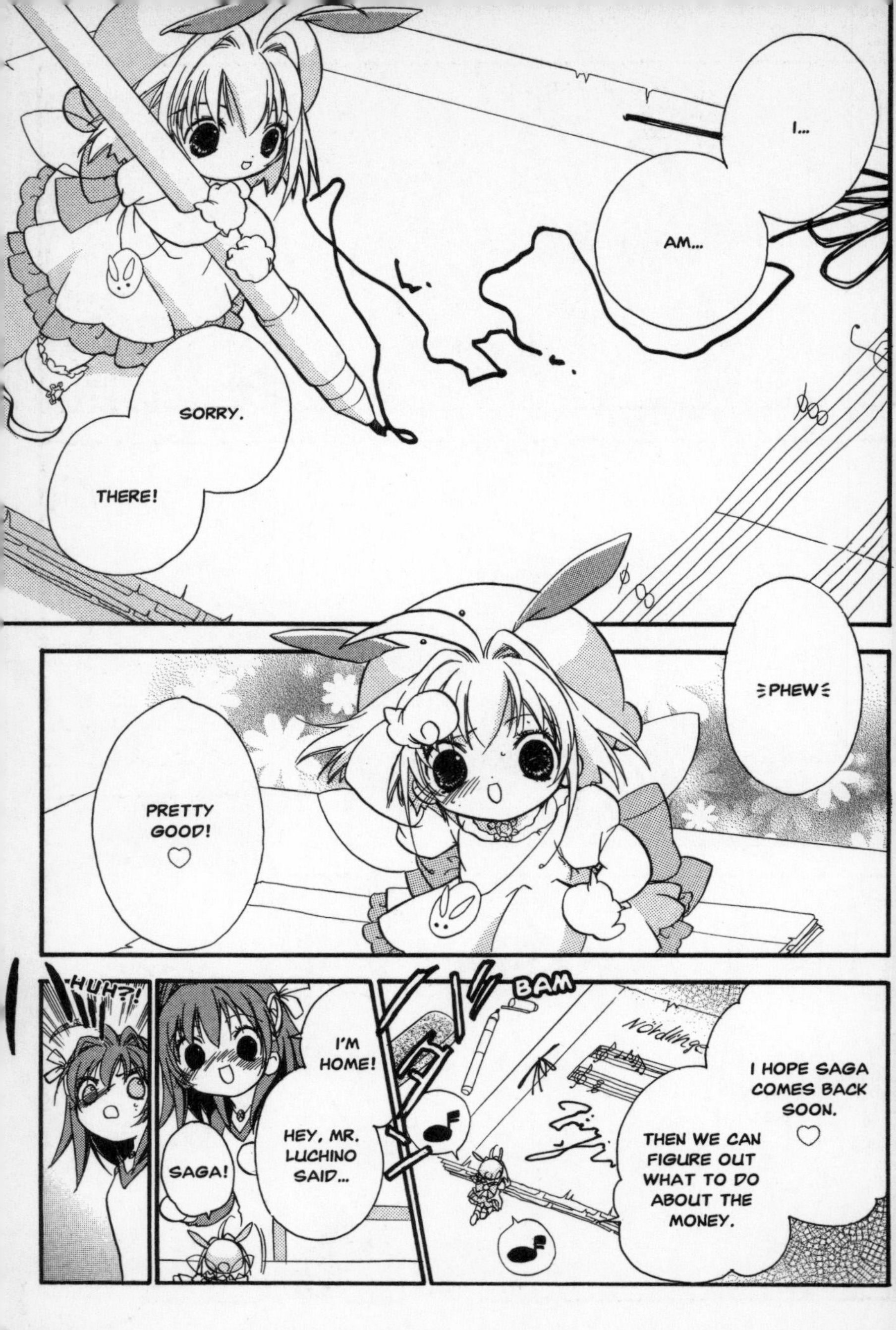
I...
AM...
SORRY.
THERE!
PHEW
PRETTY GOOD! ♡
BAM
I HOPE SAGA COMES BACK SOON. ♡
THEN WE CAN FIGURE OUT WHAT TO DO ABOUT THE MONEY.
I'M HOME!
HEY, MR. LUCHINO SAID...
SAGA!
HUH?!

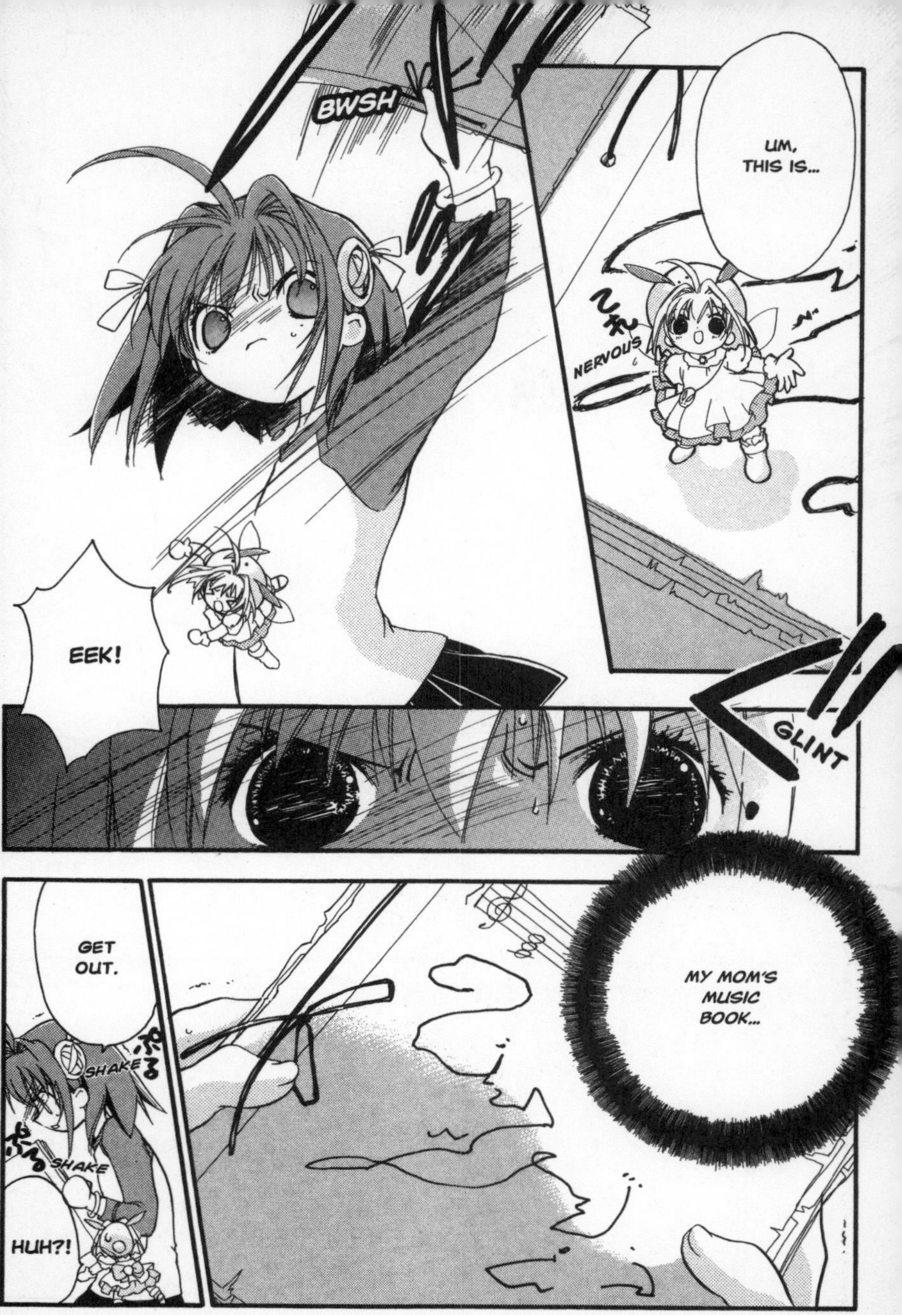
UM, THIS IS...
NERVOUS
BWSH
EEK!
GLINT
MY MOM'S MUSIC BOOK...
GET OUT.
SHAKE
SHAKE
HUH?!

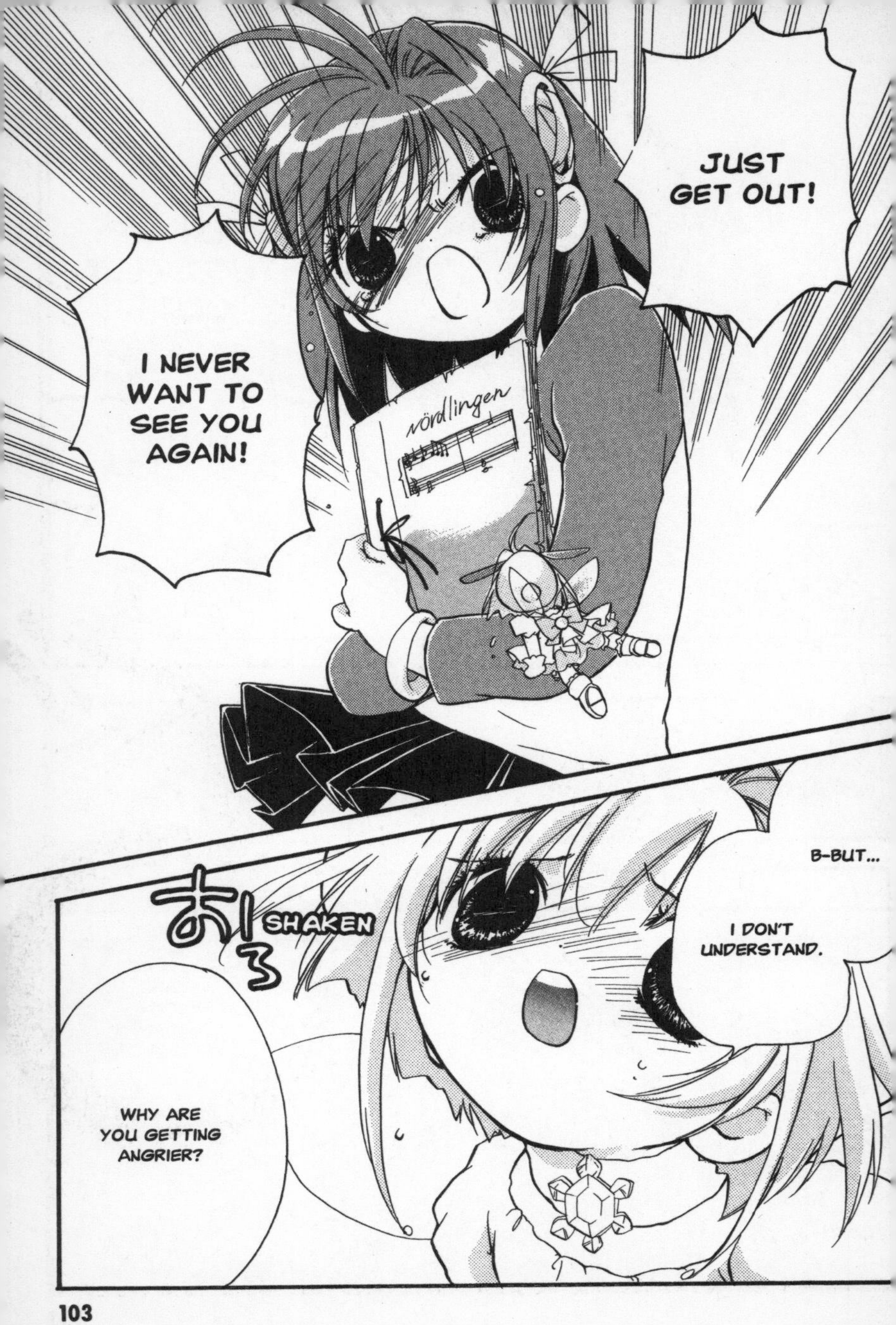
JUST GET OUT!
I NEVER WANT TO SEE YOU AGAIN!
nördlingen
B-BUT...
I DON'T UNDERSTAND.
おろ SHAKEN
WHY ARE YOU GETTING ANGRIER?

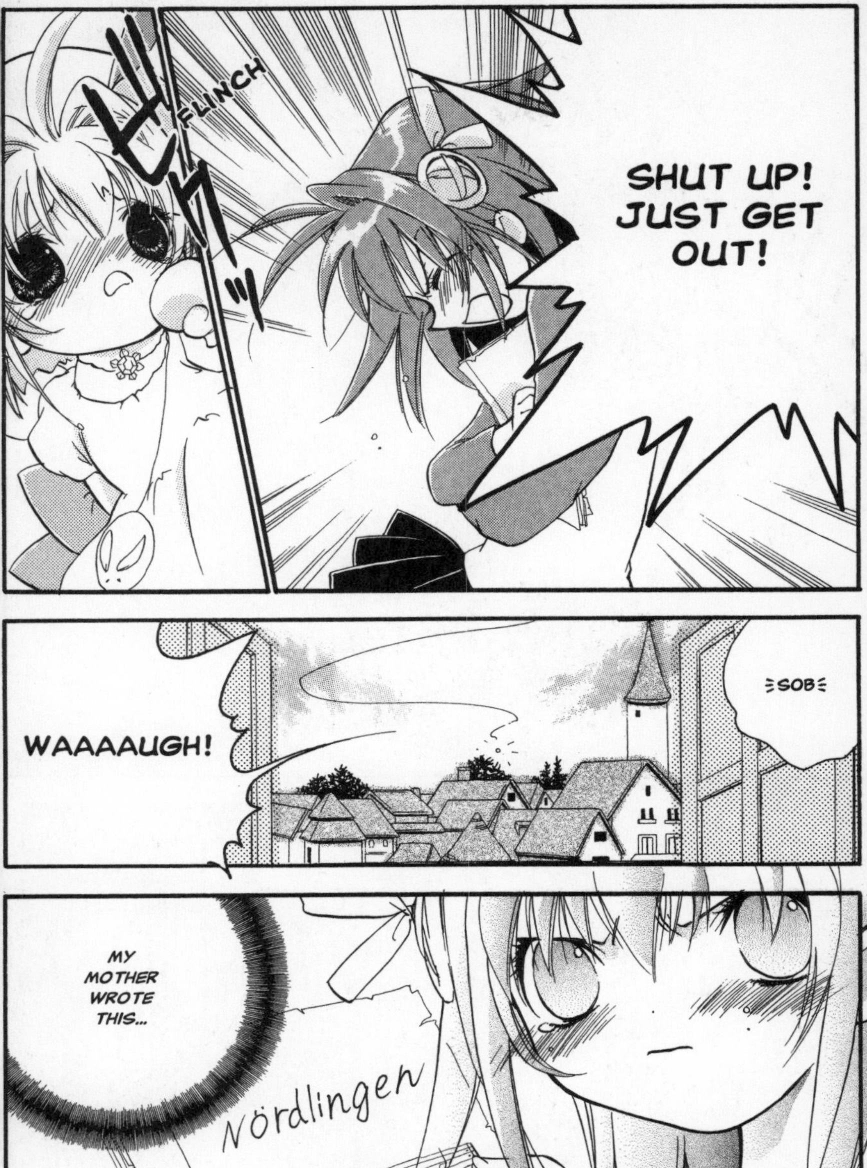

SHUT UP! JUST GET OUT!
FLINCH
SOB
WAAAAUGH!
MY MOTHER WROTE THIS...
Nördlingen

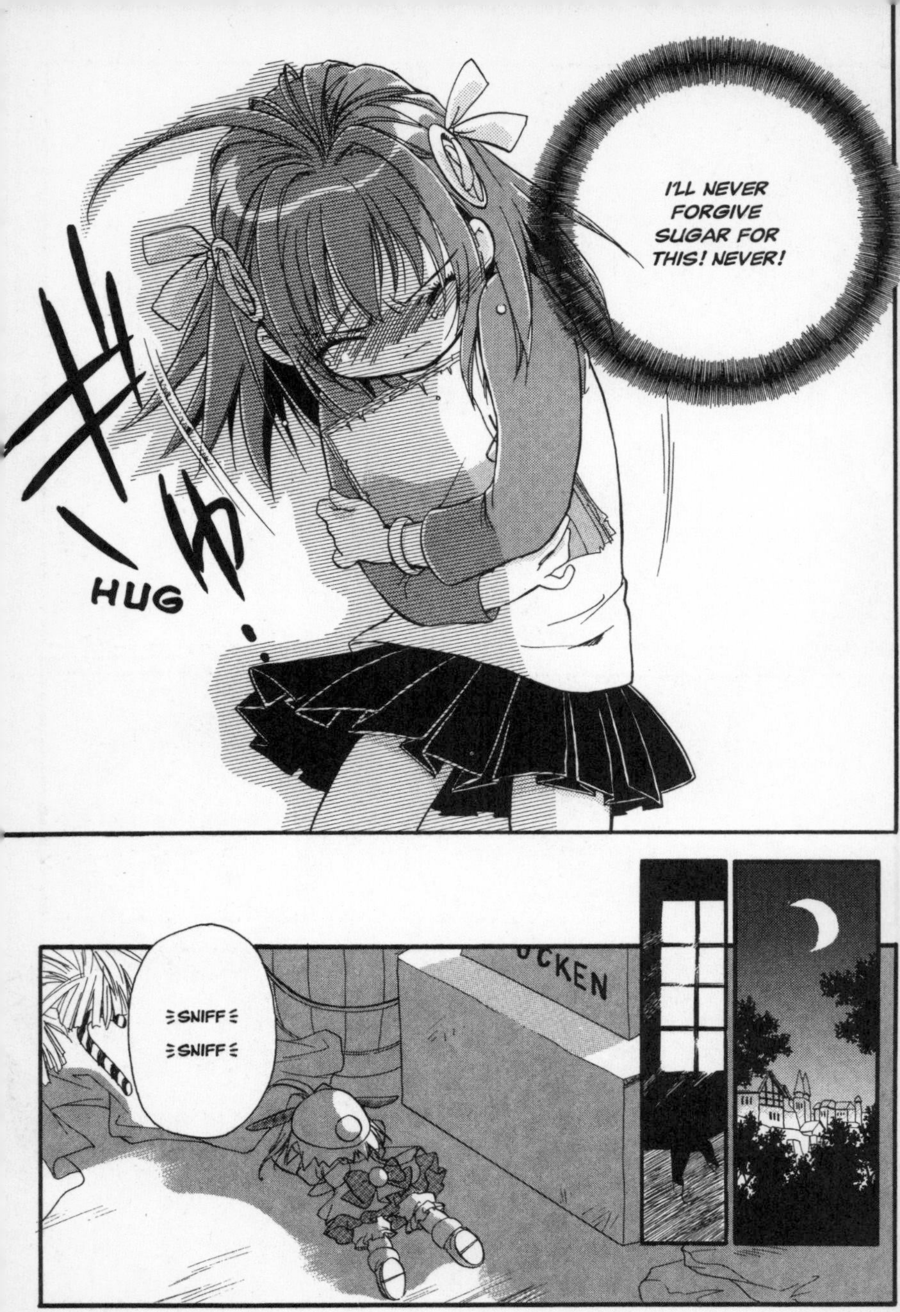
I'LL NEVER FORGIVE SUGAR FOR THIS! NEVER!
HUG
SNIFF
SNIFF

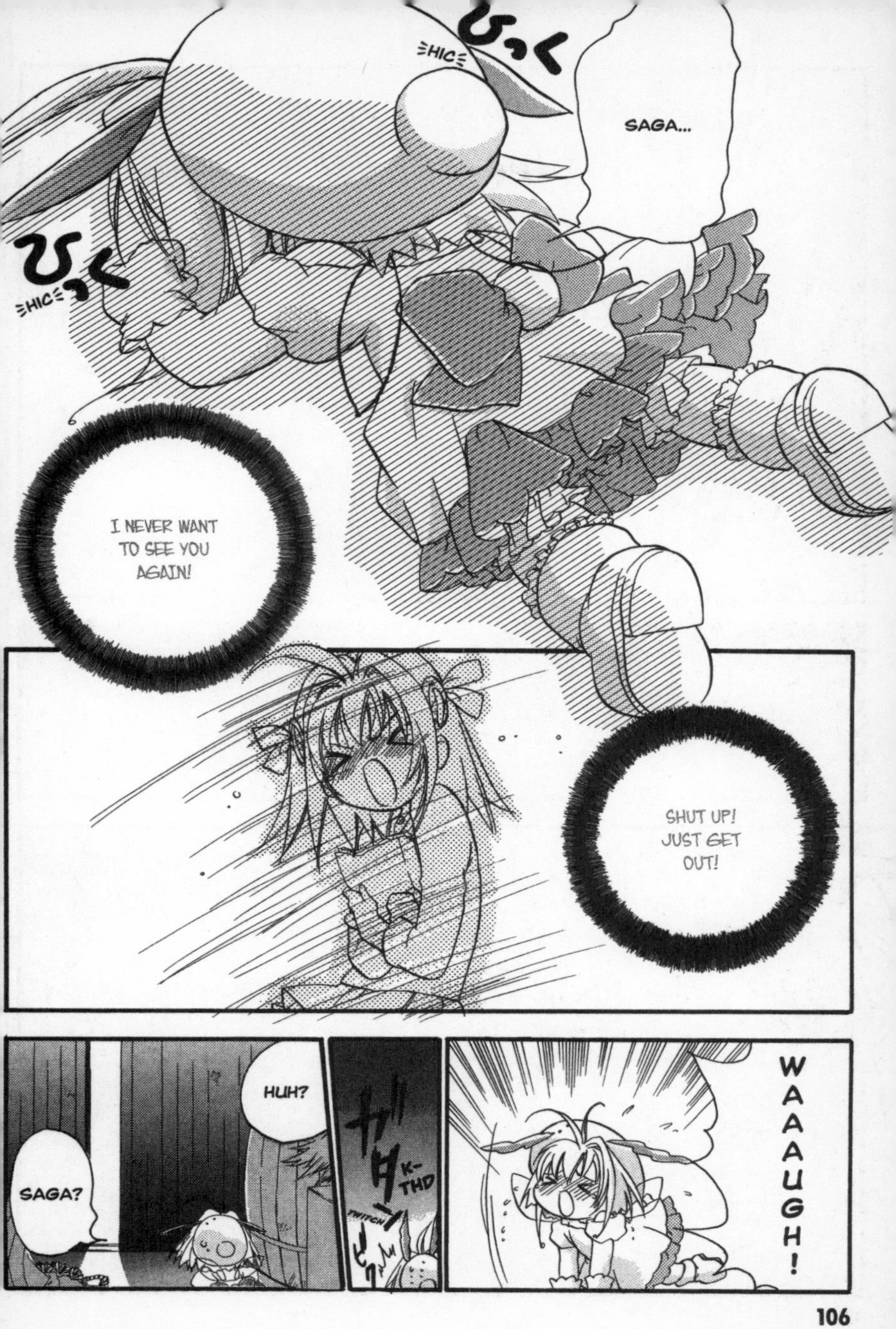
SAGA...
ひっく
HIC
ひっく
HIC
I NEVER WANT TO SEE YOU AGAIN!
SHUT UP! JUST GET OUT!
WAAAAUGH!
K-THD
TWITCH
HUH?
SAGA?

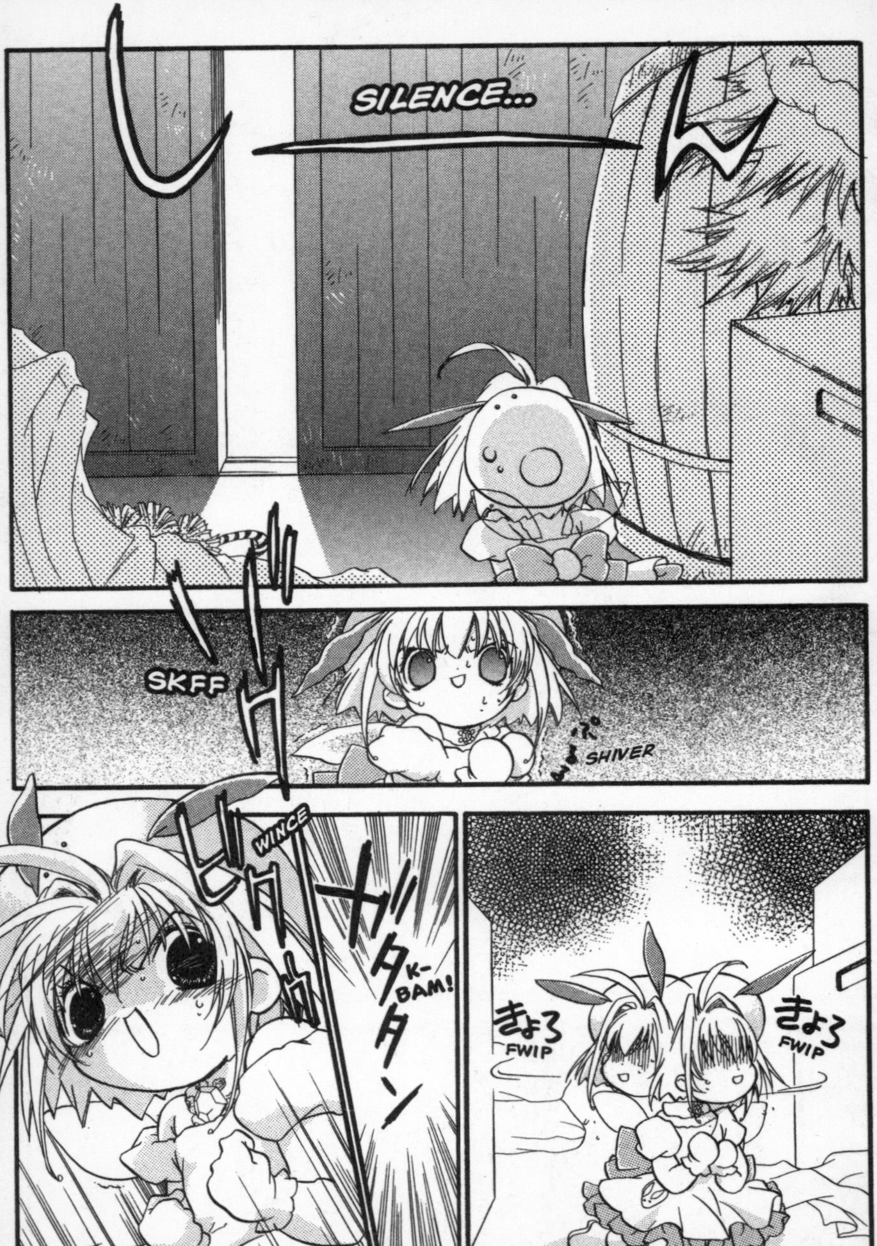
SILENCE...
SKFF
SHIVER
きょろ
FWIP
きょろ
FWIP
WINCE
K-BAM!

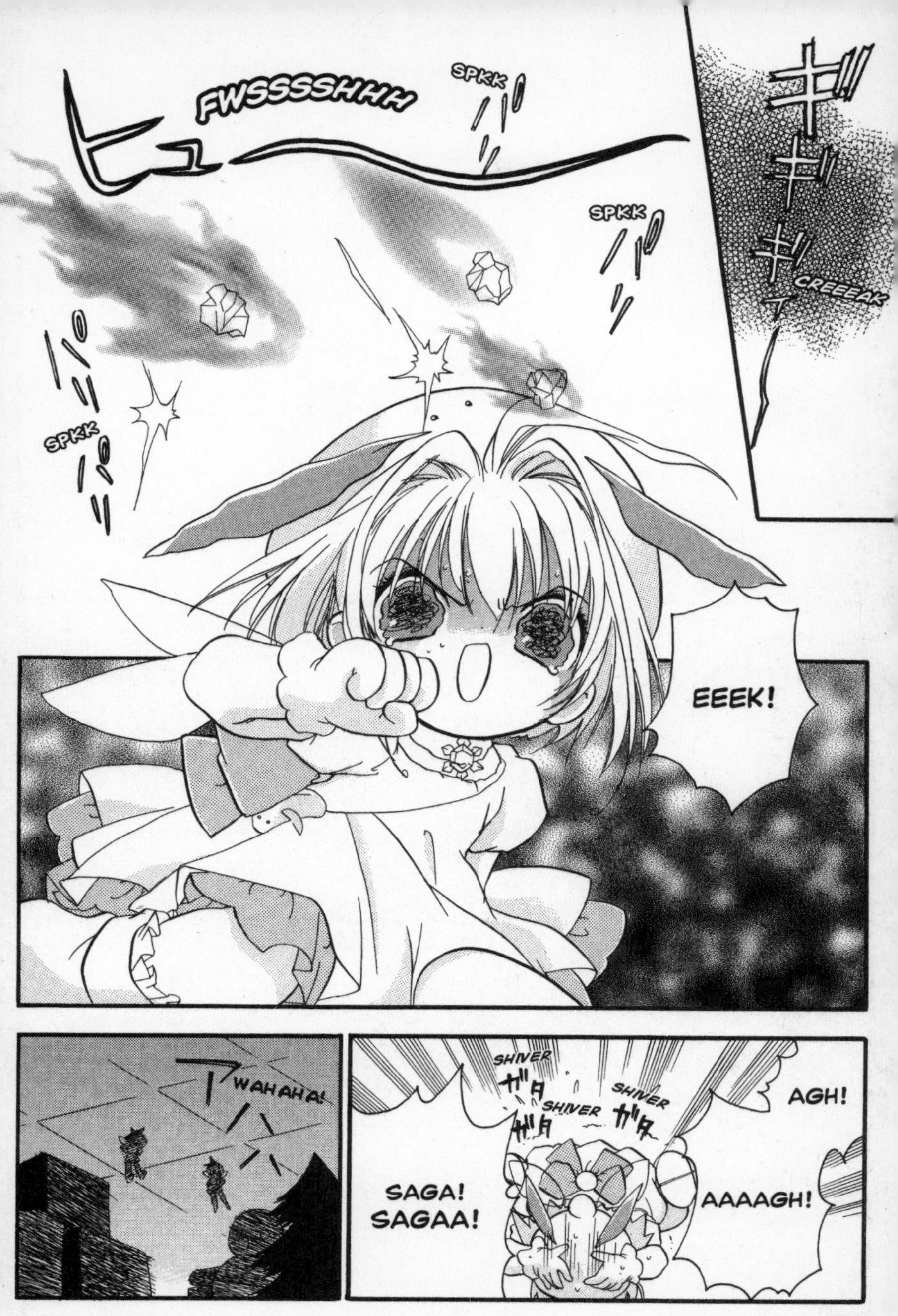
CREEEAK
FWSSSSHHH
SPKK
SPKK
SPKK
EEEK!
SHIVER
SHIVER
SHIVER
AGH!
AAAAGH!
SAGA! SAGAA!
WAHAHA!

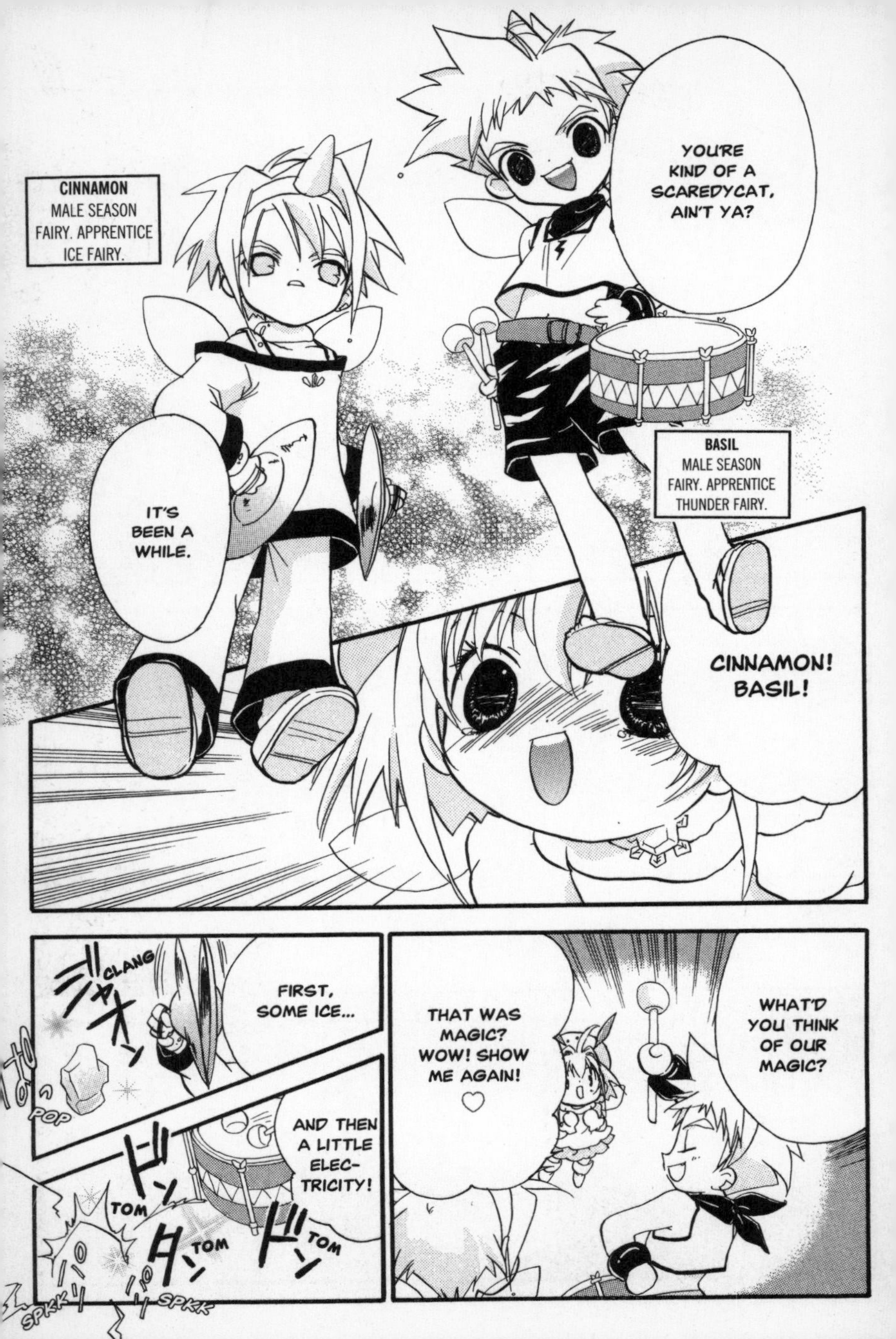
YOU'RE KIND OF A SCAREDYCAT, AIN'T YA?
BASIL
MALE SEASON FAIRY. APPRENTICE THUNDER FAIRY.
CINNAMON
MALE SEASON FAIRY. APPRENTICE ICE FAIRY.
IT'S BEEN A WHILE.
CINNAMON! BASIL!
WHAT'D YOU THINK OF OUR MAGIC?
THAT WAS MAGIC? WOW! SHOW ME AGAIN! ♡
FIRST, SOME ICE...
CLANG
POP
AND THEN A LITTLE ELEC-TRICITY!
TOM
TOM
TOM
SPKK
SPKK

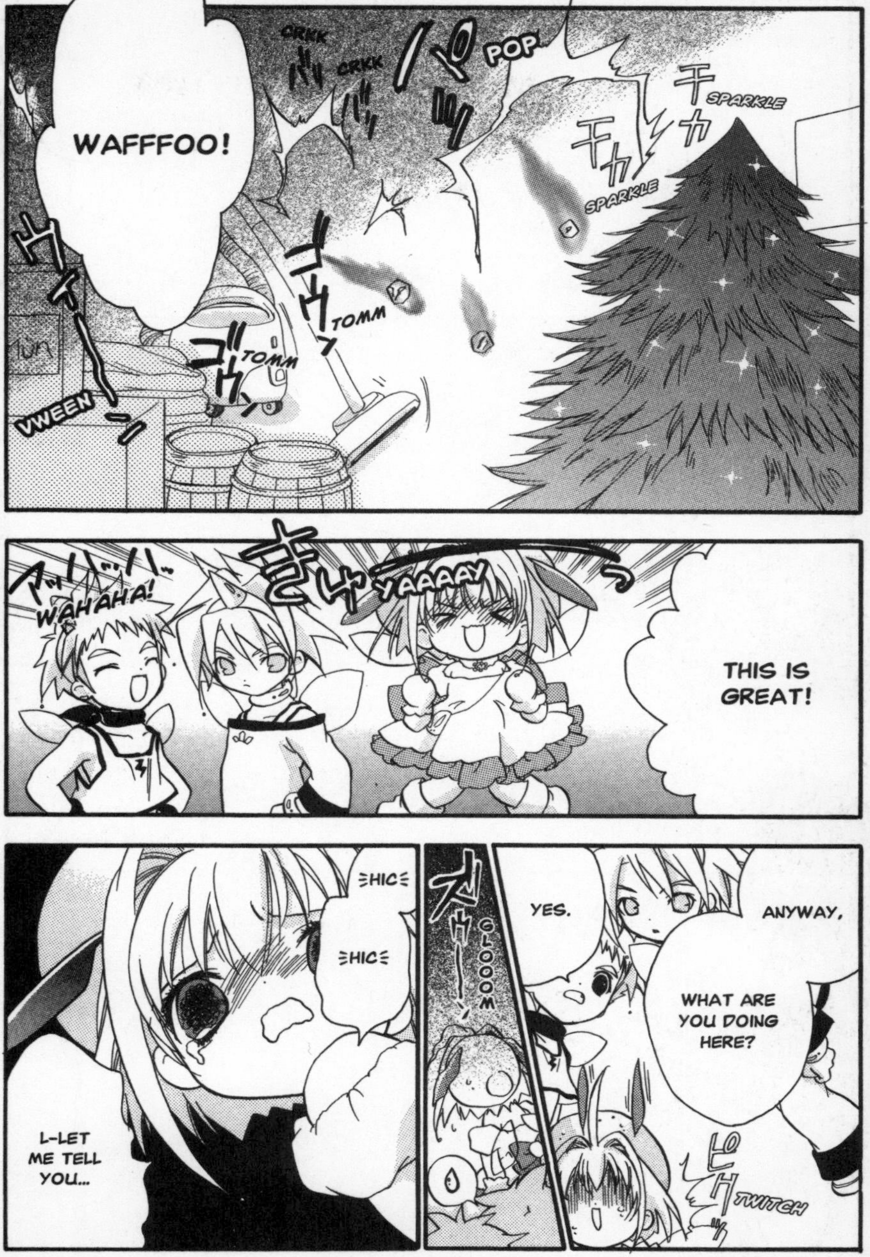
SPARKLE
SPARKLE
POP
CRKK
CRKK
TOMM
TOMM
WAFFFOO!
VWEEN
THIS IS GREAT!
YAAAAY
WAHAHA!
ANYWAY,
WHAT ARE YOU DOING HERE?
YES.
TWITCH
GLOOOOM
HIC
HIC
L-LET ME TELL YOU...

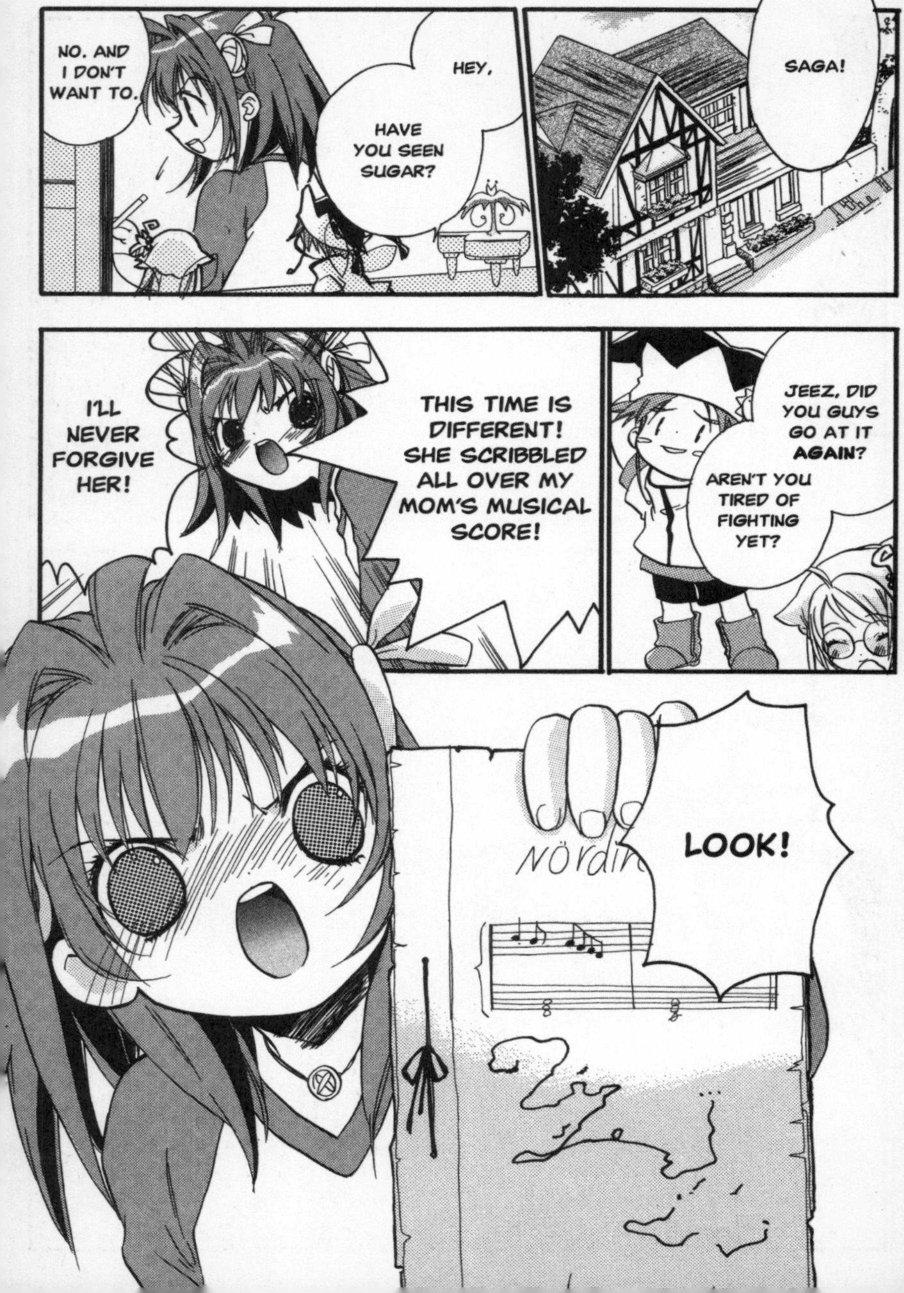
SAGA!
HEY,
HAVE YOU SEEN SUGAR?
NO. AND I DON'T WANT TO.
JEEZ, DID YOU GUYS GO AT IT AGAIN?
AREN'T YOU TIRED OF FIGHTING YET?
THIS TIME IS DIFFERENT! SHE SCRIBBLED ALL OVER MY MOM'S MUSICAL SCORE!
I'LL NEVER FORGIVE HER!
LOOK!

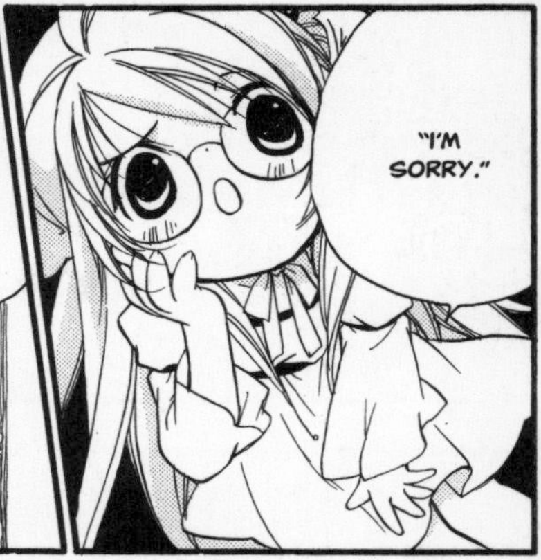
"I'M SORRY."

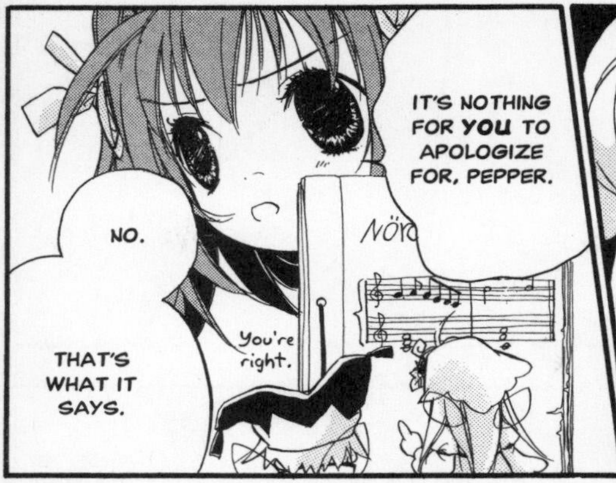
IT'S NOTHING FOR **YOU** TO APOLOGIZE FOR, PEPPER.
NO.
You're right.
THAT'S WHAT IT SAYS.

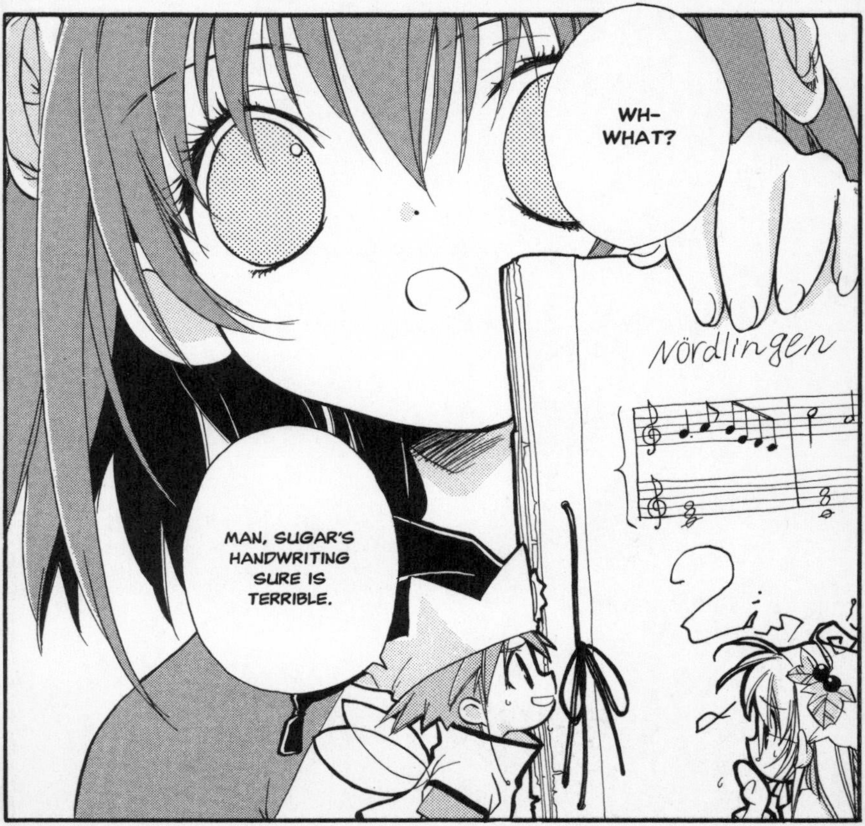
WH- WHAT?
Nördlingen
MAN, SUGAR'S HANDWRITING SURE IS TERRIBLE.

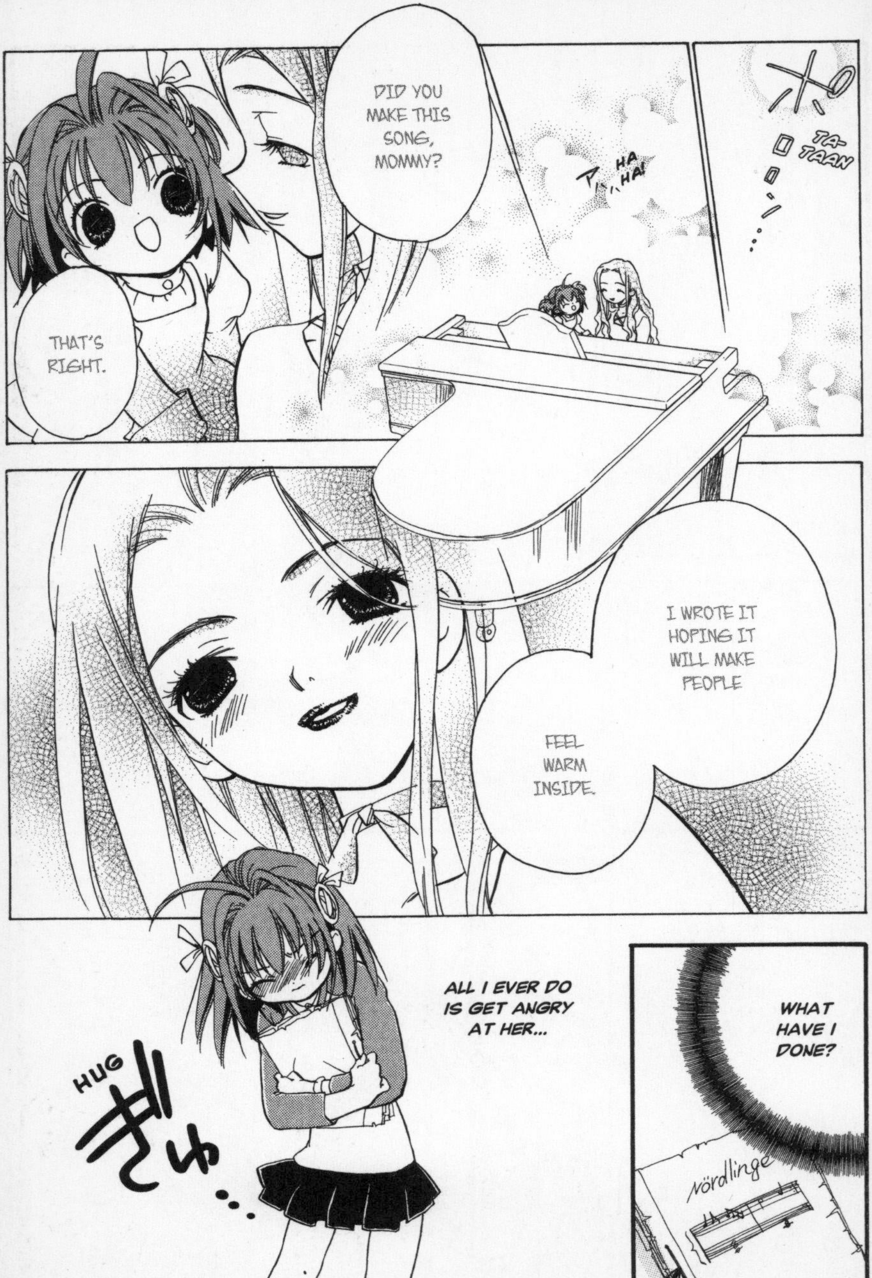
TA-TAAN
HA HA!
DID YOU MAKE THIS SONG, MOMMY?
THAT'S RIGHT.
I WROTE IT HOPING IT WILL MAKE PEOPLE
FEEL WARM INSIDE.
WHAT HAVE I DONE?
Nördlinge
ALL I EVER DO IS GET ANGRY AT HER...
HUG

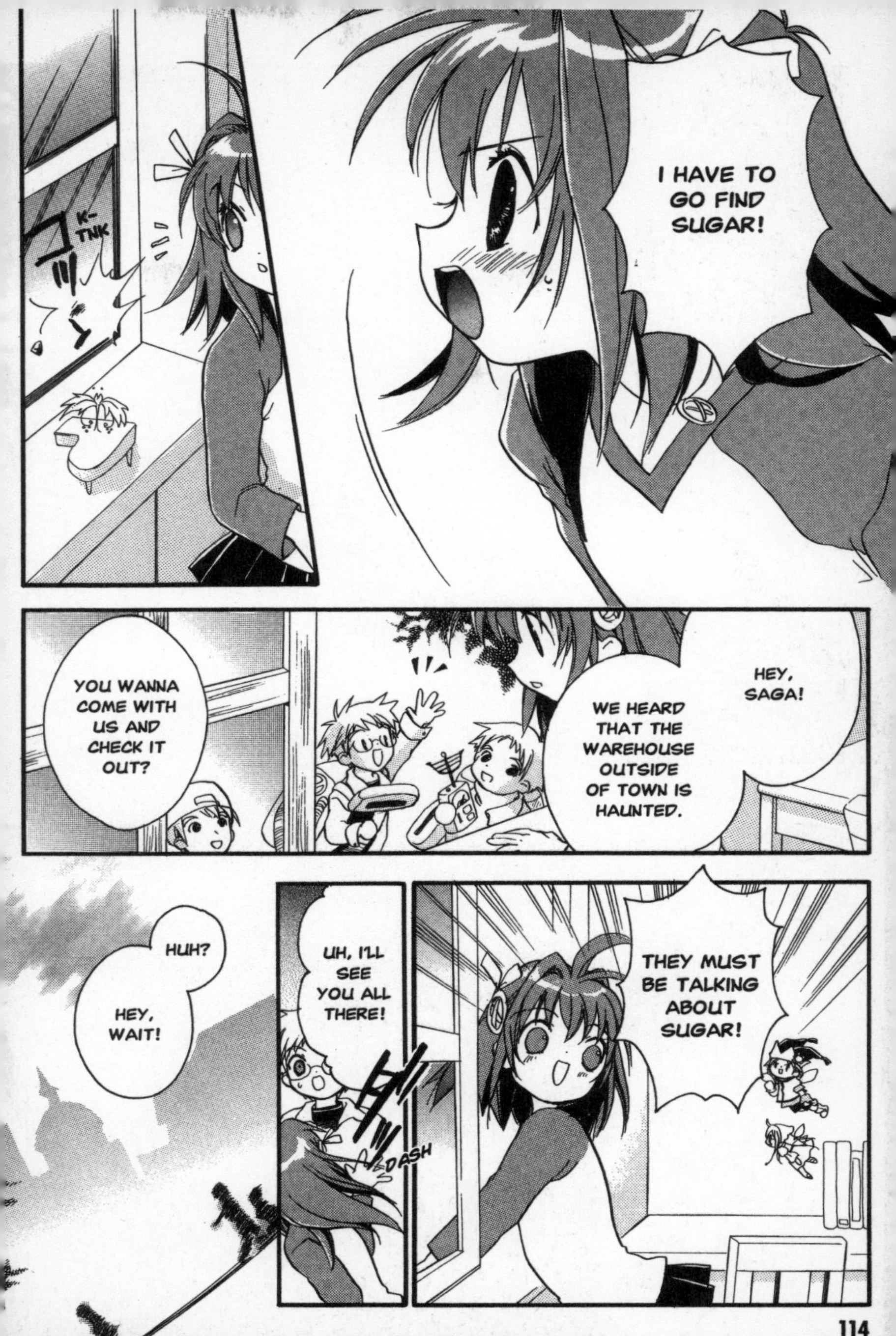
I HAVE TO GO FIND SUGAR!
K-TNK
HEY, SAGA!
WE HEARD THAT THE WAREHOUSE OUTSIDE OF TOWN IS HAUNTED.
YOU WANNA COME WITH US AND CHECK IT OUT?
THEY MUST BE TALKING ABOUT SUGAR!
UH, I'LL SEE YOU ALL THERE!
DASH
HUH?
HEY, WAIT!

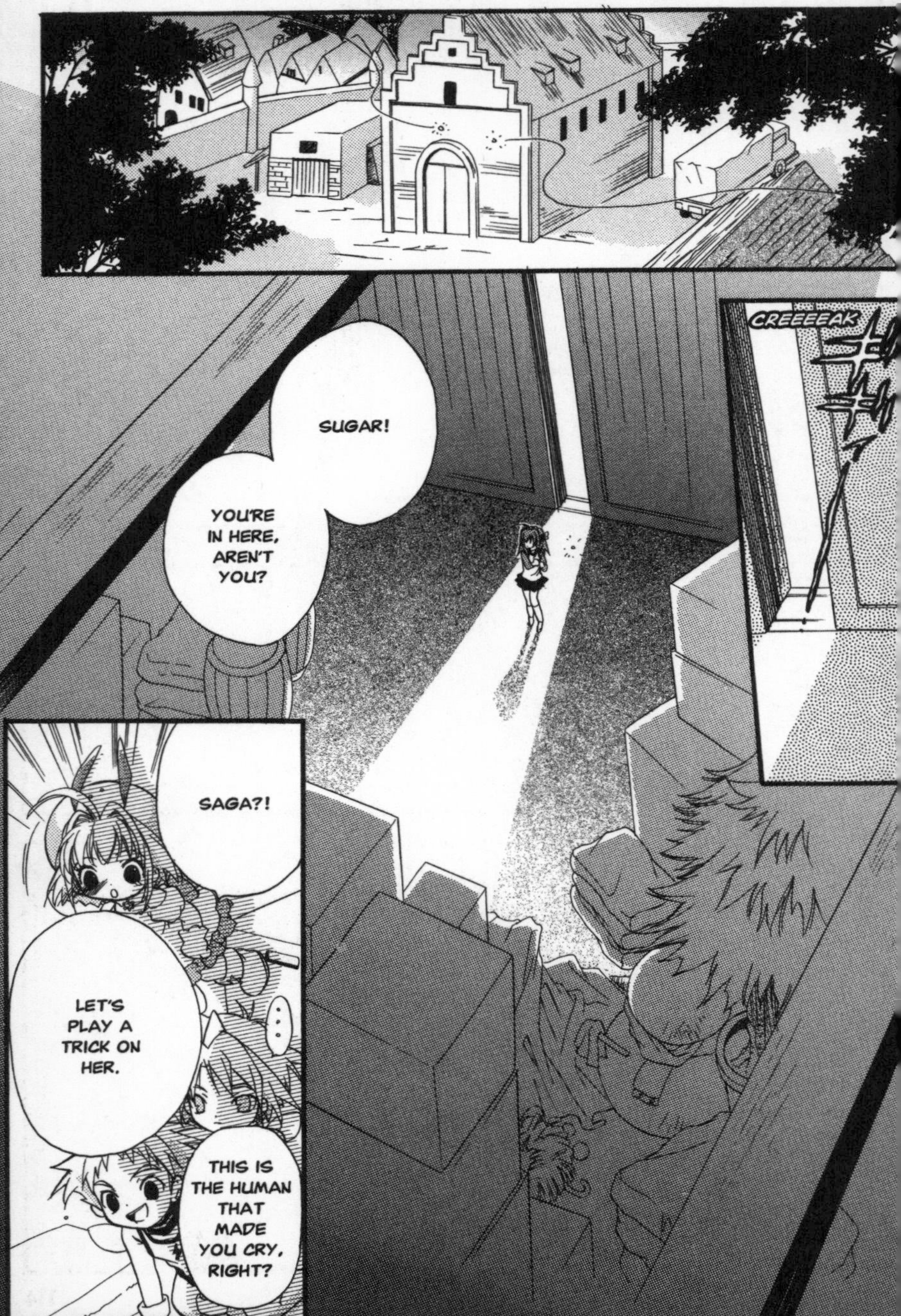
CREEEEAK
SUGAR!
YOU'RE IN HERE, AREN'T YOU?
SAGA?!
LET'S PLAY A TRICK ON HER.
...
THIS IS THE HUMAN THAT MADE YOU CRY, RIGHT?

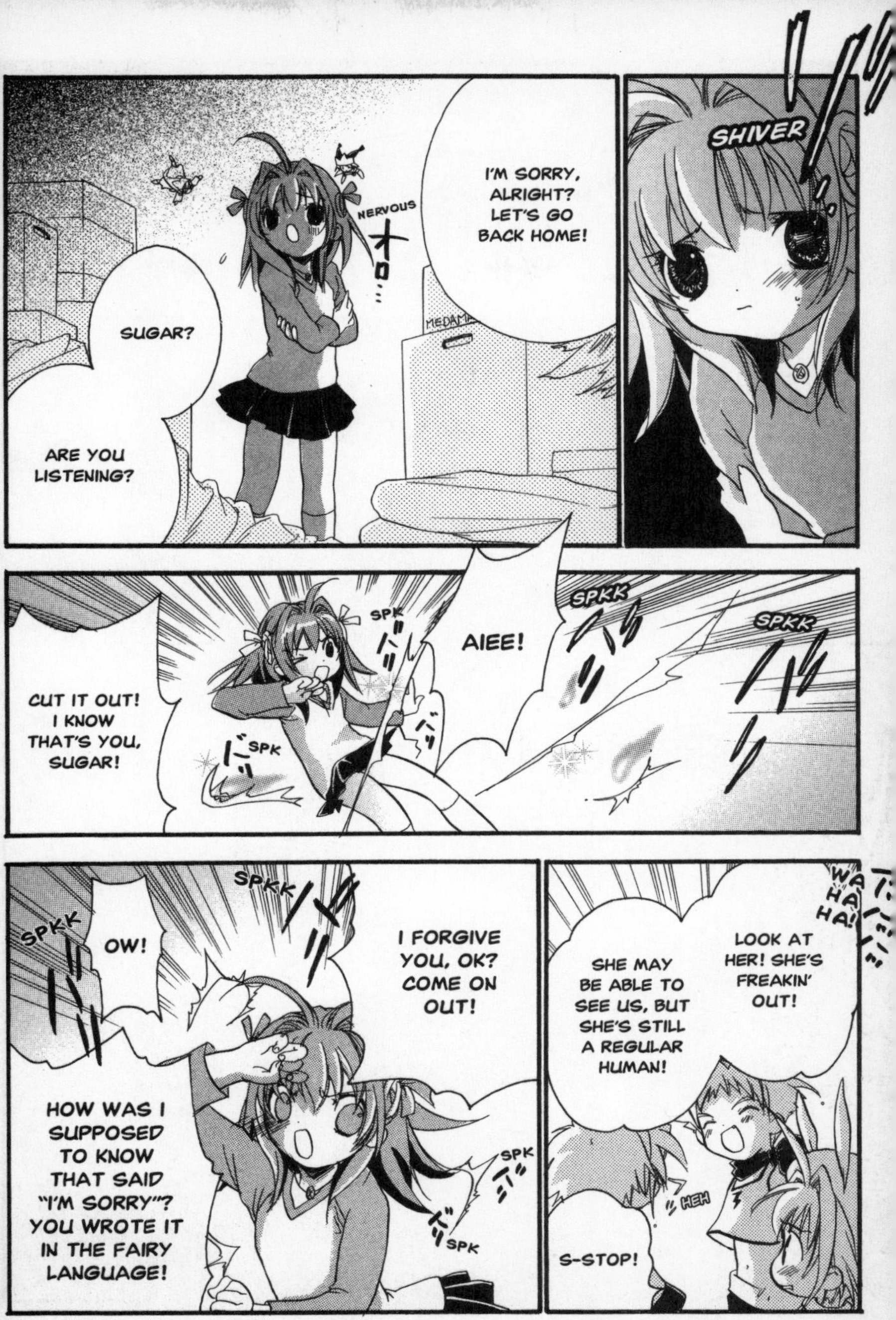
SHIVER
I'M SORRY, ALRIGHT? LET'S GO BACK HOME!
NERVOUS
SUGAR?
ARE YOU LISTENING?
SPKK
SPKK
AIEE!
SPK
CUT IT OUT! I KNOW THAT'S YOU, SUGAR!
SPK
WA HA HA!
LOOK AT HER! SHE'S FREAKIN' OUT!
SHE MAY BE ABLE TO SEE US, BUT SHE'S STILL A REGULAR HUMAN!
HEH
S-STOP!
SPKK
I FORGIVE YOU, OK? COME ON OUT!
SPKK
OW!
HOW WAS I SUPPOSED TO KNOW THAT SAID "I'M SORRY"? YOU WROTE IT IN THE FAIRY LANGUAGE!
SPK
SPK

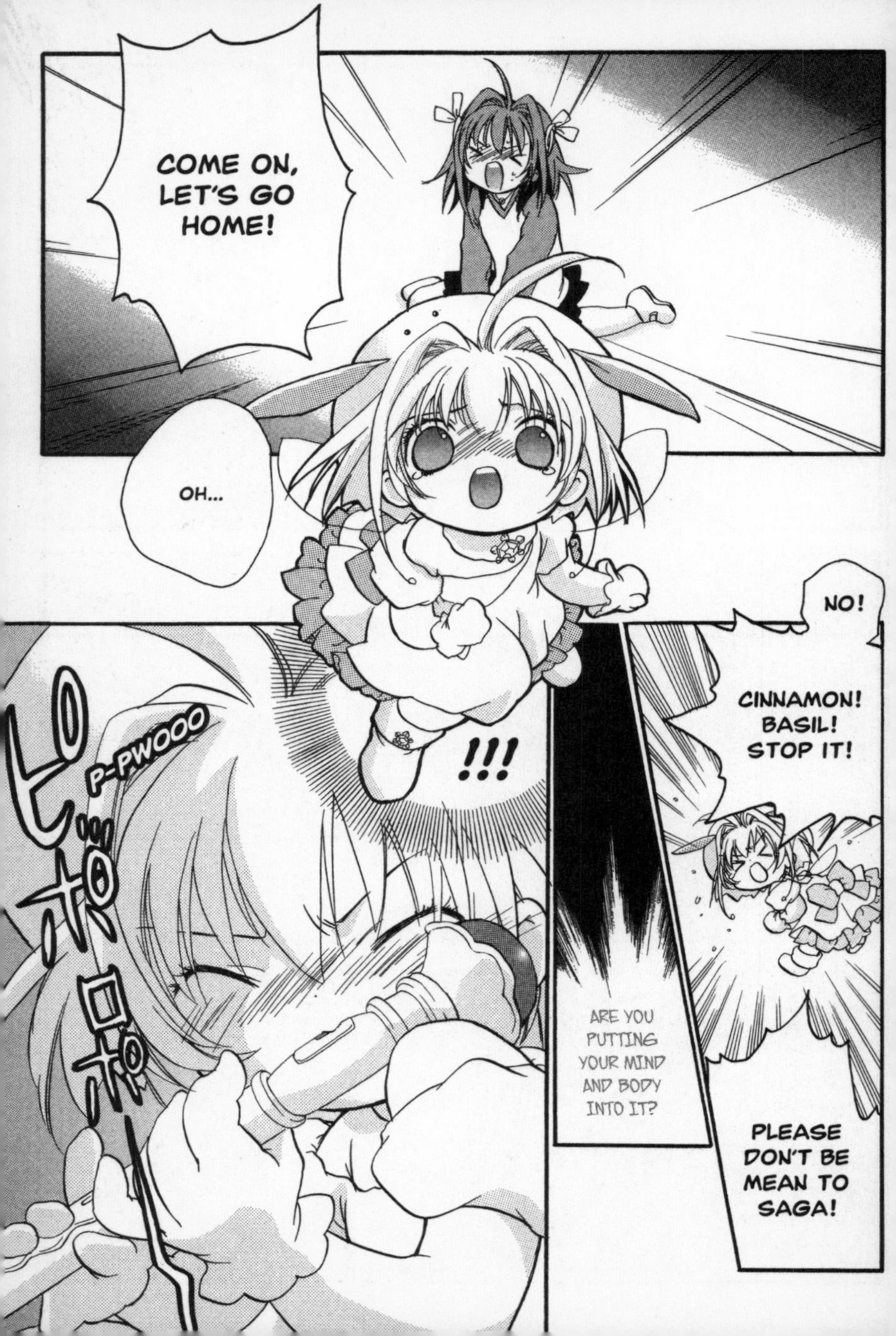

COME ON, LET'S GO HOME!
OH...
NO!
CINNAMON! BASIL! STOP IT!
PLEASE DON'T BE MEAN TO SAGA!
ARE YOU PUTTING YOUR MIND AND BODY INTO IT?
!!!
P-PWOOO

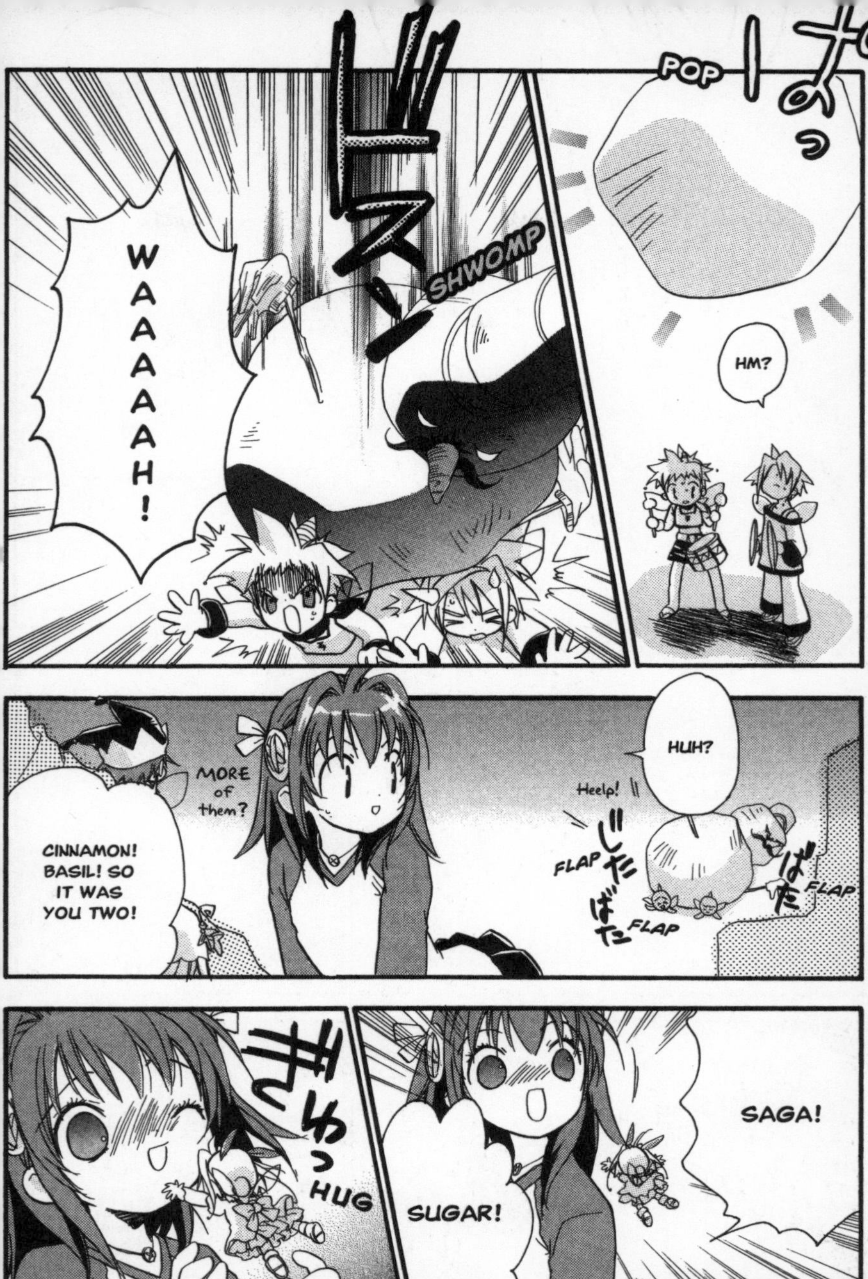
POP
ぽっ
HM?
ドスッ
SHWOMP
WAAAAAAH!
HUH?
Heelp!
じたばた
FLAP
FLAP
ばた
FLAP
MORE of them?
CINNAMON! BASIL! SO IT WAS YOU TWO!
SAGA!
SUGAR!
ぎゅっ
HUG

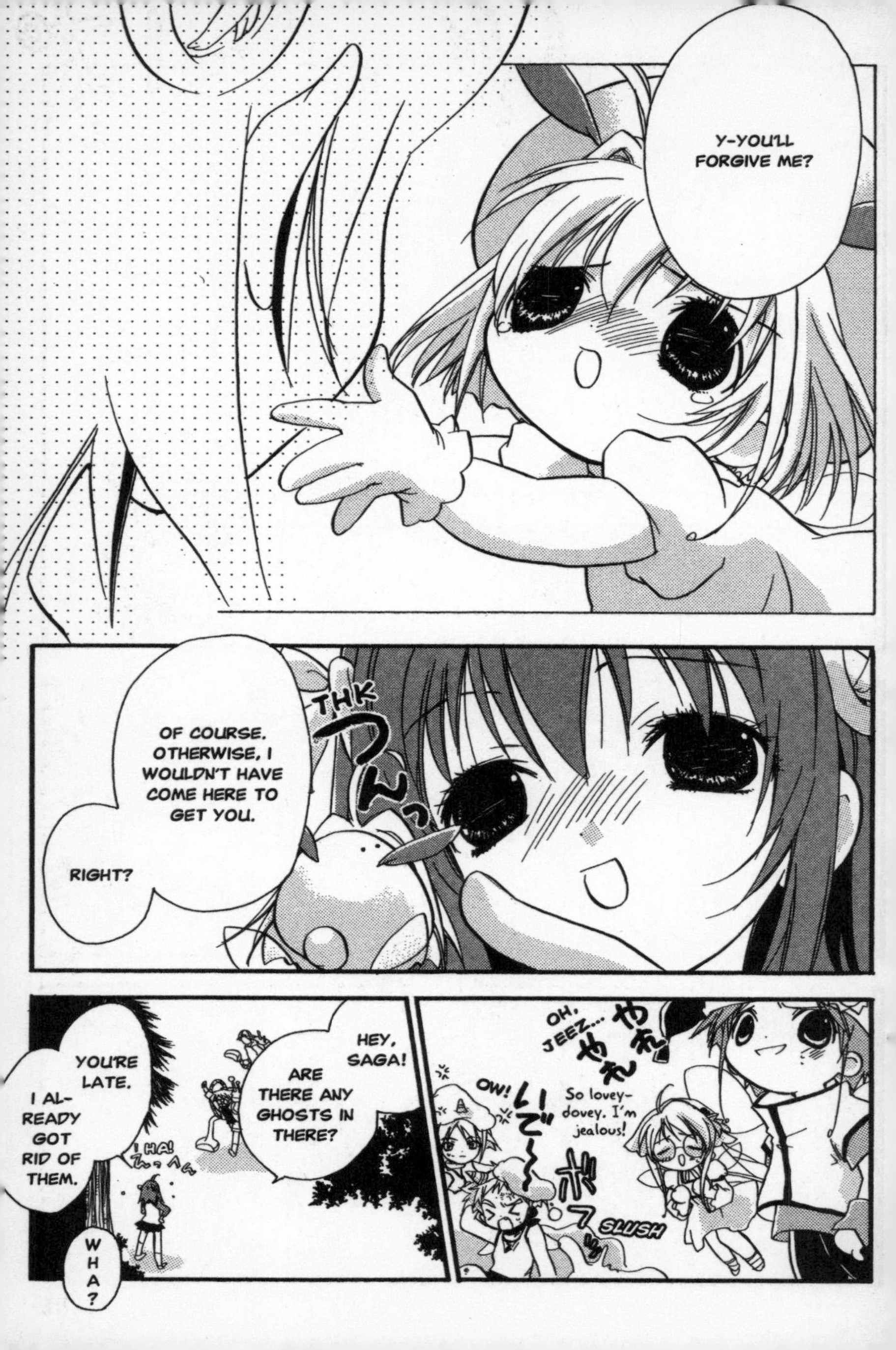
Y-YOU'LL FORGIVE ME?
OF COURSE. OTHERWISE, I WOULDN'T HAVE COME HERE TO GET YOU.
RIGHT?
THK
OH, JEEZ...
So lovey-dovey. I'm jealous!
OW!
SLUSH
HEY, SAGA!
ARE THERE ANY GHOSTS IN THERE?
YOU'RE LATE.
I AL-READY GOT RID OF THEM.
HA!
WHA?

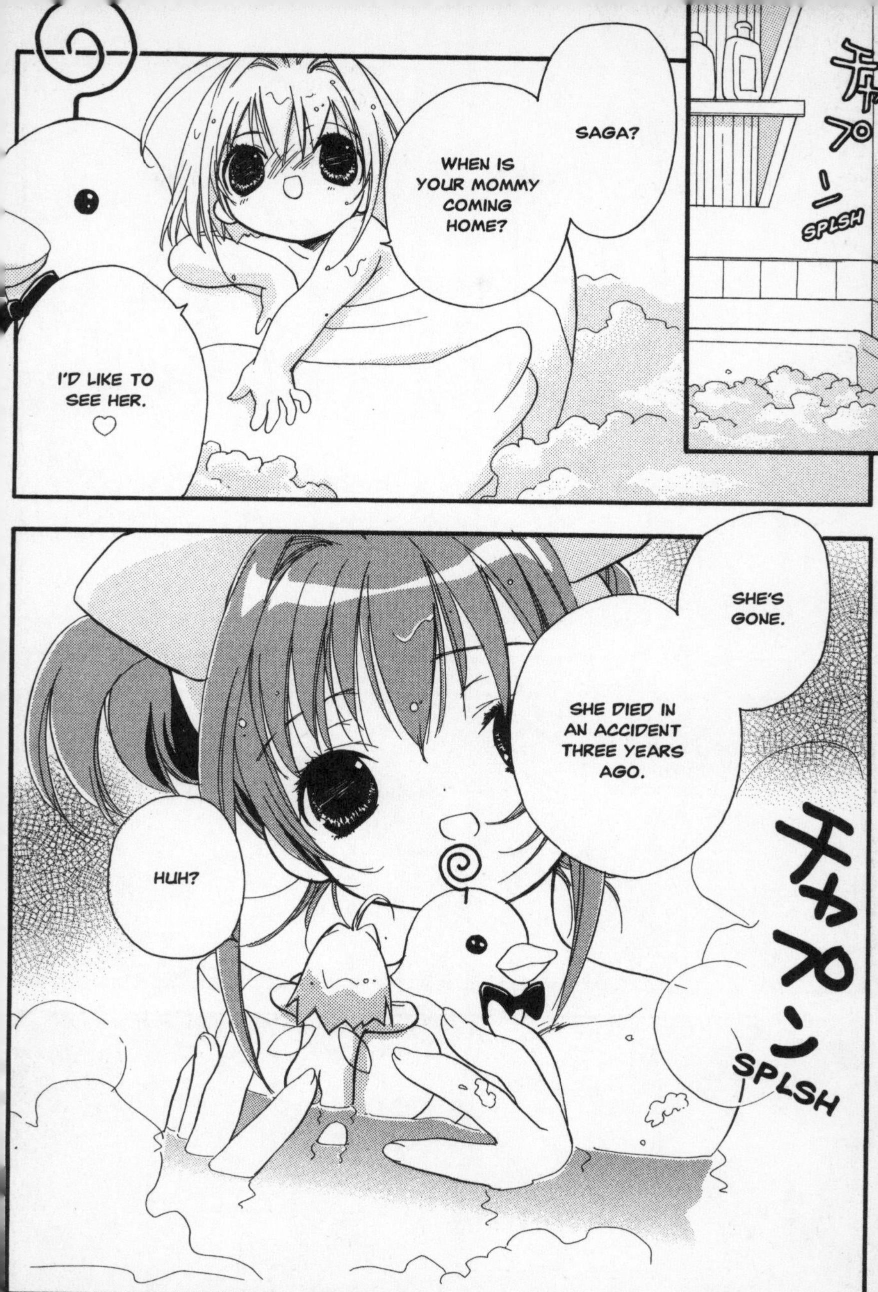
チャプーン
SPLSH
SAGA?
WHEN IS YOUR MOMMY COMING HOME?
I'D LIKE TO SEE HER. ♡
チャプン
SPLSH
SHE'S GONE.
SHE DIED IN AN ACCIDENT THREE YEARS AGO.
HUH?

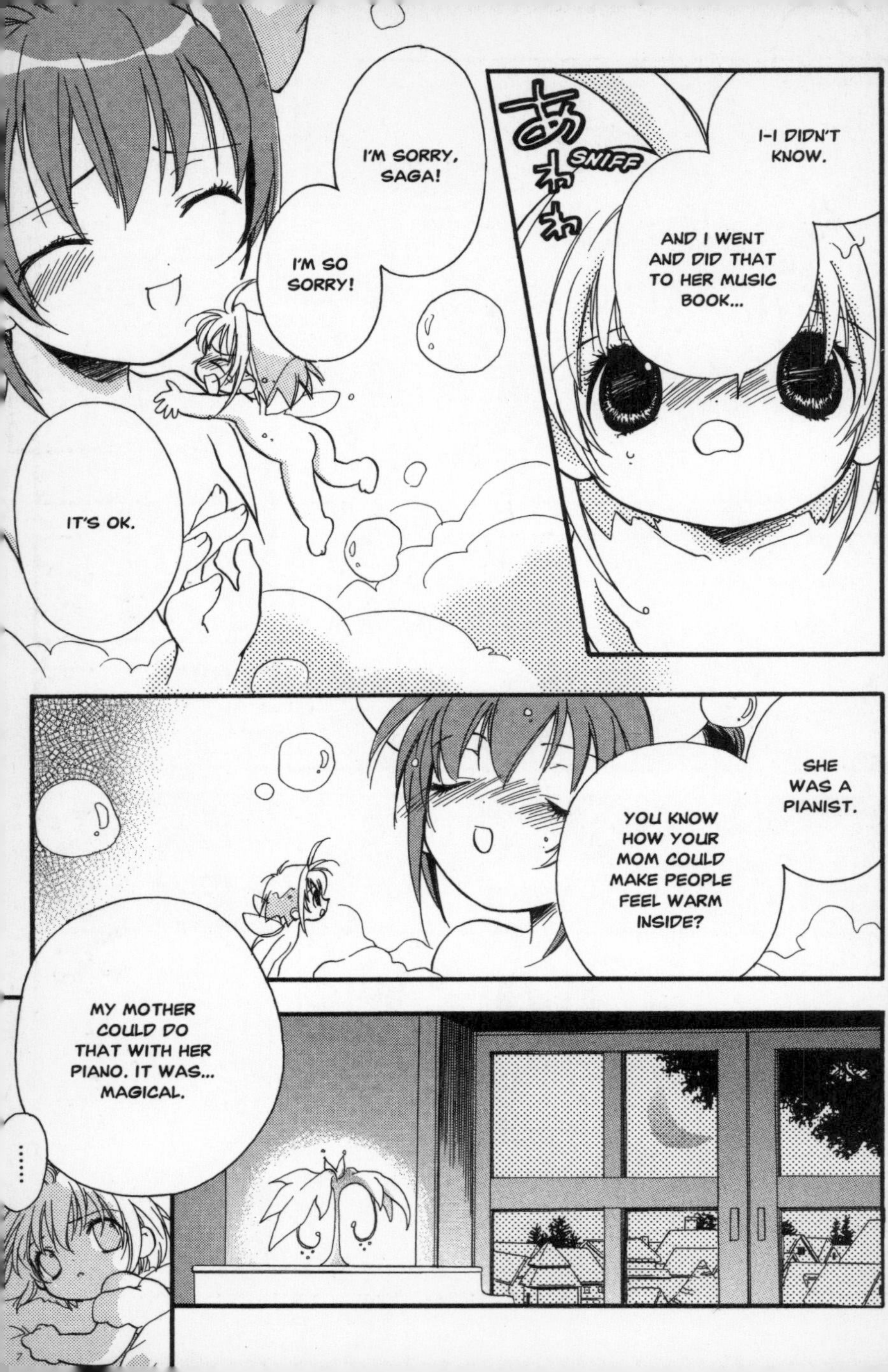
SNIFF
I-I DIDN'T KNOW.
AND I WENT AND DID THAT TO HER MUSIC BOOK...
I'M SORRY, SAGA!
I'M SO SORRY!
IT'S OK.
SHE WAS A PIANIST.
YOU KNOW HOW YOUR MOM COULD MAKE PEOPLE FEEL WARM INSIDE?
MY MOTHER COULD DO THAT WITH HER PIANO. IT WAS... MAGICAL.
......

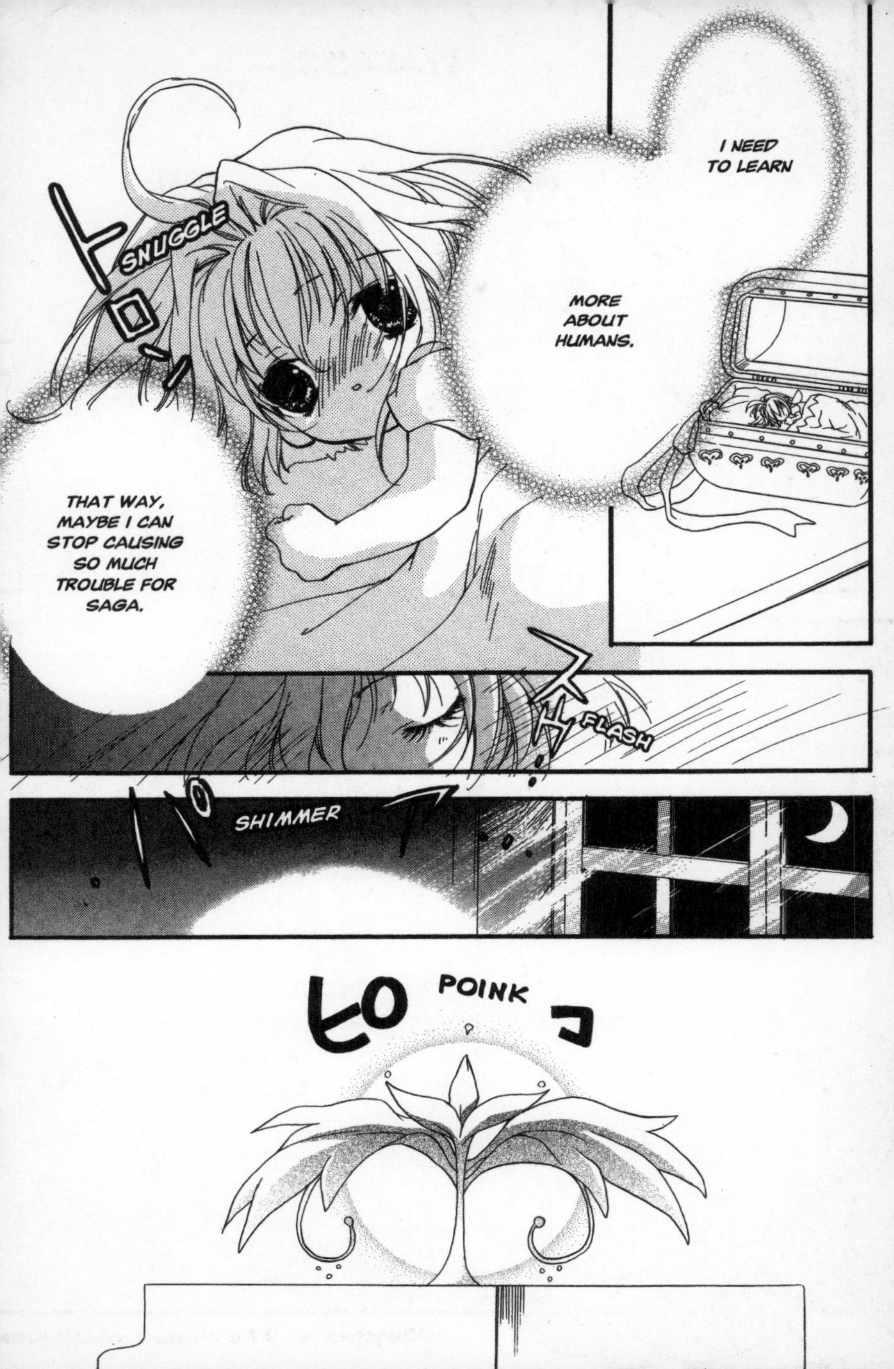
I NEED TO LEARN
MORE ABOUT HUMANS.
SNUGGLE
THAT WAY, MAYBE I CAN STOP CAUSING SO MUCH TROUBLE FOR SAGA.
FLASH
SHIMMER
POINK

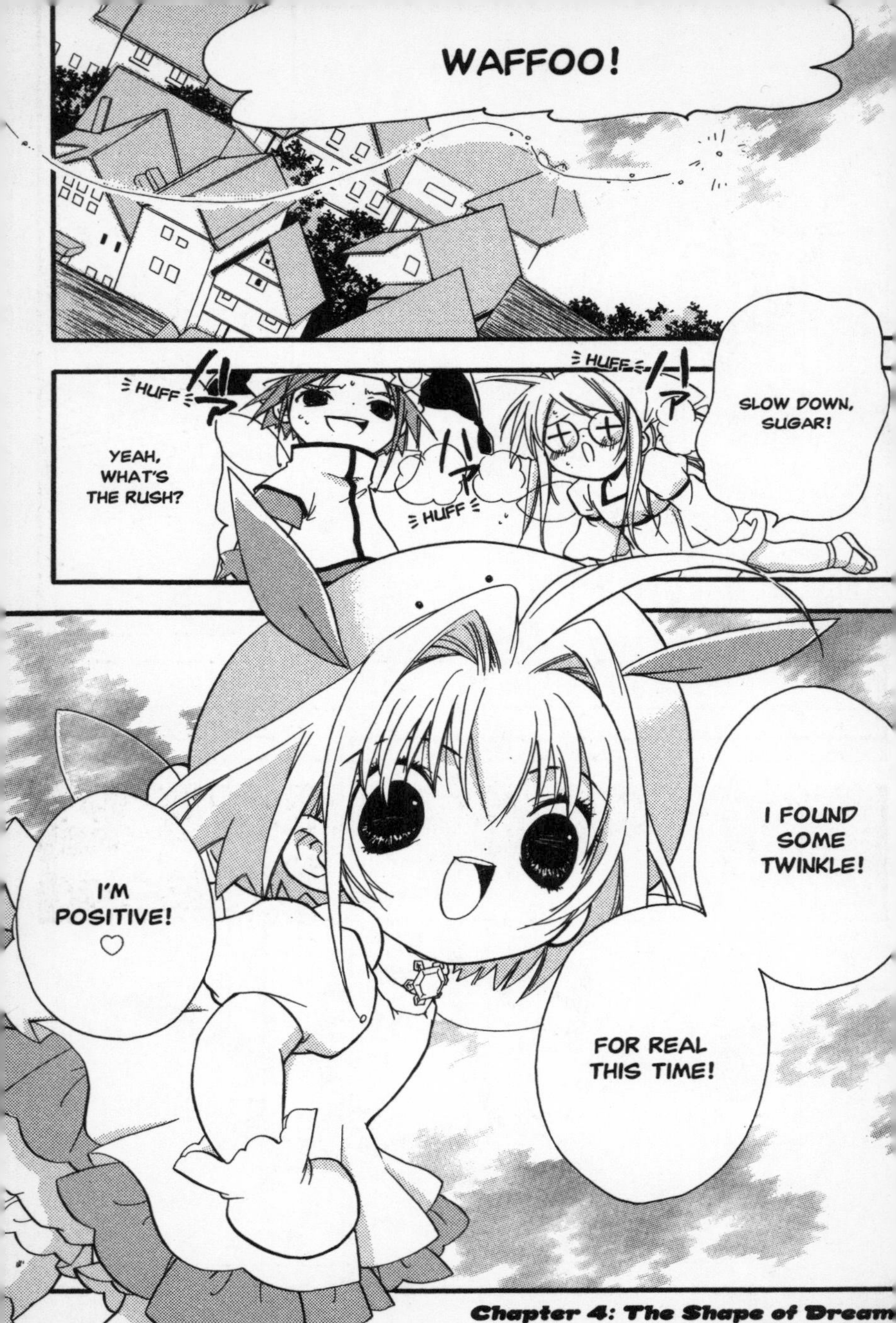
WAFFOO!
HUFF
SLOW DOWN, SUGAR!
HUFF
YEAH, WHAT'S THE RUSH?
HUFF
I FOUND SOME TWINKLE!
FOR REAL THIS TIME!
I'M POSITIVE! ♡

Chapter 4: The Shape of Dream

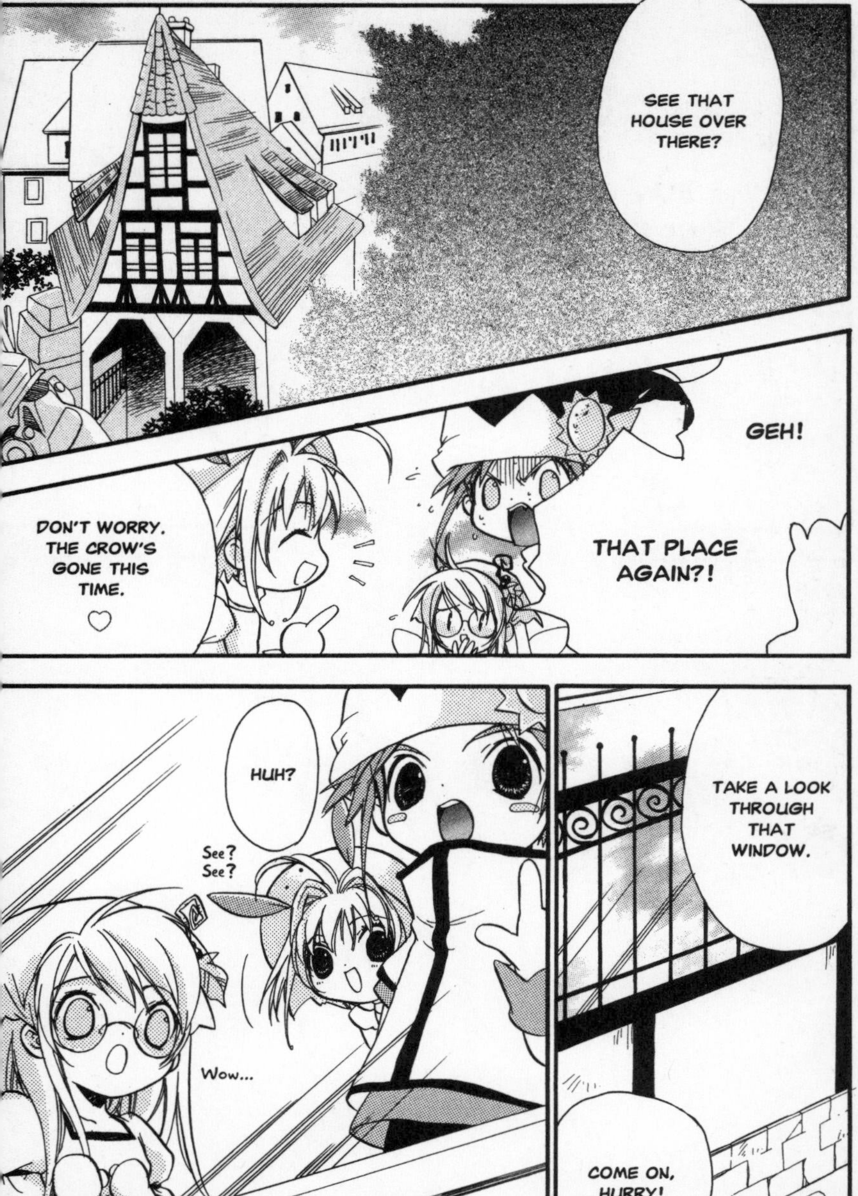
SEE THAT HOUSE OVER THERE?
GEH!
THAT PLACE AGAIN?!
DON'T WORRY. THE CROW'S GONE THIS TIME. ♡
TAKE A LOOK THROUGH THAT WINDOW.
COME ON, HURRY!
HUH?
See? See?
Wow...

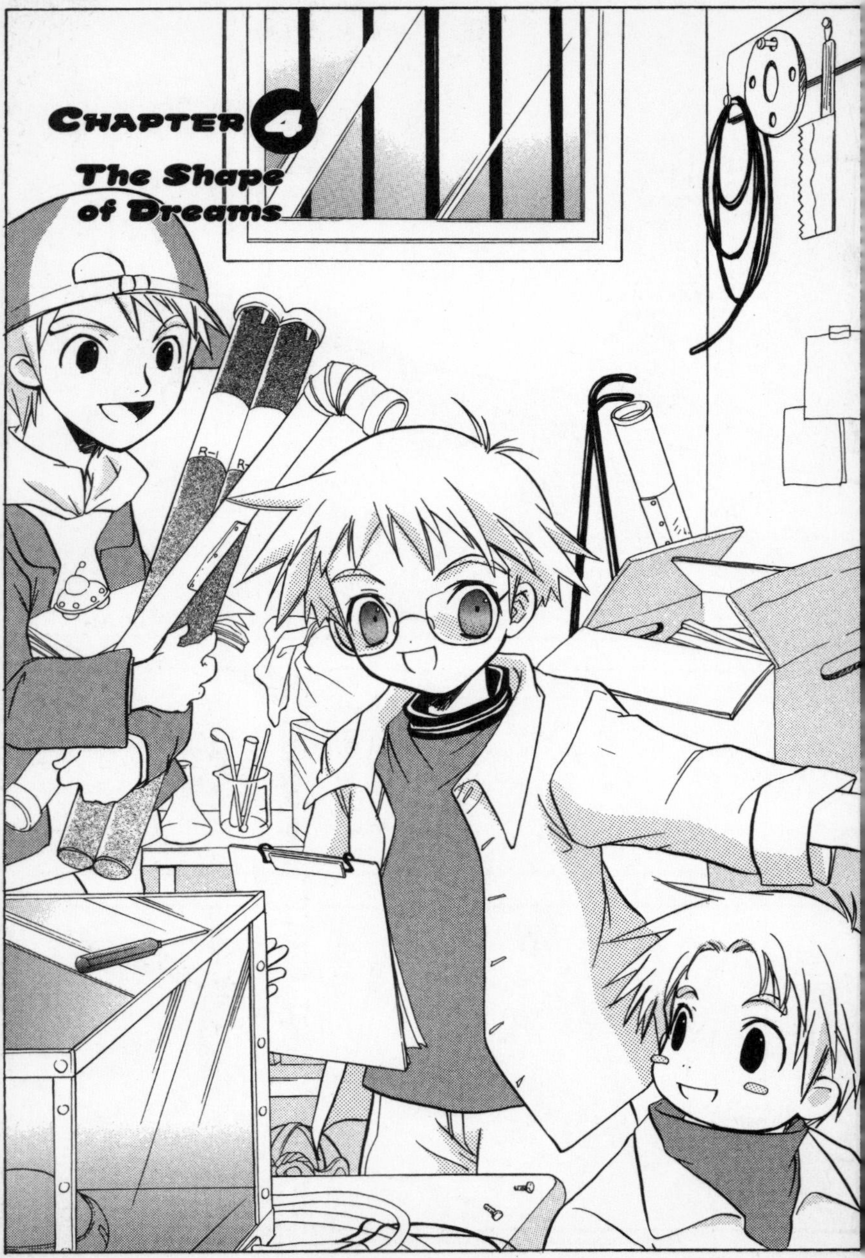
Chapter 4
The Shape of Dreams
R-1

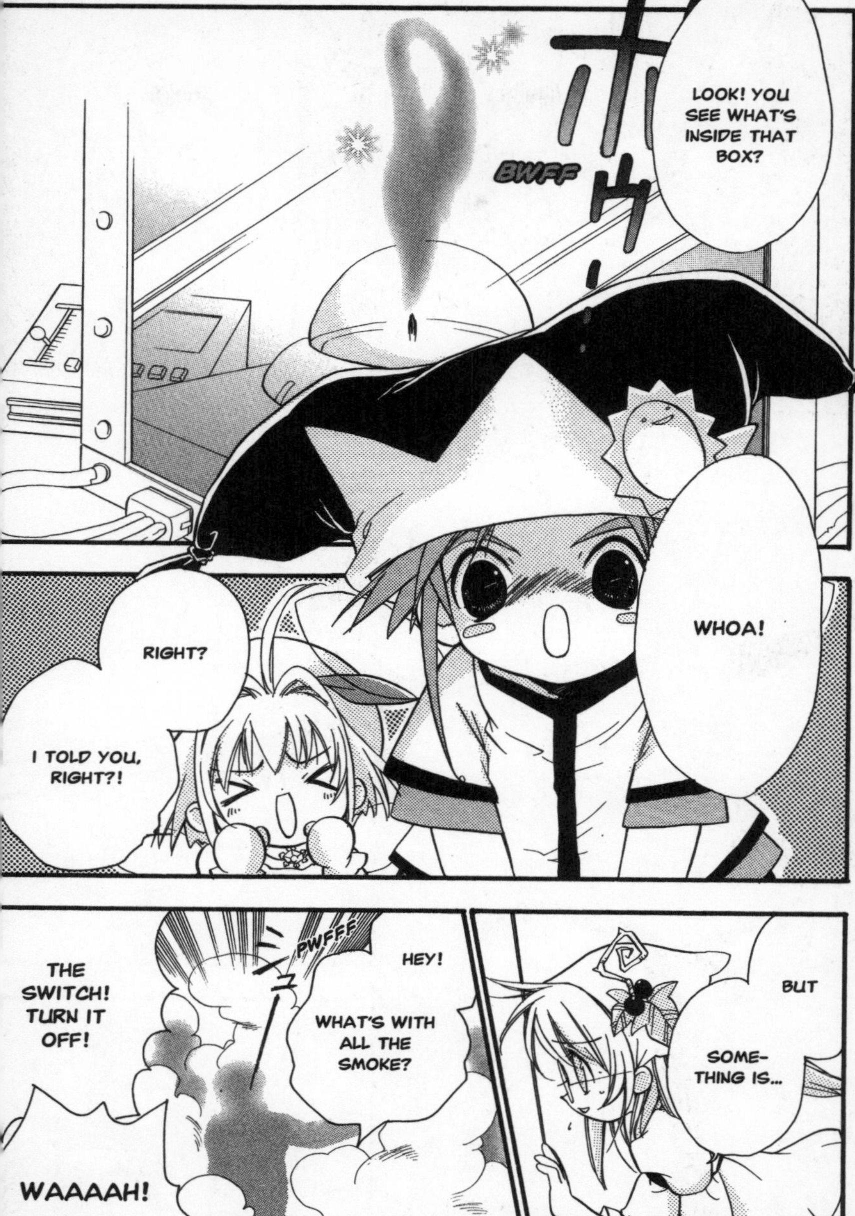
LOOK! YOU SEE WHAT'S INSIDE THAT BOX?
ホウ
BWFF
WHOA!
RIGHT?
I TOLD YOU, RIGHT?!
BUT
SOME-THING IS...
HEY!
WHAT'S WITH ALL THE SMOKE?
PWFFF
THE SWITCH! TURN IT OFF!
WAAAAH!

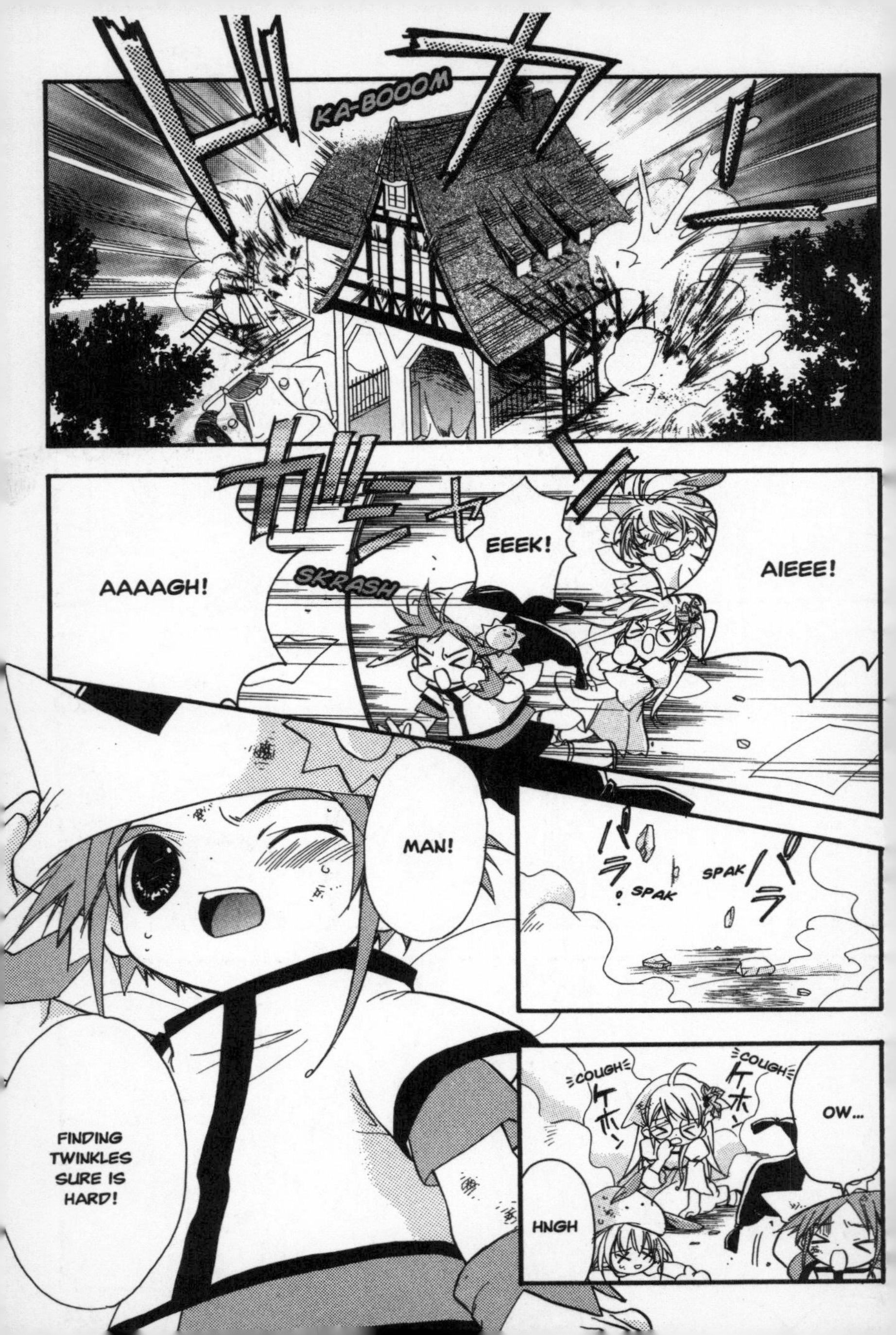
KA-BOOOM
AIEEE!
EEEK!
SKRASH
AAAAGH!
SPAK
SPAK
OW...
COUGH
COUGH
HNGH
MAN!
FINDING TWINKLES SURE IS HARD!

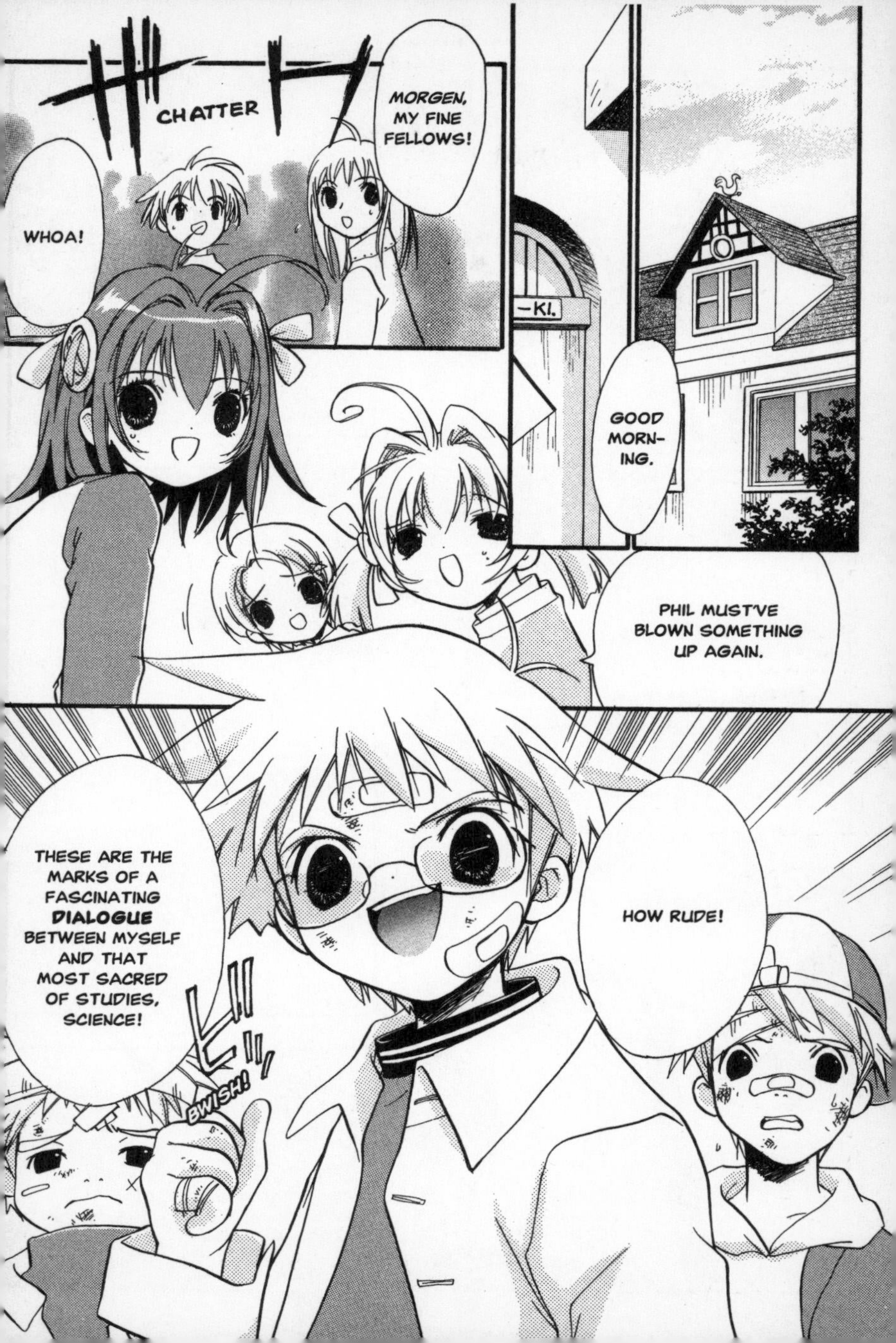

–KI.
GOOD MORN-ING.
MORGEN, MY FINE FELLOWS!
CHATTER
WHOA!
PHIL MUST'VE BLOWN SOMETHING UP AGAIN.
HOW RUDE!
THESE ARE THE MARKS OF A FASCINATING **DIALOGUE** BETWEEN MYSELF AND THAT MOST SACRED OF STUDIES, SCIENCE!
BWISH!

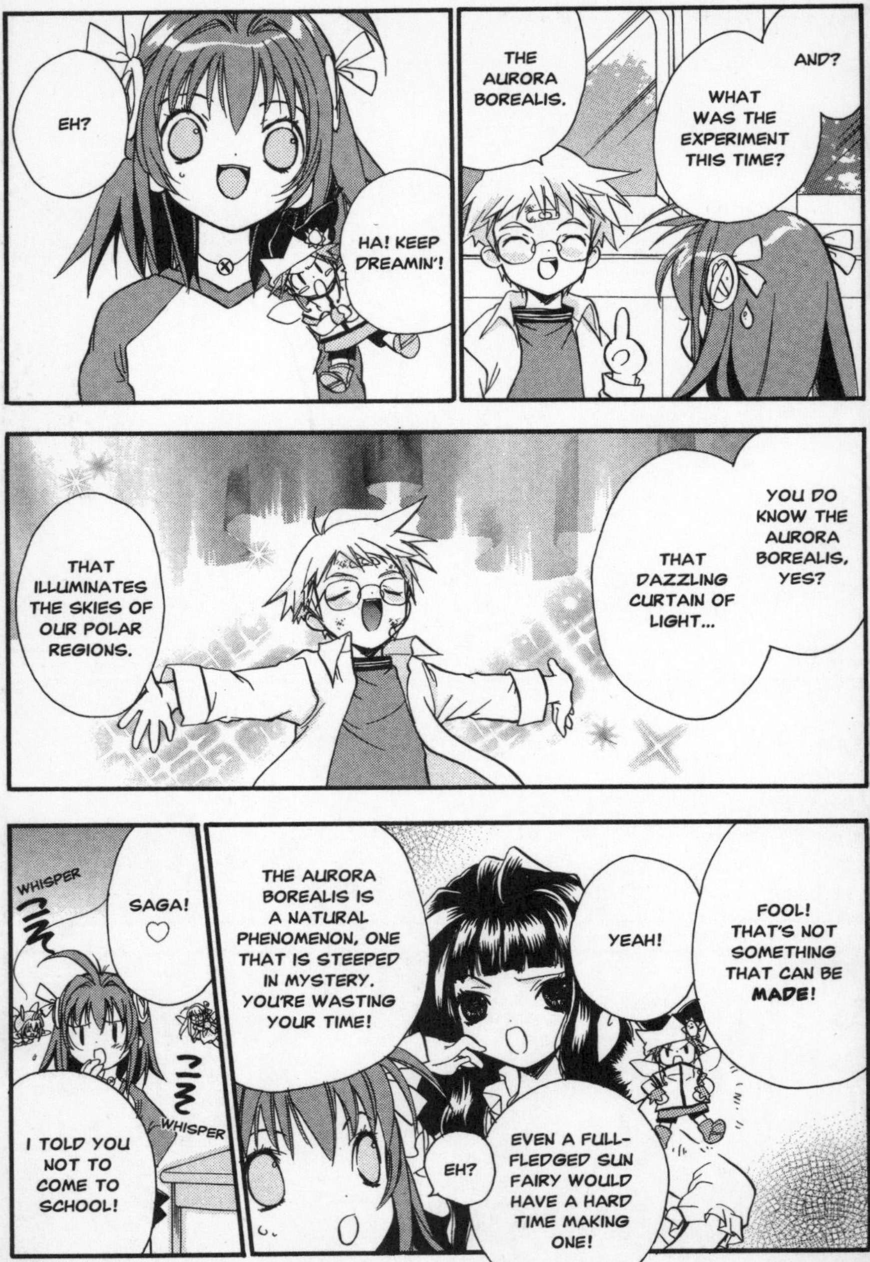
AND?
WHAT WAS THE EXPERIMENT THIS TIME?
THE AURORA BOREALIS.
EH?
HA! KEEP DREAMIN'!
YOU DO KNOW THE AURORA BOREALIS, YES?
THAT DAZZLING CURTAIN OF LIGHT...
THAT ILLUMINATES THE SKIES OF OUR POLAR REGIONS.
FOOL! THAT'S NOT SOMETHING THAT CAN BE **MADE**!
YEAH!
THE AURORA BOREALIS IS A NATURAL PHENOMENON, ONE THAT IS STEEPED IN MYSTERY. YOU'RE WASTING YOUR TIME!
EVEN A FULL-FLEDGED SUN FAIRY WOULD HAVE A HARD TIME MAKING ONE!
EH?
WHISPER
SAGA! ♡
WHISPER
I TOLD YOU NOT TO COME TO SCHOOL!

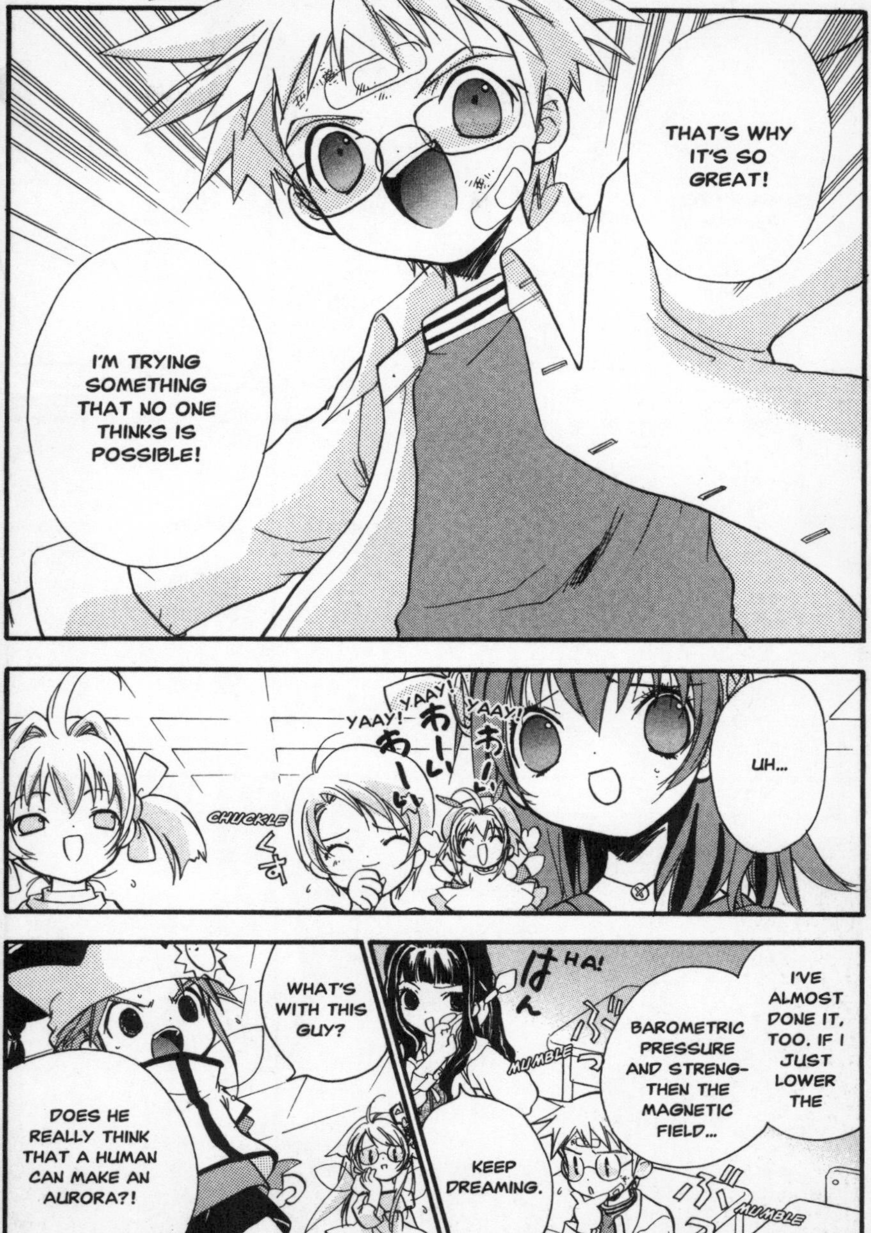
THAT'S WHY IT'S SO GREAT!
I'M TRYING SOMETHING THAT NO ONE THINKS IS POSSIBLE!
UH...
YAAY!
あーい
YAAY!
あーい
YAAY!
あーい
CHUCKLE
くす
I'VE ALMOST DONE IT, TOO. IF I JUST LOWER THE
BAROMETRIC PRESSURE AND STRENG- THEN THE MAGNETIC FIELD...
HA!
はん
MUMBLE
KEEP DREAMING.
MUMBLE
WHAT'S WITH THIS GUY?
DOES HE REALLY THINK THAT A HUMAN CAN MAKE AN AURORA?!

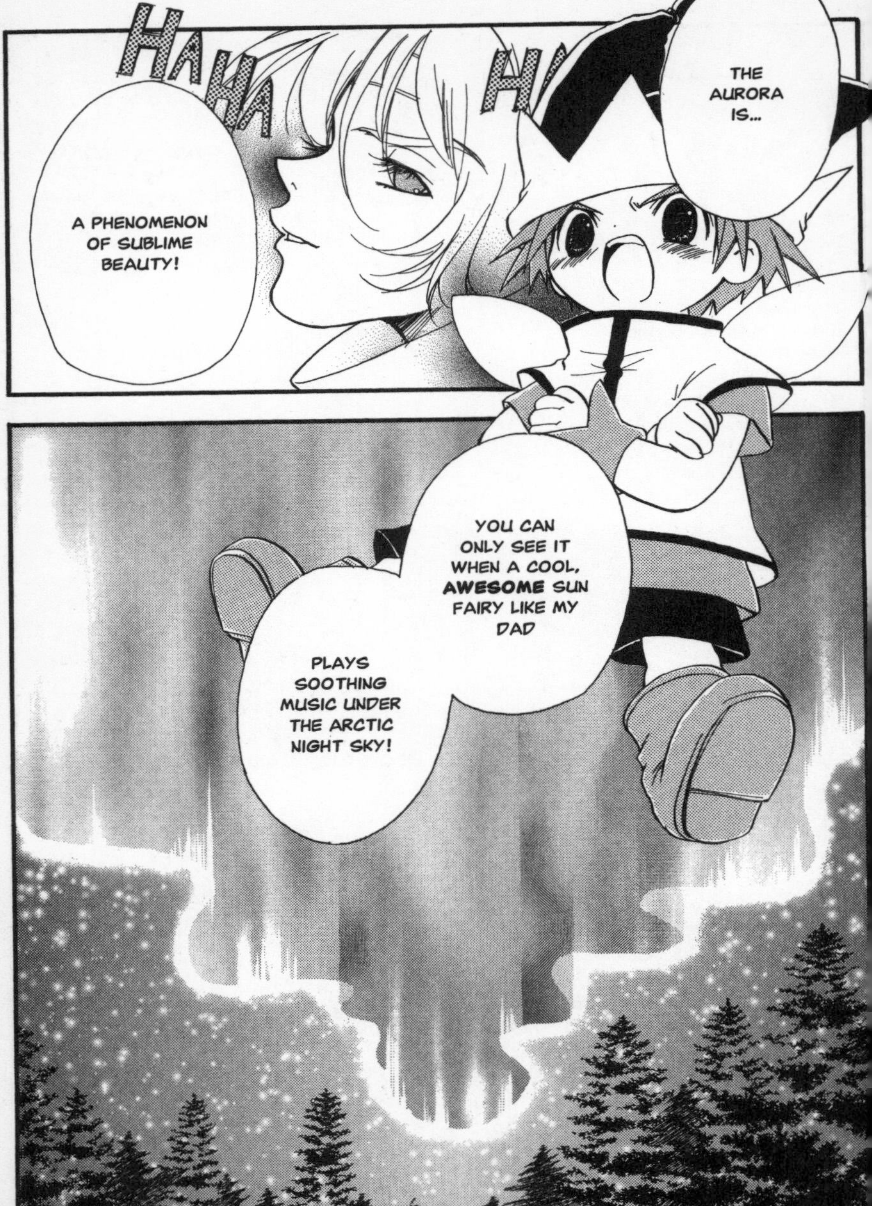
THE AURORA IS...
HAHA
A PHENOMENON OF SUBLIME BEAUTY!
YOU CAN ONLY SEE IT WHEN A COOL, **AWESOME** SUN FAIRY LIKE MY DAD
PLAYS SOOTHING MUSIC UNDER THE ARCTIC NIGHT SKY!

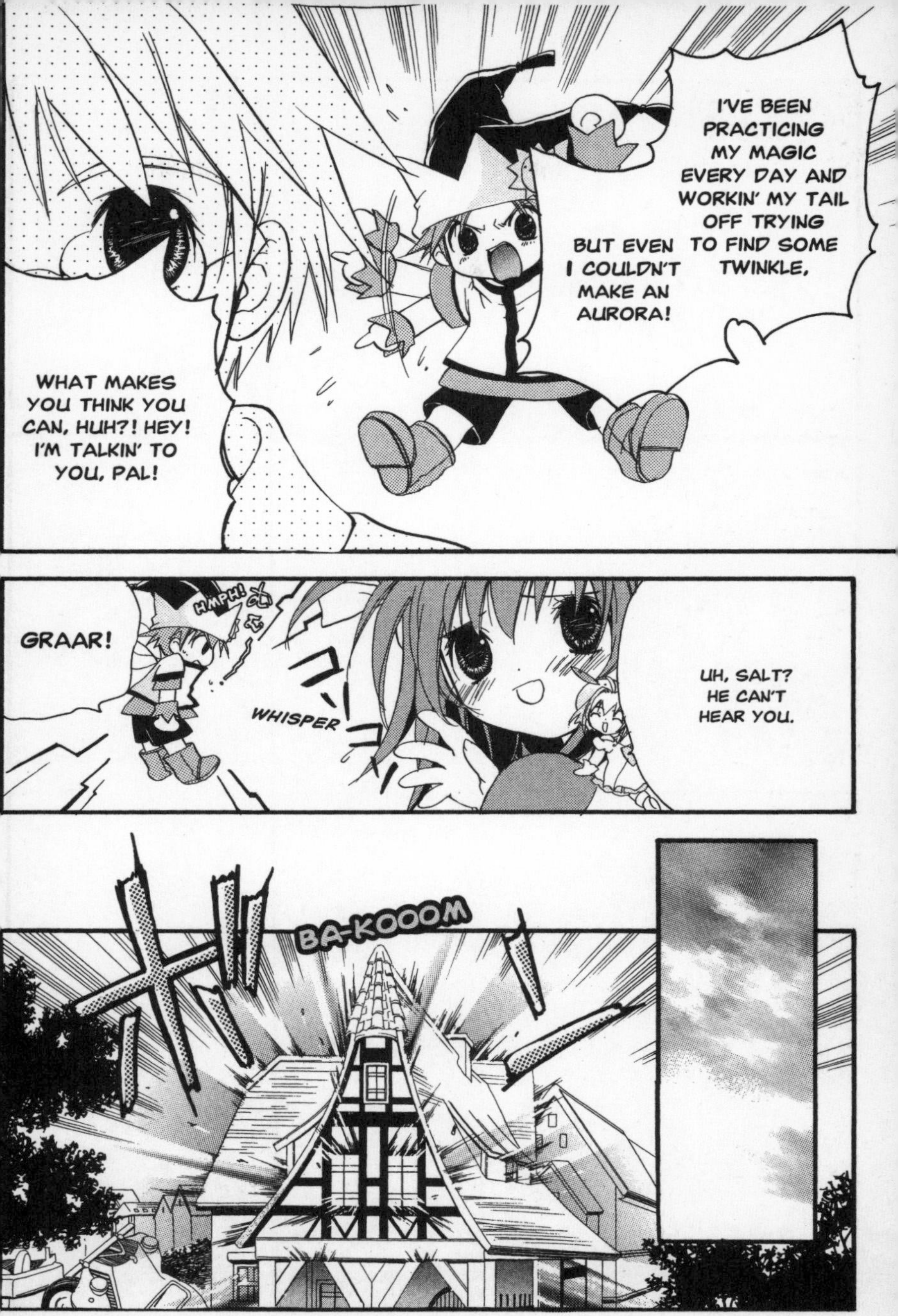
I'VE BEEN PRACTICING MY MAGIC EVERY DAY AND WORKIN' MY TAIL OFF TRYING TO FIND SOME TWINKLE,
BUT EVEN I COULDN'T MAKE AN AURORA!
WHAT MAKES YOU THINK YOU CAN, HUH?! HEY! I'M TALKIN' TO YOU, PAL!
UH, SALT? HE CAN'T HEAR YOU.
HMPH!
WHISPER
GRAAR!
BA-KOOOM

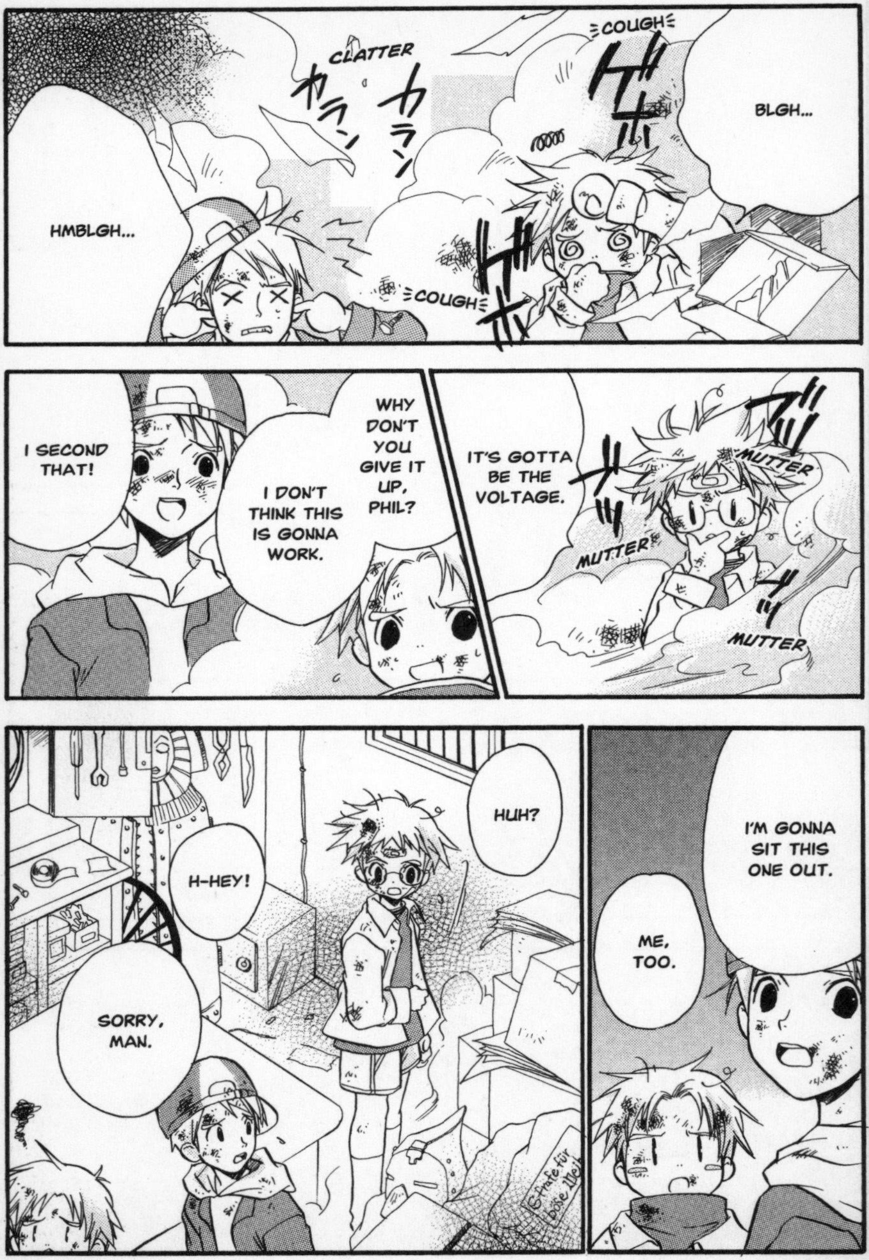
COUGH
ゲホ
BLGH...
CLATTER
カラン カラン
COUGH
ゲホ
HMBLGH...
MUTTER
IT'S GOTTA BE THE VOLTAGE.
ブツ ブツ
MUTTER
MUTTER
WHY DON'T YOU GIVE IT UP, PHIL?
I DON'T THINK THIS IS GONNA WORK.
I SECOND THAT!
I'M GONNA SIT THIS ONE OUT.
ME, TOO.
HUH?
H-HEY!
SORRY, MAN.

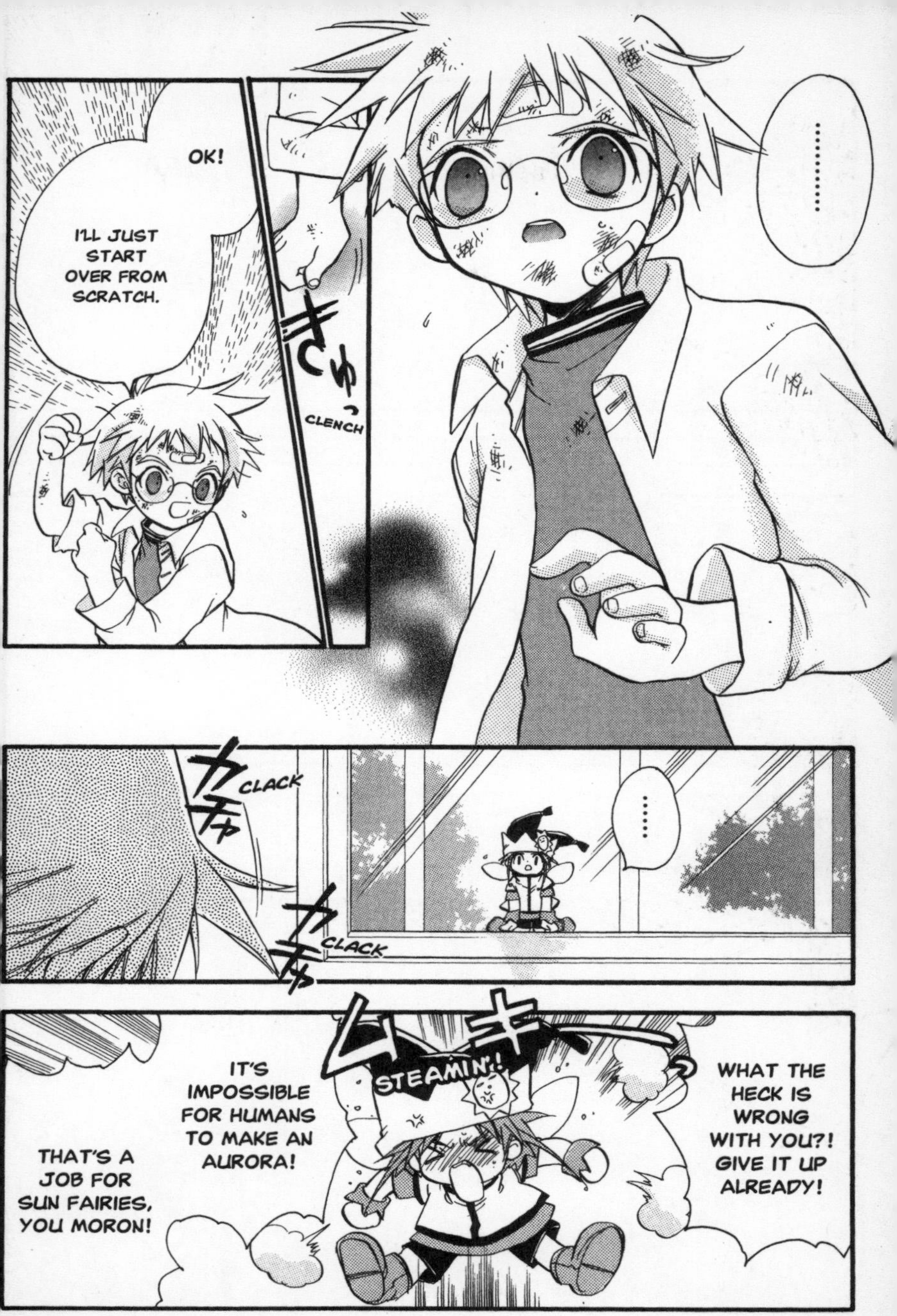
......
きゅっ
CLENCH
OK!
I'LL JUST START OVER FROM SCRATCH.
......
カチャ
CLACK
カチャ
CLACK
WHAT THE HECK IS WRONG WITH YOU?! GIVE IT UP ALREADY!
ムキー
STEAMIN'!
IT'S IMPOSSIBLE FOR HUMANS TO MAKE AN AURORA!
THAT'S A JOB FOR SUN FAIRIES, YOU MORON!

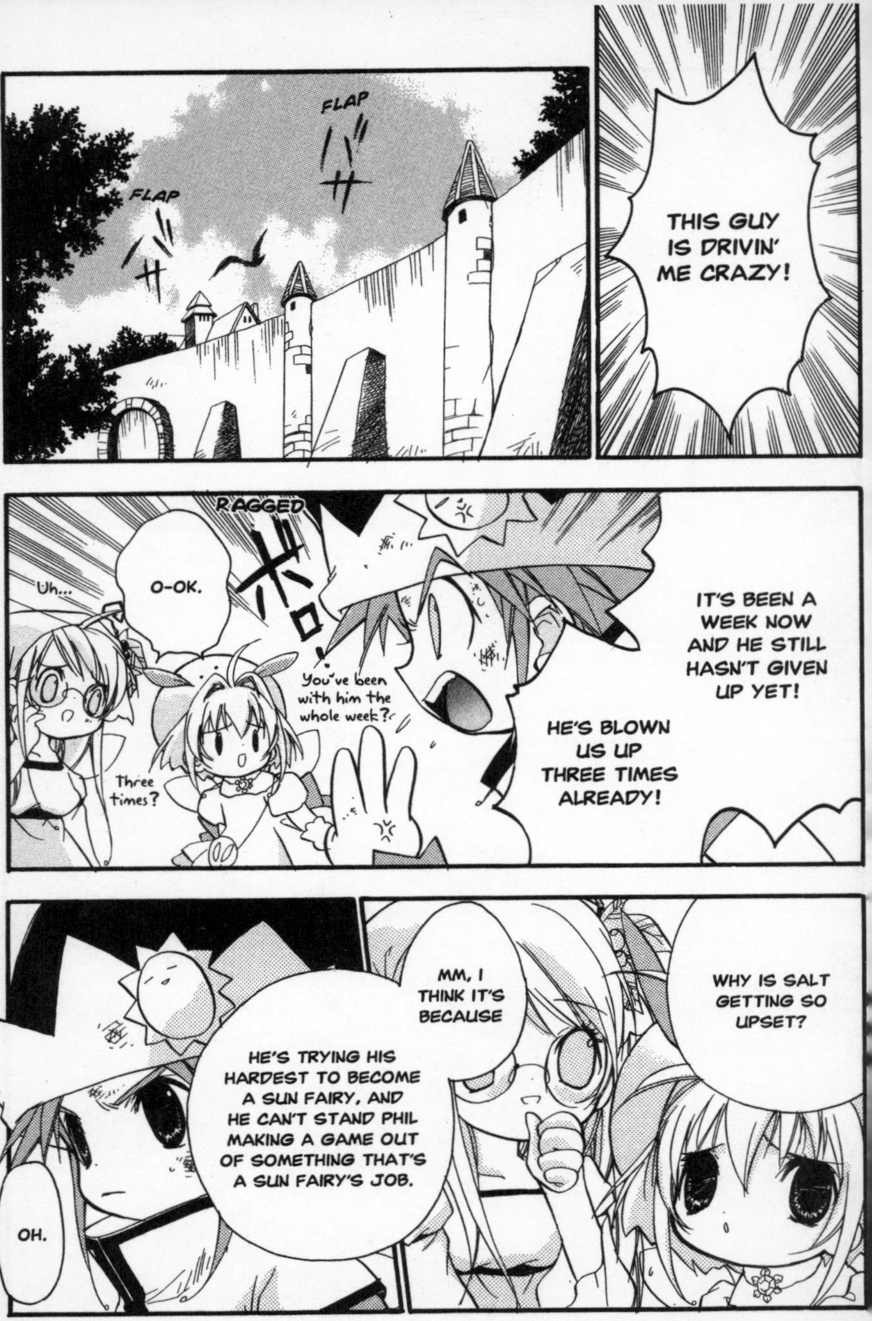
THIS GUY IS DRIVIN' ME CRAZY!
FLAP
FLAP
IT'S BEEN A WEEK NOW AND HE STILL HASN'T GIVEN UP YET!
HE'S BLOWN US UP THREE TIMES ALREADY!
RAGGED
You've been with him the whole week?
O-OK.
Three times?
Uh...
WHY IS SALT GETTING SO UPSET?
MM, I THINK IT'S BECAUSE
HE'S TRYING HIS HARDEST TO BECOME A SUN FAIRY, AND HE CAN'T STAND PHIL MAKING A GAME OUT OF SOMETHING THAT'S A SUN FAIRY'S JOB.
OH.

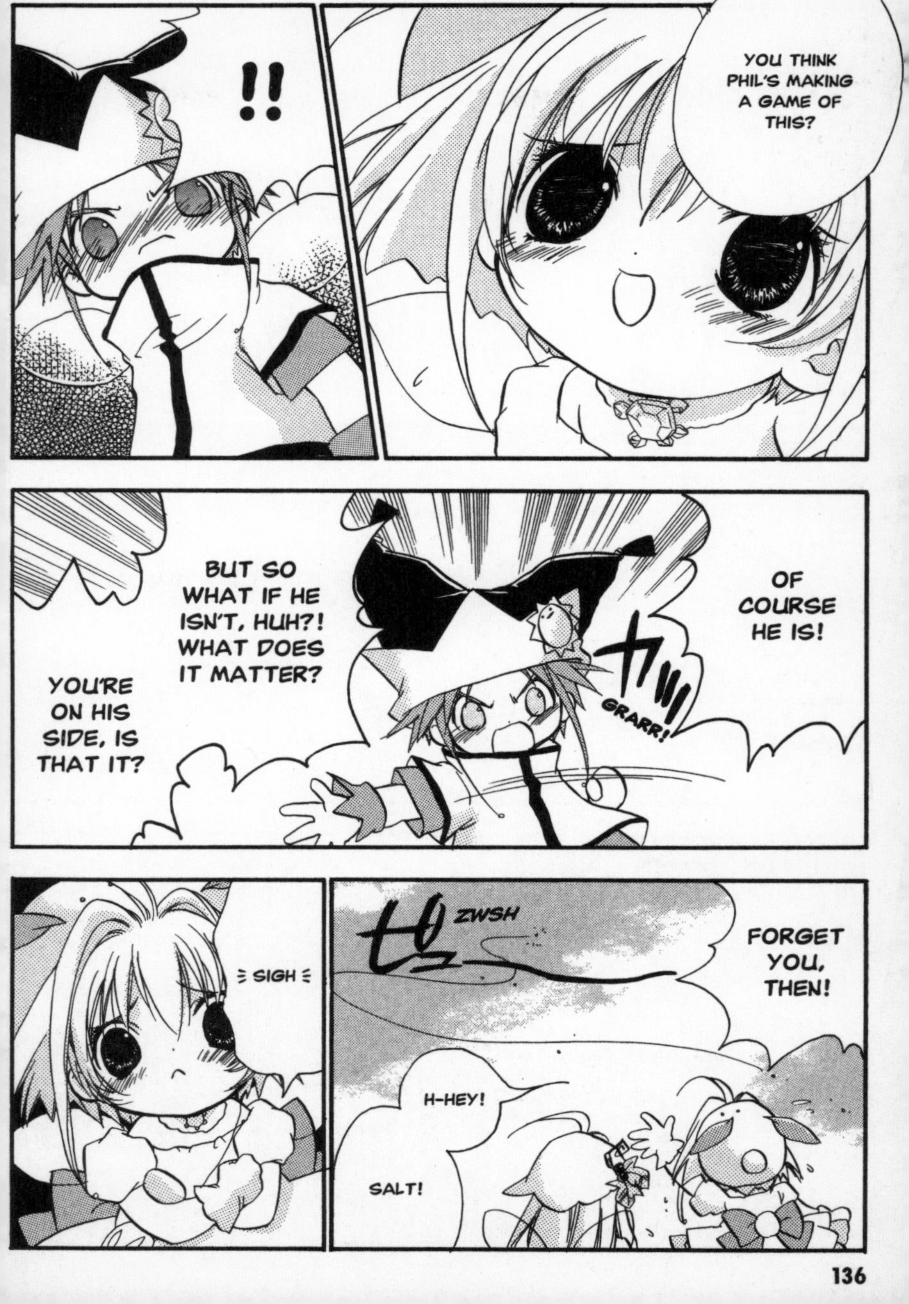
YOU THINK PHIL'S MAKING A GAME OF THIS?
!!
OF COURSE HE IS!
GRARR!
BUT SO WHAT IF HE ISN'T, HUH?! WHAT DOES IT MATTER?
YOU'RE ON HIS SIDE, IS THAT IT?
FORGET YOU, THEN!
ZWSH
H-HEY!
SALT!
SIGH

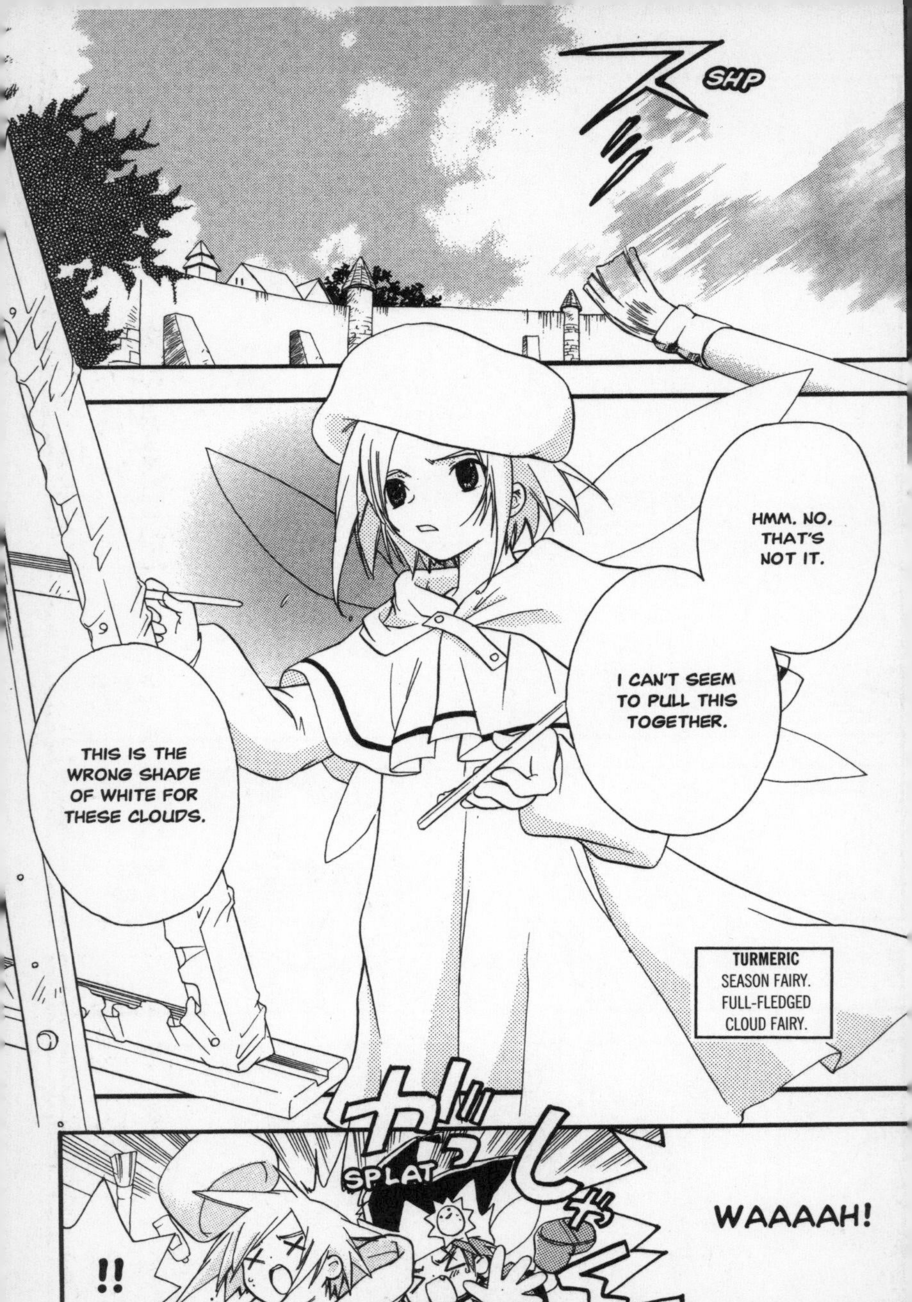
SHP
HMM. NO, THAT'S NOT IT.
I CAN'T SEEM TO PULL THIS TOGETHER.
THIS IS THE WRONG SHADE OF WHITE FOR THESE CLOUDS.
TURMERIC
SEASON FAIRY.
FULL-FLEDGED CLOUD FAIRY.
WAAAAH!
SPLAT
!!

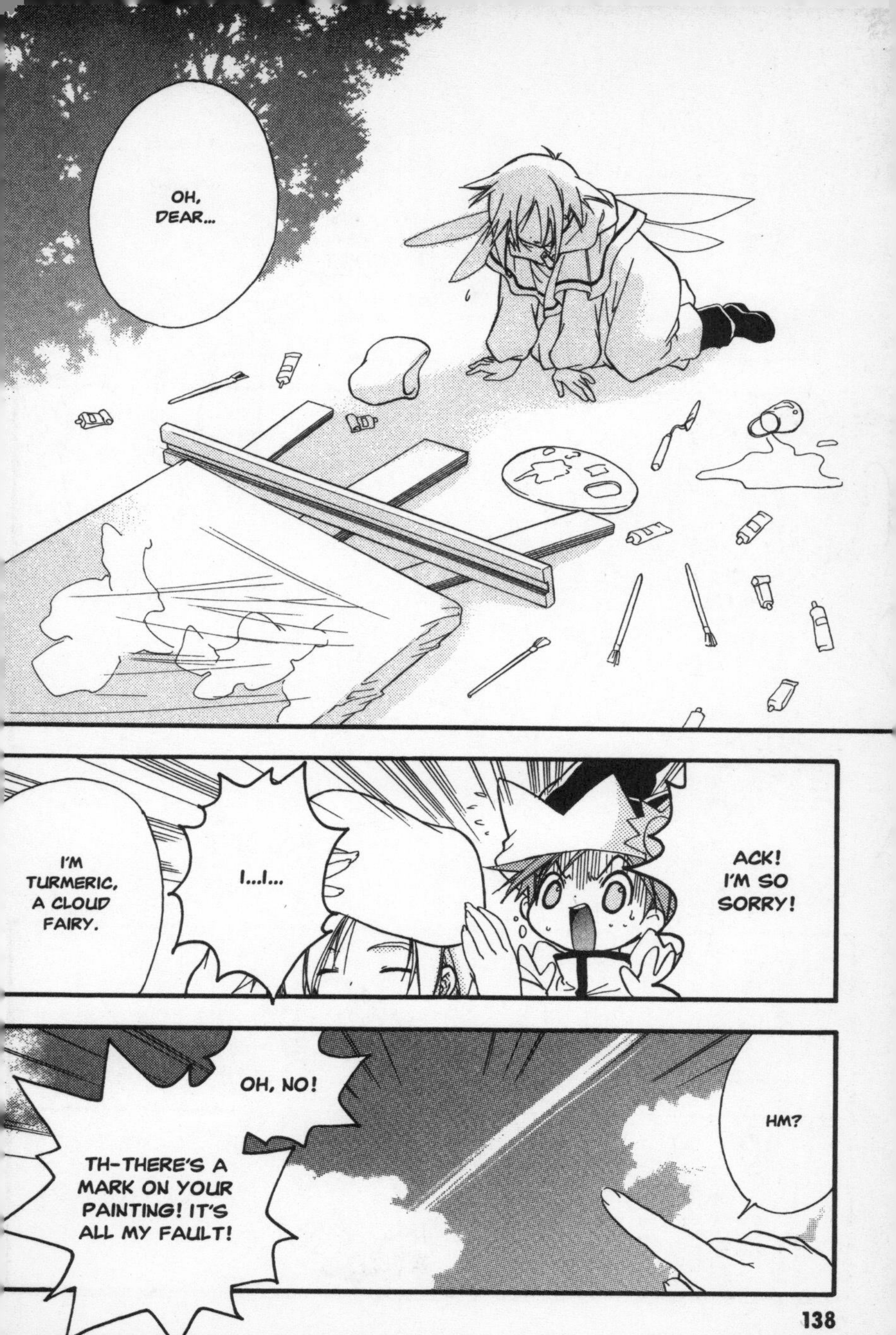

OH, DEAR...
ACK! I'M SO SORRY!
I...I...
I'M TURMERIC, A CLOUD FAIRY.
HM?
OH, NO!
TH-THERE'S A MARK ON YOUR PAINTING! IT'S ALL MY FAULT!

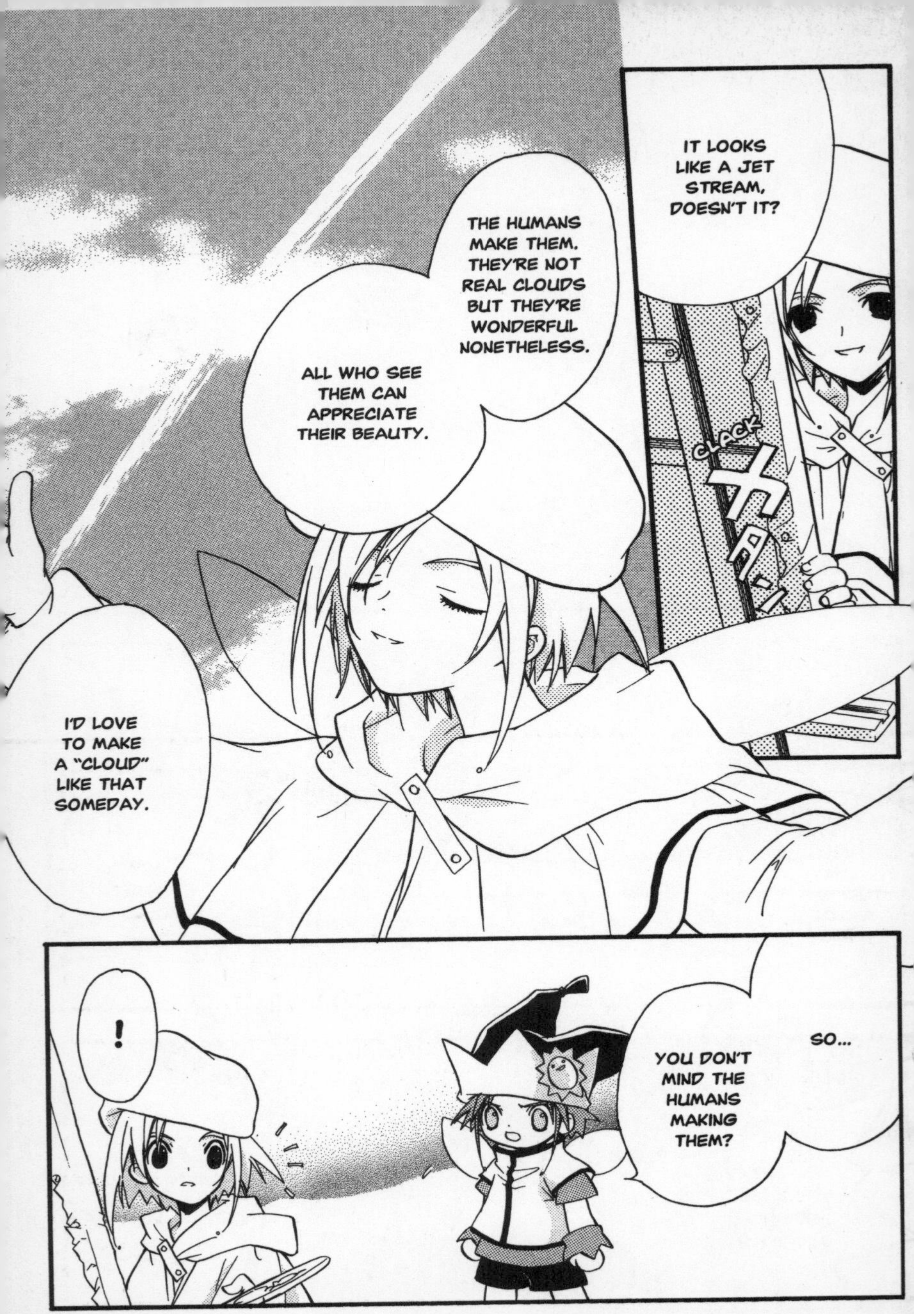
IT LOOKS LIKE A JET STREAM, DOESN'T IT?
CLACK
THE HUMANS MAKE THEM. THEY'RE NOT REAL CLOUDS BUT THEY'RE WONDERFUL NONETHELESS.
ALL WHO SEE THEM CAN APPRECIATE THEIR BEAUTY.
I'D LOVE TO MAKE A "CLOUD" LIKE THAT SOMEDAY.
SO...
YOU DON'T MIND THE HUMANS MAKING THEM?
!

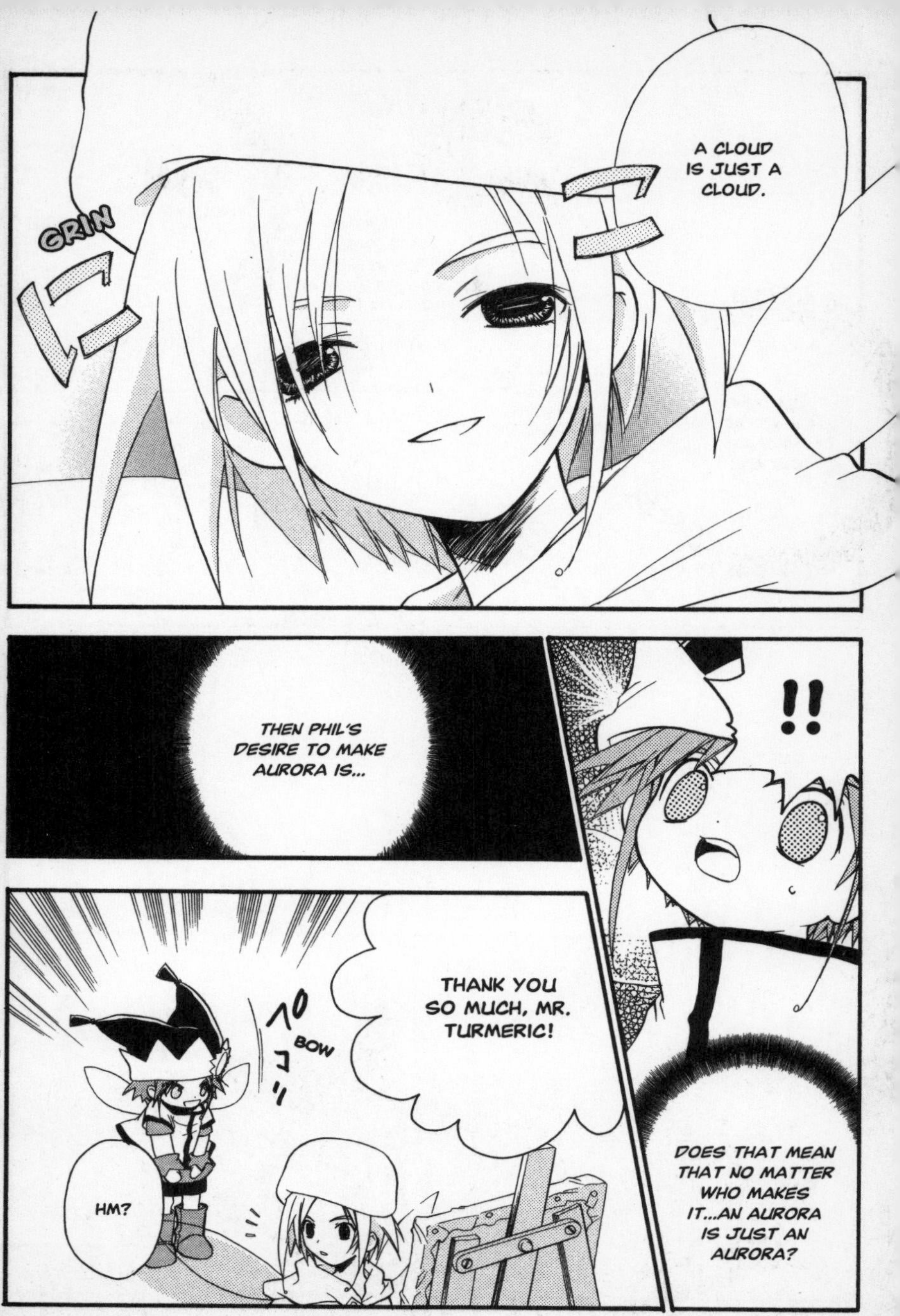
A CLOUD IS JUST A CLOUD.
GRIN
!!
DOES THAT MEAN THAT NO MATTER WHO MAKES IT...AN AURORA IS JUST AN AURORA?
THEN PHIL'S DESIRE TO MAKE AURORA IS...
THANK YOU SO MUCH, MR. TURMERIC!
BOW
HM?

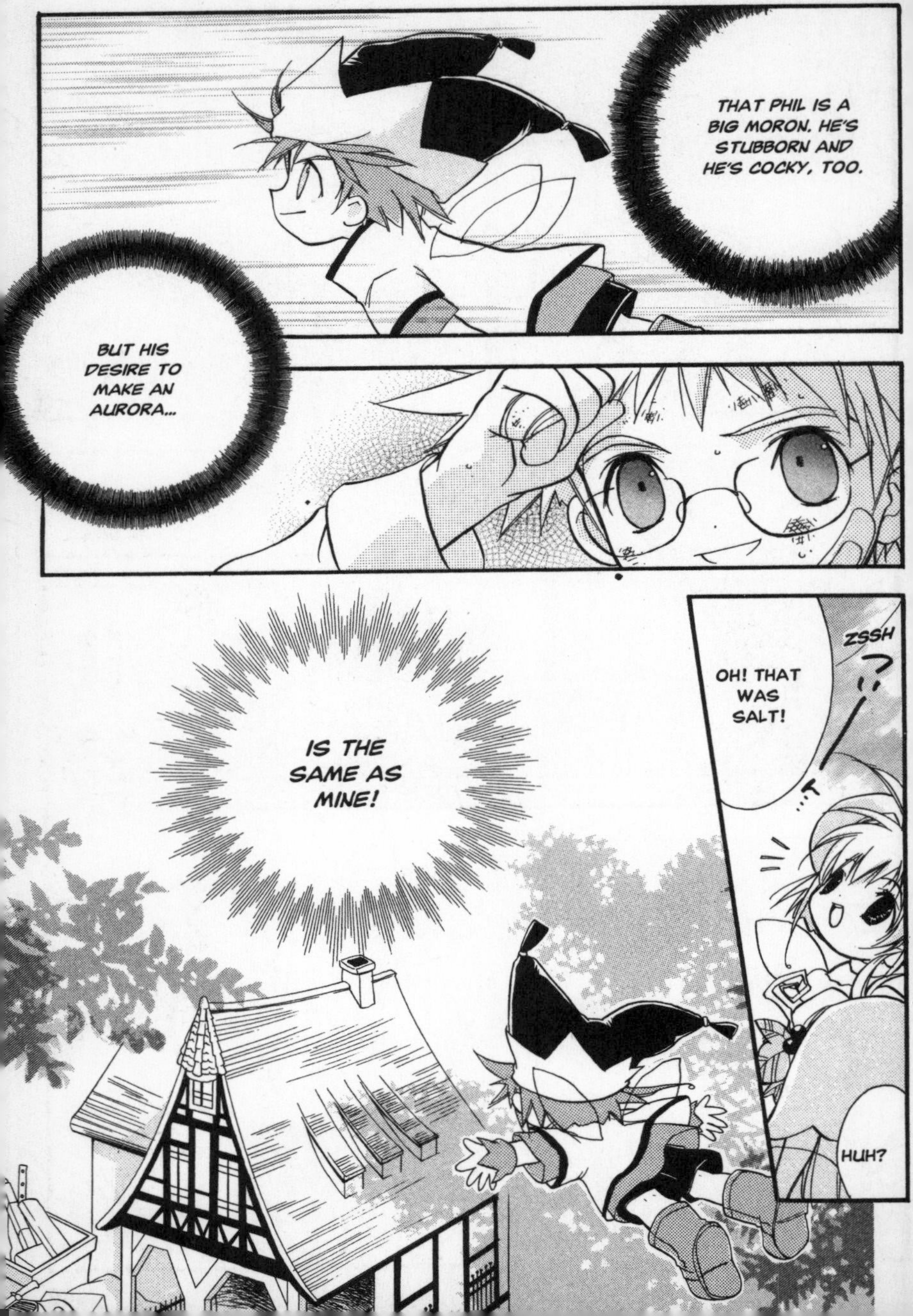
THAT PHIL IS A BIG MORON. HE'S STUBBORN AND HE'S COCKY, TOO.
BUT HIS DESIRE TO MAKE AN AURORA...
IS THE SAME AS MINE!
ZSSH
OH! THAT WAS SALT!
HUH?

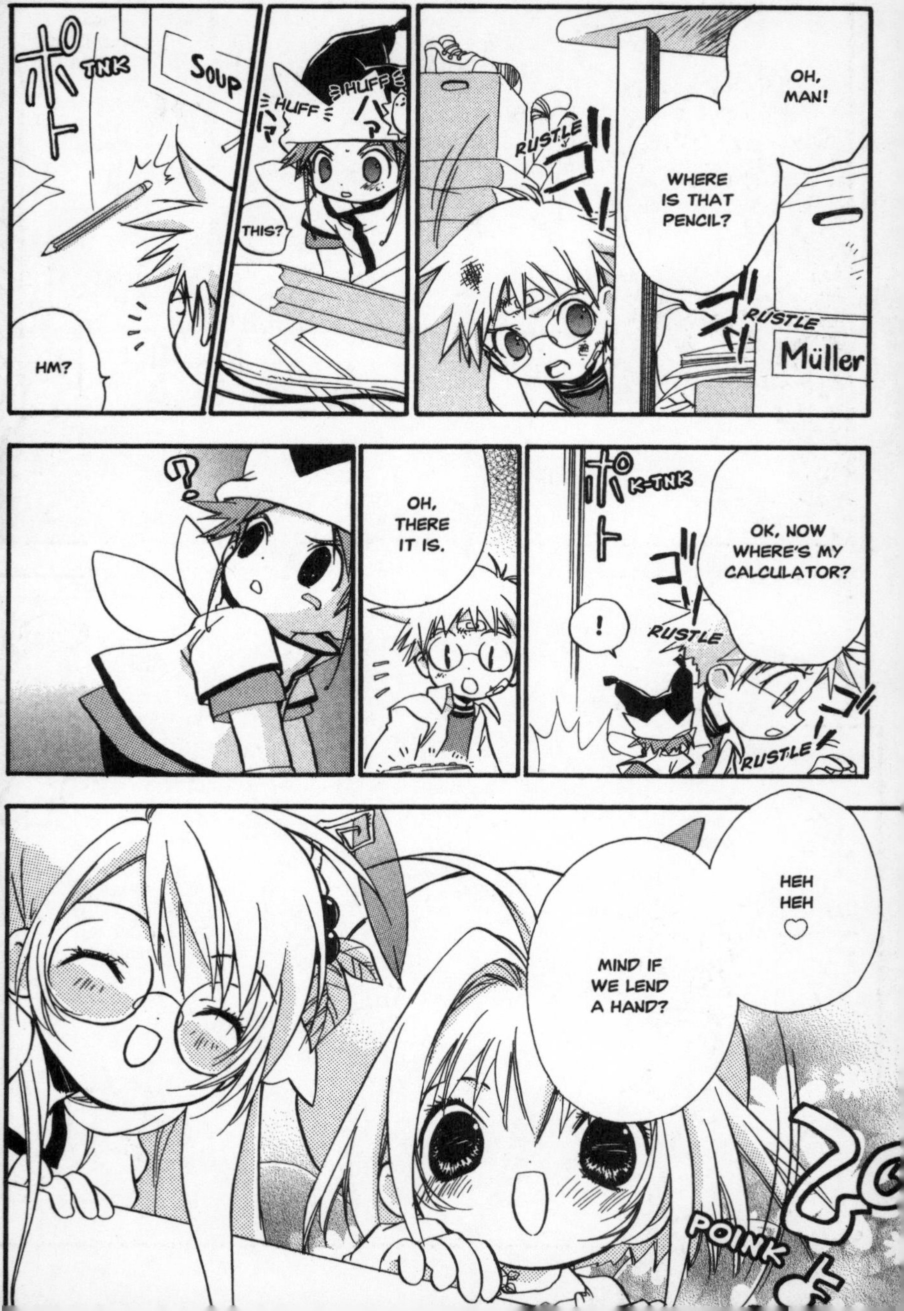

OH, MAN!
WHERE IS THAT PENCIL?
RUSTLE
RUSTLE
Müller
HUFF
HUFF
THIS?
TNK
Soup
HM?
K-TNK
OK, NOW WHERE'S MY CALCULATOR?
!
RUSTLE
RUSTLE
OH, THERE IT IS.
?
HEH HEH ♡
MIND IF WE LEND A HAND?
POINK

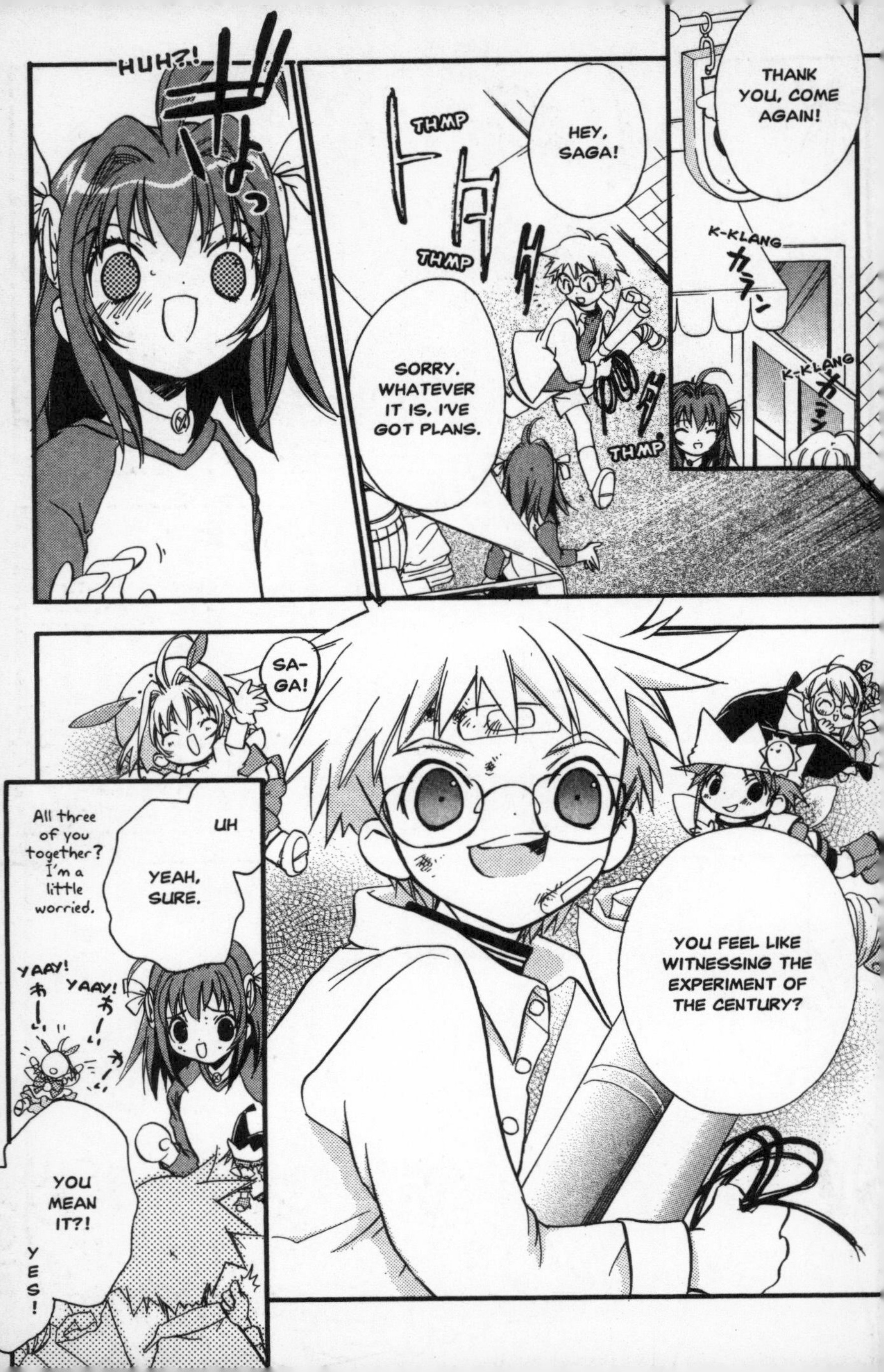
THANK YOU, COME AGAIN!
K-KLANG
カラン
K-KLANG
HEY, SAGA!
THMP
THMP
SORRY. WHATEVER IT IS, I'VE GOT PLANS.
THMP
HUH?!
SA-GA!
YOU FEEL LIKE WITNESSING THE EXPERIMENT OF THE CENTURY?
UH
YEAH, SURE.
All three of you together? I'm a little worried.
YAAY!
YAAY!
YOU MEAN IT?!
YES!

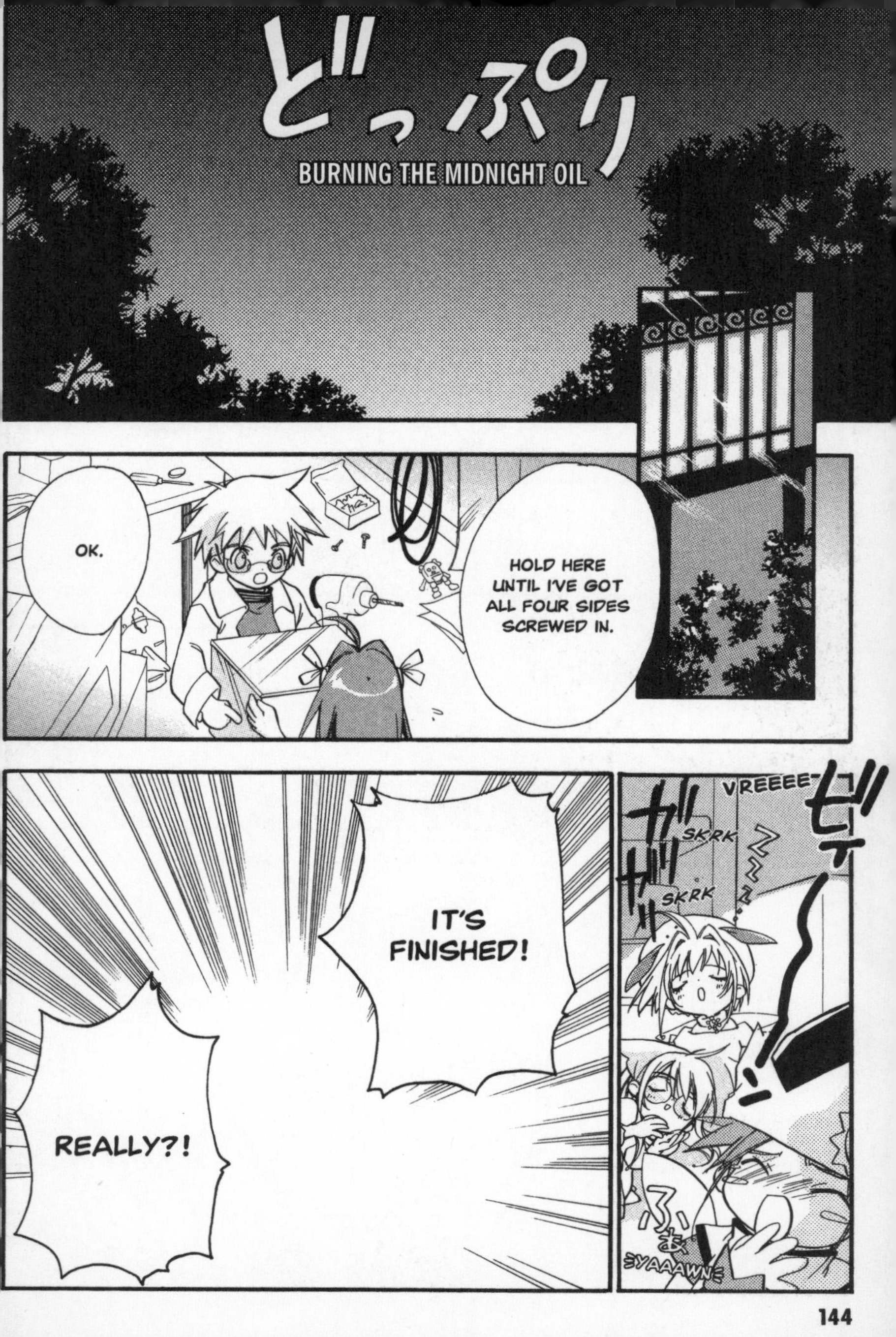
どっぷり
BURNING THE MIDNIGHT OIL
HOLD HERE UNTIL I'VE GOT ALL FOUR SIDES SCREWED IN.
OK.
VREEEE
SKRK
SKRK
YAAAWN
IT'S FINISHED!
REALLY?!

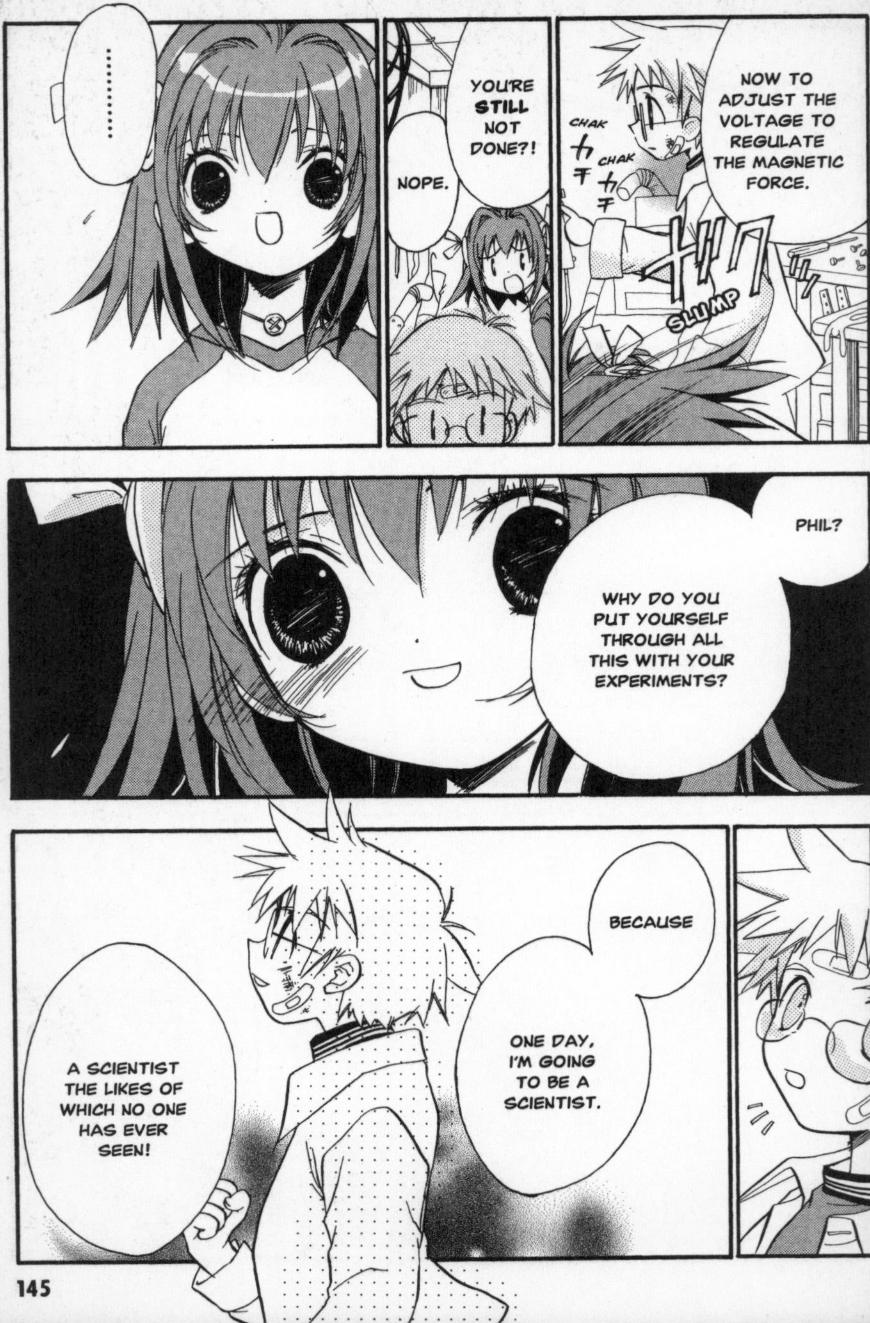
NOW TO ADJUST THE VOLTAGE TO REGULATE THE MAGNETIC FORCE.
CHAK
CHAK
SLUMP
YOU'RE **STILL** NOT DONE?!
NOPE.
......
PHIL?
WHY DO YOU PUT YOURSELF THROUGH ALL THIS WITH YOUR EXPERIMENTS?
BECAUSE
ONE DAY, I'M GOING TO BE A SCIENTIST.
A SCIENTIST THE LIKES OF WHICH NO ONE HAS EVER SEEN!

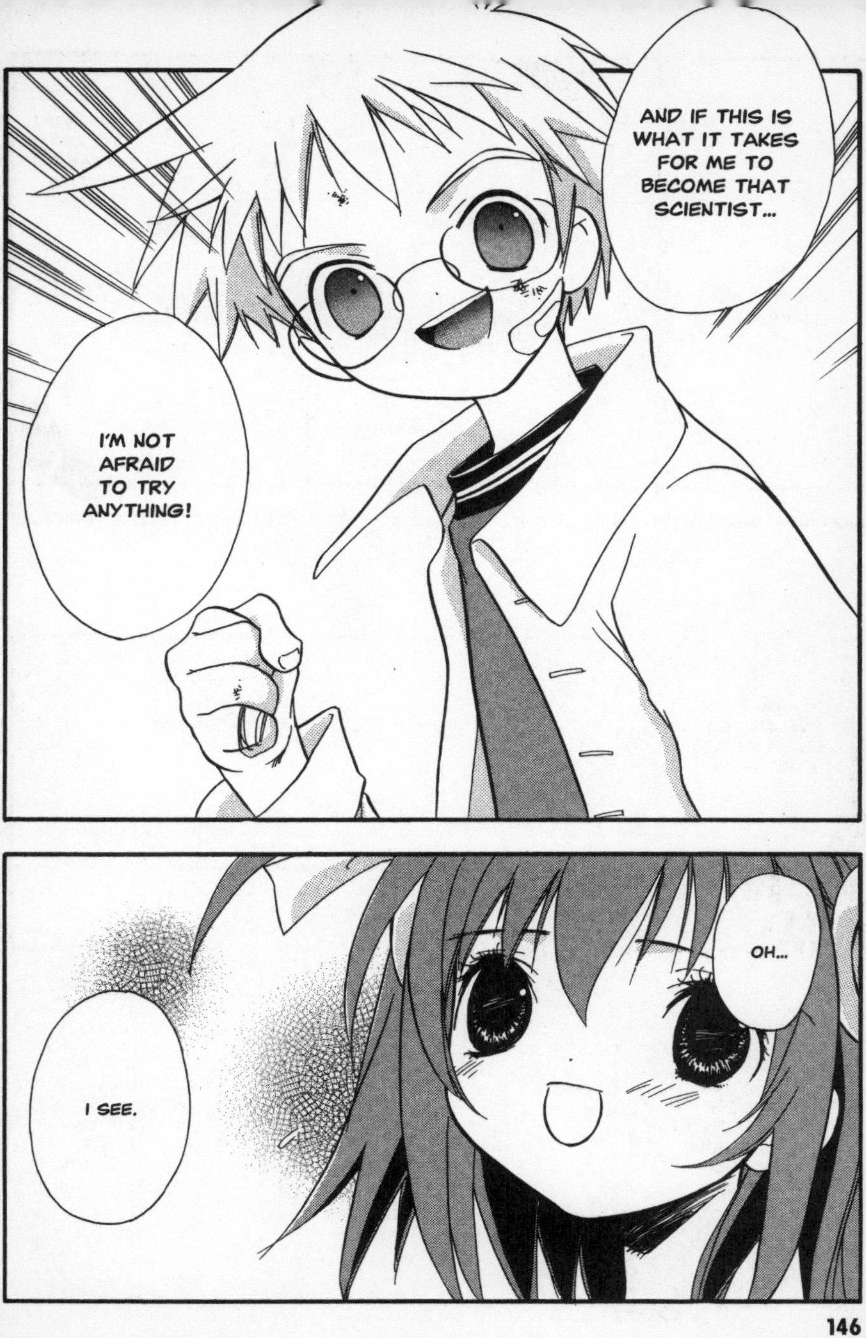
AND IF THIS IS WHAT IT TAKES FOR ME TO BECOME THAT SCIENTIST...
I'M NOT AFRAID TO TRY ANYTHING!
OH...
I SEE.

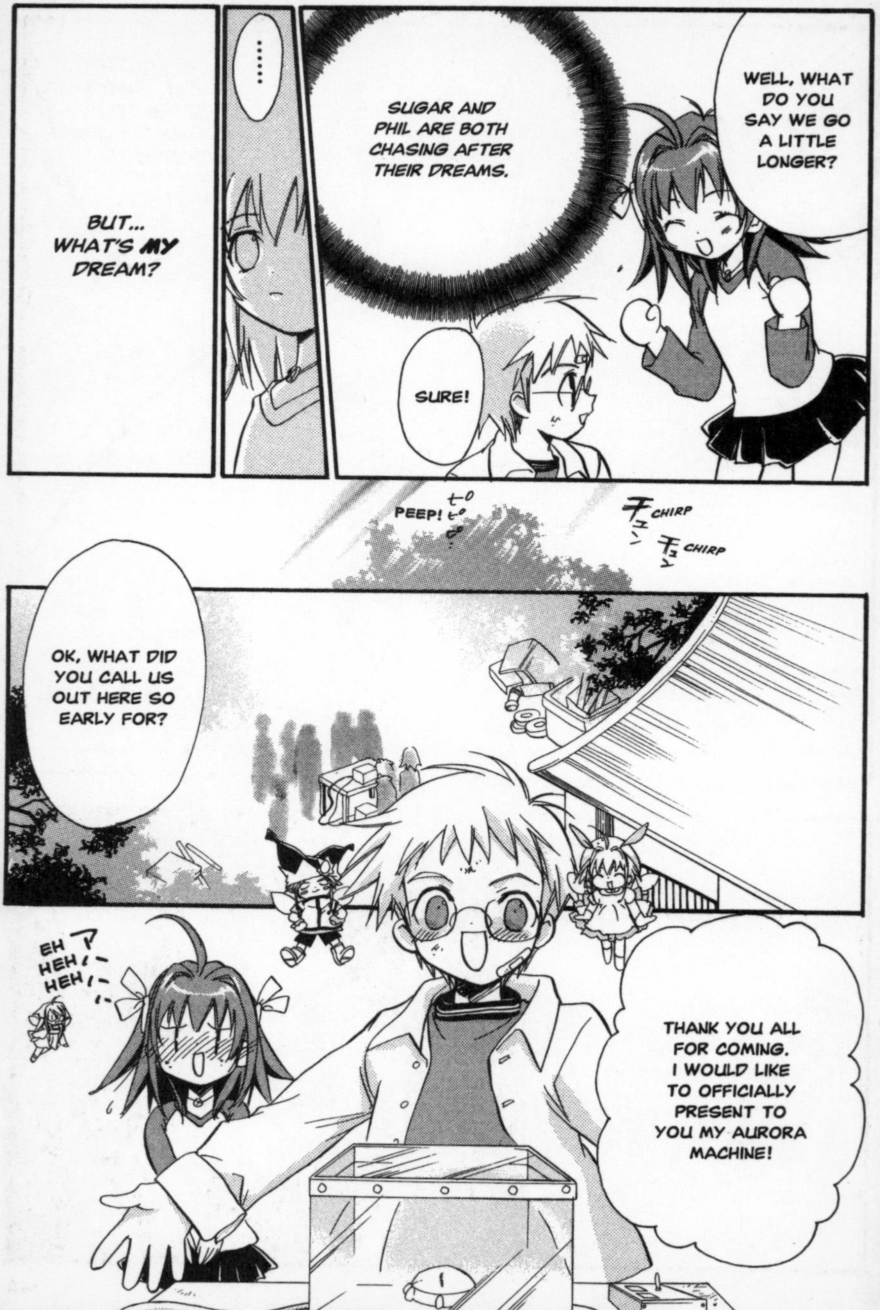

WELL, WHAT DO YOU SAY WE GO A LITTLE LONGER?
SUGAR AND PHIL ARE BOTH CHASING AFTER THEIR DREAMS.
SURE!
……
BUT... WHAT'S MY DREAM?
CHIRP
CHIRP
PEEP!
OK, WHAT DID YOU CALL US OUT HERE SO EARLY FOR?
THANK YOU ALL FOR COMING. I WOULD LIKE TO OFFICIALLY PRESENT TO YOU MY AURORA MACHINE!
EH HEH HEH

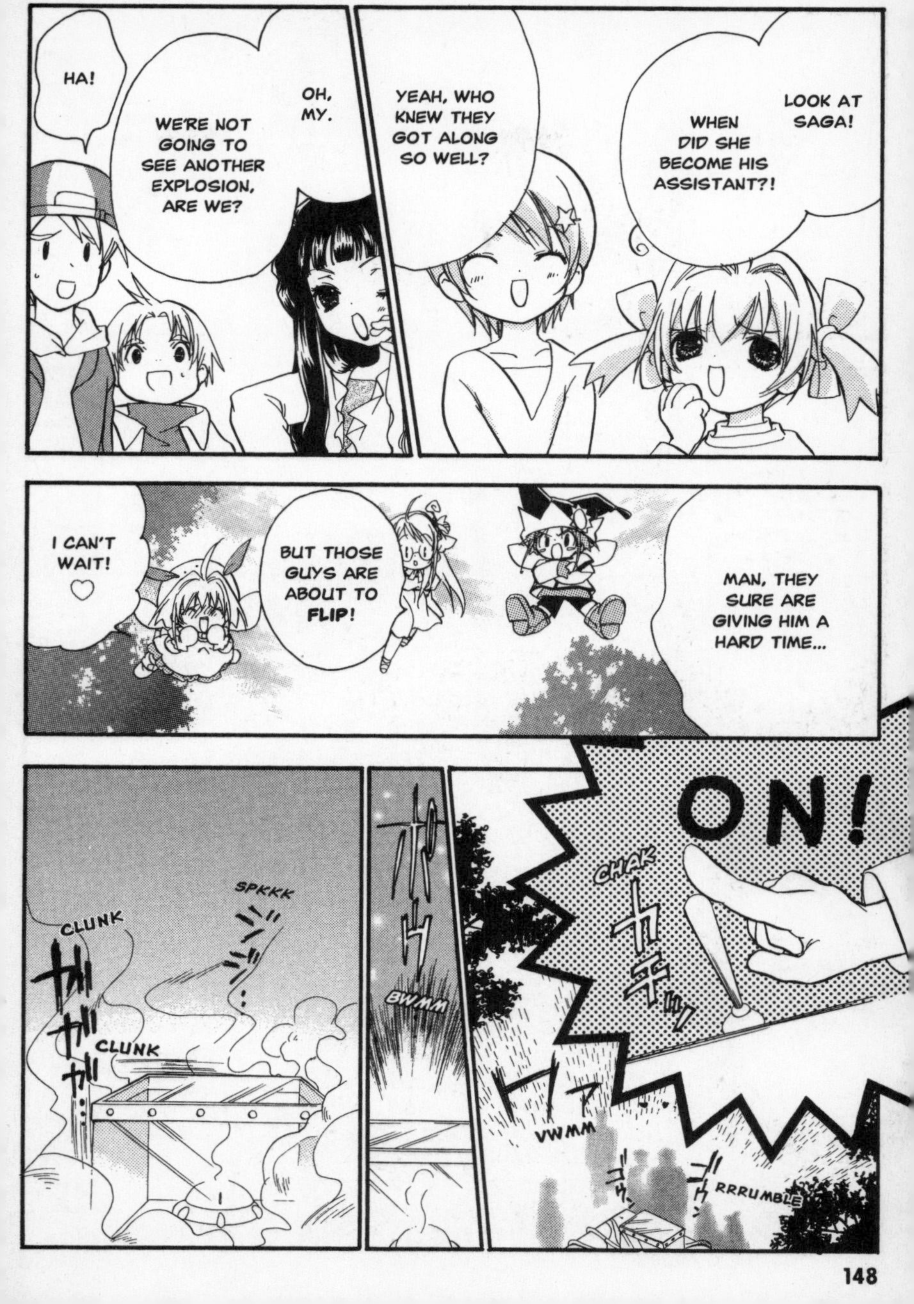

LOOK AT SAGA!
WHEN DID SHE BECOME HIS ASSISTANT?!
YEAH, WHO KNEW THEY GOT ALONG SO WELL?
OH, MY.
WE'RE NOT GOING TO SEE ANOTHER EXPLOSION, ARE WE?
HA!
MAN, THEY SURE ARE GIVING HIM A HARD TIME...
BUT THOSE GUYS ARE ABOUT TO FLIP!
I CAN'T WAIT! ♡
ON!
CHAK
VWMM
RRRUMBLE
BWMM
SPKKK
CLUNK
CLUNK

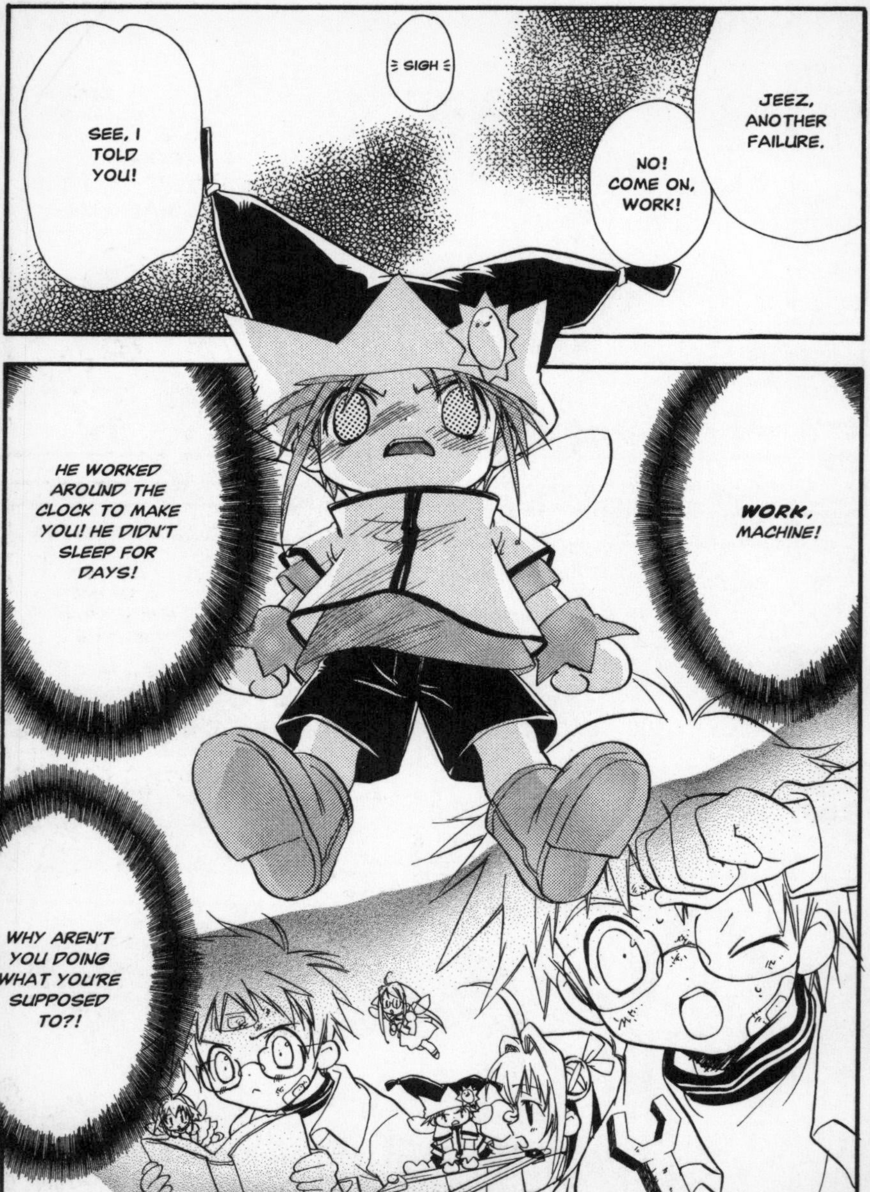
JEEZ, ANOTHER FAILURE.
NO! COME ON, WORK!
SIGH
SEE, I TOLD YOU!
WORK, MACHINE!
HE WORKED AROUND THE CLOCK TO MAKE YOU! HE DIDN'T SLEEP FOR DAYS!
WHY AREN'T YOU DOING WHAT YOU'RE SUPPOSED TO?!

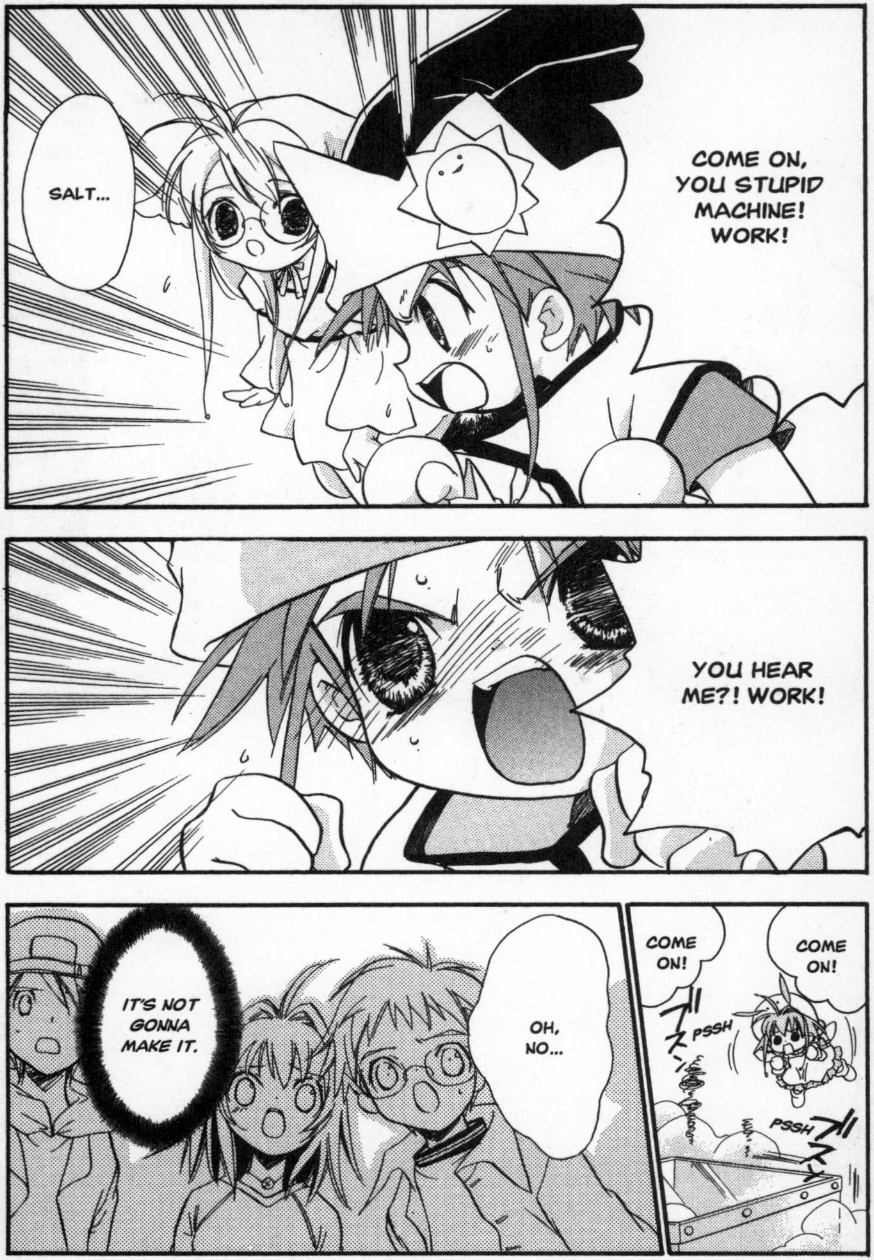
COME ON, YOU STUPID MACHINE! WORK!
SALT...
YOU HEAR ME?! WORK!
COME ON!
COME ON!
PSSH
PSSH
OH, NO...
IT'S NOT GONNA MAKE IT.

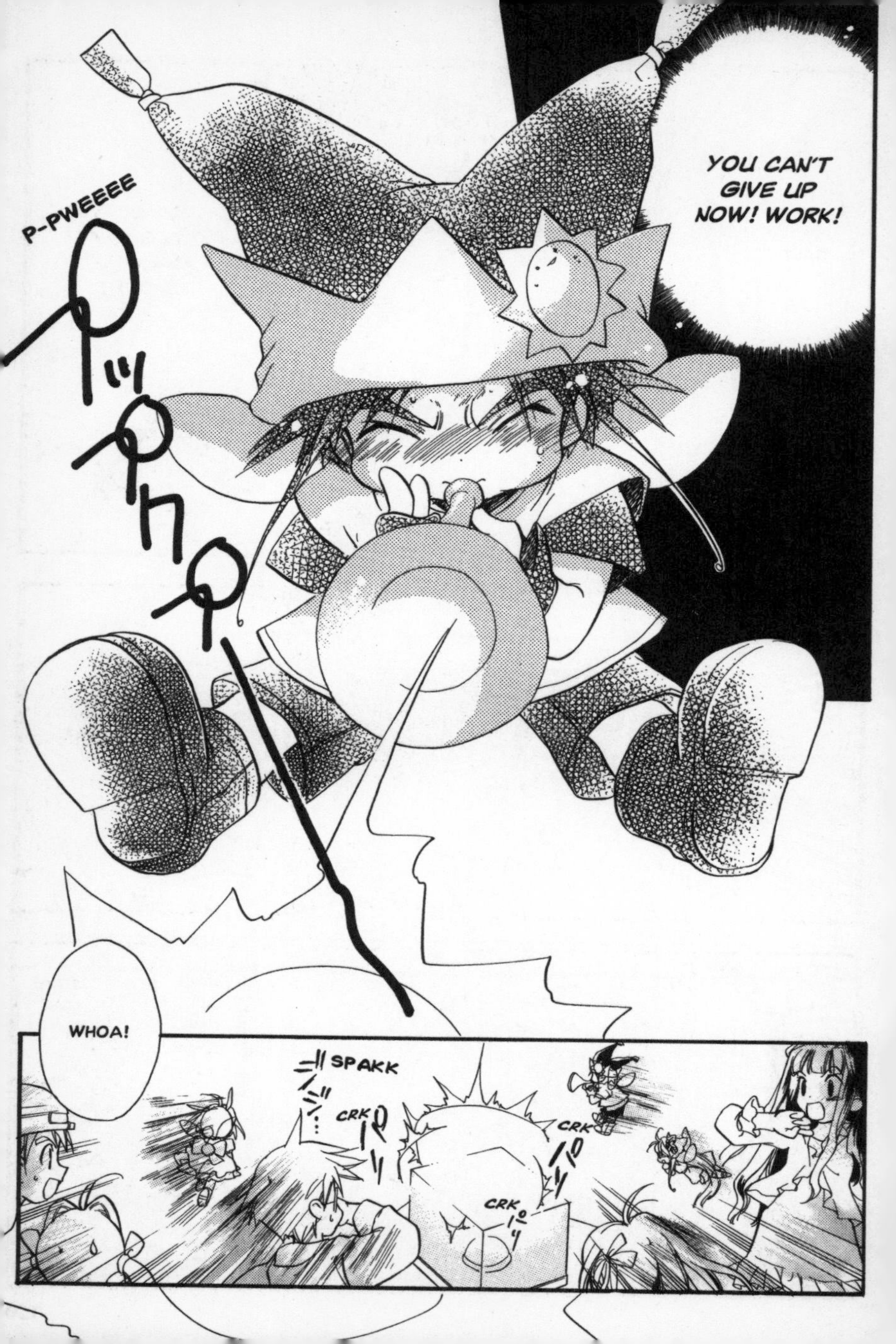
YOU CAN'T GIVE UP NOW! WORK!
P-PWEEEE
WHOA!
CRK
SPAKK
CRK
CRK

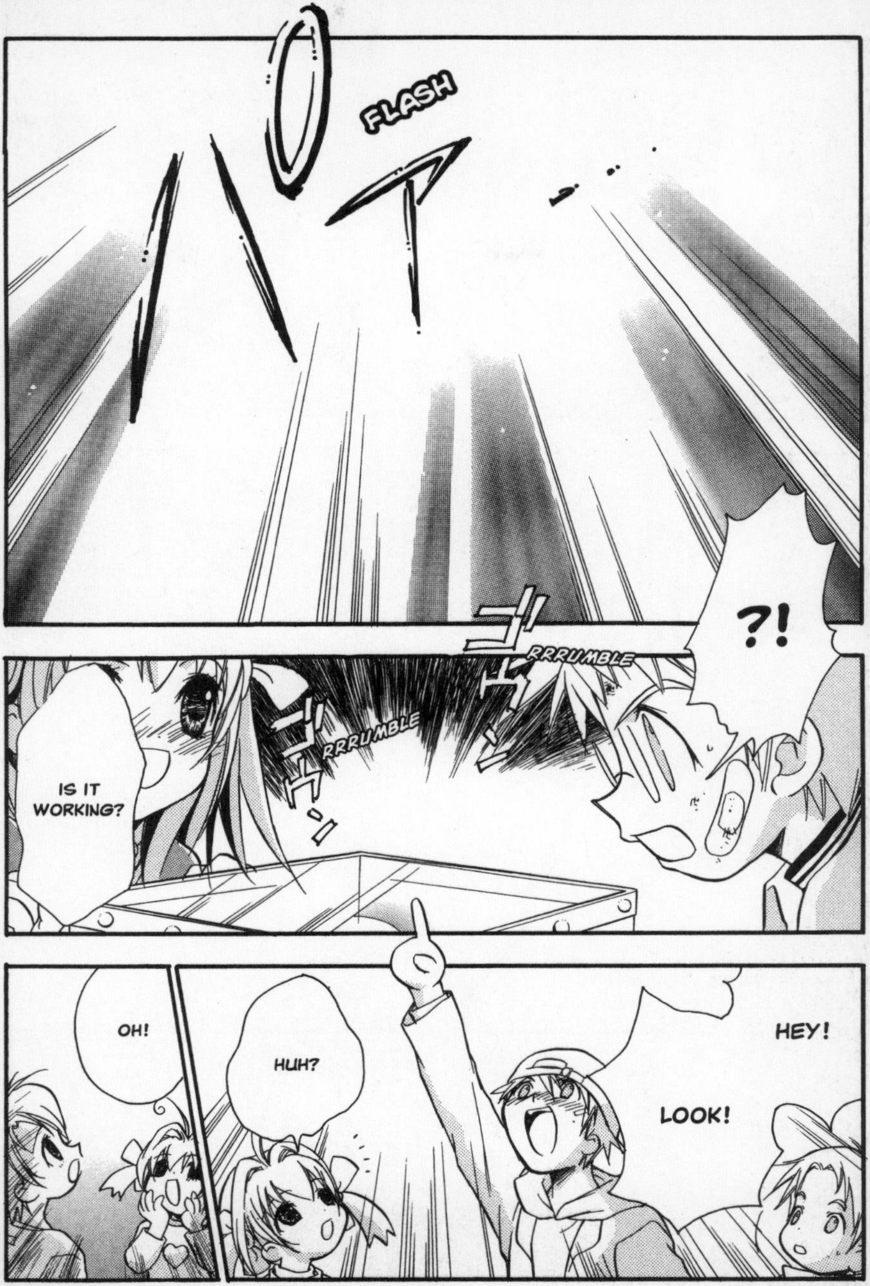
FLASH
?!
RRRUMBLE
RRRUMBLE
IS IT WORKING?
HEY!
LOOK!
HUH?
OH!

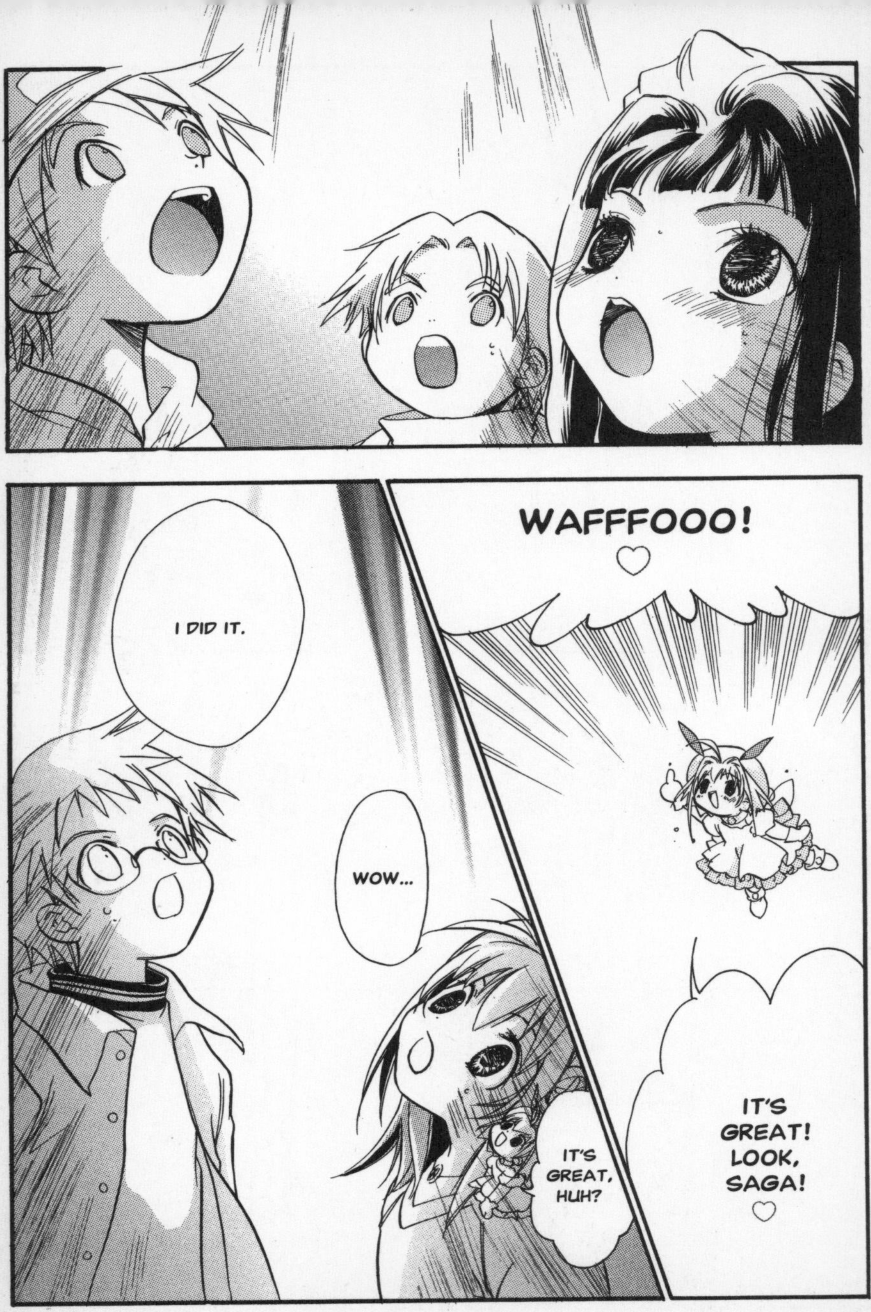
WAFFFOOO! ♡
IT'S GREAT! LOOK, SAGA! ♡
I DID IT.
WOW...
IT'S GREAT, HUH?

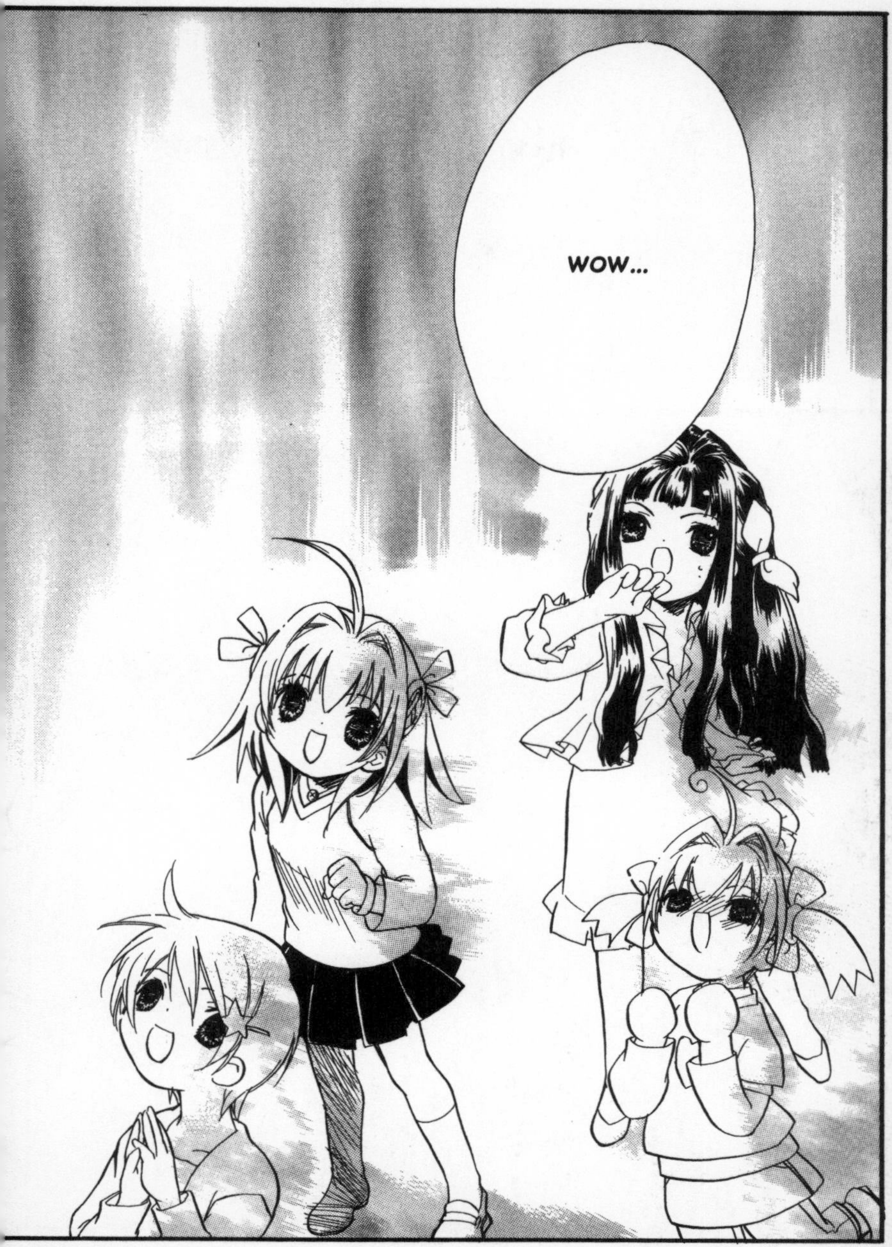
WOW...

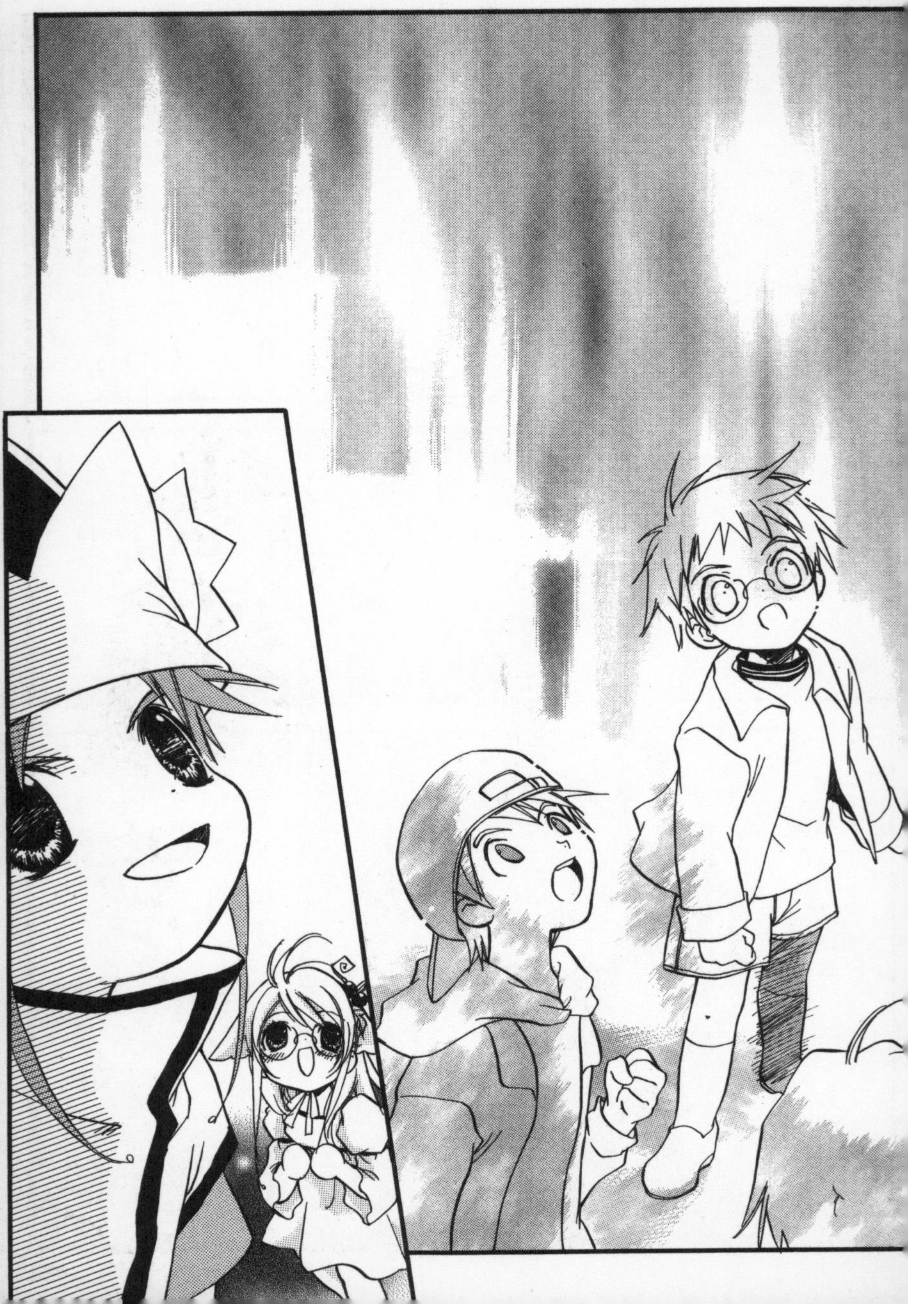

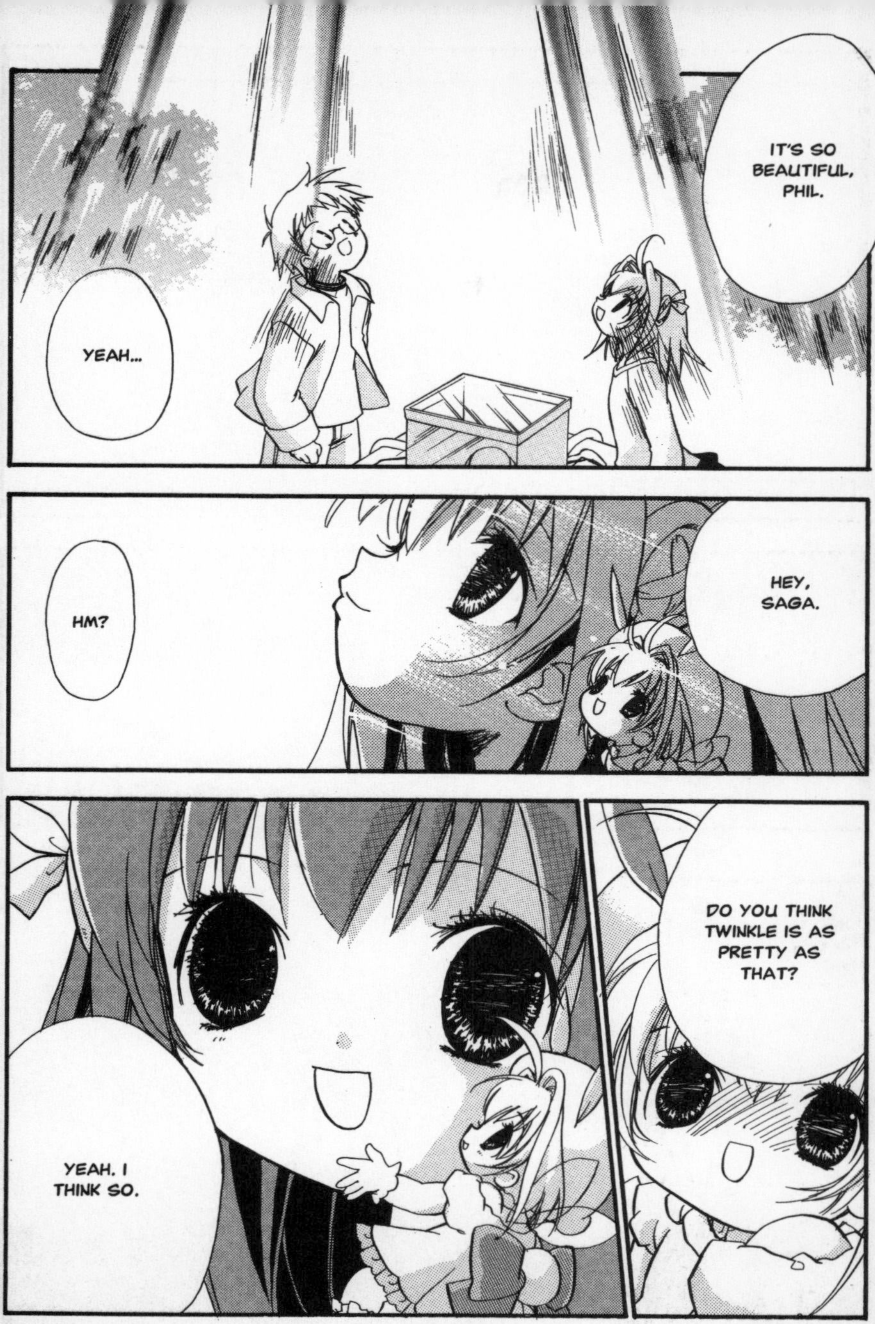
IT'S SO BEAUTIFUL, PHIL.
YEAH...
HEY, SAGA.
HM?
DO YOU THINK TWINKLE IS AS PRETTY AS THAT?
YEAH. I THINK SO.

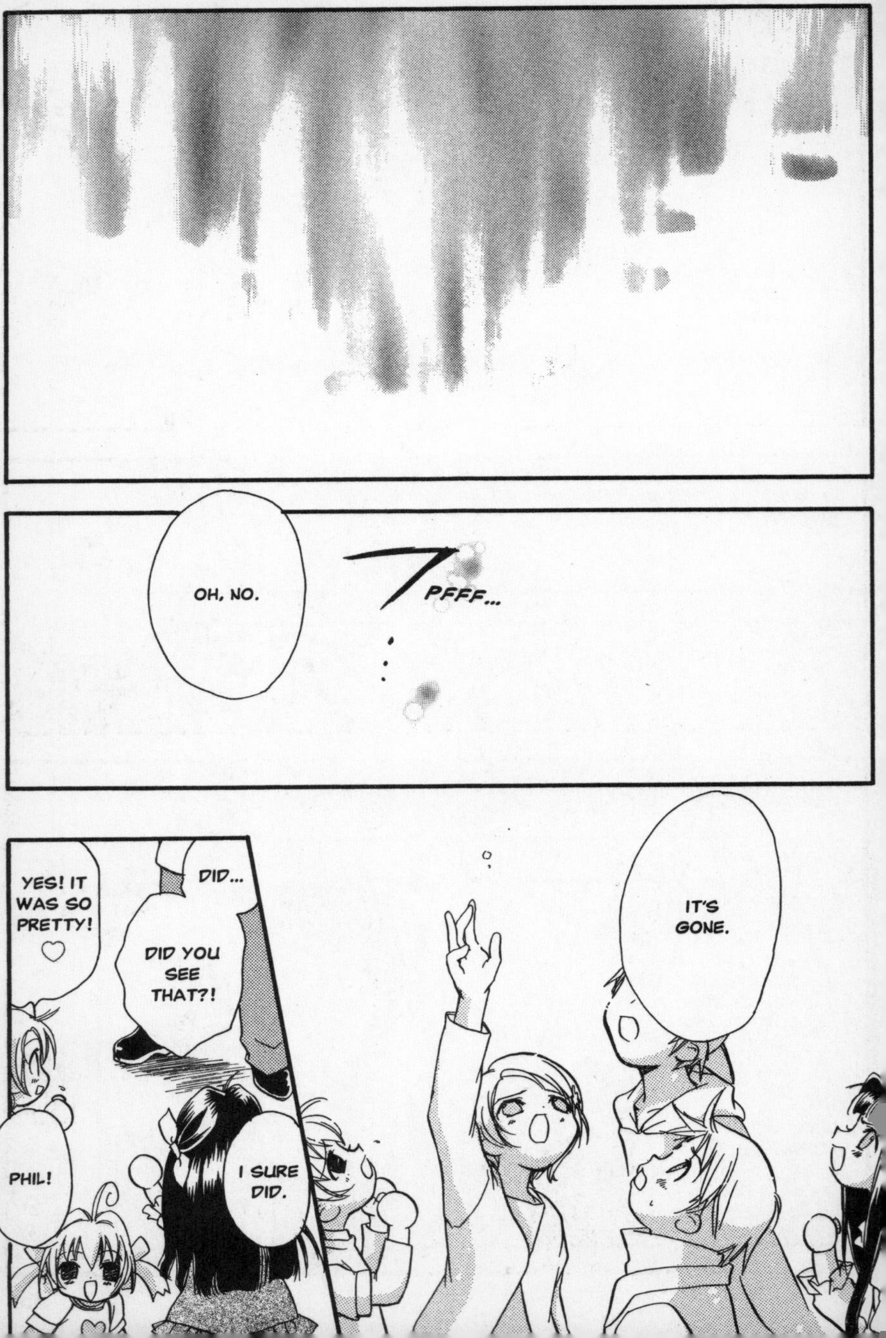
PFFF...
OH, NO.
IT'S GONE.
I SURE DID.
DID...
DID YOU SEE THAT?!
YES! IT WAS SO PRETTY! ♡
PHIL!

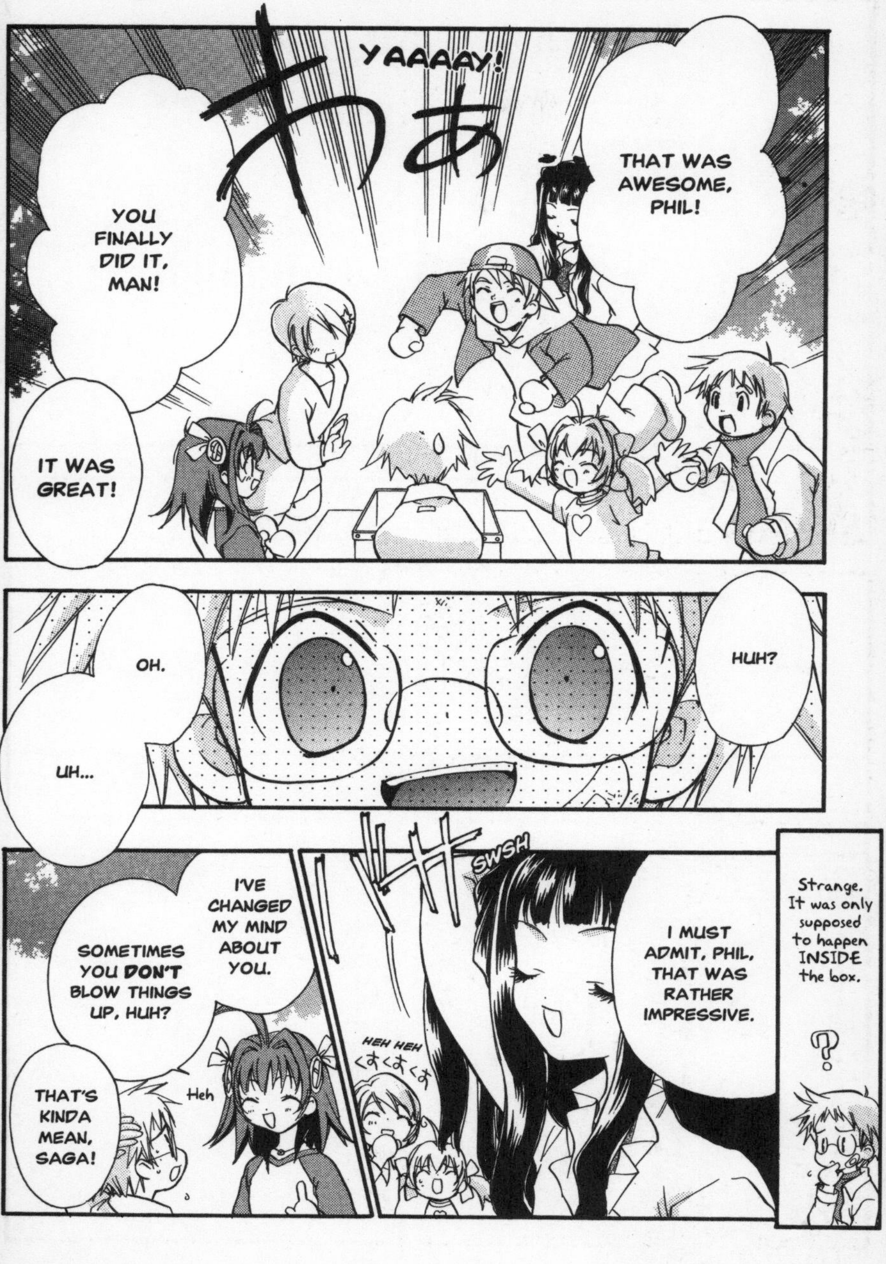
THAT WAS AWESOME, PHIL!
YAAAAY!
わあ
YOU FINALLY DID IT, MAN!
IT WAS GREAT!
HUH?
OH.
UH...
Strange. It was only supposed to happen INSIDE the box.
?
SWSH
I MUST ADMIT, PHIL, THAT WAS RATHER IMPRESSIVE.
HEH HEH
くすくすくす
I'VE CHANGED MY MIND ABOUT YOU.
SOMETIMES YOU **DON'T** BLOW THINGS UP, HUH?
Heh
THAT'S KINDA MEAN, SAGA!

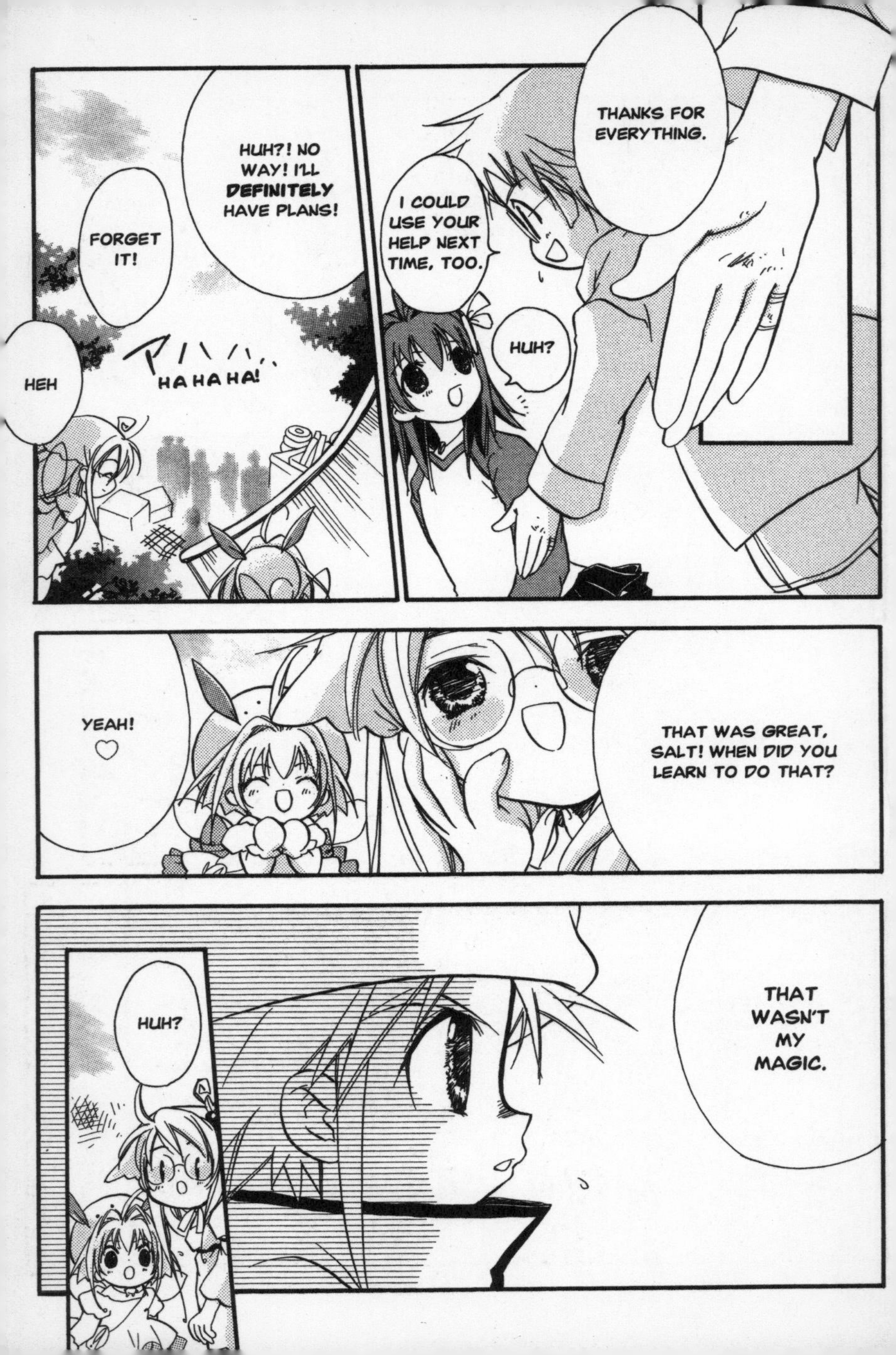
THANKS FOR EVERYTHING.
I COULD USE YOUR HELP NEXT TIME, TOO.
HUH?
HUH?! NO WAY! I'LL **DEFINITELY** HAVE PLANS!
FORGET IT!
HEH
アハハ..
HAHAHA!
THAT WAS GREAT, SALT! WHEN DID YOU LEARN TO DO THAT?
YEAH! ♡
THAT WASN'T MY MAGIC.
HUH?

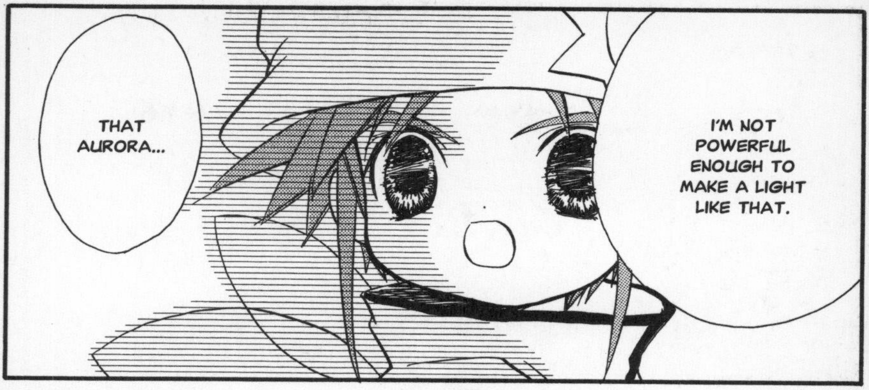
I'M NOT POWERFUL ENOUGH TO MAKE A LIGHT LIKE THAT.
THAT AURORA...

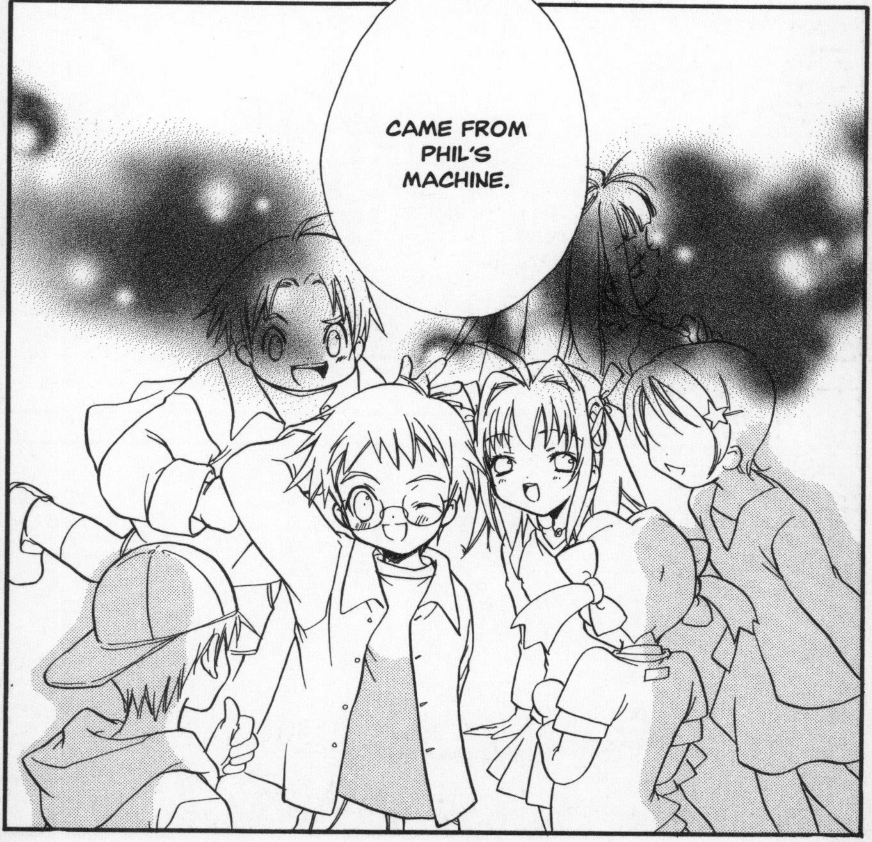
CAME FROM PHIL'S MACHINE.

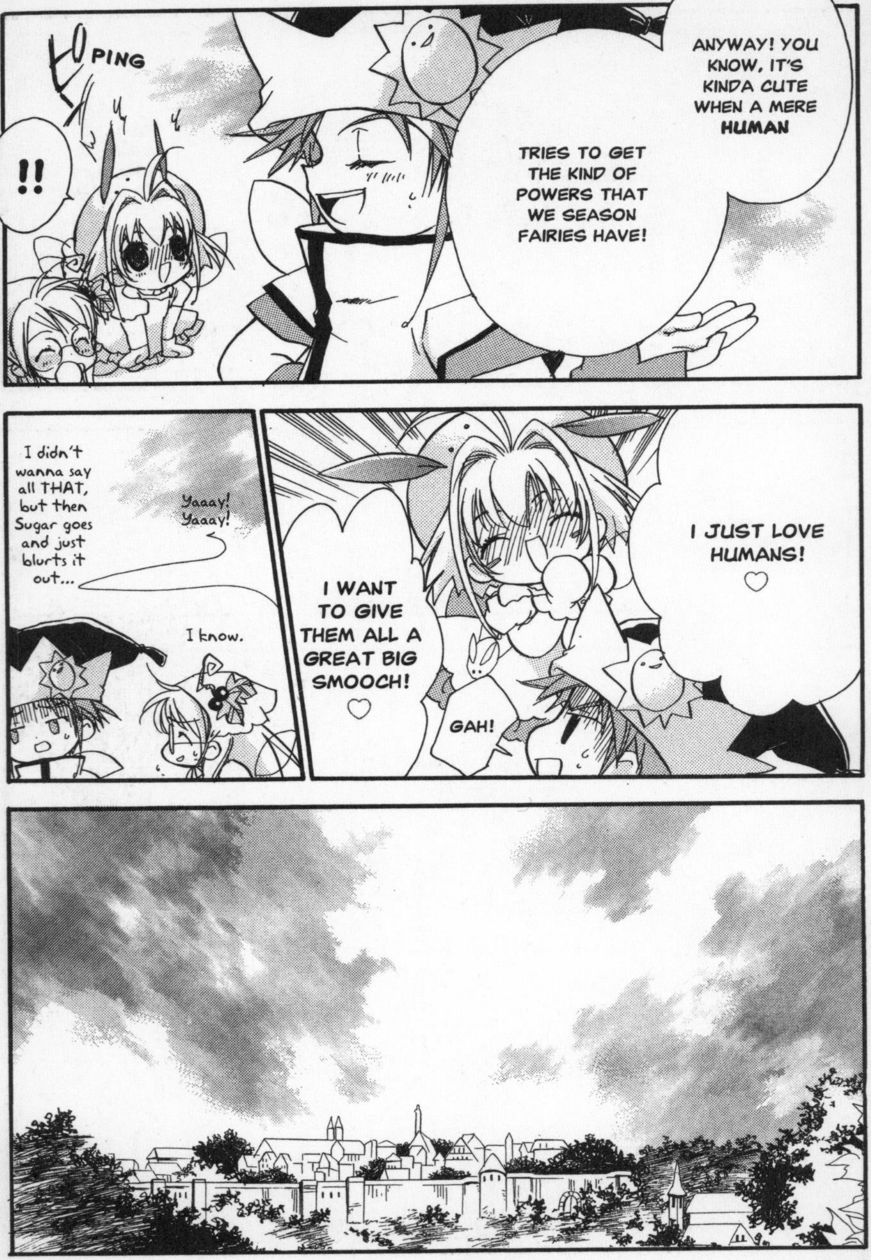
ANYWAY! YOU KNOW, IT'S KINDA CUTE WHEN A MERE HUMAN
TRIES TO GET THE KIND OF POWERS THAT WE SEASON FAIRIES HAVE!
PING
!!
I JUST LOVE HUMANS! ♡
I WANT TO GIVE THEM ALL A GREAT BIG SMOOCH! ♡
GAH!
I didn't wanna say all THAT, but then Sugar goes and just blurts it out...
Yaaay! Yaaay!
I know.

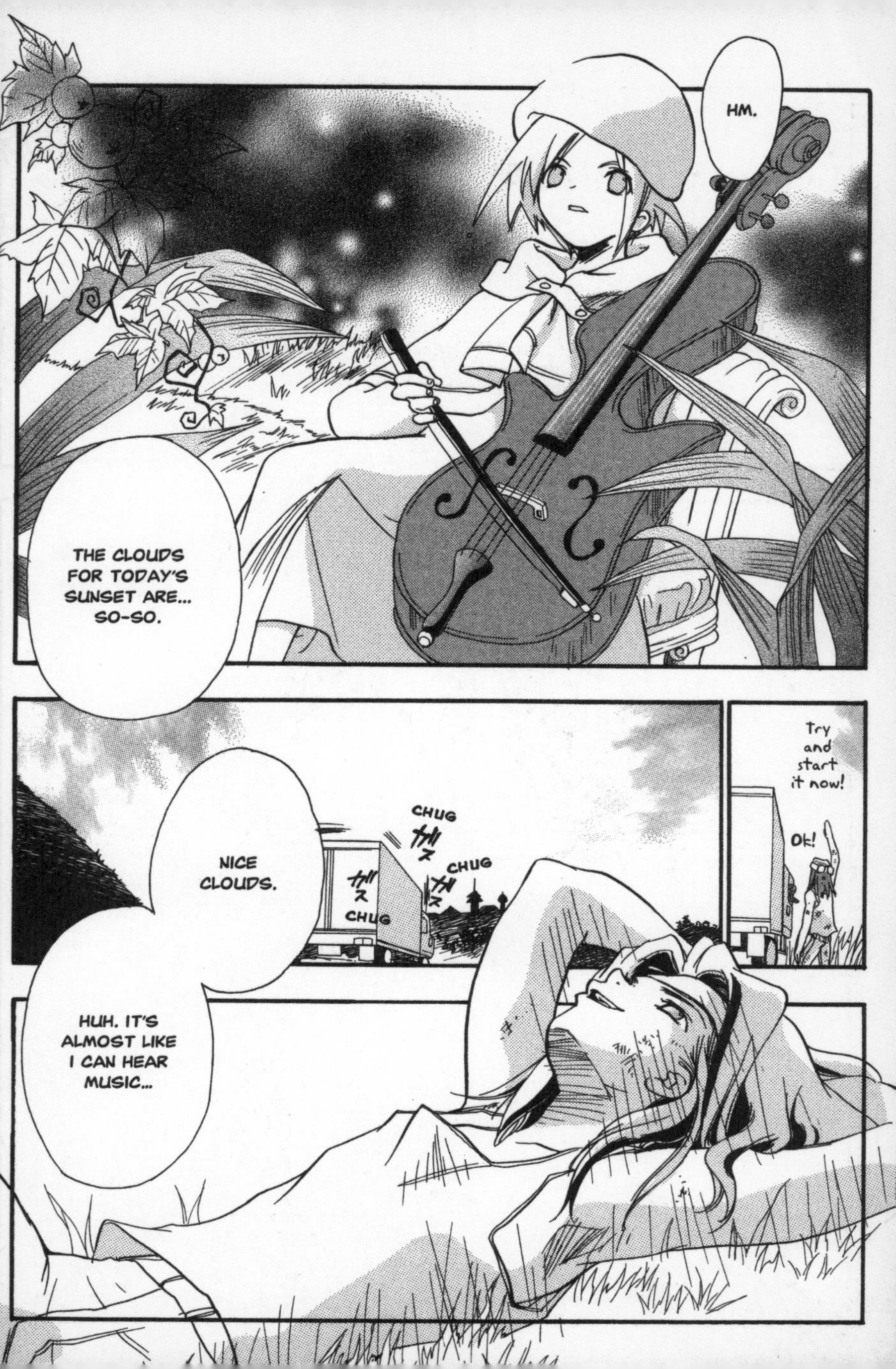
HM.
THE CLOUDS FOR TODAY'S SUNSET ARE... SO-SO.
Try and start it now!
Ok!
NICE CLOUDS.
CHUG
CHUG
CHUG
HUH. IT'S ALMOST LIKE I CAN HEAR MUSIC...

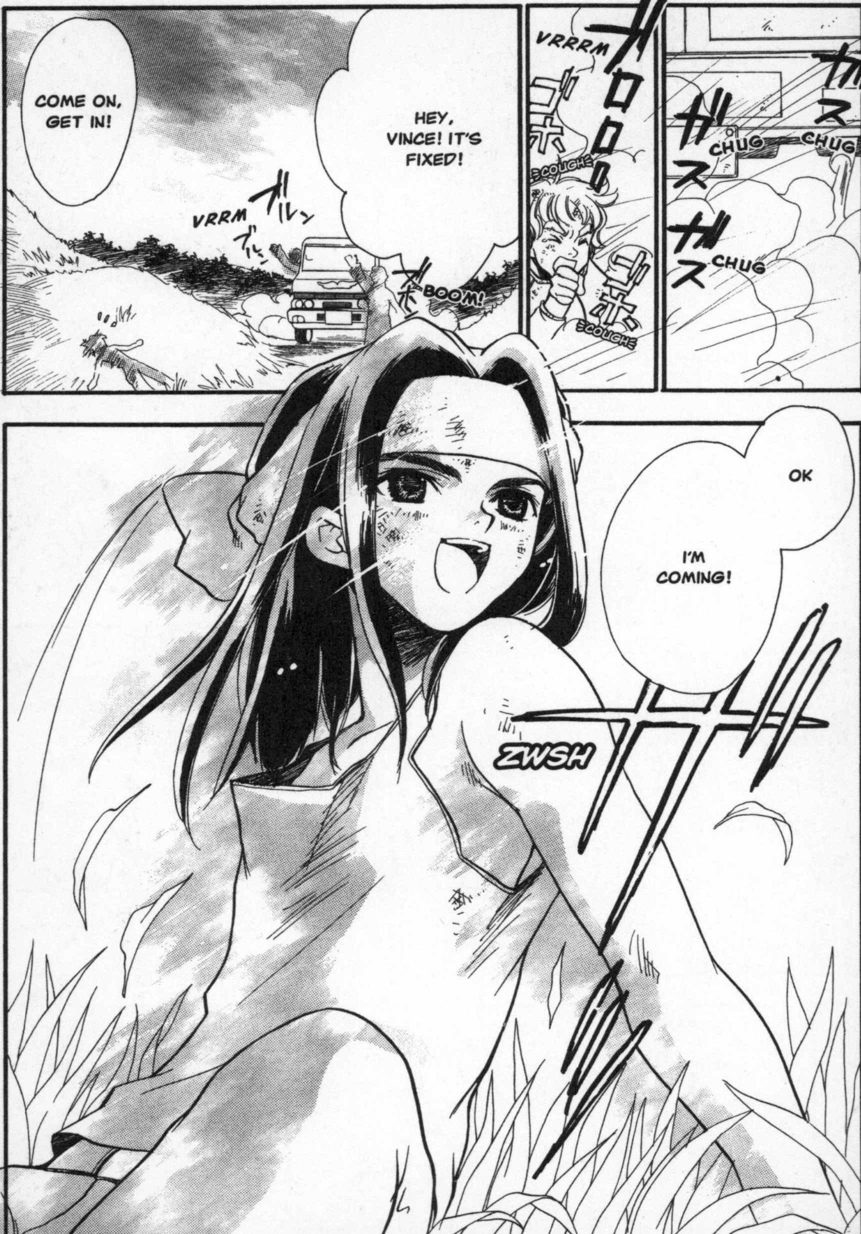
CHUG
CHUG
CHUG
VRRRM
COUGH
COUGH
HEY, VINCE! IT'S FIXED!
COME ON, GET IN!
VRRM
BOOM!
OK
I'M COMING!
ZWSH

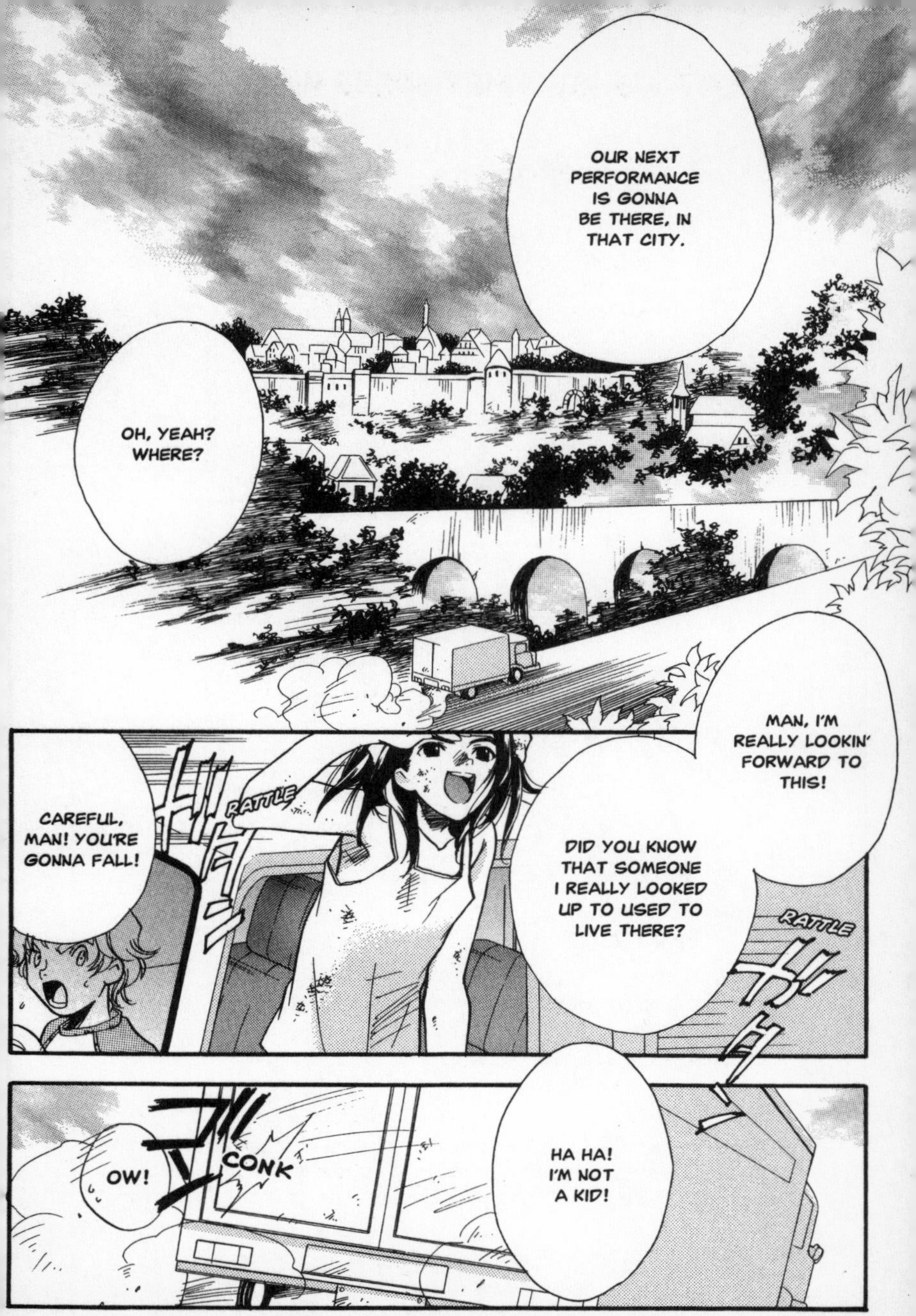
OUR NEXT PERFORMANCE IS GONNA BE THERE, IN THAT CITY.
OH, YEAH? WHERE?
MAN, I'M REALLY LOOKIN' FORWARD TO THIS!
DID YOU KNOW THAT SOMEONE I REALLY LOOKED UP TO USED TO LIVE THERE?
RATTLE
RATTLE
CAREFUL, MAN! YOU'RE GONNA FALL!
HA HA! I'M NOT A KID!
CONK
OW!

A Little Snow Fairy Sugar / To Be Continued in Volume 2

A LITTLE SNOW FAIRY SUGAR VOLUME ONE

© 2001 HARUKA AOI/TBS
© 2001 BH SNOW + CLINIC
Originally published in Japan in 2001 by
KADOKAWA SHOTEN PUBLISHING CO., LTD., Tokyo.
English translation rights arranged with
KADOKAWA SHOTEN PUBLISHING CO., LTD., Tokyo.

Editor **JAVIER LOPEZ**
Translator **KAORU BERTRAND**
Graphic Artist **SCOTT HOWARD**

Editorial Director **GARY STEINMAN**
Creative Director **JASON BABLER**
Print Production Manager **BRIDGETT JANOTA**
Production Coordinator **MARISA KREITZ**

International Coordinators **TORU IWAKAMI & MIYUKI KAMIYA**

President, CEO & Publisher **JOHN LEDFORD**

Email: editor@adv-manga.com
www.adv-manga.com

www.advfilms.com

For sales and distribution inquiries please call 1.800.282.7202

ADV ™
MANGA
is a division of A.D. Vision, Inc.
5750 Bintliff Drive, Suite 210, Houston, Texas 77036

English text © 2006 published by A.D. Vision, Inc. under exclusive license.
ADV MANGA is a trademark of A.D. Vision, Inc.

ISBN: 1-4139-0333-9
First printing, August 2006
10 9 8 7 6 5 4 3 2 1
Printed in Canada

TRANSLATOR'S NOTES

A Little Snow Fairy Sugar

P. 6 **1) Guttenburg**

While the anime version of *A Little Snow Fairy Sugar* is set in Mühlenburg, the manga version chose Guttenburg as its setting.

2) *Morgen*

Short for *guten morgen*, or "Good morning."

P. 13 **DM**

The sign in the shop window uses the denomination DM, which is short for deutschemark, Germany's former currency. The deutschemark was rendered obsolete with the introduction of the Euro in 1999, and phased out entirely in 2002.

P. 21 **Waffo!**

When Sugar becomes overly pleased about something, she tends to exclaim "waffo!", a slightly muffled version of the Japanese equivalent of "yippee." (Some have opined that waffo is a corruption of "waffle," Sugar's favorite snack, but in fact she exclaimed "waffo!" before she ever knew what waffles were called.)

P. 25 **Season Fairy**

While *kisetsu-tsukai*, the Japanese term for Season Fairy, does indeed include the word for "season," the names of the fairies are those of *seasonings*, such as salt, basil, pepper and turmeric.

P. 87 **Nördlingen**

The musical score written by Saga's mother bears the name of a town in Bavaria, Germany. Nördlingen is also sometimes referred to as the "Romantic Road."

P. 142 **Soup**

For some inexplicable reason, Phil seems to have amassed boxes of *Leberknödelsuppe*, a liver-dumpling soup flavored with onion, garic, parsely and marjoram.

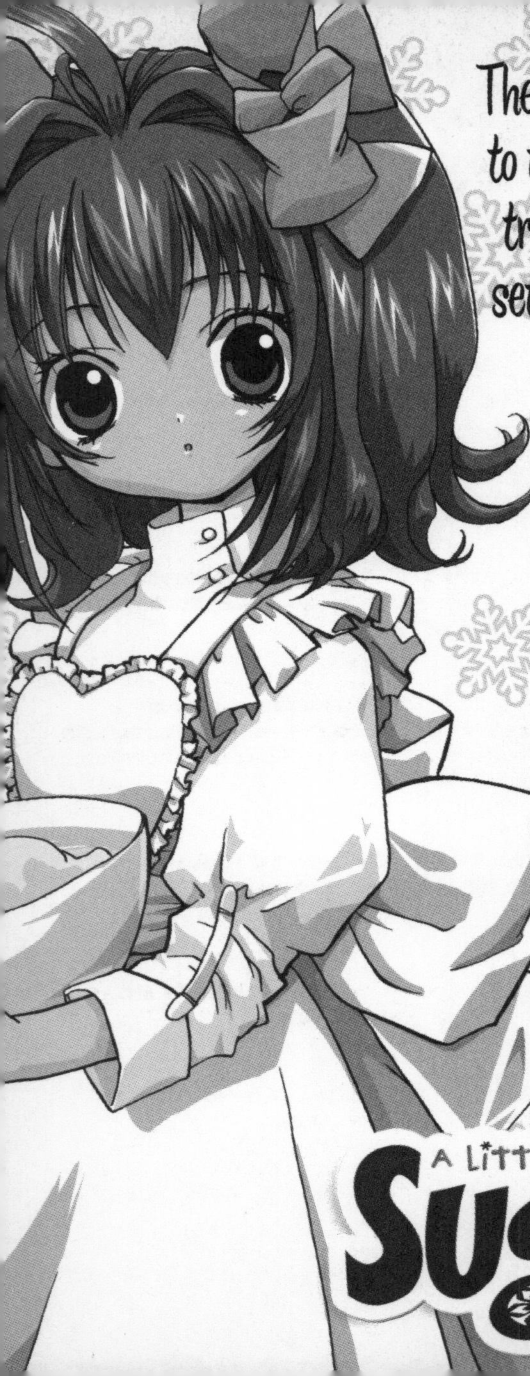

The Bear Pianist has come to town, and this traveling troubadour has his eyes set on a duet with Saga!

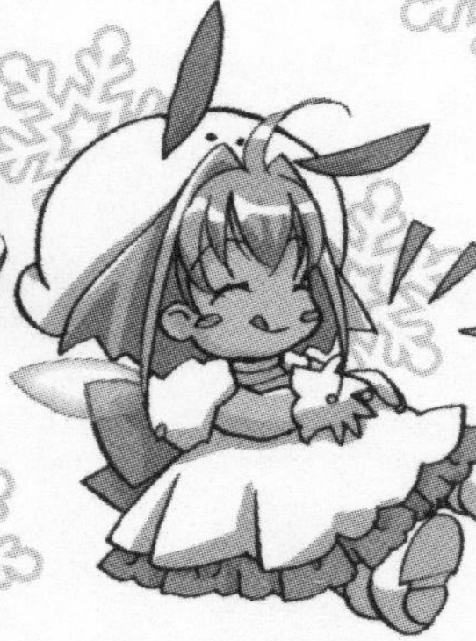

As if that weren't enough, the Elder Season Fairy drops in (literally) with some ominous news—Sugar's flower is sick, and what happens to the flower happens to Sugar!

Have Sugar's plans been nipped in the bud, or will she find some Twinkle in time to brace her blossom?

A Little Snow Fairy
Sugar
2

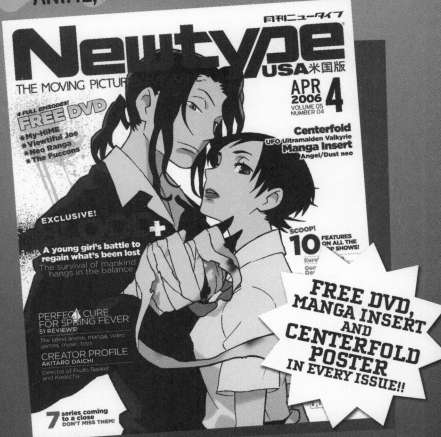